THE GOVERNMENT AND
POLITICS OF ISRAEL

Third Edition

The Government and Politics of Israel

Don Peretz and Gideon Doron

WestviewPress

A Division of HarperCollins*Publishers*

Copyright © 1997 by Westview Press, A Division of HarperCollins Publishers, Inc.

Published in 1997 in the United States of America by Westview Press, 5500 Central Avenue, Boulder, Colorado 80301-2877, and in the United Kingdom by Westview Press, 12 Hid's Copse Road, Cumnor Hill, Oxford OX2 9JJ

Library of Congress Cataloging-in-Publication Data
Peretz, Don, 1922–
   The government and politics of Israel / Don Peretz and Gideon
Doron. — 3rd ed.
      p.   cm.
   Includes bibliographical references and index.
   ISBN 0-8133-2408-4 (hardcover).—ISBN 0-8133-2409-2 (pbk.)
   1. Israel—Politics and government.   I. Doron, Gideon.
II. Title.
JQ1830.A58P47   1997
320.95694—dc20
                                                                    96-35240
                                                                    CIP

The paper used in this publication meets the requirements of the American National Standard for Permanence of Paper for Printed Library Materials Z39.48-1984.

10   9   8   7   6   5   4   3   2   1

Contents

Tables and Figures

Tables

Figures

Preface

This book aims to familiarize those interested in Israel's government with that country's origins; the way its political institutions, practices, and traditions have evolved; and the way the government works today. The book demonstrates that the country's political and social systems have been transformed from a nonliberal democratic-socialist orientation during its formative years to one based on territorial nationalism and conservative socioeconomic policies with a more liberal, individual-centered open society.

The first edition of this book, published in 1979, introduced the reader to a political system dominated by one party. Between its independence in 1948 and 1977, Israel was ruled by the Mapai (the Israel Workers' Party), which later became the Ma'arach (Labor Alignment). Little structural political change occurred during that period. The second edition of this book, published in 1983, added a new chapter, "The Begin Era," which traced the reasons for Labor's inability to regain its traditional political leadership in 1977 and 1981.

Since 1983, Israeli government and politics have undergone significant changes. Labor shared power with Likud in both 1984 and 1988 in wall-to-wall coalitions. Israel withdrew from Lebanon and survived runaway three-digit inflation. It absorbed hundreds of thousands of new immigrants from the collapsed Soviet Union and from Ethiopia. Israel began peace negotiations with its Arab neighbors in Madrid during November 1991, and in September 1993 it decided to shift the responsibility for Arab residents of the occupied West Bank and the Gaza Strip to the Palestinians. At the end of October 1994 a peace treaty was signed with Jordan; other Arab and Muslim countries including Morocco, Tunisia, and the Gulf states became active in reconciliation with the Jewish state.

These events were possible as Labor resumed its historical role as the country's leading party. The transition was preceded by several institutional, legal, and normative changes in the political system during the second half of the 1980s and the early 1990s.

Updating the information included in the second edition of this book is only one objective of the third edition. Chapters from earlier editions have been rewritten to include new information and interpretations of topics previously covered. The present volume also includes new issues that were not salient before but that, over the years, have become central in the study of Israeli national political systems. For example, Chapter 2 surveys the problem of national identity as it relates to the people of Israel, the position and status of women in politics, and the process that led to the emergence of a vital civil society—topics that received little attention in the study of politics during the 1970s. Finally, the book discusses these issues as they relate to the future of politics in Israel.

Several individuals have been helpful in commenting on and preparing the manuscript, although the authors alone are responsible for its contents. Special thanks go to Rebecca Kook, Maoz Azaryahu, Maya Peretz, and Martin Sherman for their useful suggestions and to Moti Levi and Penina Elkis for assisting in research.

Gideon Doron, Tel Aviv
Don Peretz, Washington, D.C.

1

Historical Origins of Israel

No other nation of Israel's size is as well-known throughout the world or as influential in its relations with other countries. During the early days of the state, a delegation from the U.S. Congress visited the country and concluded, "What Israel needs is a good mayor and a good sheriff." Israel is a very small country in both area and population. Its area of nearly 8,000 square miles (about 28,000 square kilometers) makes Israel similar in size to New Jersey, Slovenia, Wales, or El Salvador; it is considerably smaller than countries like Belgium and is half the size of the Netherlands or Denmark. A person driving 55 miles an hour could cross Israel from Metula in the north to Eilat in the south in about four hours and could travel the width from Netanya on the Mediterranean coast to the Jordan River in less than an hour. Among its Middle East regional neighbors, Israel is larger than Lebanon, Qatar, and Kuwait. Jordan is almost five times larger than Israel, however; Syria is nine times as large, Iraq is twenty times as large, Turkey is forty times as large, Egypt is fifty times as large, Iran is eighty times as large, and Saudi Arabia is over one hundred times as large.

The Centrality of Israel

With a population of over 5.3 million in 1994, Israel has fewer or the same number of people as at least thirty-five of the world's largest cities, including London, Paris, Moscow, Los Angeles, Chicago, and New York. Three Middle Eastern cities—Cairo, Teheran, and Istanbul—have up to twice the number of inhabitants as Israel. Its population equals 15 percent of California's, or a little under 2 percent of that of the United States. Iraq and Iran, two of Israel's declared regional enemies, have about four and twelve times more people, respectively, and Egypt, an active enemy until 1979, is more than ten times larger.[1]

Although it is one of the smaller political entities in both the region and the world, Israel has become a focus of unusual attention, especially since independence in 1948. Israel's conflict with surrounding Arab states, its central role in major Middle Eastern crises, and its social, economic, and political development constantly arouse interest around the globe— particularly in the United States and Europe. Some studies place Israel among the ten countries with the largest foreign press corps during 1992; 270 news organizations keep a permanent representation there. When a superstory breaks in times of war or other major crises, Israel becomes, after the United States, the country most covered by the foreign press. There are several reasons for this phenomenon.

First, Israel is the birthplace of the two Western monotheistic religions, Judaism and Christianity, and it is also sacred to Islam. Events that affect the "land of the Bible" and its holy sites are of major interest to believers of these three faiths. Tom Friedman, the noted U.S. journalist, defined events in Israel during 1987 as "the translation of the Bible to news items."[2] Events that involve the resurrection of the Jewish people in their native home are theologically problematic for Catholics; they are significant, however, for fundamentalist Protestants who see their religious visions approaching fulfillment in Israel's revival.

Second, Israel has acquired prominence in Western consciousness because it shares similar values with the West. Israel is one of the most democratic countries in the Middle Eastern region. Much of Israel's political and economic leadership is either Western-born or Western-oriented. Indeed, many enemies as well as friends tend to perceive Israel as an extension of Western civilization or even as a colonial outpost of late European imperialist expansion to the Third World. In addition, the trauma or perhaps some profound guilt over the actions and inactions taken during the Holocaust draws sympathy and support from Europeans. In 1992 fifty-one German news organizations had representatives in Israel, second only to the fifty-six U.S. representatives.[3] The transformation of yesterday's victims into a vibrant force has been noted with great interest and even with respect, if not admiration. Until 1967 Israel was generally perceived as the weak David facing the mighty Goliath but able to overcome him. After Israel's victory in the 1967 war, the power and moral equations seem to have been reversed; in the eyes of the world, Israel's sheer power replaced its moral strength.

Intellectually, Israel constitutes an exciting social and political experiment. Its propelling national ideology, Zionism, is no doubt the most important underlying force that has profoundly revolutionized Israelis' private and collective lives. There is no historical parallel for an ethno-religious group that for two millennia was placed in an exilitic situation and was ef-fectively able to restore its independent national life. The process of Jewish resurrection also includes the revival of a "dead language," Hebrew, which, like Latin, was used primarily for religious rituals and is now the principal means of daily communication. Experimentation in various forms of col-lective living—most notably the kibbutz communal arrangement, which re-lies on the principles of equality among members, joint property, and direct democracy—also draws attention to this old-new society.

Strategically, Israel's importance belies its size. Located at the crossroads of three continents—Asia, Africa, and Europe—in ancient times the land of Israel became a common battlefield for ambitiously expanding nations, a situation that changed little during the second half of the twentieth century. Israel's several rounds of all-out wars with some of its Arab neighbors and many violent border and terrorist incidents constituted a risk that these conflicts would not be contained within the region but would spill over to the international level as well. This risk became acute when Israel sided with the Americans and against the Soviet Union and its Arab clients dur-ing the Cold War. The fact that Israel is generally perceived as one of the nations with nuclear weapons has intensified the potential danger to inter-national security. Moreover, its special economic, military, and diplomatic relationships with the United States are not unnoticed by other nations.

The development of the U.S.-Israeli friendship rests on several factors, in-cluding the support Israel has traditionally obtained from American Jews. By 1992 one-third of the world's Jewry lived in Israel, a number almost equal to the U.S. Jewish community. Israel is the world's only state in which the majority of citizens and many national institutions such as holidays, diet (Kashrut) laws, and regulations over personal affairs (including birth, mar-riage, and death) are Jewish; thus, Jews everywhere are interested in Israel. Whether because of sympathy, identification, or a direct interest in creating a shelter in case of persecution, events in Israel are discussed regularly in U.S. synagogue meetings, and requests to assist the country in overcoming its mounting challenges are important in Jewish communal life. U.S. Jewish organizations and individuals help financially, but more important, they use their influence in the political system to rally various forms of support for Israel.

Large concentrations of Jews are found in New York, Los Angeles, Lon-don, and Paris—cities that are national and international centers for printed and electronic media. Local Jewish residents' demand for news about Israel is transformed to the national level. Thus, for example, the *New York Times* often carries as many detailed accounts of Israeli issues as do Israeli newspapers. The existence of such a large market for news about Israel is the prime reason major U.S. and European television networks keep per-manent crews in Israel.

Wars, terrorist activities, heroic behavior, and human despair tend to produce "good" stories. Likewise, acts of reconciliation between enemies draw much media coverage because of the hope that if protracted conflict, however complex, can be solved in one place, then perhaps other conflicts can also be resolved.

A Changing Society and Its Problems

What is actually known of this popular political entity? Some preliminary generalizations are in order. First, the formal name of the Jewish state is not Israel but rather "the State of Israel" (Medinat Israel). This distinguishes the political entity of the state from the physical and spiritual entity of the Land of Israel (Eretz Israel). Eretz Israel is a biblical territory that includes both banks of the Jordan River (and thus the Kingdom of Jordan) according the League of Nations Mandate for Palestine, discussed later. Jews maintain internationally recognized political sovereignty only in the state; although since June 1967 they have also lived in the West Bank (captured from Jordan), which was part of the land, and the Gaza Strip (captured from Egypt), these territories do not legally belong to Israel. In July 1967 Israel annexed East Jerusalem to its state. Fourteen years later, in December 1981, the Golan Heights, an area belonging to Syria, also became part of the state.

By the end of 1994, Israel had internationally agreed and fixed borders with only two neighbors: Egypt and Jordan. The border with Egypt was determined by the March 1979 peace treaty and that with Jordan by the October 1994 peace agreement. In the second half of the 1990s, Israel was still waiting to alter the status of the "armistice lines" (the so-called green lines) to define its borders with Syria and Lebanon and to redefine borders with the emerging Palestinian entity. The armistice lines were drafted in 1949 armistice agreements with Egypt, Jordan, Lebanon, and Syria following the 1948 Arab-Israeli war.

Although most citizens of Israel are Jews, about 18.5 percent of the population is non-Jewish (i.e., 77 percent Arab-Moslem, 14 percent Arab-Christian, and 9 percent Arab-Druse).[4] A small, undetermined number of residents is neither Jewish nor Arab. Most of the latter group arrived in Israel because they married a member of the Jewish faith or came to find work in the labor market. Although most Arab citizens were born in Israel, that is not the case for the Jews. Only during the 1980s did the number of Jewish natives surpass the number of those born beyond Israel's borders. Between 1948 and 1994, more than 2.35 million Jews arrived in Israel from 130 countries.[5] Prior to 1948, most immigrants had come from Europe. Immediately after independence they came primarily from Middle Eastern countries—including Egypt, Syria, Iraq, and Yemen—and from North

Africa. Between 1960 and 1990, most immigrants came from countries belonging to the Soviet bloc (Poland, Romania, Russia, and Georgia) and from the United States. The largest single wave of immigration (about 500,000 people, or over 10 percent of the population) came during the period 1990–1993 from the collapsing Soviet Union and from Ethiopia.[6]

A creation of the Zionist movement, the State of Israel does not officially belong to all its citizens but belongs to the Jewish people, an undetermined entity that also includes individuals and groups that are explicitly anti-Zionist (like the Satmar Hasidim of Brooklyn, New York) or that never plan to visit the land of their "forefathers." According to Israeli law, however, these people potentially have more legal rights in many matters in Israel than do the country's indigenous non-Jewish citizens. As a nonliberal democracy whose basic values and laws are deduced from a commitment to the interests of Jewish people, Israel has no written constitution. Its single-chamber parliament, the 120-member Knesset, serves as both a legislature and a constituent body. Regular laws, regulations, and acts are drafted through the first function, and basic laws embodied with constitutional status are enacted through the second. The Knesset also selects, approves, and supervises the operations of the government.

Representation in the Knesset is obtained through election. The entire country constitutes one voting district. Voters cast their preferences among party lists rather than for individual candidates. Because no party has ever obtained a majority of votes in an election to the Knesset, public policy has been conducted by coalition governments. Through membership in the world Zionist movement, most parties included in this extensive multiparty system (on average, twelve parties are represented in the Knesset) have overseas affiliates in the Americas, Western Europe, and South Africa.

Since independence, the country and its people have experienced tremendous change. The population has increased nearly ninefold. Excluding the 1991 Gulf War, when Israel's role was that of a "passive victim," Israel experienced major wars in 1948, 1956, 1967, 1973, and 1982, as well as the War of Attrition with Egypt (1969–1971). As a result, Israel has become a garrison state whose society constantly encounters security tensions exacerbated by frequent guerrilla and terrorist activities.

In spite of this violent background, Israel has built a relatively sound economy, moving from an agriculturally based Third World type to a modern industrialized system based on the most advanced communication infrastructure. This situation has made Israel the principal, if not the largest, economic power in the Middle East region.

Demographically, Israel has been transformed from a country whose Jewish population was mostly European to one in which Jews of Afro-Asian origin constitute nearly half the citizenry, thereby strengthening the Middle Eastern element in the culture and society. Among the Jews, until the end of the 1980s immigrants from Arab countries constituted the largest subgroup, compared to those of European, American, or Israeli origin. By 1994, however, Afro-Asian Jews were outnumbered by the Russian Jews, who began pouring into the country during the 1990s and became the largest subgroup—replacing those who came from North Africa during the 1950s. Regardless of their original background, most latecomers were able to adjust—often with difficulty—to the basic political, cultural, economic, and military norms and institutions laid down by Western Jews during the prestate era.

European Zionists who immigrated to Palestine before or soon after World War I dominated Israeli leadership until the early 1970s. Only after the 1973 October War was there a native-born prime minister (PM). Until 1996, Yitzhak Rabin was the only Israeli-born prime minister among the seven men and one woman (i.e., Golda Meir) who served in that position. The gerontocracy of the early twentieth-century Zionists, which was so influential in party leadership, the Knesset, and other political institutions, has largely disappeared. The first generation of leaders, the founding fathers and mothers of modern Israel, has faded. Even in 1994, some of the country's most prominent politicians—Rabin, Shimon Peres (foreign minister and former PM), Yitzhak Shamir (former PM), Ezer Weizman (president), and others—were past age seventy.

Despite the changes in social composition, in most aspects of life leadership is still either Western or of Western origin. Most members of the cabinet and Knesset, the party leadership, and high-ranking public administrators, as well as those in state-owned enterprises, large industrial companies, the Israeli Defense Force (IDF) high command, academic institutions, and the like, are Western Ashkenazi (of European origin) males. The Afro-Asians (Mizrachim) dominate local-level politics and many small businesses. Tensions created by the resulting economic and cultural disparities are often transformed into political issues. For example, the Likud's Ashkenazi leadership, headed by Menachem Begin (1948–1983), was able to upset Labor's domination in 1977 and to control the government until 1992 by mobilizing the political support of the Mizrachim, especially those of North African origin.

The non-Jewish citizens of Israel present two of the most serious dilemmas to maintaining political stability. In 1994 they constituted about 18.5 percent of the total population and were divided into three subgroups: Muslims, Christians, and Druze. On one level there is a problem of the relationship between state and religion. Because these two are not separate, non-Jews who are not Arabs find it difficult, if not impossible, to legally conduct their personal affairs through state institutions. Attempts to obtain citizenship, to marry, or even to find a burial plot can become major obstacles. The only branch of Judaism recognized by the state is the Orthodox.

Consequently, Reform and Conservative Jews, the two largest U.S. Jewish movements, are denied the freedom to conduct certain religious functions in Israel.

The Israeli Arabs encounter problems on a different level. Residing largely along or near the borders of the adjoining countries with which until recently Israel was in a formal state of war, the Arab minority has been perceived by many to represent a potential security problem. But tensions between Jews and Arabs in Israel would remain high even if Israel did find peace with its enemies because Israel is legally a Jewish state in which no separation exists between religion and nationality. The Arabs are therefore excluded from many basic institutions of the state, from the state's collective memory, and from most national symbols. No Arab citizen of Israel has ever held a leading position in any state political institution. The highest ranks obtained by an Arab have been deputy minister, mayor, or district court judge. Socioeconomic, cultural, linguistic, and political differences between Jews and Arabs in Israel have increasingly politicized the situation and have raised serious questions about the future of Israel as a Jewish state or, alternatively, as a democracy.[7]

The protracted war with the surrounding Arab states has been decisive in shaping Israel's economic structure and policies. In some years, especially during the first half of the 1970s, levels of expenditures on security relative to the country's gross national product were among the highest in the world. In addition, the national goal of bringing all Jewish exiles to their promised land, coupled with a fundamentally socialist ideology, greatly strained the economy. Since 1948 Israel has almost cyclically muddled through one economic crisis after another, albeit with relative success. Instrumental to this success were the millions of new immigrants who came to the country without material resources but with advanced knowledge and high levels of motivation.

At the same time, the state has maintained a very generous welfare system, which directly supports many new immigrants for extended periods. Widows, orphans, invalids, veterans, elderly people, single-parent families, and the like are assisted by the welfare system. Living standards of most citizens are maintained at Western levels through government subsidy of many necessities such as food, housing, transportation, and education. As inflation and soaring defense costs increased, however, economic pressures—especially during the 1970s and 1980s—created tension between the government and organized labor that was manifest in frequent strikes.

Closely related to the dilemma of economy and ethnicity is the issue of class. Since independence, when most of the Jewish community was relatively close-knit and homogeneous, class distinctions have become more visible and politically relevant. A new bourgeoisie has emerged, and enough people have become rich to almost constitute a class. On the other hand, with the immigration from Arab countries, especially from North Africa, Oriental Jews have found themselves at the bottom of the social and economic scale, and poverty has become commonplace. Urban and rural slums have sprung up, and tensions have grown between the Mizrachi poor and the affluent Ashkenazi. Generous government measures undertaken during the 1980s in the form of neighborhood renewal programs somewhat eased the tension. However, the half million immigrants who came to Israel from the former Soviet Union and Ethiopia during the first half of the 1990s revived the tension between those who have and those who have not.

During the entire period since independence, the Arab minority in Israel has remained the lowest class as defined by all relevant socioeconomic indicators. In 1994, the average earnings of an Arab family in Israel were about half those of an average Jewish family.[8] It is thus little wonder that many Arab families were below the poverty line. This situation has added yet more tension and affected social and political stability in Israel.

Geopolitical Setting

Israel is a country with no fixed borders. Even in biblical times, the boundaries of the land in which the people of Israel resided were largely undefined: They expanded and contracted in accordance with the ambition and strength of local or external rulers. The borders of modern Israel were carved from mandatory Palestine in a series of international agreements and wars. At the end of 1994, Israel's northern and eastern borders were still largely in a state of flux. The issue of the Golan Heights remained unresolved, Israel still occupied its "security zone" in Lebanon, and no decision had been reached regarding the eventual international border between Israel and the Palestinian entity. Prior to World War I, Palestine was a southern province of the Ottoman Empire. Thus, although the terms *Palestine* and *Israel* both have ancient historical antecedents, they are new political entities created during the twentieth century.

Since the November 1947 UN partition of the area west of the Jordan River into Jewish and Arab political entities, Israel has considerably increased its territory. The country expanded by around 2,000 square miles between 1947 and 1948 as a consequence of the first Arab-Israeli war. In 1956 Israel seized the Sinai Peninsula in the south from Egypt, but under superpower pressures it quickly returned the area. Israel regained control over the Sinai in the 1967 war, adding to the territories captured from the two other antagonists—Jordan (the West Bank) on the east and Syria (the Golan Heights) in the northeast. Altogether, the Jewish state added about 35,000 square miles to its original holdings, thus controlling over four times more land than it had in 1948. In 1973, as a result of the October War, Israel captured even more Egyptian land west of the Suez Canal. Israel retreated in 1974, and following the 1979 peace treaty the rest of the territory taken from Egypt, except for the Gaza Strip, was surrendered. Between 1982 and 1985, Israel dominated southern Lebanon. Since then it has maintained a several-kilometer-deep "security zone" supervised directly by the IDF and the IDF-financed South Lebanon Army.

Following the accord signed in Oslo in September 1993 between Israel and the Palestine Liberation Organization (PLO), management of the Gaza Strip and of the town of Jericho in the West Bank became the PLO's responsibility. This accord, and others signed in 1994 in Washington, D.C., and Cairo, specified the process by which most of the West Bank would eventually come under the authority of the Palestinians. Likewise, the October 1994 peace agreement with Jordan determined the international borders between Israel and Jordan. By 1996, negotiations with Syria and Lebanon had not resulted in a clear solution to border problems.

Geographically located as it is on the western shore of the Mediterranean, Israel lies at the crossroads of three continents: Asia, Africa, and Europe. This location provides commercial advantages, but it creates disadvantages from a security point of view. Spatial attributes were manifest in ancient times. Located at the center of the Old World, the region often became a battleground for advancing empires from the east (Assyrians, Babylonians, Persians, and Ottomans), the south (Egyptians and Arabs), and the west (Macedonians, Romans, and, later, French and British). Political sovereignty in the area was often conditioned by international developments. Even during the golden biblical years, until the destruction of the first temple, the Hebrews maintained only partial political control of the area. They resided in the inner lands and for over two hundred years shared the coastal area with the Philistines, a nation of seafarers, with whom they fought for territorial supremacy.

Israel's location makes the country vulnerable to attack from different directions. The first full-scale Arab attack took place in 1948 but failed, resulting in 570 miles of armistice frontiers. In the 1967 war with Egypt, Syria, Jordan, and Iraq, the size of Israel's territory was increased, but the length of its borders was reduced by around 50 miles. This represented a major strategic benefit to Israel: Large cities like Jerusalem and Tel Aviv, as well as many smaller settlements, were no longer within easy reach of neighboring armies. Moreover, Israeli control over the Golan Heights removed a direct military threat to its northern residential cities and placed the IDF only 30 miles from the Syrian capital of Damascus. The security or "buffer zone" Israel maintains in Lebanon provides similar advantages. Yet, as Israeli military strategists learned during the 1991 Gulf War, when dozens of Scud missiles were launched against Israel's major cities from Iraq, in modern warfare geographic distance and topographical height may not carry the same security value as they did in the past.

Israel's climate, land forms, flora, and fauna are similar to those of southern California. The Mediterranean coastal plain has mild winters with moderate rainfall and hot, dry summers. The mountains and hilly areas that extend from Lebanon in the north through central Palestine and the Negev Desert in the south are sparsely settled and unproductive. The lands south of Beersheba and Gaza, the Negev and the Jordan Valley, are arid and dry throughout the year, although with irrigation they can produce high-quality crops.

As in most Middle Eastern countries on the edge of the desert, lack of water is a major barrier to growth. Rainfall is uneven, with adequate quantities in the north and almost none in some of the southern regions. Periodic droughts cause extensive damage to the country's agriculture. Throughout history, the countries of the region have quarreled over water, and these quarrels continue today. Disputes over the main water system; the Jordan River and its tributaries; the Dan, Hasbani, and Yarmuk Rivers in the north; Lake Tiberias (also called the Sea of Galilee or, in Hebrew, Kinneret); and the Dead Sea have caused frequent clashes among Israel, Syria, and Jordan. These waters are important not only for their economic value; they also have political, historical, and religious significance. Thus, one of the most important elements in the 1994 peace agreement between Israel and Jordan was cooperative water utilization.

Natural resources are modest; they include mineral deposits such as potash, phosphates, and copper ore, and natural gas and small quantities of oil that are commercially exploited. Light rainfall, a dry climate, sparse water sources, and the sandy soil of the region produce a Mediterranean-type agriculture with emphasis on field crops (cereals and grains), fruits (citrus, bananas, and avocados), vegetables, and flowers. Some crops have been raised for export to Europe. Early in the twentieth century, Jewish farmers introduced extensive irrigation and scientific agricultural methods that greatly increased productivity of the land. By the 1990s, Israel was commonly considered one of the world's leading sources of knowledge of intensive agriculture and water utilization through the use of sophisticated electronic or computerized irrigation systems and advanced desalinization methods. Over the years, however, with the expansion of other sectors of the economy and the decline of manpower requirements in agriculture, farming has diminished in relative importance, providing only 3.5 percent of domestic product and national income in 1991 and employing only 55 thousand workers in a labor force of over 1.5 million.[9]

In 1994, nearly 90 percent of Israel's total population lived in 178 urban localities. About 28 percent (1.2 million people) of the Jewish population lived in the three major cities: Jerusalem, Tel Aviv–Jaffa, and Haifa.[10] Jerusalem, the capital, had 568,000 residents, of whom 407,000 were Jews. The coastal area between the two seaports, Haifa and Ashdod, contains the greatest concentration of Jewish inhabitants, as well as most industries, commerce, and other vital sectors of the economy.

Most Arabs live separated from the Jewish population, largely because of historical circumstances and the fact that in the Middle East ethnic and religious groups tend to live in their own exclusive locations. In urban centers, where there are mixes of Jews, Muslims, Christians, and their respective subgroups, each group often has its own "quarter," or city district. Thus, Arabs live alongside Jews in separate sectors of six mixed cities: Haifa, Jerusalem, Jaffa, Acre, Rammle, and Lydda. Nazareth, Taybe, Um el Fahem, and Rahat (a Bedouin town in 1994) are exclusively Arab cities within the green line. Nearly half of Israeli Arabs live in rural areas, most in Galilee villages and along the pre-1967 frontiers with Jordan.

Heavy Arab concentrations in the north, where Arabs outnumber the Jewish population, have raised the possibility that in the future the minority may demand cultural and even political autonomy. To prevent such actual or potential demands and also for security reasons, the government has attempted to disperse Jews in vacant regions along the borders and in areas where large numbers of Arabs reside. Consequently, urban and rural sites have been established as border settlements inside Israel and, after 1967, in the West Bank, the Gaza Strip, and the Golan Heights. Likewise, "development towns" like Dimona and Yerucham, inhabited by new immigrants who arrived from North Africa in the 1950s and from the Soviet Union in the early 1990s, have been built in the Negev (where most Bedouins reside) and in Galilee. In Arab cities like Nazareth, where no Jews used to reside, the government has set up an adjunct independent Jewish Upper Nazareth.

Origins of Modern Israel

A Jewish presence existed in Palestine before Great Britain assumed the Mandate for Palestine, but few Jews were associated with Zionist institutions. By 1914, the forty-four Jewish settlements, with a total population of about 12,000, constituted only 14 percent of the Yishuv (Jewish community). Most Jews lived in the four Jewish holy cities—Jerusalem, Hebron, Safed, and Tiberias—where Jews had lived for centuries. In Jerusalem, they had formed the majority of the population since the mid-nineteenth century.

How could such a small group of people establish a country that became a regional power within a single generation? The question is even more provocative when we consider Israel's sparse natural resources and scarcity of water, its relative smallness, and its precarious situation in a region that is not only inhospitable geographically but that was also surrounded by a hostile Arab population with much more extensive territories, many more people, and richer natural endowments.

Modern political Zionism was a European nationalist movement linked to the land of Israel by history, tradition, and mythology. After the Roman conquest of Palestine during the first century, destruction of the second temple, and the forceful dispersion of a large part of the population in A.D. 70, Palestine was no longer the center of organized Jewish life. But Jewish communities continued to survive in Galilee, parts of the coastal plain, and Judea. One version of the Talmud (studies of Jewish history and law), compiled in Palestine between 200 B.C. and A.D. 500, mentions over four hundred Jewish settlements there. Such major historical events as the Bar Kochba rebellion against Rome (A.D. 132–135) and the Masada episode at the end of that period, when Jewish zealots committed mass suicide to avoid captivity, became an important part of Jewish collective memory. "Masada shall not fall again" is a motif often used by Israeli politicians and soldiers in times of extreme threat to national survival.

Separated physically from the Land of Israel, Jews scattered in the diaspora retained close traditional and emotional ties with Palestine, chiefly through the Bible and other Jewish religious literature that became the basis of communal life for two thousand years. Some historical theories maintain that through conversion, many non-Semitic peoples became Jews and that few direct descendants of the ancient Hebrews remain. At the same time, over the years many Jews have either voluntarily or by force abandoned their faith and become Christian or Muslim. What is of immediate political relevance, however, is that most Jews are attached to their Jewish identity regardless of their historical origins.

The largest Jewish communities were established in Europe, although Jews were dispersed as far as China, Ethiopia, and central Asia. They continued to live in separate communities where life was based on the laws, traditions, and customs of ancient Israel. In the Byzantine, Christian nations of medieval Europe that had state religions, Jews were prevented from participating in communal life. They could not hold public office or own land and were usually excluded from the mainstream of social life. Frequently, they were expelled or became victims of political persecution. Nearly every major European nation—Spain, France, Portugal, England, Romania, and Germany—exiled its Jewish community at one time or another.

Thus, the nineteenth-century Jews were a people apart; they never really became Frenchmen, Englishmen, Poles, Germans, or Russians. Not only were they regarded as a distinctive people by those around them, but they also thought of themselves as such. Jews and non-Jews (Gentiles) came to regard each other with mutual suspicion: Gentiles perceived the Jews as a foreign element in their midst, and Jews believed the Gentiles were determined to persecute them, if not eliminate them. As a result of their exclusion from landholding and such primary occupations as agriculture, Jews often gravitated toward work others would not do. They frequently became skilled middlemen, merchants, and money lenders or, at intermediate and lower levels of the economy, craftspeople, tailors, and the like, and a number of characteristically Jewish occupations developed. Social isolation and economic exclusion became hallmarks of the Jewish condition in Europe and, to some degree, in the Arab world, where Jewish communities lived apart from their neighbors—a fact that later became significant in Zionist ideology. These conditions intensified the closeness within the Jewish communities and their inner-directed perceptions of the world and also strengthened the emphasis on ancient Israel and glories of the past. Jewish tradition, observance, and custom were central to the lives of Jews until modern times; all abided by Jewish law and followed the leadership of their rabbinical elders.

Most Jews did not distinguish between the spiritual and the physical Palestine. In Palestine, although not in Russia or Poland, holidays, feasts, and fasts commemorated biblical events such as Moses's flight across the Sinai Desert from Egypt to Canaan (Passover and Sukkot), the destruction of the first and second Jewish temples in Jerusalem (Ninth of Av, Tenth of Tevet, Seventeenth of Tamuz), and the harvest season (Shavuot). The annual Passover festival ended with the hopeful prayer "next year in Jerusalem!" Jewish religious ties with Eretz Israel were more than formal or ritualistic: There was a mystical quality about the intensity and depth of Jewish attachment to the Holy Land.

After the French Revolution, new ideas swept across Europe, and the life of European Jewry was transformed. The most important changes were the destruction of the ghetto walls that had physically isolated Jews from their Gentile neighbors and the growing acceptance of Jews in Western Europe as equal citizens. By the mid-nineteenth century, many of the restrictions on Jews had been removed. In varying degrees, Jews were permitted to own property, practice law, teach at universities, and hold government posts. Jews became involved in political life, stood for office, and entered military service.

Integration into the mainstream of civil life led to new forms of Judaism. Notable was the rise of Reform Judaism, which sought to separate religious practice and observance from the requirements of daily life. As Jews became integrated with others and were accepted, they found it increasingly difficult to follow all of the customs and practices required by Orthodox rules. Reform Judaism was an attempt to modernize observance and adapt it to the lifestyles and manners of the predominantly non-Jewish environment.

The French Revolution and the Napoleonic concept of equality for all citizens, regardless of religious practice, were not accepted in czarist Eastern Europe, which responded to Western reform by imposing new restrictions and intensifying the fight against subversive liberal ideologies. The Jews became the chief victims, as fresh restrictions were imposed on Jewish movement, places of residence, and employment. In the 1880s, Russian anti-Semitism erupted into sporadic pogroms, with officially sanctioned attacks on lives and property. These pogroms reached such proportions in Russia by the end of the nineteenth century that the Jewish community was thrown into turmoil. Response to czarist persecution took diverse forms. The most common was immigration to the West. Most of the large Jewish communities in the United States, Great Britain, and France increased vastly during this period.

Some Jews joined indigenous protest movements including social democratic organizations, labor unions, and radical secular movements. Other Jews preferred Jewish organizations in the common struggle against reactionary forces. Secular socialist parties, like the Bund, and labor groups retained a distinctive Jewish identity. Only a small number were attracted to Jewish nationalism, which in many ways resembled other nineteenth-century national movements. Like these other movements, Jewish nationalism was a product of both negative and positive forces: a response to oppression and a revival of Jewish pride in the ancient culture. This nationalism also had deep religious roots and affinities with the organized religious institutions of the community. Although there was no Jewish national church similar to the Greek, Romanian, or Bulgarian Orthodox Churches, many Eastern European rabbis played a prominent role in the revival of Jewish nationalism.

Identification with a specific territory was an integral part of nineteenth-century nationalist movements. One major difference between the newly awakened Jewish nationalism and the other movements was that the Jewish followers were far removed from the homeland with which they identified. This fact did not diminish the fervent attachment of Jewish nationalists to the Holy Land, however. Separation not only intensified their longing for their land but often resulted in false perceptions of realities in Palestine. To some it was a "land of milk and honey," to others "a land without a people waiting for a people without a land." Many believed Palestine had been abandoned since biblical times.

The reality, as the first Zionist settlers were to find out, was rather different. A substantial Arab population was living in Palestine at the end of the nineteenth century, with a peasantry that cultivated large stretches of land. In the villages and larger towns such as Jaffa, Hebron, and Nablus, local gentry were fairly visible—many as leaders of a nascent Arab nationalist movement. Much of Palestine was desert, and cultivation was primitive by European standards, leaving most of the villagers in dire poverty.

Initially, Jewish nationalism was poorly developed and loosely organized, with no central movement or leadership. Jewish intellectuals in various parts of Europe wrote tracts propounding a Jewish homeland as the answer to the Jewish condition. Among these writers were Moses Hess (1812–1875), author of *Rome and Jerusalem* (1862), and Leo Pinsker (1821–1891), author of *Autoemancipation* (1882); these works became the foundation of later Zionist writings. Hess, a German socialist inspired by the reunification of Italy in 1857, proposed a similar Jewish "national renaissance." He believed in the "creative genius of the nation" and called the Jewish cause "the last national problem." Pinsker, a Russian physician who was stirred by the pogroms of the 1880s, gave currency to a new term, "anti-Semitism," which he described as "Judeo-phobia." The Jews—everywhere a minority, nowhere a majority—were a "ghost-nation," an abnormal phenomenon, always "guests" and never "hosts." No matter how hard they tried, Jews would be unable to become like their Gentile neighbors and gain acceptance. Forever alien, Jews were inassimilable and hated and thus were forced to find their own homeland.

Asher Ginsberg (1856–1927), who hebraicized his name to Ahad Ha'am (One of the People), emphasized the cultural aspects of Jewish nationalism. He envisioned Palestine as the center of Hebrew literature and learning, "a true miniature of the people of Israel as it ought to be which will bind all Jews together."[11] His focus on Jewish ethics led him to deemphasize Zionist political aspirations for a national state.

One of the first movements to evolve from early Jewish nationalist writings was Hovevei Zion (Lovers of Zion, another name for Israel), established in Russia during the early 1880s. Its members, striving for a cultural revival and self-determination, advocated Jewish settlement in Palestine as a practical relief measure rather than a religious ideal. Inspired by Pinsker, they argued that legal emancipation in Russia, even if it stemmed from humanitarian motives, was useless. Only a "land of our own," whether on the banks of the Jordan or the Mississippi, was the true solution.

One student member of Hovevei Zion traveled throughout Russia and recruited five hundred fellow enthusiasts determined to settle in Zion. The group, called the Bilu from the Hebrew initials of their rallying call in the Old Testament, "O house of Jacob, come, let us go forth," succeeded in sending a few youths to Palestine, where they laid the foundations for the first Zionist town, Rishon le-Zion (First in Zion), in 1882. By the end of the nineteenth century, a few dozen other small Jewish settlements, or colonies (*moshavot*), had been established by young Jewish intellectuals from Russia and Poland.

Initially, the early Zionists constituted a small minority group among European Jews. Only a handful of young people actually went to Palestine. Many supporters left with the millions of Jews who fled czarist persecution and immigrated to the United States and Western Europe. Difficult living conditions in Palestine, the problems of obtaining entry into the Ottoman

Empire, and the uncertainties of life there were deterrents to a mass movement to the East. Economic difficulties and problems of adjusting to the arduous pioneer life stunted the new Zionist colonies, and few ever developed into major Jewish centers. Although Zionism advocated a return to the land in a physical as well as a historical sense, it was not easy for lower-middle-class Jews, unaccustomed to rigorous toil, to work the land. Many Bilu settlers hired Arab labor rather than till the earth with their own hands. Thus, many of the early efforts were unsuccessful not only economically but also ideologically as far as Zionist theory was concerned.

The Zionist Movement and Political Zionism

Within fifteen years after the establishment of Hovevei Zion, the diverse groups coalesced into a single, large, and unified world Zionist organization. Ironically, this group's founder did not come from the ghettos of Eastern Europe. Theodore Herzl, born in Budapest in the Austro-Hungarian Empire in 1860, was an assimilated Western Jew. In his youth, he admired Prussian culture and Teutonic might and found little to attract him in Jewish tradition. Throughout his life, he remained rather ignorant of Jewish customs and practices.

As a correspondent for a Viennese newspaper, Herzl attended the 1894 Paris trial of Captain Alfred Dreyfus, a French Jewish army officer falsely accused of selling military secrets to Germany. Dreyfus was sentenced to imprisonment on Devil's Island. His trial stirred humanitarian protest in Western Europe and sparked waves of anti-Semitism in France. Herzl was deeply affected by the virulent manifestations of the hatred of Jews, such as the cry "Death to Jews!" at the ceremony at which Dreyfus was stripped of his rank. The incident aroused Herzl's memories of anti-Semitism he had experienced as a youth.

Shortly after the Dreyfus trial, Herzl began work on a pamphlet that became the basic document of the new Zionist movement. Published in 1896, *Der Judenstaat* (The Jewish State) laid out Herzl's perception of the Jewish problem and proposals for a solution.[12] He believed Jews were a unique part of society, alienated from the mainstream. Therefore, they would never be accepted and were destined to be universally hated. Where Jews go, Herzl argued, they carry the virus of anti-Semitism; hence they must either leave non-Jewish society or become totally assimilated into that society. Even immigration to supposedly friendly nations would not exempt Jews from eventual anti-Semitism. If they were not persecuted or discriminated against for two generations, Jews might perhaps become part of a new liberal society, Herzl added, but it seemed unlikely that they could be free from persecution for so long. The Jewish problem was not religious or social, he concluded; the Jews were a "nation without a land." Therefore, the world powers should grant them a territory to fulfill the needs of a nation. "Let sovereignty be granted us over a portion of the globe large enough to satisfy the rightful requirements of a nation," he wrote, "and the rest we will arrange ourselves."

In his book, Herzl presented an action plan to establish a Jewish state. A "Society of Jews" would organize the Jewish masses for emigration from Europe and would negotiate with the European powers for acquisition of a national territory. Any territory was acceptable as long as it met the requirements for a Jewish national home. Herzl, who had none of the Orthodox Jews' deep religious attachments to the Holy Land, suggested either Palestine or Argentina—the latter because of its rich undeveloped area. Jewish public opinion and the Society of Jews would make the final determination.

After publication of his volume, Herzl traveled through the Jewish communities of Eastern Europe to propagate his ideas. He also arranged audiences with the most powerful political figures of the time, seeking their support. Most Jewish leaders in Western Europe and North America, who felt secure in their liberal environments, were skeptical. They believed Herzl's program was unrealistic and that it would jeopardize their own integration into Western societies. Herzl's approaches to Jewish financial magnates such as the Rothschilds and the Hirsches—two philanthropic families that had helped to finance Jewish settlement projects in Palestine and Argentina, respectively—were unsuccessful, providing few if any of the funds required for the venture.

The masses of Eastern European Jewry, on the other hand, lionized Herzl as a new Moses. He was driven by a frenzy of compassion for the oppressed Jews of Russia and Romania, warning frequently that disaster awaited them within a generation if nothing was done about their plight. In his efforts to convince those in power of the merits of his scheme, Herzl gained access to the German kaiser, the Ottoman sultan, the pope, and the chief political figures of Great Britain. Unable to convince imperial Germany to become the protector of the Jewish state, he turned to Great Britain. Rejected by the sultan, Herzl tried to negotiate for other territories in the British Empire—East Africa, Sinai, or Cyprus.

Enthusiasm for the Jewish state among Jews in Russia, Poland, and Romania was so great that Herzl was able to convene the First World Zionist Congress in Basle, Switzerland, during August 1897. This was an international gathering of over two hundred delegates from all over the world, with the largest representation coming from Eastern Europe. Those attending were a cross-section of Jewish society, representing Orthodox and Reform sects, Eastern and Sephardi Jews, and a variety of political persuasions and social classes.

The major accomplishments of the First Zionist Congress were the organization of an official Zionist movement and the establishment of a formal credo that later became the foundation of Zionist nationalism and of the State of Israel. The credo stated that "the aim of Zionism is to create for the Jewish People a home in Palestine secured by public law." To attain this objective, Jews would be organized, as in Herzl's *Jewish State,* to promote the systematic settlement of farmers, artisans, and craftspeople in Palestine. Jewish consciousness and national identity were to be strengthened, and efforts were to be made to raise the funds necessary to achieve Zionist objectives. A Zionist was thereafter officially defined as a dues-paying member of the organization who supported the Basle program.

Shortly after the congress, in late 1897, Herzl wrote in his diary: "If I were to sum up the Basle Congress in one word—which I shall not do openly—it would be this: at Basle I founded the Jewish State. If I were to say this today, I would be met by universal laughter. In five years, perhaps, and certainly in fifty, everyone will see it. The State is already founded, in essence, in the will of the people of the State."[13]

In 1902, Herzl persuaded the British government to offer Uganda for Jewish settlement. The offer nearly split the new movement between those inclined to accept any territory and those—mostly from Eastern Europe and with deep religious ties to the Promised Land—who would accept only Palestine. Because of his support for the Uganda project as a temporary shelter for the Jewish oppressed, Herzl, respected leader that he was, fell victim to the sharp disputes within the movement, although he remained its leader until his death in 1904. Herzl is regarded as the founder of modern Jewish nationalism, as expressed in the Zionist idea, and as the father of modern Israel. His picture hangs in Israel's government offices, schools, and public places and adorns the state's postage stamps and currency. Thousands of Jews every year visit his burial shrine in Jerusalem.

Herzl's *Jewish State* and the Basle Congress planted the seeds from which have grown organizations and ideas that are still vital to the movement and to Israel. These include organizations for fund-raising and mass recruitment, representative bodies such as the Knesset, and the concept of proportional representation in both the Israeli electoral system and the World Zionist Congresses.

After Herzl's death, new leaders with a variety of views about the Jewish state emerged inside the movement. In less than a decade, a wide range of viewpoints representing diverse social, economic, and religious philosophies developed. Some of these evolved into distinct groups or parties. Others were merely philosophical trends unrepresented by any formal organization. Most are represented in Israel today in either political parties or political movements and intellectual groups. The common denominator of all Zionist parties and groups—whether religious, socialist, radical, secular, militant, or moderate—is the Basle program conceived by Herzl in 1897. In fact, since 1987 it has been illegal in Israel to form a political party or movement whose explicit or intended goal is to deny the Zionist nature and ideology of the state.

Among the early divisions within Zionism were those between the cultural and the political Zionists. The "culturals" were concerned less about establishing a political entity than with reviving Hebrew identity. In the words of Ahad Ha'am, one of the cultural leaders, the crux of the problem was less "the need of the Jews" than "the need of Judaism."

Zionism's task was to devise new structures to contain the separate identity of the Jews. In Ha'am's view, the Jewish "national spirit" was more important than the God of Israel. Religion was merely an instrument through which to preserve Jewish national identity and the special role of Jews in society. Jewish identity was to be expressed through the revival of Hebrew as a modern tongue and through the establishment of a Hebrew university where the finest Hebrew culture in literary, scientific, humanistic, and other fields would be preserved and developed. The culturalists saw Palestine as the spiritual center of Jewish culture rather than as a political state.

Political Zionists emphasized the immediate need for a physical refuge for Jews, for a territorial solution of the Jewish problem. A few were willing to accept any land in which large numbers of Jews could be settled, but for the overwhelming majority only Palestine was acceptable because of its centrality in Jewish consciousness. Herzl, the political Zionist par excellence, had conceived of a Jewish state with institutions that included an army, a parliament, a constitution, and the other trappings of Western nations. Throughout his career, his driving ambition was to obtain a charter that gave international recognition to Zionist claims. A handful of "territorialists" were so determined to attain a piece of exclusive Jewish national property that they severed relations with the Zionist movement when it rejected Great Britain's Uganda offer in 1903. They virtually disappeared within a few years, leaving only a few hundred followers.

Another group of Zionists stressed practical achievements in Palestine. They emphasized "creating facts," new Jewish settlements with expanding agriculture and industry, ports, roads, transportation, communication, and other aspects of a national infrastructure that would give viability and validity to Jewish identity in Palestine. In the words of Chaim Weizmann, Israel's first president, the goal was to create an "absorptive capacity" for new Jewish immigrants on the land and in the cities. The "practicals" placed less emphasis on political achievements than on physical expansion of the Jewish presence in Palestine.

Still other trends developed, some shaped by political philosophies like Marxism and socialism, some by controversies between secularist and Orthodox Jews. One of the strongest trends was the Zionist labor movement, which developed several political parties. Religious Jews, who were less strong than the Zionist socialists, also formed their own parties.

As distinctive political parties emerged within the movement, different aspects of Zionism were stressed. Parties in the militant nationalist wing, for example, were more inclined to strive for international political acceptance than for developing new settlements or expanding Jewish agriculture.

As the nationalist ideology solidified, a Zionist organizational apparatus developed along with other permanent institutions. At the apex was the World Zionist Congress, which met every year or two depending on international circumstances. The congresses represented Zionist groups, national federations, and other subsidiary affiliates such as political parties of religious, labor, or general Zionists; these meetings set the general outlines of policy. Dues-paying members could vote for representatives from their respective countries to the world congress. Most countries in Europe and the Americas had federations of Zionist groups that were affiliated with the world movement. The number of members expanded rapidly, growing from over 164,000 in 1907 to more than 2 million by the late 1960s. Herzl and his associates founded a newspaper in 1899, *Die Welt,* which became the movement's official organ.

Between congresses, movement affairs were carried out by an institutional bureaucracy and by subgroups such as an Actions Committee, later called the Zionist General Council, and its executive, known initially as the Small Actions Committee. In accord with Herzl's blueprints, the Zionist organization established its own bank in 1899. The bank was called the Jewish Colonial Trust and was registered in England; it became an Israeli company in 1955. The Jewish National Fund was founded at the Fifth Zionist Congress in 1901 to acquire, develop, and afforest land in Palestine. A substantial part of the funds were collected in small contributions from world Jewry in blue-and-white boxes, later a common feature in Jewish homes and synagogues.

Since its inception, the Zionist movement and its organizations have been international in character, representing Jews from dozens of different countries and with headquarters and offices in several places. Because of Herzl's domination, Zionist headquarters were located initially in Vienna where he lived. After his death, they were transferred to Cologne, the residence of his successor, David Wolffsohn, who headed the movement from 1905 to 1911. With the advent of the next president, Otto Warburg, head of the organization between 1911 and 1920, Berlin became the center. During World War I, the movement was divided, and an Allied branch was set up in London. A liaison office was organized in 1915 in neutral Copenhagen to facilitate contact across the battle lines. During the presidencies of Chaim Weizmann and Nahum Sokolow, spanning the years from 1920 to 1946, London became the capital of world Zionism. In 1936, many activities of the organization were transferred to Jerusalem, although the presidential organization and several members of the executive remained in London.

Although great activity and large memberships were generated in Europe and the United States during the first twenty years of Zionism, the situation in the Middle East was different. There was still no political entity called Palestine; it was merely a vague geographic term indicating the area where the ancient Philistines and, later, Jews had lived. The largely Arab population, not yet known as Palestinians, referred to itself as Syrians. After the Ottoman conquest in 1517, the land had been divided and redivided among several provinces until 1864, when it was partitioned between the two Ottoman *vilayets* (provinces) of Beirut and Syria and the smaller *sanjak* (administrative subdivision) of Jerusalem. The special status of the land was guaranteed by the European Christian powers after their intervention to protect Christians in the Levant during the 1860s.

Despite Herzl's fervent pleas to the sultan, the Ottoman authorities were reluctant to grant any special political consideration to Jewish settlers. The Ottomans were suspicious of Zionist connections with the Western powers and feared any further European intervention in their already disintegrating empire. When the Turks did intervene, it was not to the advantage of the new Jewish settlers, who the indigenous Arabs perceived as infidel intruders.

When Napoleon invaded the area in the early nineteenth century, there were only 5,000 Jews. By mid-century the number had doubled, and it had doubled again by the 1880s, when the first Zionist settlers arrived. Between 1882 and 1914, the number of Jews in the region grew from 24,000 to 85,000, most of whom were pious and elderly Jews who had come to die in the Holy Land. Most Jewish residents of the country were protected by various European powers; only 10 percent were Ottoman subjects.

The 600,000 Christian and Muslim Arab inhabitants had not yet developed a strong nationalist sentiment. Ethnic identity was based on religious affiliation with Islam, Judaism, or one of the many Christian bodies recognized as a *millet* (national community) by the Ottoman authorities. There was little Ottoman intervention into the lives of most Arab villagers and practically none into the lives of the roaming Bedouin in the south and along the edges of the cultivated areas. Contacts between Jews and local Arabs were rare. Few of the early Zionist leaders recognized the significance of Arab-Jewish relations. Instead, they concentrated on contacts with the European powers whom they believed would further their goals. After Herzl's visit to Palestine, he barely mentioned the Arab population in his diary or written reports.

During World War I a large number of Jewish settlers were Russians or citizens of other Allied powers that were at war with Turkey; thus, many were deported, imprisoned, or executed. The Zionist movement was charged with subversion and with intent to dismember the Ottoman Empire. Institutions such as the Jewish Colonial Trust and the Anglo-Palestine Bank were banned, and public use of Hebrew was forbidden. Natural disasters including drought, a locust plague, and famine added to the miseries of the populace. By the time General Edmund Allenby, commander of British forces in the area, entered Jerusalem in 1917, the total population in Palestine had diminished by nearly one-fifth, and the Jewish population had diminished by about one-third to only 55,000.

Jewish Opposition to the Zionists

Despite many controversies around and within the movement, Zionism gradually became the strongest unifying force among world Jewry. Until World War II, however, it had to compete with other Jewish movements and trends. The opposition that had developed could not ignore the conceptual thesis put forward by the Zionists, which consisted of three elements: (1) Jews are a separate people, and their common religious and cultural characteristics qualify them to be perceived as a national entity; (2) because of the prevailing anti-Semitism rooted in gentile society, Jews cannot expect to be treated as equals by their European "host" nations; and (3) the only solution to Jews' aspirations to equality and normalcy is to establish somewhere, preferably in Palestine, a national "homeland." Thus exclusion, inequality, and the need for independence were the three components of the Jewish problem and its solution as defined by Zionism. This approach claims that Jews are a "territorial nation" aspiring to return home; they should uproot the past and begin communal life again by creating a realm that is free of anti-Semitism.

The essence of this nationalist approach was developed during the time of European emancipation. The approach was, however, only one prevailing option among several available to the Jews during that period. Prior to emancipation they had virtually no options. Their identity as Jews, as a distinct group of people, was secured if not only from within and by themselves then from the outside by their gentile hosts. Now, when freedom of choice prevailed, the Jews were required—in some regions more than others—to define who they were and how they wished to conduct their private and collective affairs. For those who stayed within their religious communities, practicing their ancient rituals and conducting their lives in accordance with traditional disciplines, these new freedoms constituted little problem. Their identity, and hence their position in society, was firmly defined by the dictates of their forebears and the rabbis. The issue of equality mattered little; it meant they had new personal rights but also new civil obligations (like military duty), an option they wished to avoid. Those who moved out of the traditional community could choose one of several possibilities: immigration to the United States or Western Europe (the restriction on Jewish immigration to England, for example, was lifted in 1826), assimilation into the gentile society as individuals, or coexistence with that society in one form or another, thus abandoning their Jewish identity.

At the beginning of the nineteenth century, some estimates placed the number of Jews in the world at about two and a half million. Almost 90 percent of Jews lived in Europe, most in the countryside because in some countries they were forbidden to reside in cities. By the end of the nineteenth century there were about 10 millions Jews worldwide. During that century and until 1925, when restrictions were imposed on free immigration to the United States, around 4.5 million Jews left Central and Eastern Europe for the West, where they could sustain their identity. Most emigrated after the 1880s, when pogroms and persecutions were at their peak.

Among the millions of Jews who stayed in Europe, several thousand decided to assimilate into the Christian world to enhance their personal welfare. During the nineteenth century, around 250,000 East and Central European Jews converted. This was not the first massive Jewish conversion; in the Middle Ages such conversions were common in the Iberian Peninsula. In some places in Europe it took little for a Jew to be officially considered a non-Jew and hence to be recorded as a convert. In Austria and Prussia, for example, Jews could cease paying taxes to the Jewish community by declaring themselves "without religion." In Germany and other regions, active assimilation was easily achieved and even officially encouraged. Thus, for example, Jews who wanted to hold public office in Prussia were required to convert to Catholicism or Protestantism. Heinrich Marx, in order to hold public office, baptized himself and his son Karl in 1824; a year later the poet Heinrich Heine did the same. Abraham Mendelssohn-Bartholdy, the father of the composer Felix, became a Christian in 1822. Jews could become members of the British Parliament only in 1858, but Benjamin Disraeli's father, Issac, had baptized and qualified him for a possible political post in 1817.

Those who refused to convert but who, unlike the Zionists or the immigrants, wished to stay in Europe learned that gentile society was not ready to accept them as equals. The principles of emancipation assert that in the modern secular state the law protects the rights of private opinion and free association, including religious worship. The practice of religion was confined to the private domain and was therefore not in conflict with public order. Public order entailed civil obligations, and many nonnationalist Jews understood that to coexist with the Gentiles they needed to accept the Christian dogma and make the proper adjustments in their methods of worship. The evolving Jewish Reform movement placed among its guiding principles a strong patriotic identification with the state. This movement became a major Jewish force in Germany and later, through immigration, in the United States.

Many other Jews joined general revolutionary and reform movements whose principle aim was to make society more egalitarian. These Jews thought the collective goal, even when abstractly defined, would help to resolve their personal identity problem. By moving away from specific concerns for their own people to concerns of the general community and shifting from the battle for Jewish rights to the battle for all humankind, they hoped to resolve their own problems. They understood that "a new beginning" was called for. They considered the bourgeoisie the enemy of equality. Moreover, among the principal revolutionary thinkers, some of Jewish origin—such as Marx and, later, Rosa Luxembourg—identified Jews as an integral component of the society they wished to change. Their arguments added a problematic dimension to those made by the anti-Semitic ideologues of the time. Naturally, the attempt to establish a separate secular identity as Jews was opposed by revolutionaries as a reactionary trend. Lenin, the leader of the Soviet revolution, favored the assimilation of Jews and their complete disappearance into society. On the one hand, he denounced all forms of anti-Semitism; on the other, he opposed separatism, including Jewish nationalism.

The percentage of Jewish founders, leaders, and rank-and-file members of the socialist and social democratic parties of Central and Eastern Europe far exceeded their percentage in the population. Leon Trotsky, founder of the Red Army and second in command to Lenin; Lev Kamenev and Grigori Zinoviev, who together with Stalin constituted the Troika that ruled the USSR after Lenin's death; Maxim Litvinov, the Soviet Union foreign minister; Lazar Kaganovich, a member of the Communist party Central Committee; and Bela Kun, the Hungarian Communist dictator in 1919, are a few of the notable Jews who believed a workers' victory would resolve the Jewish problem as well.

Others chose to maintain their distinct, although nonreligious, Jewish identity and to obtain their goals within the framework of their own community. Many upheld the concept of diaspora nationalism in two significant groups: the Autonomists and the Yiddishists. Jews who refused to accept the notion that they were alien in their place of residence or that anti-Semitism was eternal and could not be avoided considered themselves to be one of the European national groups with the same rights as other groups. They rejected the idea of reviving Hebrew as a national language and argued that they already had Yiddish, with its rich culture, as their national tongue.

Simon Dubnow (1860–1941), who published a multivolume account of Jewish history, was the most important theoretician of the autonomous concept of diaspora community life.[14] According to Dubnow, Jews, as a consequence of their exile, moved into an advanced stage of human existence and became the only true "international" nation. Dubnow felt Jews should therefore attempt to coordinate their efforts and establish their own cultural institutions everywhere, especially an educational system with Yiddish as its language. His followers organized a party in Poland (Peoples' Party) and a newspaper (*Der Monet*) that fought for domination of the Jewish public and aimed to establish a system of Jewish "parliaments" (diets) to coordinate and guide the affairs of the various European communities. All nations, the autonomists believed, would progress toward this Jewish modality of human association.

The greatest rival of the Zionists in Eastern Europe, except for Orthodox Judaism, was the Jewish socialist Bund, established in 1897—about the same time Herzl founded the Zionist movement. Unlike many Jews who joined the general revolutionary movements and the newly established socialist and social democratic parties, the Bundists felt their activities should be conducted only in Yiddish.

The Zionists, perhaps because of a clearer guiding concept and better organization, were gradually able to increase their power relative to the other Jewish groups. By 1917, over half of the 500 members of the all-Russian Jewish Congress were Zionists; only 9 percent were Bundists. Likewise, among the 133 members of the Association of Jewish Communities in Moscow, 53 were Zionists, 16 were Bundists, and 20 were Orthodox. Among the 55 Jews represented in the 809-member Ukrainian parliament (Rada), 18 were Zionists and 13 were Bundists. In other representative bodies in Eastern Europe, similar proportions existed between Zionists and their opponents.[15]

All of these Jewish secular factions were either suppressed by the Stalin regime or destroyed by the Nazis. The opposition presented by the Orthodox group, however, became the most durable and extends into the present. For the Orthodox, Hasidim, and others, Zionism was perceived to be far too secular and hence as destructive of Jewish tradition and values. The Zionist goal of restoring national life in Eretz Israel was considered counter to religious dictates. Devoted Jews should await the coming of the Messiah to guide them to the Holy Land. Speeding up the process of restoration, as the Zionists proposed, was a sin. Several current Orthodox sects, such as the Satmar Hasidim in New York and Naturei Karta (Keepers of the Gate) in Jerusalem, would gladly see the State of Israel—the product of "godless" Zionism—destroyed and its governing authorities transferred to non-Jewish hands, either Christian or Muslim.

Not all Orthodox are or were so radically opposed to Zionism. Some from Eastern Europe and Germany who wished to protect their own version of Judaism formed Agudat Israel in 1912, with branches in Eretz Israel. This organization later became an Israeli political party. For others, especially the Mizrachi, which later became the largest faction within Israel's National Religious Party (Mafdal), contradictions between traditional values and Zionism were resolved by a conceptual bridge that was formulated by, among others, Rabbi Avraham Kook. Essentially, Kook argued that the Zionist return to Eretz Israel signified the beginning of the divine redemption and renewal of the Jewish people. He felt the secular Zionists should not be opposed and that attempts should be made to emphasize the spiritual aspects of the national revival. Theologically, Kook suggested, Zionists who labored over the construction of the "Holy Land" should be regarded similarly to the foreign artists and builders who erected the Holy Temple in Jerusalem during biblical times. Kook, a nonpartisan, became the spiritual leader of the Mizrachi and the first chief rabbi in Palestine.

The Balfour Declaration

In the international political arena, World War I was the occasion for spectacular Zionist advances. Despite the division of the movement into Allied, Central Power, and neutral camps, it achieved the recognition Herzl had striven for but never acquired. Both Germans and British sought the support of their respective Jewish communities and those on the opposite side (Allies and Central Powers, respectively) through statements that recognized Zionist aspirations. Zionist leaders in Allied capitals pressed their claims to Palestine by organizing special Jewish units to assist the war effort. Joseph Trumpeldor gathered nine hundred troops in the Zion Mule Corps, which served with the British against the Turks in Gallipoli. Another Russian Zionist, Vladimir Jabotinsky, who later became the nationalist leader, headed a campaign to create a Jewish Legion. Although they were never organized on the scale conceived by Jabotinsky, two battalions of Jewish volunteers from Russia, England, and the United States, called the Judeans, were attached to General Edmund Allenby's forces. Another volunteer Jewish battalion brought the number of Jewish forces in Palestine to about five thousand.

The major political efforts were made in Great Britain and the United States, where Zionism won official approval. Chaim Weizmann, a Russian-born chemistry lecturer at Manchester University, became the focus of these activities. After settling in England, Weizmann became an active Zionist leader. As a young man he attended the Basle conference, and he remained active in the newly established Zionist organization. Next to Herzl and David Ben-Gurion, Israel's first prime minister, Weizmann is probably the individual associated the most strongly with the establishment of modern Israel. Among his scientific accomplishments was the development of a process to produce acetone, an essential ingredient for manufacturing the cordite required in British artillery shells during World War I. Weizmann's scientific work brought him into close contact with high-level British officials, and he persuaded them to support Zionism.

After months of lengthy discussion and despite divisions in the British cabinet and within the Jewish community, a compromise formula was reached in which Great Britain officially recognized and supported Jewish aspirations in Palestine. Some cabinet members were reluctant to adopt this formula because of fears that support of Zionism would alienate both Arabs in the Middle East and Muslims elsewhere in the British Empire. Non-Zionist Jewish leaders, including Edwin Montagu, the only Jew in the British cabinet, were apprehensive about repercussions for their identity as loyal British subjects. But expectations that support of Zionism would result in large-scale Jewish support finally led to the Balfour Declaration, published November 2, 1917.

The declaration was a watered-down version of what Weizmann and his colleagues had desired. The wording was sufficiently vague to cause numerous future debates. The declaration took the form of a public letter from Lord Alfred Balfour, the British foreign minister, to Lord Lionel Walter Rothschild, a prominent British Zionist leader. It stated that "His Majesty's Government view with favour the establishment in Palestine of a national home for the Jewish people, and will use their best endeavours to facilitate the achievement of that object, it being clearly understood that nothing shall be done which may prejudice the civil and religious rights of the existing non-Jewish communities in Palestine, or the rights and political status enjoyed by Jews in any other country."[16]

In deference to non-Zionists, the wording of the declaration was changed to call for the establishment of "a national home" in Palestine rather than "*the* national home of the Jewish people." The existing communities in Palestine, as well as Jewish rights in the diaspora, were to be safeguarded.

The British Information Ministry created a special Jewish department to follow through on the declaration. This department prepared leaflets containing the text of the Balfour Declaration to drop over enemy territory and spread word about it both in Eastern Europe and in the United States, where Jewish sentiment was strongly antipathetic to czarist Russia, which was Great Britain's ally until the 1917 revolution. If an alliance could be contracted with a variety of Jewish interest groups, it might strengthen the pro-Allied sentiment of many influential Jews and weaken those opposed to the war. Some British officials even hoped to win German Jewish support.

At the same time, however, in other statements, agreements, and contractual arrangements with France and with Arab nationalist leaders, Great Britain made a variety of promises about the future of the Ottoman Empire after an Allied victory. Some British leaders asserted that the diverse promises could be reconciled, whereas to many they seemed contradictory. British involvement in the Middle East became even more complicated following General Allenby's conquest of Palestine. Zionist leaders demanded and received British permission for a Zionist Commission of Jews from Allied countries, which would visit the occupied areas. At the same time the Arabs, who believed the Balfour Declaration conflicted with British wartime promises to them, were beginning to ask embarrassing questions about Jewish activities.

The Zionist Commission was the first official organization of the Zionist movement in Palestine that had international recognition. Established as an advisory body to the British occupation forces, the commission was to represent both Palestinian and world Jewish concerns. From the beginning, the commission was at odds with British officials. The latter saw their primary responsibility as maintaining a politically stable environment in which British interests could flourish. The Zionists believed Great Britain was obligated to implement the Balfour Declaration, with its emphasis on developing the Jewish national home.

Following an interruption during the war, meetings of the World Zionist Congress were resumed in 1921, and functions of the Zionist Commission were absorbed by the Zionist Executive of the Congress. Major decisions for the Jewish community in Palestine, the Yishuv, and the world Zionist movement continued to be made at European headquarters by leaders such as Weizmann, who lived in Europe. The Yishuv was viewed as the "vanguard of world Jewry," laying the groundwork for the Jewish state, which in the future would, it was hoped, absorb most of the world's Jews. According to Zionist dogma, Jews in the diaspora were obliged to support the national home financially and politically.

Locally, the Yishuv attempted to organize its own representative bodies. After the British seized Jerusalem in 1917, the Jews, who then constituted a majority of the population, set up a city council. Later, a countrywide provisional council was organized to prepare the way for an elected Jewish constituent assembly; however, the assembly was blocked by British authorities who felt it was premature. By 1918, when the rest of Palestine was captured from the Turks, a national conference made up of several Jewish settlements chose Weizmann and his Russian Zionist colleague, Nahum Sokolow, to represent it at the Paris peace talks. However, not until British military authorities turned the country over to civil rule in 1920 was a Jewish constituent assembly formally recognized.

By the end of World War I, Weizmann had become the true successor to Theodore Herzl as the world Zionist leader. Although Weizmann still lived in England, the Yishuv and the Zionist Congress called upon him to negotiate the future of Palestine with Great Britain and Arab nationalists. Through British intercession, Weizmann conducted several parleys with King Faisal of Syria to mollify growing Arab concerns about Zionist plans for Palestine. At meetings in London and in Aqaba in southern Palestine, Faisal recognized the Balfour Declaration and the need for cooperation with the Zionists, and he encouraged Jewish immigration, provided it did not jeopardize Arab rights. In return, Weizmann promised Jewish economic and technical assistance in developing an Arab state. Both agreed that the British would arbitrate disputes. As a caveat to their written protocol, Faisal insisted that if Arab nationalist aspirations were not fully realized, he would "not then be bound by a single word of the present Agreement which shall be deemed void and of no account or validity, and I shall not be answerable in any way whatsoever." This appended clause was later cited by Arab nationalists as justification for disregarding the agreement; they argued that the French conquest of Syria in 1922 and the fall of Faisal invalidated the pact.

It soon became evident that Faisal did not represent an Arab consensus concerning Palestine. Syrian nationalists warned that Palestine was incontestably a part of their country. Jews would be permitted to settle in an autonomous Palestine, but they would be tied by a bond of federation with Syria. By 1918, nationalism was also stirring the Palestinian Arab consciousness. Sparked by repressive Ottoman measures and Allied promises of self-determination, associations of Christian and Muslim notables were formed in several Palestinian towns during 1919 and 1920. These groups were sent to the nationalist congresses in Damascus to introduce anti-Zionist platforms. During this era, most Arabs in the country's 850 villages did not yet consider themselves separate Palestinians but felt they were part of the new Syrian Arab kingdom.

Zionist leaders urged the Paris peace conferees to turn Palestine over to the newly created League of Nations. The international community, they argued, was obligated to consult world Jewry about the country's future and to support the establishment of an autonomous Jewish commonwealth. In return, they promised full religious freedom for Muslims and Christians and protection of sites that were sacred to all religions.

Palestine's immediate fate was determined by neither Zionists nor Arab nationalists. British and French negotiations over their respective imperial interests in the Middle East were decisive. New Palestinian borders were the result of compromises based on French demands in the north and promises to Arab nationalists in the south. Since no previous international frontier defined Palestine, during 1921 the British subdivided their area into Transjordan and Western Palestine. Faisal was compensated for the loss of Syria to the French by being given the new kingdom of Iraq.

Transjordan was turned over to Faisal's brother, Abdullah, as a reward for services the Hashemites—who had ruled Mecca in the Arabian Peninsula prior to the war—had rendered to the British during that war. Following the military occupation, Transjordan and Palestine were both governed by a single British high commissioner under the Colonial Office, but the east bank of the Jordan River was excluded from commitments related to the establishment of a Jewish national home. This unilateral British separation of Palestine from Transjordan raised no strong protests among mainstream Zionist leaders because there were no Jewish settlers on the east bank. However, militant nationalists, especially Vladimir Jabotinsky's followers, strenuously protested the division of the country into the east and west banks. Their objections later became the basis for a new Zionist political party of Revisionists, whose chief raison d'être was to revise Palestine's borders to include both the east and west banks of the Jordan River.

The Mandate for Palestine

After Great Britain and France agreed on the frontiers of Palestine at the San Remo Conference in 1920, Palestine received its first civilian high commissioner, Herbert Samuel, an English Jew who was a leader of the Liberal party and an avowed Zionist. Samuel had played a significant role in framing the Balfour Declaration and at first was considered to be sympathetic to development of the Jewish home. Zionists were enthusiastic about his appointment, believing he would carry out mandatory policies that were favorable to them.

Although it was administered by Great Britain, according to international law the Mandate for Palestine was the ultimate responsibility of the League of Nations. The mandate system was established by the league in 1922 to avoid quarrels over colonial territory conquered by the Allies and to replace imperialism with a more enlightened policy. Each of the Allied victors entrusted with former German colonies or pieces of the Ottoman Empire was to assist the "liberated" countries in developing self-governing institutions, leading to eventual independence. In the Middle East, France was entrusted with Syria and Lebanon, whereas Great Britain received Iraq, Transjordan, and Palestine.

The Mandate for Palestine gave special recognition to Zionist claims and emphasized rights and privileges of the Jewish community. The preamble incorporated the Balfour Declaration verbatim. There was no specific reference to the country's Arab population by name; instead, these Arabs were called "the inhabitants of Palestine." Whereas Great Britain was vested with "full powers of legislation and administration," special emphasis was placed on British responsibility "for placing the country under such political, administrative and economic conditions as will secure the establishment of the Jewish national home." Local autonomy was to be encouraged "so far as circumstances permit."[17]

The mandate formally recognized the Zionist movement, which was declared the appropriate Jewish agency in matters affecting the establishment of the national home and the interests of the Jewish population in Palestine. Outside Palestine, the Zionist organization was authorized to take steps "to secure the cooperation of all Jews who are willing to assist in establishment of the Jewish national home."

Great Britain was assigned to "facilitate Jewish immigration . . . and encourage, in cooperation with the Jewish Agency [the Zionist organization] . . . close settlement by Jews on the land, including State lands and waste lands not required for public purposes." The nationality law was to include "provisions framed so as to facilitate the acquisition of Palestinian citizenship by Jews who take up their permanent residence in Palestine." Hebrew, English, and Arabic were recognized as the official languages: "Any statement or inscription in Arabic on stamps or money in Palestine shall be repeated in Hebrew and any statements or inscriptions in Hebrew shall be repeated in Arabic."

Requirements protecting the civil and religious rights of "existing non-Jewish communities in Palestine," as stated in the Balfour Declaration, were reemphasized in the mandate. Respect for the religious practices "of the various people and communities" in Palestine was to be guaranteed. Foreign relations were entrusted to the mandatory authority, as was the protection of Palestinian citizens when abroad. In all matters of responsibility related to the "Holy Places and religious buildings or sites in Palestine, including that of preserving existing rights and of securing free access to the Holy Places, religious buildings and sites and the free exercise of worship," the mandatory authority "shall be responsible solely to the League of Nations." A special commission was to be appointed by the mandatory authority "to study, define and determine the rights and claims in connection with the Holy Places and the rights and claims relating to the different religious communities in Palestine." Freedom of worship and conscience was guaranteed: "No discrimination of any kind shall be made between the inhabitants of Palestine on the ground of race, religion or language. No person shall be excluded from Palestine on the sole ground of his belief."

The Mandate for Palestine was sufficiently vague to stimulate years of controversy over its intent. Zionists insisted that it obligated Great Britain to further develop their commonwealth with all due haste. Arab nationalists protested that if it was not an outright violation of the League of Nations covenant that guaranteed their independence, at the least the mandate was discriminatory because it emphasized Jewish rights and failed to even mention Arab rights. Furthermore, they argued, the mandate could not be carried out evenhandedly because of internal inconsistencies. The mandate prohibited discrimination against any group in Palestine, yet it clearly guaranteed certain economic and political advantages to the Jewish community.

The British, caught in the middle of this dilemma, improvised a wide range of means to reconcile their policies with the demands of both Arabs and Jews. The fact that there were three tiers of administration of the mandate added to the diffusion of responsibility and the lack of clarity about final authority. British colonial administrators at the local level in Palestine often differed with each other in carrying out their tasks. Some were sympathetic to Jewish aspirations; others favored the Arabs. Both groups were frequently at odds with, or received unclear signals from, London, where officials in the Colonial Office or the military frequently disagreed with the policies laid out by Parliament. Finally, the British government, which was ultimately responsible to the Permanent Mandates Commission of the League of Nations, became determined to devise policies in Palestine that were consistent with its larger imperial interests in the Middle East.

Throughout the mandatory era, Palestine was run like a British Crown colony. The high commissioner, appointed by the British Crown, had all of the power and authority of a colonial governor or viceroy in India. The commissioner was responsible only to London, not to the population of Palestine or to any world Jewish organization. Authority delegated by the commissioner through his staff or executive council composed of mostly British officials was also legally unchallenged. District commissioners, who were also British, ruled the three principal subdivisions of the country. There was Herbert Samuel and six more high commissioners, mostly generals who had served in other colonial posts.

Of the 10,000 or so employees in the Palestinian civil service, only about 250 were British. By May 15, 1948, the end of the mandate, about one-third of the civil service employees were Jewish and two-thirds were Arab, although proportions varied from department to department. Although major decisions were made by high-ranking British officials, the day-to-day implementation was carried out by Palestinian Jews and Arabs. At first, all of the district officers responsible to the three district commissioners were also British, but several were later chosen from the local Arab and Jewish populations.

The legal basis of British authority was the 1922 Palestine Order in Council, passed by the Parliament in London. In effect, it served as Palestine's constitution during the mandatory era, supplemented by laws published in the *Palestine Official Gazette*. This legislation, based mostly on English law, pertained to administration, crime, commerce, labor, and similar matters. Other legislation pertaining to land and personal status was taken over from the Ottoman rulers by the British administration.

Ottoman law relating to personal-status matters—including marriage, divorce, inheritance, and provision for orphans—was continued under the British administration, which assigned jurisdiction in these affairs to the Jewish, Muslim, and Christian religious courts. The British, reluctant to surrender their political authority, recognized the communities in Palestine as religious rather than political entities. Under the Religious Communities Organization Ordinance, Muslims, Jews, and Christians were identified with their respective religious communities. Land law was also borrowed from the Ottomans; thus, various categories of property and their use, taxation, and inheritance were prescribed according to Ottoman tradition. Some elements of both British and Ottoman legislation are still included in the Israeli legal code.

Under the mandate, major progress was made in developing the country. New roads and railways extended the communications network and linked formerly isolated regions. Health and educational facilities were expanded by the British in the Arab sector and by the Yishuv institutions among the Jews. Agricultural and industrial productivity increased substantially in both sectors. Zionist leaders claimed credit not only for the growth of the Yishuv but also for development of the rest of the country. The British credited their own administration with these achievements. Arab nationalists discounted any advance, asserting that the country could have made far greater progress if it had been independent. These perceptions proved to be a major factor in creating separate national identities and driving the ethnic groups apart.

The mandatory government's efforts to create stable self-governing institutions were ineffective. The British failed to balance the conflicting communal interests of both the Jews and the Arabs. Consequently, Samuel formed an advisory council made up of British officials, Palestinian Jews, and Arabs. Originally, the council was to have been replaced by an elected legislative council, but the latter was stillborn. Until 1936, several more efforts were made to form a legislative council, all of which were aborted by disagreements between Jews and Arabs. In the earlier proposals for local representation, the Jews would have been outvoted. Arab nationalists nevertheless charged that because they were the majority, they were underrepresented. The most militant among them refused to recognize any British authority; consequently, there was little local input into major government decisions. Most decisions were taken by the high commissioner and his staff, restricted only by directives from London, or by popular outbursts.

The Yishuv in Palestine

Within this system, the Yishuv was able to lay foundations for the future Jewish state, to establish its presence in Palestine as a viable and powerful entity, and to achieve national recognition from Jewish communities abroad and from the Western world as a whole. The various factions within the Zionist movement continued their ideological disputes during the mandate, but all made progress. The "politicals" achieved the international recognition of a Jewish national identity for which Herzl had struggled. The "practicals" saw the expansion of the Yishuv from a tiny minority of the population. The number of Jewish settlements increased tenfold, and a Jewish economic infrastructure developed, with its own agriculture, industry, trade, and commerce. "Cultural" Zionists could boast that the Hebrew language had taken root, the number of newspapers and publishing houses had multiplied, and an educational system—capped by the Hebrew University in Jerusalem—had developed.

By the end of the mandate, the Jewish population had increased—largely through immigration—from 65,000 in 1919 to about 650,000 in 1948.[18] Territorially, the Yishuv still occupied less than 10 percent of Palestine. By far the largest areas were lands that belonged to the government—including nearly the entire southern half of the country, called the Negev.

The majority of the Yishuv were Eastern European Jewish immigrants, mostly from Poland and Russia, although smaller groups came from Romania, Bulgaria, and Hungary. There were also a few Middle Eastern immigrants, mainly from Yemen. After Hitler's rise, a new wave of refugees arrived from Germany and Austria. In 1948, more than two-thirds of the Jews were recent immigrants who had come since 1919; of these, 90 percent were European. Immigration was a reaction to the burst of Polish nationalism after World War I, to anti-Semitism in the Nazi-ruled areas after 1933, and to deteriorating economic conditions in Central Europe. Nevertheless, in the interwar period, most Jewish migration still flowed westward to the United States and Western Europe. Despite the development of the Yishuv, life in Palestine remained difficult, and political unrest caused frequent "troubles" or "disturbances," as the British called the strife with Jews and Arabs.

The Yishuv referred to the successive waves of migration as *aliya* (ascent), since the arrivals were considered to be "going up" to the Holy Land. An immigrant was called *oleh,* and immigration was *aliya.* An Israeli Jew who left the country to settle abroad was called *Yored* (descender), and the phenomenon was *yerida.*

Five waves of Jewish immigration, or *aliyot,* are traditionally recorded prior to 1948. The first *aliya* consisted of small groups of Bilu from Russia, who founded the early Jewish colonies during the 1880s, and other Jewish settlers who arrived before 1905. In July 1882, fourteen Biluim arrived in Jaffa to start the process. By 1903, the Bilu had established a score of new settlements and brought around 10,000 Jews to Palestine. Only half became farmers; the others began new Jewish urban settlements—notably in Jaffa, which had 3,000 settlers.

The failure of the 1905 Russian revolution brought about a somewhat larger *aliya* of young workers and socialist Zionists. Thus, between 1905 and 1919 around 30,000 Jews came, mostly from Russia and its adjunct Polish territories. According to some estimates, because of the difficult living conditions they encountered in Palestine, as many as 90 percent of the newcomers returned home or left for the West. Those who stayed emphasized the realization of Zionist-socialist goals—especially the use of Hebrew labor on Jewish land—in contrast to the Bilu, who often followed the traditional colonial pattern of using local Arabs to farm their fields. Many of Israel's founders—including the first three prime ministers, Ben-Gurion, Moshe Sharett, and Levi Eshkol, and the second and third presidents, Itzhak Ben Zvi and Zalman Shazar—were from the second *aliya.* They laid the foundations for a vibrant political system, a security system, the unionization of workers, and the establishment of the original collective agricultural settlements (kibbutzim)—a symbol of Zionist activity in the country. They are often referred to as the founding fathers of Israel, and from a political perspective they are called "the first generation."

The third *aliya,* between 1919 and 1923, came from Poland and other Eastern and Central European nations where economic pressures on the lower-middle-class Jewish communities and increased anti-Semitism made life difficult. Ideologically akin to settlers from the second *aliya,* many in this wave became active in the formation of labor organizations and in providing *halutzim* (pioneers) in agriculture and in the new industries being formed by the Yishuv. About 35,000 immigrants arrived during this period.

Larger numbers, about half from Poland, came in the fourth *aliya.* Many had been impoverished by economic crisis and by discriminatory measures clamped on Jews by Poland's finance minister, Wladyslaw Grabski. Some called the fourth *aliya* the Grabski *aliya* because of his role in driving Jews from Poland. The U.S. closed door policy to large-scale immigration began after 1925, which turned many Jews toward Palestine. A larger number of immigrants from the fourth *aliya* brought capital, which they invested in small businesses in Palestine. Between 1926 and 1929, Palestine experienced a severe economic crisis, resulting in the departure of thousands of the new Jewish immigrants. By 1927 there were nearly twice as many *yordim* as *olim,* and a net decline was seen in the Jewish population.

No sizable immigration occurred again until Hitler's rise to power in 1933 precipitated the fifth and largest *aliya.* Between 1933 and 1936, 164,000 Jews immigrated to Palestine. Nazi persecution changed both the demography and the outlook of the Yishuv.

Until the arrival of middle-class German Jews, the Yishuv had been a fairly homogeneous community, with no significant class differences and no great diversity in social structure. Jewish immigration during the previous half century had come largely from an area of only a few hundred square miles in Eastern Europe. A kind of frontier camaraderie existed in which Jews addressed each other informally as *haver* (comrade). Scorn for formality was epitomized by calling the necktie a herring (*dag maluah*). Standard male dress was khaki shorts and open-necked work shirts. The work ethic, with an emphasis on agriculture, was dominant, although the Jewish population was concentrated in three large cities—Tel Aviv, Jerusalem, and Haifa.

With a total population smaller than that of many European cities, in the 1920s and 1930s the Yishuv enjoyed essentially the atmosphere of a town. In this small, closely knit community, it was easy to develop a strong spirit of national identity. Furthermore, the community was separated from the non-Jewish population by its economic and social life. In Arab and Jewish communities alike, the average individual grew up with little outside contact. Jews were born in Jewish hospitals, studied in Jewish schools, and attended the Hebrew University. Social activity revolved around Zionist youth clubs or Jewish scout groups. Work was done in Jewish businesses, trades, or public enterprises. Jews were employed in Jewish factories with Jewish bosses and a Jewish trade union organization, the Histadrut. Finally, Jews were buried in Jewish cemeteries.

Education played an important role in developing a national consciousness. A British royal commission observed in 1936 that from the education melting pot emerged a national self-consciousness of unusual intensity. Jewish educational institutions, from preschool to university, used the Hebrew language, thereby fostering the development of a strong cultural identity and institutions.

With the fifth *aliya* and the arrival of many professionals from Germany, the demographic and class structure of the Yishuv was altered. Among the arrivals from Central Europe were physicians, engineers, musicians, and other well-educated people with diverse skills. The distinctly middle-class, liberal, Western European viewpoints of the German Jews helped to broaden the perspectives and outlooks of the Yishuv. The German settlers brought new ideas and organizational and managerial skills and began to temper the largely Eastern European Jewish community. Most Germans were identified more closely with the mainstream of traditional European culture than were the immigrants from Russia and Poland. Among the notable cultural contributions of the Germans was the development of a new philharmonic, which became one of the most acclaimed orchestras in the world. German accents provided nuances to the Hebrew language, and German customs identified the Germans as a distinct cultural group. The expression *yekeh* (a contraction from jacket) was applied to German Jews because of their formal attire and manners. Politically, they strengthened the nonsocialist liberal political orientation of the Yishuv through the establishment of the New Immigrant (Aliya Hadasha) party, a forerunner of the Progressive and the Independent Liberal movements.

During the mandate, about 45,000 non-Western Jews came to Palestine, constituting just over 10 percent of the migrants. Many came from Yemen, where Jews had lived before the rise of Islam. Known as excellent craftsmen and arduous laborers, they did little to influence the mainstream of cultural and political development. By the end of the mandate, the 650,000-member Yishuv was definitely European in composition, outlook, and social orientation.

The most important local representative body was the National Council (Vaad Leumi) of between 23 and 42 members, established in 1920 under British mandatory regulations authorizing each religious community to organize its own institutions—a policy the British had adapted from the Ottoman era. The council was chosen by the Elected Assembly (Asefat ha-Nivharim), composed of between 170 and 300 representatives elected nationally by Knesset Israel, the organized Yishuv. Under mandatory regulations, membership in Knesset Israel was voluntary, although few among the Orthodox anti-Zionist Agudat Israel opted out. To exclude oneself from the Yishuv meant, in effect, to be cut off from community activities and services such as education, social welfare, and even normal social life.

Nearly every member of the Yishuv belonged to some organized group within the official Israeli community. There were myriad youth groups, sports organizations, labor activities, social welfare services, and political parties connected to one or another of the Zionist political parties, which were part of the world movement. Parties were both national—because they elected delegates to the National Council—and international, by virtue of representation in the World Zionist Organization and Congress. Some Zionist parties with headquarters either abroad or in Palestine had branches in many countries, including the United States and Great Britain. Many were members of international federations or confederations; others maintained only loose ties with their associates abroad.

Rather than representing separate geographic districts in Palestine, party candidates were elected by the entire Yishuv in a system of proportional representation. When casting a ballot, the voter chose a list of candidates representing a party rather than selecting individual candidates. Party leaders determined who would be on the ballot. When all returns were in, the number of votes required to elect a candidate was obtained by dividing the total number of valid ballots cast by the number of offices to be filled. Replacements between elections were chosen by the party rather than in by-elections. With some modifications, this practice continued until the 1996 general elections.

Because of the great variety of political views in the Yishuv and the world Zionist movement, views that represented many shades of opinion from various parts of Europe, this system of strict proportional representation produced an unusually large number of parties. By 1936 there were ten main parties, each uniting two or more subgroups. At the end of the mandate, the total number of parties was nearly three dozen. The main trends were, and still are, labor, centrist, Orthodox, and national rightist. The strongest trend was the labor movement, which had control of most political institutions such as the National Council. Its base was the Histadrut, or General Federation of Jewish Workers in Palestine. The movement controlled the agricultural sector, including the kibbutzim, and the largest labor unions in the industrial sector. As its strength expanded, the labor movement developed its own industries, marketing cooperatives, transportation systems, banks and financial institutions, and social service network. Most Yishuv leaders came from the labor movement and its affiliated institutions.

True power in the community was wielded by the National Council Executive, a group of six to fourteen leaders who headed departments organized much like a cabinet, including education, health, social welfare, and political affairs. The council also organized the clandestine recruitment and military training of Jewish youth in the Haganah (Defense), which later became the basis for Israel's national security forces. By 1936 the Haganah had about 10,000 well-trained and relatively well-equipped members. Some of the Haganah units were organized with British assistance during the Arab revolt against the mandate between 1936 and 1939.

Deliberations of the National Council, its Executive, and diverse operational or cabinet departments reflected the major issues of the day in the small Jewish community. Relative homogeneity and a large measure of social equality notwithstanding, many controversial issues arose during the quarter century of prestate political existence. For example, should membership in the small community be obligatory or voluntary? Although the great majority favored obligatory membership in the Yishuv because of its small numbers, some dissidents wanted membership to be voluntary. The small Communist movement opposed direction by the "bourgeois" National Council. Was the nature of identity in the community to be personal or territorial; that is, would membership automatically include all who lived within the boundaries of the Jewish community? Should the growing number of settlements and the new towns have greater authority over local affairs, or should control be centralized in the National Council? Debates over such issues as the position of women continued after the state had been established, and some have yet to be resolved.

One of the most strenuous debates concerned the role of religion. The Zionist religious parties strongly emphasized the Jewish content of the Zionist movement; at the other end of the political spectrum, Marxist Zionists perceived class struggle and rights of Jewish workers to be elemental. Zionist socialists advocated the establishment of a welfare system, a planned economy, and greater equalization in society, in contrast to nonsocialists, who believed a major responsibility of the Yishuv was to concentrate on economic expansion by encouraging private investment in agriculture and industry.

Zionist interests abroad were sustained and developed through the World Zionist Organization and the Jewish Agency for Palestine. By the time Israel was founded, the World Zionist Organization and its institutions had become a far-reaching network with branches in around fifty nations and approximately a million members. The Zionist Executive had established its seat in Jerusalem by the late 1930s, with departments that handled immigration and absorption, youth and immigration, education and culture, settlement, and information. These departments supplemented the local activities of the National Council, for which the Yishuv was responsible.

To rally the support of non-Zionist Jews in building the national home, in 1929 Zionist President Chaim Weizmann urged the movement to establish the Jewish Agency for Palestine. The agency was established on the principle of parity between Zionists and non-Zionist Jews, who supported building a national home without accepting the political aspirations of the movement. The Jewish Agency for Palestine assumed the activities of building a national home in which all Jews, even non-Zionists, could participate. It conducted negotiations with the Palestinian mandatory government, with Great Britain, and with the League of Nations. The agency's attempts to negotiate with the Arab leaders were unsuccessful, however. The agency's most important offices—including its presidency and heads of the political, finance, labor, trade, industry, and statistical departments—were held by Zionists. Only those offices concerned with agricultural settlement and the problems of German Jewish immigration were directed by non-Zionists. Zionists and non-Zionists shared direction of the important immigration department, whose task was to determine which Jews could come to Palestine within Great Britain's strict quota system.

With the growth of the Yishuv, its leaders attained positions of increasing influence in the World Zionist Organization and the Jewish Agency for Palestine. By the 1930s, most affairs of importance concerning the Jewish national home were directed by Jews from Palestine. Differences between Zionists and non-Zionists gradually disappeared. In 1947, following the resignation of the last non-Zionist, the Jewish Agency for Palestine and the World Zionist Organization merged. Participation in the National Council, the World Zionist Organization, and the Jewish Agency for Palestine had given hundreds of Palestinian Jews experience in the theoretical and practical problems of statecraft and had helped to create the cadre for the extensive civil service that was to become part of the new Israeli government in 1948. Israel's first four prime ministers, most of its cabinet members during the first generation, and a large number of its top officials, party leaders, and members of parliament received their experience in the prestate Yishuv and in the Zionist movement.

Only at the peripheries of society and in the mixed cities such as Haifa and Jerusalem did extensive contact occur between Jews and non-Jews. Contacts with Arabs or British officials were generally business rather than social occasions. Language also divided the groups. Hebrew was the principal means of communication in Jewish educational and cultural life. Yiddish was considered the language of the diaspora, and its use was discouraged in public, although it continued to be the home tongue of many Eastern European families. With thousands of Jews working for the British mandatory government, English became the second language for many. Only a handful of Jews knew more than a few words of Arabic. A parallel situation prevailed in the Arab community, where English rather than Hebrew became the second language.

A major characteristic of this system of Jewish political and social organization was its isolation from non-Jewish life. Under British rule, the Palestinian Arabs also organized their own separate and distinct communal establishment, although the Arabs were not as well financed, cohesive, or closely knit as the Yishuv. By the end of the mandate, the Arab two-thirds of the population was more spread out geographically and more divided politically and socially than the Yishuv. However, the regional class, religious, and familial or clan differences within Arab society did not prevent it from uniting in its opposition to Jewish immigration and settlement in Palestine. The country's history during the mandate was one of strife and dissension between Jews and Arabs and between each of these groups and the British mandatory government.

Each community perceived the other to be a threat to its existence and its national aspirations. Both Arabs and Jews in Palestine also perceived the British as antagonistic to their respective goals.

From Mandate to Jewish State

At the end of World War II, several factors converged to end the British Mandate for Palestine, which led to the establishment of the Israeli republic. The most powerful of these factors was the wartime experience of European Jewry. After the outbreak of World War II in 1939, anti-Semitism in Hitler's Germany became increasingly virulent. Nazi policy changed from persecution to the outright liquidation of Jews. Hitler's goal was no longer merely to uproot but to totally exterminate the Jews. During the resulting Holocaust, 6 million Jews were slaughtered: about 90 percent of the Jews in German-controlled Europe, or about one-third of world Jewry.

When the word leaked out about the death camps, most Westerners, including many Jews, received it with disbelief. Attempts to bring word of the horrors to the U.S. public and the U.S. Congress—made by a small group of Jews from Palestine, the Bergsonites (after the group's leader, Peter Bergson, also known as Hillel Kook)—encountered bitter opposition from the Zionist establishment. According to David Wyman, with no significant public pressure on the U.S. administration, the only effective Western body at the time that could help save European Jewry, President Franklin Roosevelt decided to ignore the Jews.[19] The small Yishuv was also not engaged in a serious coordinated effort to save the Jews, although many of its members joined the Allied forces. Several local Arabs led by the mufti of Jerusalem, Haj Amin al-Husayni, actively supported the German war efforts. By the end of the war, the horrifying truth of the genocide was all too apparent.

The Holocaust intensified Jewish nationalistic fervor and galvanized most organized Jewish communities behind Zionist demands for a Jewish state in Palestine. Competing nationalist ideologies such as the Bund lost support. Most opponents of Jewish nationalism abandoned their opposition, and even indifferent supporters rallied behind the idea of the Jewish state. Influential non-Zionist Jewish organizations in the West, such as the American Jewish Committee, not only abandoned their opposition but actively supported the creation of Israel.

Within the Zionist movement, the trend was toward more militant activism. Organizational aims were sharpened and focused on the immediate needs of European Jewry. At an emergency meeting held at the Biltmore Hotel in New York in May 1942, a new platform was adopted that served as the basis of mainstream Zionism until the establishment of Israel in 1948. The Biltmore Program urged that the gates of Palestine be opened, that the Jewish Agency for Palestine be vested with control of immigration into Palestine, and that Palestine be established as a Jewish commonwealth integrated into the structure of the new democratic world.[20]

In the face of conflicting promises and responsibilities, British power and prestige declined precipitously. Plagued by war weariness and financial pressures, Great Britain began to withdraw from its most troublesome and expensive imperial outposts. India, Pakistan, Burma, and Ceylon became independent. In the Middle East, British control was loosened in Egypt, Iraq, and Transjordan, and in England pressure increased to give up the Mandate for Palestine. Intensification of Jewish nationalism and demands to remove restrictions on immigration and physical expansion of the Jewish homeland led to clashes between British forces and the Yishuv. In desperation, Great Britain turned the problem over to the new United Nations in 1946.

The United Nations, successor to the League of Nations, was still Western-dominated. In an attempt to deal with Arab opposition to the establishment of a Jewish state in all of Palestine, on November 29, 1947, the UN General Assembly recommended a compromise partition resolution dividing the country into a Jewish state, an Arab state, and an international enclave around Jerusalem. In a rare display of unity, the United States and the Soviet Union both supported the resolution; the ten Arab and Muslim members of the assembly voted against it. Great Britain, the mandatory power, refused to support partition because of Arab opposition.

The resolution precipitated a civil war in Palestine. The Yishuv, elated with the result of the UN debate, demonstrated its joy with victory celebrations and parades. Many who had never expected to see a Jewish state were astonished at the speed with which their dream was about to be fulfilled. For the Palestinian Arabs, however, the UN resolution was a nightmare. Crowds poured into the streets in demonstrations of opposition. Inevitably, tensions between the two communities escalated into violent incidents. Jews quickly retaliated against Arab attacks, and within days the country was plunged into civil war.

Great Britain still refused to cooperate in implementing the partition resolution. Its official goal was to leave Palestine by May 15, 1948, the last day of the mandate. No effort was made to effect an orderly transition. Instead, thirty years of British administration ended in total chaos. Government offices, equipment, and records fell into the hands of whatever forces happened to fill the vacuum left by departing British officials.

Between November 30, 1947, and May 15, 1948, when the mandate officially ended, Arab leaders in Palestine organized local militia forces to prevent the establishment of a Jewish state. They were aided by guerrillas from the surrounding Arab countries; on May 15 the armies of Egypt, Syria, Lebanon, Jordan, and Iraq officially joined the battle. Israelis called this first in a series of wars between Israel and the surrounding Arab states the War of Independence. It ended in 1949, when Israel signed separate armistice agreements with Egypt, Syria, Jordan, and Lebanon. These agreements solidified Israel's frontiers with its Arab neighbors for nearly twenty years, until the third Arab-Israeli war in 1967.

The State of Israel was declared, and its first government was established amid war and chaos on May 14, 1948. Actually, a de facto government had begun to function several months earlier in anticipation of the end of the mandate. The United Nations had sent a Palestine commission to implement the partition plan. Since neither the Arabs nor the British would cooperate with the commission, it worked exclusively with the Jewish community through the National Council and the Jewish Agency for Palestine to form the Jewish government as described in the UN resolution. A Jewish Provisional Council, chosen from National Council and Jewish Agency for Palestine executive members, was organized in March 1948 and assumed control of many areas as they were abandoned by the British. When the British withdrew, the Provisional Council provided the services and administrative apparatus necessary to maintain a semblance of normal life. Thus, education, sanitation, social welfare, and public law and order were maintained in Jewish-controlled regions. The Jewish Agency for Palestine also organized a provisional post office to replace the mandatory system.

As the date for termination of the mandate and departure of the British grew closer, opinion in the Provisional Council was divided as to whether to declare independence. Many countries, including the United States, which only a few weeks earlier had supported partition, now urged the Zionist leaders to postpone independence. They wanted to avoid further escalation of the war, fearing its consequences for the entire Middle East. In the end, David Ben-Gurion, chair of the Jewish Agency for Palestine and leader of the Yishuv, insisted that the opportunity to declare independence should not be lost. The council decided to issue its Declaration of Independence on May 14 and transformed itself into the new Provisional Council of State, Israel's first government. The name State of Israel was chosen because it was closest to the Hebrew term *Eretz Israel* (Land of Israel).

The Declaration of Independence became the statement of principles of Israel's new political system. Like Great Britain, Israel has no formal written constitution; rather, an accumulation of basic laws forms the legal basis of the government and the constitutional system. The Declaration of Independence emphasized the historical claims of the Jewish people to the Land of Israel and the confirmation of those claims in the Balfour Declaration, the League of Nations mandate, and the UN partition resolution. It defined Israel as a Jewish state "representing the Jewish people in Palestine and the World Zionist movement" and declared that Israel "be open to the immigration of Jews from all countries of their dispersion." The "Jewish people all over the world" were called "to rally to our side in the task of immigration and development, and to stand by us in the great struggle for the fulfillment of the dream of generations for the redemption of Israel." Special emphasis was placed on Israel's relationship to the survivors of the Holocaust and "the need to solve the problem of the homeless and [the] lack of independence of the Jewish people."

Non-Jewish rights were guaranteed, and the declaration promised that the country would be developed "for the benefit of all its inhabitants . . . on the principles of liberty, justice and peace as conceived by the Prophets of Israel." All citizens were promised "full social and political equality . . . without distinctions of religion, race, or sex." The declaration also promised to secure "freedom of religion, conscience, education and culture . . . [to] safeguard the Holy Places of all religions; and . . . [to] loyally uphold the principles of the United Nations Charter."

Arab inhabitants of the state were called upon "to preserve the ways of peace and play their part in the development of the State, on the basis of full and equal citizenship and due representation in all its bodies and institutions—provisional and permanent." All of the neighboring states and their peoples were invited to cooperate "with the independent Jewish nation for the common good of all." Israel offered to "make its contribution to the progress of the Middle East as a whole." A formal constitution was "to be drawn up by the Constituent Assembly no later than the 1st October, 1948."[21]

The Declaration of Independence reflected a number of ideological and political compromises among the diverse factions of the Yishuv and the Zionist movement. It made no reference to boundaries or frontiers. Although the Jewish Agency for Palestine and the National Council had accepted the UN partition plan, the term *Land of Israel* referred to all of Palestine. The Revisionist faction of the Zionist movement still regarded the east bank of Jordan as a rightful part of the Jewish patrimony. Furthermore, Israel was in the midst of a war with surrounding Arab states, the outcome of which had not yet been determined.

The role of religion in the Jewish state presented another dilemma. Orthodox Jewish leaders wanted the declaration to emphasize formal religion and to recognize explicitly not merely the Jewish ethnicity of Israel but also Israel's intimate ties with the Jewish faith. At the other end of the political spectrum, Marxist-oriented members of the Mapam party opposed any deference to Orthodoxy. They wanted a Jewish secular state in which religion was separate from politics and God was not mentioned. A compromise was reached using Old Testament phraseology in which signers of the declaration placed their "trust in the Rock (*zur*) of Israel."

The State of Israel and its new government replaced the British mandatory government in most of Palestine. Areas not under Israeli control by the end of the War of Independence were divided among various Arab armies, principally those of Jordan, Egypt, Syria, and Lebanon. When the 1949 armistice agreements were signed, Israel controlled four-fifths of Palestine's 10,000 square miles, Jordan held the largely Arab regions west of the Jordan River, and Egypt occupied the Gaza Strip.

Challenges of the New State

While the War of Independence was still underway, the new Jewish government began to take steps for establishing the state. Immediate choices had to be made: How could the new government win the war with scarce ammunition and untrained soldiers? What resources should be spared to bring in the thousands of Holocaust survivors whom the British had placed in Cyprus camps or displaced persons' camps in Europe? What should be done with the Arab minority: the many who left and became refugees and the few who stayed behind? How could a central government and authority be installed over groups and individuals who refused to submit to the dictates of the Yishuv leadership?

The basic attributes of the new society had to be agreed upon. What type of political system (including the nature of the representative bodies and electoral methods) should be used? What type of economy should be encouraged: planned, capitalist, or a mixed system? What should be the nature of the relationship between state and religion and between religion and nationality? How much effort should be invested in immigration, especially from Arab countries where the position of Jews had dramatically worsened as their governments waged war with Israel? What international orientation should be adopted: pro-Western, pro-Soviet, or neutral? What cultural character was desirable, Western or Mediterranean? How extensive should public administration be, and what degree of military and civilian control should be imposed? Many of these basic questions were not resolved then and are still outstanding. The following chapters address these issues and show how problematic their resolution has been in the evolving Israeli society and state.

2

Political Culture

The characteristic nature and dynamics of Israeli society are outcomes of its history, the specific environmental constraints it encounters, and the challenges it must overcome. In itself, Israel's political system is not unique; its components are those of similar multiethnic immigrant societies that have one dominant ethnic or religious group. But the particular context in which Israel's Western-type democracy developed is distinctly its own.

An Immigrant Society

In October 1994, Israeli Minister of Labor Ora Namir suggested in a newspaper interview that some selective measures should be taken with regard to Jewish immigration from Russia. She argued that many Russian Jewish immigrants were unproductive. The old, the sick, and single mothers with dependent children were enjoying the benefits of the elaborate Israeli welfare system. Young productive Jews stayed behind or immigrated to the United States. Such conduct, she argued, was a practice of the young Russian Jews that was "unfair" to their elders and to economically strained Israel.

The public uproar over the minister's words spread across the entire political spectrum. How dare she propose implementation of discriminatory measures against Jews? How could she go against the very essence of the Zionist credo? How could she place major emphasis on the economic dimension of immigration rather than on its ideological or humanitarian aspects?

As it turned out, the data upon which the minister relied were simply inaccurate. Indeed, because it increases the country's Jewish population, immigration is the lifeblood of Israel. It is the raison d'être and the single most important objective of the Zionist movement in establishing the Jewish state.

Throughout the mandatory period, disputes over Jewish immigration were the main cause of tension between the British and Zionist leaders. Fear of being outnumbered was a primary factor in the development of the Arab nationalist movement, which demanded that Great Britain halt the flow of Jews into the country. This fear has not disappeared. In the late 1980s, when Palestinian and other Arab leaders learned that the Soviet Union might open Jewish immigration to Israel, they flew to Moscow to argue against such a decision.

From the early days of the movement, the Zionists understood that if they were not to remain a small and beleaguered enclave in a hostile environment, they had to become an independent Jewish commonwealth that was free to determine its own immigration policies. They believed that with more Jews in the country it would be easier to maintain a qualitative edge over the Arabs in security, settlement, and other government policies.

British restrictions on Jewish immigration and land purchases in Palestine, imposed in the 1939 White Paper, were a decisive factor in intensifying militancy and led to the 1942 Biltmore Program discussed in Chapter 1. Immigration was essential not only to protect Jews from anti-Semitism and extermination in Europe but also to continue the development of the Jewish national home. Therefore, one of the first official acts of the new government in 1948 was to repeal the 1939 restrictions on Jewish immigration. Shortly thereafter, on July 5, 1950, the Knesset unanimously passed the Law of Return.

The Law of Return is one of Israel's basic constitutional anchors. It confirms provisions made in the Declaration of Independence guaranteeing that "every Jew has the right to immigrate to the country" except for those who "acted against the Jewish nation" or who "may threaten public health or State security." In presenting the law to the Knesset, Ben-Gurion observed: "This law lays down . . . this right [which] is inherent in every Jew by virtue of his being a Jew if it but be his will to take part in settling the land. This right preceded the State of Israel; it is that which built the State."

From 1948 until 1994, the number of immigrants varied from year to year. During that period about 2.35 million Jews entered Israel from all over the world. This represented nearly four times the number of Jews in Israel at independence and about six times the number who arrived during the mandate. The largest wave of immigration—from May 1948 through 1951—doubled the Jewish population. Almost 688,000 people—an average of 172,000 new immigrants per year—arrived, with the highest number, 240,000, immigrating in 1949. This group emptied the displaced persons' camps in Europe, which housed refugees from Nazi concentration camps, and closed the interment centers on Cyprus, where the British kept "illegal" Jewish immigrants.

The second-largest number of immigrants came during the period 1990–1993, mostly from the collapsing Soviet Union. Over 507,000 people arrived, with the largest numbers—199,000 and 176,000—coming in 1990 and 1991, respectively.

Table 2.1 provides data on immigration to Israel between 1948 and 1991. The periods shown include years when significant fluctuations occurred in the intensity of immigration. The table also shows the distribution of immigrants by place of origin. This information will serve as the basis for the analysis in the remainder of this section.

By the early 1950s, most European Jews had been resettled, and a new wave of immigrants came, mostly from Iraq and Arab North Africa. During the next twenty years, the number of these Jews nearly equaled the number of European immigrants. However, few Jews remained in Asia and Africa, and Western Jews continued to arrive in increasing numbers; thus, the Ashkenazim remained the largest group. Between 1948 and 1991, almost 63 percent of the newcomers were from Europe and America.

The first immigration wave from Arab countries was Operation Magic Carpet from Yemen. Most of that country's approximately 47,000 Jews were flown to Israel during 1949 and 1950. When the operation ended, only a few hundred Jews remained in Yemen, a few of whom were "bought" from their government and covertly brought to Israel during the early 1990s. In 1950, Iraq abruptly enacted a law authorizing Jewish emi-

TABLE 2.1 Jewish Immigrants by Period and Continent of Origin, 1948–1991 (%)

		Continent of Origin	
Period	*Number of Immigrants*	*Asia-Africa*	*Europe-America*
1948–1951	687,624	49.9	50.1
1952–1954	54,676	76.4	23.6
1955–1957	166,492	68.3	31.7
1958–1960	75,970	36.0	64.0
1961–1964	228,793	59.4	40.6
1965–1968	82,244	49.7	50.3
1969–1971	116,791	37.3	72.7
1972–1974	142,755	9.2	90.8
1975–1979	124,827	14.3	85.7
1980–1984	83,637	27.1	72.9
1985–1989	70,196	20.4	79.6
1990–1991	375,612	7.0	93.0

Source: Statistical Abstract of Israel (Jerusalem: Government of Israel, Central Bureau of Statistics, 1992).

gration, and its Jews were flown to Israel in Operation Ezra and Nehamia, named after the two Old Testament patriarchs who migrated to the Holy Land from Mesopotamia. Consequently, nearly 121,000 Jews left some of the oldest Jewish settlements, leaving behind a few who were later smuggled across the Iraqi borders.

Growing political unrest, economic insecurity, and the Arab-Israeli wars were the prime incentives for the departure of most Jews from Arab countries in the Middle East (Iraq, Yemen, Syria, Lebanon, and Egypt) and North Africa (Morocco, Tunisia, Algeria, and Libya). By the early 1970s, few Jews remained in the Arab world. Of the 750,000 Arab-speaking Jews who arrived in Israel during the 1960s, about one-third came from Morocco, leaving behind only about 30,000 Jews. The few hundred Jews who remained in Syria were brought in, again in a covert manner, during 1994.

Among the 37,000 Jews who arrived in Israel during 1983 and 1984, around 12,000 were brought secretly from Ethiopia in Operation Moses. The relationship between these newcomers, "Beta Israel" (or Falasha), and Judaism was questioned by some Orthodox rabbis, who concluded that they were descendants of one of the Bible's twelve lost Hebrew tribes. In 1991, 20,000 more Jews were flown covertly from Ethiopia during Operation Solomon; an additional 3,600 Jews came in 1992.

According to World Jewish Congress population statistics, there were about 13 million Jews worldwide by the end of 1990. One-third lived in Israel, making it the second-largest Jewish community after the United States. Another large group lived in Europe, mostly in France (about 600,000), Great Britain (315,000), Russia (close to 600,000), and the Ukraine (450,000). Of the millions of Jews in Poland prior to World War II, fewer than 10,000 remained. Other significant concentrations of Jews were found in Latin America (about 500,000, half in Argentina and a quarter in Brazil), Canada, South Africa, and Australia with 360,000, 114,000, and 100,000, respectively. The rest were scattered in small numbers in over eighty countries.[22]

The experience over four decades of immigration shows that Israel's "pull" power was generally much weaker than the "push" factor. Anti-Semitism and deteriorating economic conditions were the two main factors that caused Jews to leave the diaspora for Israel. Zionist ideology and love of Zion were not strong enough to attract them; nor were the benefits and care the state offered to newcomers. The prevailing economic conditions in Israel, as well as its security situation, constituted another deterrent. The economic recession of the early 1950s, for example, caused a sharp decline in immigration; fewer than 12,000 immigrants came in 1953, which is less than the number who arrived illegally during some of the mandate years. Likewise, when Jews were permitted to leave the Soviet Union during the mid-1970s by obtaining Israeli visas, most went to the United States. Because of tightened U.S. immigration restrictions during the late 1980s, most

Jews leaving the Soviet Union at that time ended up in Israel. For some, Israel was a transition station; for most, it became a permanent home.

Ethnic Composition

Like most other immigrant societies, Israel is made up of a mosaic of groups—Jew and Arab, Oriental and Western, cosmopolitan and parochial, rich and poor. Essentially, one can easily distinguish between two of these groups: those who are Jews and those who are non-Jews, mostly Arabs. This section examines the ethnic composition of the first group; the next section deals with the second group.

To the extent that demographic, social, and economic data can offer some insight into the life of a country, the following statistics are informative. Jewish society in Israel is customarily divided according to country of origin. Three groups are thus defined: those born in Israel, those born in Asia-Africa, and those born in Europe-America. The members of the first group are called Sabras (after the fruit of the cactus—"sweet on the inside, prickly on the outside"); those of the second group are the Sephardim, also called Mizrachim (Easterners) or Orientals; and members of the third group are the Ashkenazim (Westerners). By 1991 there were 1,137,400 Jewish households in the country. They included 448,600 Sabra households, 286,300 Sephardi, and 402,500 Ashkenazi. The "typical" Israeli Jewish family had 3.4 members. Sephardi families were the largest (3.75 persons), next were the Ashkenazim (2.83), then those with fathers born in Israel (2.76). About 45 percent of the households headed by an Israeli-born father had a Sephardi grandfather, so they were often also perceived as Sephardim. Similarly, an Israeli-born father whose own father came from the West was generally considered to be Ashkenazi. Sephardi Jews tended to have more children and earn less money than Ashkenazim. About half had at least three or four children per family, compared with only about one-third of the Ashkenazim. However, some Ashkenazim also had large families (six or seven children or more), especially in the ultra-Orthodox households whose heads perceive having large families to be a religious obligation.[23]

By 1993, an average wage-earning family made as much as $2,000 per month at current levels; after income tax and social security payments, such a family was left with about 20 percent less, or close to 4,900 new Israeli shekels (NIS) per month.[24] This places Israel among the wealthier Western countries.

Household density is another indicator of living standards. Forty percent of the Jews had homes with less than one person per room, and only one percent lived with three people per room.[25]

Another indicator is the number of private autos per person. In 1976 just over 8 percent of the population owned private automobiles, five times more than the number in 1960. By 1991 there were almost 850,000 cars in Israel, just under one for every Jewish household. Personal possessions such as refrigerators, televisions, and washing machines are found in almost every Jewish home.[26]

Among 1991 wage earners, 37 percent were in public and communal services, over 21 percent were in industry, 14 percent in trade, 10 percent in finance, 6 percent in both construction and transport, and only 3.5 percent in agriculture.[27] Clearly, the gradual annual increase in living standards has affected Jewish occupations and transformed the pattern from blue-collar labor to more service-oriented, white-collar, and middleman work. Although this trend is common in other economically advanced countries, in Israel it has a special meaning. The Zionist goal was, among other things, to construct "a new Jew" close to the soil and to the means of production, but this goal has not been achieved. Israeli Jews of the 1990s earn their living in occupations essentially similar to those of their grandfathers in Europe. Twice as many Jews were working in finance in 1991 as had been in 1970; the number who actually worked in the fields decreased by almost 500 percent. In Israel in the 1990s agriculture and construction relied heavily on Arabs from the West Bank and the Gaza Strip and on labor imported from other countries.

The gini coefficient, which measures the extent of inequality in the distribution of income in a given society, showed some improvement in 1993: It was 0.343, compared to 0.352 in 1992 (a 0.0 coefficient indicates a perfectly equal society).[28] The state of urban Sephardim (salary earners and unemployed) improved over the years compared to that of urban Ashkenazim. Together, these two groups constituted about 90 percent of Jewish households. Thus, whereas in 1985 an average Sephardi family made as much as 63 percent of the average Western income, eight years later that figure had risen to 83 percent.[29]

Interestingly, the gap between Israeli-born Sephardi and Ashkenazi Sabras is greater than that in the previous generation born abroad. This is a result of several factors, including the higher percentage of unemployed among the Sephardi Sabras, the type of professions they choose as a result of inferior education, and their concentration in economically disadvantaged places.

By 1991 the median schooling for a person age fifteen and over was more than nine years (i.e., one year of high school) for Sephardim and twelve years for Israeli-born and Western Jews. Over 16 percent of Sephardim had never attended school, compared to just over one percent of Ashkenazim. Likewise, whereas about 27 percent of Israeli-born Jews had attended post-secondary institutions, just over 6 percent of the Sephardim had done so. (There are six universities in Israel: the Hebrew University, Tel Aviv University, the Technion, Haifa University, Bar Ilan University, and Ben-Gurion

University. Students can also study in several undergraduate, professional, and general colleges.)[30]

The information presented here clearly shows a distinct societal gap. According to most indicators, Western Jews dominate the Sephardim. How and why did this gap evolve? To understand this and other changes in Israeli ethnic composition, substantive differences between the two groups should be clarified.

Ashkenazi and Sephardi are more cultural than any other categorization. Ashkenazi Jews originated in Europe, where they spoke Yiddish, or "Jewish" that is German-based. Because most U.S. Jews, as well as those from South Africa and Latin America, originated in Europe, they are also considered Ashkenazi regardless of whether they speak or have ever heard Yiddish.

Ashkenazi Jews initiated the Zionist movement to resolve their personal and communal problems without considering Jews who lived beyond their cultural regions. They established the Yishuv and dominated the Israeli polity. They also revived Hebrew as the official language of Israel, largely replacing Yiddish as the spoken means of communication. Today, only a few old people, Orthodox families who consider Hebrew to be too holy for daily use, and some new Ashkenazi immigrants speak Yiddish; most Sabras are completely unfamiliar with it.

But the Ashkenazi are by no means unified. They came from many areas, and they formed communities in Israel that reflected the cultural outlooks, preferences, and prejudices of the countries from which they emigrated. Traditional regional animosities—such as those between Hungarians and Poles or Czechs and Slovaks or even between regions within the same country, such as Galicia and Warsaw in Poland—have sometimes continued among these Jewish immigrants and their children. Ashkenazi Jews who came to Israel from the United States and those who came from Russia frequently have little in common. Nonetheless, their European heritage runs deep through Israel's emerging culture. Despite attempts to assimilate or even to adopt some elements of Sephardi culture, the mainstream of Israeli cultural and social life is still very much European.

The Sephardim are equally diverse. In fact, this group consists of at least two principal subgroups: those whose main diaspora language was Ladino, and those whose spoken tongue was Arabic. There are other smaller groups whose diaspora language was Persian or Amharic (from Ethiopia). Ladino is a medieval Spanish dialect used by Jews who lived in various Mediterranean countries. When they were expelled from the Iberian Peninsula at the end of the fifteenth century, many moved to North Africa and the Balkans; some established communities in Palestine and in North America. Over the years, Ladino-speaking Jews, who are essentially of European origin, became a minority in Israel.

During the Ottoman era, the Sephardim considered themselves an elite group and regarded Ashkenazi newcomers as abrasive, overzealous in their dedication to the idea of labor, and ignorant of local traditions. The dichotomy between the Sephardim and the Ashkenazim is institutionalized in religious organization by separate synagogues and communal practice, a heritage of the Ottoman period when each group had its own official chief rabbi. The religious differences between these two groups, however, are based less on fundamental dogma (both are considered Orthodox rather than Reform or Conservative) than on style. The two chief rabbis generally coordinate their activities and conduct them in relative harmony, but clashes on matters of religious interpretation and personal honor do occur. Many of the ultrareligious Jews in Israel discredit the status of the two chief rabbis and consider them to be merely clerks appointed to their positions by an essentially secular government.

The other non-Ashkenazi subgroup is mostly from Arabic-speaking Asian and North African countries but also came from places like Iran, India, Ethiopia, and the Islamic republics of central Asia that have no Spanish ancestry and no knowledge of Ladino culture. National differences among the members are as diverse as those among the Ashkenazi. Yet they are grouped into one category together with the Sephardi, perhaps because of their darker skin and physical similarity to Arabs. This grouping definitely occurs because they are simply not "defined" as Ashkenazi.

Clearly, then, the traits cited here that distinguish the two principal Jewish groups are more impressionistic and stereotypical than they are indicators of scientific accuracy. This is the way Israelis of one group tend to see members of the other and how they were socialized to perceive themselves. It does not matter that the parents of some new immigrants from Canada spoke Arabic at home before they emigrated to North America from Morocco; statistically, they are considered Western even if they are of Sephardi origin. Nonetheless, these two principal groups do exist, and the Ashkenazim dominate the Sephardim on almost all formal indicators, as shown here. There are more of them, they are better educated at all levels of the academic scale, they live more comfortably and in economically and socially more desirable locations, and they hold higher-status and better-paying jobs.

Will these trends continue? Probably not. Social distance between the groups has narrowed over the years. The endogamy index, or rate of intergroup marriage, is constantly on the rise. In 1955 only 11.8 percent of marriages were interethnic, twenty years later the percentage had risen to 19.2, and by 1990 over 70 percent of couples married in Israel were both Israeli-born.

The early tendency to settle *olim* (newcomers or immigrants) according to their national origin was abandoned during the 1970s. The Jewish

Agency for Palestine attempted to establish new settlements based on mixed ethnic groups, but sociologists and anthropologists advised that there were advantages to preserving already existing communal structures. *Olim* were thereafter settled in national groups. This policy concentrated less affluent settlers in distinctive neighborhoods and tended to reinforce ethnic separateness. New development towns were often located far from urban economic centers and labor markets. Diaspora crafts and skills were rarely in demand in Israeli society. Public monies needed for development of modern infrastructure were not always available, especially when the regional groups supported opposition parties. Consequently, Sephardi Jewish towns and neighborhoods became poorer than others, with greater permanent unemployment and a more urgent need for social welfare services.

By the 1990s, the bulk of Jewish unemployment was still found in the development towns established during the 1950s. Since they were built with no economic rationale to guide their development, most of these towns remained dependent on government assistance. When the Likud came to power in 1977, one of its first programs was the renovation and rehabilitation of these development towns and poor neighborhoods. "Project Renewal" became a combined effort of government and, through the Jewish Agency, Jewish communities in the West. Over the years, many places benefited from the various programs of Project Renewal. Among other things, the physical appearance of buildings and streets was improved, community centers were built for cultural and sports activities for youth and adults, citizens became involved in local decisionmaking, and greater attention was directed to education.

Still, by the early 1990s, one of the most salient political and public policy issues was the condition of the poorer towns and neighborhoods. Lack of prospects for the future in these places resulted in a high percentage of empty apartments and an idle labor force. Many of the apartments became available to the thousands of Russian Jews who arrived in Israel, and by the mid-1990s most development towns had lost their former character and had become ethnically mixed.

As latecomers to the Yishuv, Sephardim found themselves outside the political establishment, as did the Europeans who immigrated after 1948 and Sabras, who were also underrepresented in the political elite and unable to obtain leadership positions in the various party machines. Of the sixty-four cabinet ministers who served during Israel's first twenty-five years, only three were of Sephardi background. The Ministry of Police was the highest "typical" ministerial post for a Sephardi politician. During that era, no more than 15 percent of the members of Knesset (MKs) were Sephardi. Since 1977, however, when the Likud assumed political power, the proportion of Sephardim among cabinet ministers and MKs has increased significantly. By 1992 Sephardi representation in the Knesset had more than doubled, and of the seventeen ministers in the government coalition, five were Sephardim. With the single exception of the National Religious Party in 1988, when Avner Shaki was placed first on the party's list of Knesset candidates, no Sephardi had ever headed a veteran Zionist party. A similar pattern has existed in the upper ranks of the civil service and the army. The number of Sephardim at the lower levels of civil service, especially in the police force, has been much higher.

Because initially the main door to national politics was closed, Sephardim entered in a fashion similar to groups in other immigrant countries: through local politics. Between 1950 and 1965, their representation in local government bodies increased from 13 percent to 44 percent. By 1970, 30 percent of Jewish mayors in Israel had come from Sephardi communities. As local power brokers, they were gradually able to penetrate party centers and party councils and, consequently, to rise to power positions at the national level. In fact, several of the current national-level Sephardi politicians are better grounded in local power bases than their Ashkenazi counterparts.

Non-Jews in Israel

Another, more serious rift in Israeli society exists between Jews and non-Jews. The latter made up about 18.5 percent of the population in 1992 and were divided into three main groups and several subgroups. The Muslims (mostly Sunnis) were the largest group, constituting 14 percent of the total population; Christians (mostly Roman Catholics and Greek Orthodox) constituted 2.7 percent; and the Druze, a distinctive Muslim sect, made up 1.7 percent. Of a total Arab population of over 950,000, about 490,000 were concentrated in the Galilee region northeast of Haifa, 160,000 lived in the Jerusalem area, about 150,000 resided in and around the region known as the Little Triangle in the center of Israel, and about 80,000 were Negev Bedouin. The rest were scattered elsewhere. Among the northern Arabs, about 15,000 were Druze who lived in the Golan Heights.[31]

At the end of the mandate, Arabs constituted two-thirds of the population of Palestine as a whole and made up nearly one-half of the residents in the area designated the Jewish state by the UN partition plan. Their number decreased greatly during the 1948 war, when more than 700,000 became refugees in the neighboring Arab countries. Under the armistice agreement, about 125,000 Arabs remained within Israel's jurisdiction. Since 1948 their number has increased as a result of one of the world's highest birth rates; additionally, 150,00 Jerusalem Arabs were incorporated after the 1967 war.

In the 1960s the average Muslim family had ten children. Continuity of traditional values; easy access to the modern and efficient Israeli health services, which decreased child mortality and improved conditions for fertility;

and better living and housing standards were among the factors that accounted for this high birth rate. Toward the end of the 1980s the rate declined. Still, in the early 1990s, Muslim women in Israel give birth to an average of 4.7 children, compared with an average of 2.7 and 2.5 children for
Jewish and Christian women, respectively.[32] With these rates, and assuming
a zero rate of Jewish immigration to Israel in the future, the number of Jews
and Arabs would become equal around the year 2015. Stated differently,
beginning in 2015, every additional 100,000 Jewish immigrants would
postpone the demographic tie between the two groups by one year. Based
on these projections, the political consequences for maintaining Israel as a
Jewish state are unclear.[33]

Except for most Arab residents of East Jerusalem, which was incorporated into Israel after 1967, the Arabs in Israel are Israeli citizens. After the
annexation of East Jerusalem, its Arabs were given the option of becoming
citizens, but most expected that the city would be returned to Arab rule and
thus retained their previous—mostly Jordanian—citizenship.

Relations between the country's Jews and Arabs have been complicated
by the state of war with surrounding Arab countries since 1948 and by
social and economic differences between the two peoples. Continued bel-
ligerency has created serious strains that have been marked by mutual
suspicion, deep antagonism, and the imposition of special security arrangements on Israeli Arab communities during the first two decades of independence. Although few incidents of Arab disloyalty or treason against
Israel have occurred, the government's security forces have remained
apprehensive because most Arab families have close relatives living in
"enemy" territory.

The official government portrait of the Arabs in Israel depicts well-being
and prosperity despite necessary inconveniences to which the minority un-
fortunately fell victim because of the war with the surrounding countries. In
its official publications, the government asserts that Israeli Arab incomes
and living standards are higher than those in other Middle Eastern countries. Through extensive government financing of irrigation, land reclama-
tion, agricultural mechanization and modernization, health services, and
village reconstruction, the Arabs in Israel have achieved an economic position superior to that of Arabs elsewhere. But the Arab community in Israel
has retained a distinctive character that is evident in its towns and villages,
which still resemble those of Palestinian Arabs living in the West Bank or in
Jordan.

Israeli Arabs were victims of deep trauma resulting from the 1948 war.
The economic and political organization of the indigenous Palestinian Arab
community was devastated. Most Arab towns, villages, farms, and property
in Israel were destroyed or taken over by the new Jewish government. Palestinian Arab intellectual, political, and religious leaders fled, leaving only a

remnant of the communal structure developed during the mandate. Those who remained in Israel were confused and uncertain about their future.

Guarantees given to the Arab population in the UN partition resolution and in Israel's Declaration of Independence were undermined by the war. Arabs were considered a security threat, and the areas in which they lived were placed under military rule. During the first years of independence, although Israeli Arab citizens had gained full legal equality, they were subject to military government controls and were required to obtain passes for travel within and beyond certain points. They were often victims of army search and seizure, arbitrary arrest, expulsion from the country, and banishment to other villages in Israel.

As security conditions improved and evidence of Israeli Arab loyalty increased, military government control was relaxed. Growing numbers of Israeli Jews pressed first for relaxation and then for total abolition of the military government. Many feared the restrictions would alienate the Arab citizenry and undermine democratic institutions, a possibility that threatened dissident Jewish groups as well as Arabs. In the late 1950s, it became easier for Israeli Arabs to obtain travel permits and move from their homes to other areas. Most restrictions were lifted on Arabs in the large Jewish population centers such as Jaffa and Haifa. In 1966 the Knesset abolished the military government altogether, and controls on those suspected of subversive activity were transferred to civil police authority.

During the first decade of Israel's existence, the government expropriated a substantial portion of Israeli Arab agricultural land. Land along the frontiers with Arab states and in other strategically located areas had been seized by Israeli forces during the 1948 war. Later, additional thousands of acres were taken for national development and were settled by new Jewish immigrants. Although it was intended to deal with the property of Arabs who had fled Israel during 1947 and 1948, the Absentee Property Law was frequently applied to Israeli Arab citizens. It authorized the seizure of land, buildings, and other possessions belonging to anyone who had been in "enemy territory" during the period specified in the law. Because many Arab areas had not come under the jurisdiction of the Israeli government until the 1948 war, Israeli Arabs who were away—even on a visit—had their land confiscated. By the 1960s, it was estimated that Israeli Arabs had lost about two-thirds of their agricultural land as a result of the Absentee Property Law and other legislation. Many Arabs were offered compensation for their property losses, but disputes over the equity of these payments continued for several years.

The loss of agricultural land radically altered the social and economic structure of the Israeli Arab community through changes in occupational distribution and landholding patterns. During the mandate, 76 to 80 percent of Palestine's Arab community had made their living from agriculture, but after the founding of Israel the proportion declined to 40 percent. As a result of diminishing agricultural employment, large numbers of former villagers worked in Jewish urban sectors of the economy. The shift from agricultural to urban pursuits changed consumption patterns and lifestyles.

After Israel's occupation of the West Bank and Gaza in 1967, Israeli Arabs entered another phase of change. Between 1948 and 1967, they had been cut off and isolated from contact with the rest of the Arab world. Only a small number of Christian Arabs were authorized to visit relatives across the border in Jordan during holidays like Christmas and Easter, an arrangement that did not apply to Israeli Muslims. Arabs in Israel were thus separated from larger family groups and from direct contact with political and social developments in the Arab world, although they could listen to radio broadcasts from surrounding countries. After the war and the occupation of the West Bank and Gaza, another one million Arabs were added to the 400,000 already under Israel's jurisdiction. When barriers to the occupied areas were removed, Israelis and Arabs from those territories reestablished direct contact. Those from the West Bank and Gaza could visit Israel, and Israelis were free to travel to the occupied regions. Gaza and West Bank Arabs were also permitted to cross the Jordan River, and many traveled to capitals in the Arab world, bringing back direct word of events in Cairo, Beirut, Damascus, and the Gulf states. Israeli Arabs were put into direct contact with families from which many had been separated and with the pulse of social and political life in the Arab world.

A humiliating Arab defeat in 1967, an apparent victory in the 1973 war, and years of direct links to the Arab world politicized many Israeli Arabs. A strong national consciousness developed; larger numbers of Israeli Arabs began to identify with the militant themes of the Palestinian movement. Prior to 1967, there had been no extensive Israeli Arab political opposition other than through the Communist party. The largest number of Arab votes went to the Labor party (Mapai) or its Arab affiliates.

After the 1967 war, a large percentage of Israel's unskilled labor in the construction, agriculture, and service industries was provided by Arabs from the occupied areas. Over a third of the non-Israeli Palestinian labor force worked in Israel, mostly in construction. Consequently, the economy of the West Bank and the Gaza Strip became largely dependent on the incomes of daily laborers in Israel; hence, it was sensitive to the government's decision to block their entry into the country in times of security tensions. To compensate for potential stoppages in the flow of workers from the Occupied Territories, the government permitted the importation of several thousand workers from countries such as Thailand, the Philippines, Romania, and Portugal.

Ethnic distinctions between Arabs and Jews are still reinforced in Israel through economic and social differences that place Arabs in a lower social stratum. In 1994 the net income of a wage-earning Arab family was about half that of a Jewish family; eight years earlier the figure was 53 percent.[34] Thus, whereas the Sephardi Jews were closing the economic gap with the Ashkenazim, the relative Arab position worsened. Part of the reason for this inability of Arabs to close the gap was the Arab disadvantage in the labor market relative to new Jewish immigrants who came in the early 1990s. For example, in 1991 the percentage of unemployed Arabs males was 10.4 percent; in 1992 it was 12.4 percent. Only 8.6 percent of Jewish males were considered unemployed in 1992.[35] As a group, the Arabs were less educated than Jews; most tended to complete their formal education after ten years, and only about 9 percent continued to study in higher institutions, compared to one-third of the Jews. This educational disparity has affected occupational opportunities. Over 80 percent of Arabs were employees, of which almost half worked in low-paying construction, agriculture, and industry jobs. Less than 4 percent held scientific and academic positions. Less than 3 percent were recorded among Israeli university graduates in 1990.[36] One major disincentive that could account for Arabs' failure to pursue advanced higher education has been the lack of available work once they graduate. There are under a score of Arab professors among the several hundred faculty members of Israeli universities, for example.

Poor living conditions and the lack of opportunity for upward mobility have radicalized the Israeli Arabs. Whereas several thousand work as teachers, police officers, or local government officials, few are found among the top state officials. No Arab has ever served as a cabinet minister, although two have served at the subcabinet level. There are no Arab members of the Israeli Supreme Court or the Security and Foreign Affairs Committee, and no Arab has ever chaired any Knesset committee, directed any state-owned enterprise, or directed a government bureau—including the branch of the Ministry of Religious Affairs that handles Arab communal and religious interests.

Superficially, life in the villages may seem the same as it has always been, but the tremors caused by Israel's new ways and its Western orientation have shaken the foundations of the patriarchal structure. Leadership is no longer the exclusive prerogative of a relatively small landowning group; in many places the younger, Israeli-educated generation has replaced the old guard. With perhaps the sole exception of some of the Druze who serve in the IDF and especially in the Border Police, almost all Israeli Arabs support the idea of an independent Palestine state coexisting with an Israel in which Arab citizens have full equality. Since the process toward achieving that goal began following the Oslo Accord signed between Israel and the PLO in September 1993, Arabs now tend to support the government's role in the peace process.

However, even if lasting peace between Israel and the Palestinians is eventually attained and the Arab minority does obtain economic and political equality, the cultural and ethnic chasm will continue. A fundamental question is whether Israel's Arabs will ever be able to identify with an exclusively Jewish milieu. Will the concept of the Jewish state ever have meaning for, or command the loyalty of, Israeli Arabs? These questions and others are addressed in the next section.

The Problem of Jewish National Identity

Even if the tensions between the Ashkenazim and the Sephardim could disappear within a generation or two as a result of mixed marriages, better education, changing neighborhoods, and the like, the rift between Jews and non-Jews is likely to continue. If one keeps in mind that Israel was established to provide a national home for the Jews, and that many state laws (e.g., the Law of Return) were drafted to facilitate Jewish citizenship and material assistance upon their arrival, one must infer that non-Jews have little reason to identify with the state. Non-Jews have no corresponding rights, and they are excluded from the prevailing communal definition of society.

The fact that the Israeli Arabs constitute a second class of citizenry has little to do with the security situation. Even when lasting peace prevails in the region or when the Israeli Arabs become equal to the Jews in their material conditions, Arabs will still remain a separate class of citizens, detached from the essence and dynamics of Israeli society. The reasons for this situation are directly related to the fusion of nationality and religion in Israeli polity that is reinforced by law, norms, and public policy.

There is no "Israeli" nationality. On ID cards, nationality is defined as either "Jewish" or "Arab"; for non-Jews who are not Arabs, the designation is their country of birth (e.g., Polish, Danish, Dutch, and so on). Israel is therefore the only country in which "Arab" is legally defined as a form of nationality.

The definition of the "Jewish" nationality is no less problematic. If nationality rests on a strictly religious definition, then a Jew is one whose mother was Jewish. According to the Law of Return, even Jewish converts to Christianity or Islam should be considered Jewish by nationality and be granted citizenship. Therefore, the fact that the question "who is a Jew" remains unsettled subjects this law to ambiguous interpretations.

The case of Brother Daniel challenged the Law of Return. Born a Polish Jew, Daniel became a Carmelite priest. His demand for citizenship was denied by the authorities, citing the Law of Return. After long deliberation, in 1962 the Supreme Court decided by a majority to uphold the government's decision, arguing that it is commonly understood that by becoming a priest Brother Daniel had removed himself from the community of Jews.

Because the question of Jewish identity is still unresolved, it often leads to government coalition crises and public unrest. In addition to the cultural-communal definition of "Jewishness," which the case of Brother Daniel underscored, several other cases do not lend themselves to easy interpretation—for example, conversions that are not conducted by a recognized Orthodox rabbi or demands of entire "Jewish" communities whose religious identity is questionable to immigrate to Israel (e.g., Ethiopian Falasha, or Beit Israel). The definition of a "Jew" in the Law of Return is secular, with little relevancy to its strict religious source; having one Jewish grandparent is sufficient to qualify for Israeli citizenship. Consequently, many people who had not previously identified themselves as Jews "returned home" to Israel from Eastern Europe and by law became "Jewish nationals."

The Jewish identity of the state and the majority of its citizens is also reinforced by several other means. Land ownership and citizenship are intraconnected. According to various estimates, only about 5 percent of lands are privately owned. The land and national resources, as defined by the Basic Law, belong to the state. Paragraph One of this law explicitly states that "ownership over these lands [which also includes houses and buildings according to Paragraph Three] will not be transferred, by sale or in any other way." People may lease land from the state and use it for an extensive period of time, but the state reserves the right to determine the ways and means by which the land is utilized and, more important, who the renters should be. Thus, non-Jews may find it difficult, if not impossible, to obtain permission to lease publicly owned lands.

All holidays and rest days are either religious or national. The new Israeli memorial days are related to the Jewish collective memory: Independence Day, Holocaust Day, Jerusalem Day, and so on. Virtually nothing refers to Israeli Arabs. No stamp has ever carried an Arab figure or an Arab-related event. Except in purely Arab localities, no new street names issued after 1948 have been Arab. Little of Arab culture has been included in the general education curricula. For all practical purposes, Israeli Arabs are excluded from society. Some are, as one Israeli author labeled them, "present absentees."

It is little wonder, therefore, that many non-Jews do not feel at home in Israel, even if their families have lived in the country for generations. Almost all Arabs support the idea of establishing an independent Palestinian state next to Israel. Such a state could help restore their split identity. Some Arab intellectuals have proposed Arab cultural and political autonomy in northern Israel. This risk to Israel's stability might be avoided if, as Rebecca Kook's 1992 study suggests, a national identity were redefined in a manner that makes room for non-Jews.

Relationship with World Jewry

The Zionist credo holds that Israel was established for world Jewry and hence should strive to "ingather" all Jews. Those who hold a less inclusive view see Israel as a cultural and spiritual homeland for all Jews but a residence for only some. Israel has become an emotional and ideological focus for Jewish communities in the diaspora, who have supported it financially and politically and are sustained by their cultural and emotional ties to it. In 1992, one-third of world Jewry lived in Israel. Most Jews outside were American, Canadian, French, British, South African, Australian, and other European. Most resided in free societies where departure was not legally prevented.

Thus, the Zionist movement, which was founded to provide a territorial solution to the problem of Europeans and was extended to include all Jews, almost completely played out its basic task. After World War II, it became apparent that to survive and live free from oppression and government anti-Semitism, Jews could either settle in the West, where immigration laws permitted, or go to Palestine. Hence, the existence of the State of Israel provided a partial, if not a total, answer to the Jewish problem. The Law of Return established the legal link and the eternal commitment between the Jewish state and the Jewish people. Although this law included all Jews, its primary application was directed toward those who continued to live in repressive societies or in places where the freedom to maintain their Jewish identity was restricted. Today, nearly all Jews are free, and the Law of Return has lost much of its original purpose. It is now used primarily to prevent non-Jews from entering Israel.

After obtaining its prime objective—the founding of a state—the Zionist movement continued to function and even grew, transferring many of its assets, such as land, and some functions to the state. It preserved other roles, especially the absorption of immigrants. The World Zionist Organization, its adjunct institutions in the various countries, and its main operative body—the Jewish Agency—maintained redundant and often competing functions with those of the state. Since the state also engaged in immigrant absorption, coordination of resources and policies became essential. Many officials of the Zionist movement were Israeli nationals, but this did not always prevent conflict. During the 1970s, for example, when transition camps for Russian Jews were established in Vienna, the state accused the Jewish Agency of not doing enough to persuade the immigrants to leave for Israel rather than for the United States.

Some Zionist leaders like Nahum Goldmann refused to subordinate themselves to the Israeli government. During the early 1950s, Goldmann distinguished himself in negotiations with Germany and Austria over reparations for Nazi victims. In 1956 he became president of the World Zionist

Congress; he criticized the Israeli leadership's overreliance on the power of the state and its military forces and leaders' insensitivity to the needs of diaspora Jews. He suggested that the government should conduct more flexible policies vis-à-vis the Arabs and should adopt a more moderate attitude toward the Soviet Union. These positions were rejected by the Israelis, and in 1970, when Goldmann sought government approval to visit Egypt to discuss peace possibilities with President Nasser, Israeli Prime Minister Golda Meir vetoed the initiative.

The national and international Zionist institutions do not legally belong to the State of Israel but belong to the Jewish people, and they can obtain access when Israel cannot. Thus, Women's International Zionist Organization (WIZO) representatives were able to function in the Soviet Union when the USSR had no diplomatic relationship with Israel and was hostile to Israel's pro-U.S. and anti-Arab policies. Similarly, the Jewish Agency was instrumental in saving Jews from repression in several Arab countries during the early 1950s and later in Iran, Argentina, and Ethiopia.

The Zionist organization is also able to mobilize resources for education, culture, settlement, welfare, and the like. The U.S. United Jewish Appeal (UJA) can generate finances that although not directly intended for the state, help nonetheless by releasing other funds for defense. Thus, for example, the UJA raised $438 million (adjusted to 1967 prices) in 1974 when Israel needed to replace its war machine, which had been destroyed in the 1973 October War. A UJA drive in 1982 yielded over half a billion dollars, which helped to ease the pressures caused by the war with Lebanon. In the past, about 60 percent of UJA collections have been transferred to Israel. The upkeep of these national institutions in 1992 was less than one percent (or 687 million NIS in current prices) of the general Israeli government expenditure.

The Status of Women in Society

The status of women is indicative of equality in a society, as well as of the efficient use of human resources.[37] Israel was designed on, among others, principles of social justice and equality between the sexes. In light of the far-reaching vision of a "national home" and with so few people to realize this enterprise, every individual's contribution became essential. One would expect, therefore, that the new Jewish society would be a model for community living under conditions of sexual equality.

This orientation was perhaps best illustrated by the collective settlement known as the kibbutz, a community in which individuals had no personal property and all decisions were made jointly in a direct, democratic fashion. In theory, communal life in the kibbutz exhibited the highest level of sexual equality, which was reflected in role distribution: Work assignments were rotated, the family as a social unit was liquidated to free mothers from the dependency of their newborn infants, and children were reared and ed-ucated by other members in special "homes." However, the more materially advanced the kibbutz became, the more equality between genders became a myth rather than a reality. In the Palmach, which consisted mostly of kibbutz members, women were involved along with men during the 1948 War of Independence, although only a handful participated in the actual fighting.

Women had attempted to secure their political rights during the election to Knesset Israel, the first assembly of Jewish settlers in Palestine, which was established in 1920 to represent the interests of the Jewish community within the framework of British rule. Fourteen women of a total of 314 del-egates were elected to the assembly. Religious Jews who opposed women's suffrage and were accustomed to casting the ballots of their wives and daughters boycotted the assembly and even attempted to dissolve it. The issue of women's suffrage was resolved through inertia. To bypass the op-position, Knesset Israel called a referendum on "women's right to vote" on November 8, 1925. Fear of losing presumably led the religious Mizrachi party to forgo its opposition.

The notion of women's equality was supported in theory, if not in prac-tice, by the founders of the Zionist movement in both Europe and the Yishuv. However, when the choice had to be made between granting women political rights versus recruiting Orthodox Jews who opposed equal rights for women, Zionist leaders opted for the latter. Consequently, women pursued independent routes through which to exercise their political influ-ence. In 1918 they established the separate WIZO, which competed with other Zionist groups for representation and power. WIZO became a polit-ical party and, together with the Women's Association for Equal Rights, ran in the 1949 election, obtaining one Knesset seat.

The 1948 Declaration of Independence forbade discrimination on the basis of sex. Yet nearly fifty years later, basic formal equality between the genders—taken for granted in Western democracies—did not prevail in Is-rael. In 1994 Israel still had no written constitution to assure gender equal-ity. Personal-status matters remained in the hands of Orthodox religious in-stitutions. Because of coalition bargaining, Orthodox religious law still determined individual civil conduct in matters involving marriage, divorce, burial, diet, citizenship, and so on. The term of military service in the IDF was shorter for women than for men. Married and self-declared religious women were not required to serve, and single women over age twenty-six were exempt from reserve duty, whereas men remained in the reserves for at least two or three more decades. At the end of the 1980s, only 225 of the 709 military occupations formally recognized by the army were open to women; none involved actual fighting or flying a military aircraft. Even though the IDF included a "women's corps," its commander was excluded from the general staff and therefore was little known to the public.

In 1992, women constituted 42.5 percent of the Israeli labor force age fifteen and above. Women were twice as likely as men to work at part-time jobs or to remain completely outside the civilian labor force. That same year only 30 percent of married women were employed, most in low-paying posts; only one percent of women were employers, compared to 6 percent of men. Men were four times more likely than women to be self-employed. The average income of men, whether computed on a monthly, weekly, or hourly basis, was considerably higher than that of women. Men earned more than women in every economic sector, and in some—such as industry, finance, and personal services—their earnings were almost twice as high. These trends indicate that traditional values still dominate Israeli society.

Israel's educational system could bring about gender equality. A comparative survey conducted during the early 1990s showed that more girls than boys were enrolled at every level except the doctoral level. In 1994, 55.8 percent of university students were women. Boys made up almost the entire student body at technical schools; and students attending nursing, secretarial, fashion, and teaching colleges were virtually all girls. Yet a closer examination over several years showed that at every level and in almost every field of study, more girls took up subjects that had previously been viewed as exclusively male and vice versa. This could mean that although differences exist between men and women in their career choices, these differences are becoming narrower over time. In some traditionally male-exclusive areas such as the legal profession, women have become the majority.

Gender equalization could be achieved through the legal system and as a result of political pressure. A sufficient number of laws and regulations are in place to safeguard against discrimination, although they are not always enforced. Of the several hundred board directors in state-owned enterprises, for example, only a handful are female. Consequently, in November 1994, the Supreme Court ruled that "a corrective policy" based on already existing law should be implemented, forcing the immediate replacement of three men with three women.

A maximum of 11 women out of 120 members have served in any of the fourteen Knessets since 1949. Likewise, no more than two women have served as ministers in any single cabinet in the 1992–1996 government. Nonetheless, there seems to be no political barrier to placing a woman at the top of a party list. Shulamit Aloni has been the leader of her left-wing Citizen Rights Movement (Ratz), which in 1992 was part of the Meretz bloc and had twelve Knesset seats and four ministerial posts. Golda Meir served as general secretary of the country's largest party, Ma'arach (Labor), and as prime minister from 1969 to 1974. These women's success, however, has had little impact on the status of women in general.

From Statism to Civil Society

The 25,000 Jews who lived in Palestine under Ottoman rule until the end of the nineteenth century functioned as a separate religious community, much like their Christian and Muslim counterparts. They and the 30,000 members of the first *aliya* (1880s–1904) had no national political aspirations; they lived under an ineffective political system and were free to pursue their own personal and communal goals. The prevailing system of capitulations, under which Europeans enjoyed extraterritorial privileges throughout the Ottoman Empire, secured these freedoms as long as the activities did not contradict the dictates of the Turkish rulers. The Jews, and to some extent the Christian community, organized various voluntary associations, whereas the Muslims relied mostly on their family networks for communal activities. This situation changed with the arrival of the young socialists during the second *aliya* (1904–1914), when Jewish communal life became highly politicized. Labor Zionists, who dominated political life in the Yishuv, promoted a collectivist approach with the idea of totally recreating in Palestine the Jewish society of the 1920s and 1930s.

Labor domination manifested itself in doctrine, ideas, methods, and style. Newcomers had to quickly develop orientations and practices similar to those of the Labor elite. This elite, which collaborated with the Mizrachi in a "Historical Alliance," supplied its supporters with most of their material and spiritual needs. The social system that emerged and that continued, with some variation, until the 1970s was highly politicized. Government intervened in many aspects of individual and group life in the name of unity and the security of the Jewish people. The economy was planned, and the welfare system was extensive and comprehensive. People were often asked by the state to contribute to the collective by undertaking pioneering tasks in risky places such as border settlements, by paying high taxes, or by serving an extended stint in the armed forces. Consequently, they were entitled to state assistance in matters considered in the West to belong in the private domain. To some degree, this "culture of entitlement" still persists.

Ben-Gurion, who masterminded many of these developments, formulated an orientation of statism, or *mamlachtiyut,* during the early years of the state. State ideology rested on two fundamental elements. The first promoted the notion that services required by all citizens should be provided by the state rather than by voluntary organizations, political parties, or the private market. The second element recognized the prerogative of state interests over those of the party and held that when the two conflicted, they had to be separated, with state interests prevailing over those of the party.

The first actual application of statism occurred during the War of Independence. To establish the IDF as the sole Jewish armed force, Ben-Gurion dissolved the Palmach, which was associated with the Mapam party and the Labor movement; the Irgun Zvai Leumi (IZL, National Military Organization), which was the military arm of the Zionist Revisionists; and Lehi (Fighters for the Freedom of Israel). Members of these groups were accepted as individuals in the new IDF, which relied largely on the Haganah, the principal armed force of the Yishuv.

Employment and education, which had been dominated by political parties in the prestate era, became immediate candidates for nationalization after independence. Employment was taken over by the government with the establishment of the Labor Affairs Ministry. In education, as a result of political pressures and coalition crises, a dual system emerged—one for secular Jews, the other for Orthodox Jews. In other areas such as health, the concept of statism could not be applied because of internal opposition from the parties—each of which had its own health insurance system—and opposition by the Histadrut (the General Federation of Workers), which kept its *Kupat Holim* (Sick Fund) as a source of funds to support other activities. Not until the 1994 Histadrut election, which resulted in the replacement of the traditional Labor leadership, was a national health law passed.

The state could not meet everyone's expectations. Many Sephardi Jews felt the distribution of resources was unfair. The need to rearm after losses in the October War, combined with three-digit inflation beginning in the mid-1970s—among other things—had a dual effect. The state began to perceive its own limitations, and citizens became increasingly self-reliant. Labor's defeat in the 1977 election and its replacement by Likud reinforced this effect. If by default rather than design, the foundations of an effective civil society were laid down during the mid–1970s and have continued to expand ever since.

Although the trend toward privatization of the economy had begun even before Likud came to power, the process of transforming government agencies into state-owned enterprises and then selling them gained ideological legitimacy after 1977. Between 1967 and 1987, the two major Israeli parties undertook approximately the same number of privatization measures. Under Likud, however, the gradual retreat of government from involvement in the economy became official policy.

Beginning in the mid-1980s, the public became increasingly convinced of the need to adopt a written constitution and to reform the electoral system. This extraparliamentary movement demanded not only a citizens' bill of rights but also a protective legal framework against the political misconduct of elected representatives. It was hoped that electoral reform would likewise make politicians more responsive to citizens' needs and citizens themselves more involved in the political process. Consequently, in 1992 Labor used a primary system that required party members to select representatives to the Knesset. Likud followed suit in 1993 with a similar method for selecting its party leader.

Because Israel lacks a constitution against which its laws and policies can be evaluated, in the early 1980s the Supreme Court began to undertake an active role in promoting liberal values and protecting human rights. In addition to its traditional role as interpreter of existing laws, the court also assumed the function of lawmaker in areas where citizens' rights conflicted with state policy.

In the 1990s the mass media greatly expanded. In addition to the single television channel initiated in 1968 that follows state preferences, the public now has access to several commercial channels, cable television, and a multitude of foreign networks. Information can no longer be blocked or manipulated by the state.

All of these factors have made Israeli citizens better informed and more protected against political arbitrariness. Many voluntary organizations have sprung up to fulfill diverse functions previously considered the responsibility of the state. In fact, it is estimated that in 1993 about 26 percent of the adult Jewish population was involved in some form of voluntary work associated with civil organizations. By another formal count, the civil society that has emerged includes 10,000 active organizations within the voluntary and nonprofit sector (VNPS), or the third sector. Established in 1986 by the Israeli chapter of the Joint Distribution Committee (part of the United Jewish Appeal), the VNPS employed about 180,000 people in 1993 in its twelve subsectors, which include education and learning, culture and arts, sports, health, community, quality of life, and citizens' rights. The VNPS lobbies on behalf of its organizations to obtain tax exemptions for contributions and helps individuals to establish and manage new associations.[38]

In 1986 Yael Yishai mapped the groups that constituted Jewish civil society in Israel. They included several categories: economic (taxi drivers and building owners), professional (lawyers and social workers) immigrants (representing cities, regions, countries, or continents), public interest (the feminist movement, or Peace Now), philanthropy (animal rights and Alcoholics Anonymous), culture and sport (Association for Basketball and Friends of Jazz), and settlement organizations (including the kibbutz movement and organizations for other forms of collective settlements).[39]

The Jewish civil network is vast. Many associations are completely independent, supported by contributions from Israeli and foreign individuals and groups. Others depend on government funding. An attempt by a Ministry of Justice committee, formed in October 1987, to evaluate the number and nature of the activities of all associations operating in conjunction with the government was inconclusive. No reliable data were obtained from any source concerning the number of associations or their relationship to the ministries supporting them. It is clear, however, that Jewish civil society is constantly expanding, even though its scope cannot be accurately assessed.

The Arab network functions with almost complete independence and is much smaller than the Jewish network. It has a number of literary, charity, scouting, and health organizations, some dating to the nineteenth century. Most of these groups were destroyed in 1948 and were not revived until the 1970s because of restrictions imposed by the state on the formation of Arab organizations, lack of proper funding, and reliance on the traditional extended family (Hamula) for civil activities.

By the mid-1970s significant changes had occurred. Security controls in the Arab community were relaxed, allowing young people—who were aware of the benefits of modernization—to replace the traditional leadership, identify local and international funding sources, and utilize the new legal framework. In 1981 the restrictive Law of Ottoman Associations was changed to the more liberal Law of Charitable Associations, thereby making it easier to form civil organizations. Two types of organizations evolved in the Arab sector: political interest groups and civil organizations that have not used politics to advance their causes.

Among the Arab groups, four are the most important. The National Committee of Chairmen of Arab Local Authorities, officially formed in 1974, mediates between citizens and the central government. The Follow-up Committee for the Interests of Arab Citizens, formed in 1982, represents all political organizations and movements in the Arab sector. The National Committee for Protection of Lands was formed in 1975 by the Communist party. The Forty Association, formed in 1988, tries to prevent the government from destroying illegally constructed buildings and helps to obtain legal recognition and state funds for Arab municipalities.

By 1991 there were 228 regional and local indigenous, nonpolitical, community-based Arab organizations—92 percent of which had been registered since the mid-1970s. They included unions, scholarship funds, intellectual and human rights associations, and women's organizations. Local groups included sectarian, academic, voluntary, and developmental organizations.

3

Political Parties and Ideologies

The Israeli party system is one of the most fractionalized among Western democracies. The system is constantly reshaping itself and seems always to be in a state of flux. Yet, the Israeli party system has exhibited remarkable stability. The principal political rivals of the 1930s were still competing sixty years later, with different names and new institutions, orientations, and personalities. In this chapter we explain the source of this apparent stability, the differences among the parties, and their place in the Israeli polity. We also address the question of why the Israeli party system of the 1990s has been transformed from one based on ideology and mass constituencies into an image-oriented system.

The Israeli multiparty system is part of the prestate political heritage, evolving from diverse ideological trends and interest groups within the Zionist movement. Until 1977, one party—Mapai (later Ma'arach [Alignment] and Labor)—dominated the system. Because of its large size and its location at the center of voters' preferences, Mapai could choose coalition partners from parties to its left or its right. Since 1977, political competition has occurred between two blocs, or camps—the left and the right.

The left camp controlled the government after the 1992 election. It consists of two principal elements. The first includes two secular Zionist parties, Labor and Meretz. The latter is a technical bloc composed of three parties: Ratz, Mapam, and Shinui. These three combined forces prior to the election and coordinated parliamentary activities while maintaining their separate organizations. The second element in the left camp consists of the Arab parties, Hadash (the New Communist List) and the Democratic Arab party.

The right camp is composed of secular and religious elements. The first group includes three nationalist parties: the Likud, which ruled between

1977 and 1992 and after 1996; the ultranationalist Tzomet; and Moledet. The right-wing religious parties are Mafdal (National Religious party), the Ashkenazi ultra-Orthodox Agudat Israel, and the Sephardi Orthodox Shas.

Twenty-one party lists participated in the January 1949 election for the First Knesset, which was also a Constituent Assembly. Only a dozen were able to capture at least one seat. Immediately after the election, the assembly declared itself the First Knesset, or parliament. Since then, no fewer than ten parties have at one time or another been represented in the Knesset. Some were splinters of older parties, some ran as a technical bloc, and others were mergers of smaller factions. Not a single party maintained its original structure or ideology from the early days of the state until the 1990s. Twenty-four parties competed in the 1961 election, and a record thirty-one were represented in 1981.

By 1992 the left camp had a "blocking coalition" of sixty-one Knesset seats; the right-religious camp had fifty-nine. One party, Shas, broke away from its eight-year alliance with the right-wing camp and joined the Labor government. In 1994, three MKs of the eight-member Tzomet formed an independent party, Yi'ud. Two of the MKs joined the Labor headed government.

Israel: A Party-State

Israel has often been defined as a party-state. From its inception as a state and even during the Yishuv era, Israeli politics have been ruled by parties. As in the West, these parties are characterized by interests, goals, strategies, resources, constraints, history, organization, memory, symbols, leaders, activists, supporters, voters—in short, by all of the elements and factors used to define politics. Several Israeli parties, large and small, were or tried to become comprehensive organizations. They had newspapers, publishing houses, sports clubs, medical insurance, housing programs, youth movements, labor unions, professional associations, settlement organizations, and even banks; they owned property, established effective organizations, and had a remarkable capacity to meet the various demands of their members. Until the 1970s, each party satisfied the needs and desires of its members and in exchange asked for political support, at least on election day— a tradeoff that was welcomed by many citizens.

Parties participating in governing coalitions were more capable than the opposition of supplying goods and services because, among other things, they used state funds. Opposition parties that lacked access to government monies had to make extensive use of symbols to provide emotional gratification in lieu of material benefits. Herut, the main opposition party, built an emotional and psychological "home" for its members, often people who felt betrayed or discriminated against by Labor movement parties. The opposition was also able to generate resources from domestic and international sources. The Communist party, for example, became a direct or indirect agent, a sort of "middleman," because it recycled financial cuts from economic transactions between an Israeli source and countries in the Soviet bloc. The money thus gathered was channeled toward financing the party's activities and improving the welfare of designated voters.

Until 1948, some parties had affiliated military or paramilitary organizations. The Irgun Zvai Leumi (IZL) (National Military Organization) was linked closely to the Revisionist movement. The Palmach, or Plugot Mahatz (Strike Forces), was linked to the Mapam and Achdut Ha-Avoda kibbutz movement, and the Haganah (Defense) was connected to Mapai. After Ben-Gurion's decision to merge these and other such forces into a national military organization, the IDF, no armed forces were controlled by political groups.

Israel's political history records many incidents in which families were split by disputes over party loyalty. Often such disputes broke out not only among members of ideological rivals, such as Mapai and Herut, but also among people in the same camp who could not agree on specific interpretations of current events. The structural split in the kibbutz movement during the early 1950s, when members left their families and homes because of ideological disputes, is a case in point.

The downgrading of political parties as suppliers of material goods and services to society is not unique to Israel. As a rule, the higher the standard of living in a given society, the more likely it is that individuals will become less reliant on parties and politics to provide their material requirements. The role of the party as a middleman, a link between the people and government, has gradually changed. Parties have become the principal interpreters and articulators of citizens' preferences, translating those preferences into collective political positions. For example, individuals' desire to improve their personal safety might be expressed in a "security program," to be implemented when the party reaches the national policymaking level. In Israel, because of the permanent need to rely on coalition governments, even a very small party can obtain a decisive position. When individuals or groups want to improve their economic well-being or their position ethnically, religiously, or genderwise, they can usually find at least one party with a platform they can support. Dependency on the political party for basic needs has been considerably weakened over the years as a direct result of voters' increasing economic self-reliance.

In addition to the established parties that strive to cover all issues in a traditional Western European manner, there are numerous small lists, which cannot even gain the one and a half percent of votes (only one percent until 1992) that guarantees a Knesset seat. The small lists offer attractive packages to potential supporters: women, the elderly, invalids, taxi drivers, mortgage holders, naturalists, prisoners, farmers, and soldiers. One candidate, Shmuel Flatto-Sharon, a new immigrant, tried to avoid extradition to France—where he had violated the law—by seeking Knesset immunity. He ran in the 1977 election and obtained enough votes for two Knesset seats, but for technical reasons he was awarded only one seat.

Israeli political parties have undergone considerable transition over the years. During the first two decades after independence, parties were largely controlled by a monolithic leadership, usually the founders and their small cadres of loyalists. David Ben-Gurion, Moshe Sharett, Levi Eshkol, and Golda Meir in Mapai; Menachem Begin and the "fighting family" in Herut; Yaakov Hazen and Meir Yaari in Mapam; and Meir Vilner in the Israeli Communist party built their parties and provided ideological leadership, but they also determined—often in a dictatorial manner—who should and who should not represent the party in various political institutions. Lists of candidates to the Knesset were selected by "arrangement committees" through a bargaining process and interparty power plays. Challenges to the leaders often resulted in individuals being removed from safe positions on the party election lists or in expulsion from the party. Shulamit Aloni, the leader of Ratz (Citizens' Rights party), was downgraded on the Ma'arach (Labor) list by Golda Meir prior to the 1973 election. Shmuel Tamir established the Free Center on the eve of the 1969 elections after he was officially removed from Herut for challenging Begin's autocratic leadership.

Leaders have been careful to adorn their party lists with candidates who appealed to certain target populations and to preserve other safe places for those without such appeal to balance the ticket. Women, Arabs, Sephardim, and others were usually the direct beneficiaries of this "quasi-representation" practice.

A survey of the most important Israeli parties and their stages of development shows great variations in most relevant activities. Some Knesset lists should not even be considered "parties" in the modern sense of the term. They are one- or two-person lists formed before an election to gain Knesset seats. Some were formed because of the personal ambition of their founder, but most often they came about because an established party needed a separate list to penetrate some target groups that could not be reached otherwise. The Arab satellite parties of Mapai are typical examples. Some parties can be considered political "branches" of certain religious leaders who select loyal followers, or "messengers," and "send" them to the Knesset. MKs who belong to Agudat Israel are "messengers" of the Council of Sages (the rabbinical leadership). Similarly, the MKs of Shas receive their directives from a rabbinical Council of the Wisest in Torah.

The Israeli polity reflects excessive democracy that includes some nondemocratic components. To bridge this seeming contradiction, the Knesset enacted the Party Law in 1992. Party laws are unfamiliar in English-speaking countries. Sweden, Benelux, and Switzerland have them, as do several regimes with short or interrupted histories of democratic culture. The German Party Law drafted in 1967 defines the legal status of parties and forbids the formation of antidemocratic political organizations. In 1952 and 1956, the law was used to ban the neo-Nazis and the Communists, respectively.

The Israeli Party Law provides a standardized legal framework for the constitution and operation of parties and the behavior of their members. Accordingly, every party must be regulated by a code that addresses the rights and obligations of members, organizational and political activities, and financial management. Each party must maintain at least three types of institutions: a center or convention, a body responsible for the management and implementation of the party's decisions, and an accounting office. A party may decide to add other types of institutions such as a members' court, a general assembly, primaries, and the like. Every political party, like other public nonpolitical associations, is obligated to open its financial records and other documents to the supervision and inspection of the State Comptroller.

A party can no longer function, either directly or indirectly, as an economic or a business unit. To finance operations, the party must rely on supporters' contributions and on the Party Financing Law (see Chapter 4).

There are three other limits to the operation of parties as expressed in the law. The first forbids the formation of any party whose explicit goal is to deny the existence of the State of Israel as both a Jewish and a democratic state. Thus, no party can be formed that seeks to alter the Jewish character of the state, such as, for example, to "a state of its citizens," as some Arab intellectuals proposed in the mid-1990s. Nor can an ultrareligious party be formed with the explicit aim of transforming the Israeli political system into a theocracy.

A second limitation bans the formation of any party with a racist message directed against either Jews or non-Jews. This provision was enforced prior to the 1988 election and denied Rabbi Meir Kahana's Kach party the right to participate because it promoted a platform that called for the removal of Israel's Arab citizens.

A third limit applies to parties believed to be a cover for illegal activities. Radical parties of all kinds could become targets of this provision and be banned from politics.

Control over the party by small groups of leaders is a thing of the past. Voters are now less dependent on parties for their livelihood, and party flexibility in selecting certain activities is restricted by law. Candidates who used to rise up the political ladder through mere loyalty to the leader have become much more independent. By using the mass media, they can now appeal directly to voters and secure positions on party lists. Physical attractiveness, media exposure, and verbal articulateness often seem to have replaced ideological proficiency and commitment.

Origins of the Israeli Party System

Multiple party systems are a function of proportional representation in which parliament members are elected at large rather than from separate constituencies. Israel's system originated in the world Zionist movement. All of the major parties in Israel descended from Zionist groups established in the diaspora, mostly in Eastern Europe. Elections to the World Zionist Congresses were determined by the World Zionist Organization, which was not a government and had sovereignty over no territory. Representatives came from dozens of diaspora countries that had small and large Jewish communities. Hence, territorial constituencies were impractical or impossible to form. A system in which constituencies were represented by those who won the most votes would have omitted a large number of significant political perspectives. Many Zionist views would have been unrepresented, and some groups might have left the organization and formed their own separate Zionist bodies—as Jabotinsky's followers did when they left the World Zionist Organization in the 1920s and formed the New Zionist Organization.

The Zionist movement organized its periodic congresses so that diverse trends and personalities would have an opportunity to be publicized. The World Zionist Organization was based on voluntary membership and could not impose majority rule. If minority rights were not respected, dissidents were free to leave the movement. However, special efforts were made to have all groups represented on the Zionist Executive and in the council that managed organization affairs.

As growing numbers of Jews accepted the Zionist credo, its constituency expanded to include many political, social, and economic orientations. There were Orthodox fundamentalists, Jewish modernists, secularists, and even atheists; protagonists of conservative, liberal, radical, and Marxist economic doctrines; some who emphasized political or territorial issues; and others for whom development of a national culture and language was paramount.

Most parties in areas of Europe in which there were large Jewish communities formed their own Zionist organizations. They established youth groups, party newspapers and periodicals, book publishing companies, financial institutions, and in a few cases, labor groups and health services. During the mandate, the leaders of many of these groups moved to Palestine and established parallel Zionist parties there. Under mandatory law, the Yishuv could levy dues on members of the Jewish community that were distributed among the parties on the basis of their strength.

Originally, the parties, influenced by the political climate in Eastern and Central Europe, strongly emphasized ideological issues. Minutiae of ideology were discussed in party organs, in daily or weekly newspapers, and in other publications such as the party dissertations issued at election time. Ideologues were trained at seminars, in study groups, and in political clubs. Before they came to Palestine, these groups could not impose levies on the community, and ideologues had to rely on moral pressure to rally support.

Despite sharp differences, ideological consensus on fundamentals of Zionism held the Yishuv together. An even stronger force than ideology was the survival instinct of the small Jewish community, which was surrounded by a hostile population. This sense of threat to its physical existence has dominated Jewish society since the early days of the Yishuv and has remained the major issue on the national agenda, with all others secondary in importance. The national dictum purports that the preservation of security must be a nonpolitical matter. The IDF is the "people's army" whose soldiers are recruited and officers advanced regardless of their personal beliefs; it is a national rather than a political service. In times of crisis, ideological differences are tabled, as was the case during the War of Independence when soldiers of all competing ideological orientations—members of Haganah, the IZL, and Lehi—fought in the same units. On the eve of the 1967 Six Day War, when there was a perceived threat to national survival, a wall-to-wall coalition formed that was made up of several groups that until then had vowed never to work together.

Differences between parties had their roots in ideological distance within the Yishuv, which persisted after independence. At one end of the political spectrum were non-Zionist and anti-Zionist parties: the Communists who believed in international revolution and the hegemony of the working class. At the other end of the spectrum were the ultrareligious groups that rejected the idea of a national home for the Jews before the arrival of the Messiah. For many, identification with the state gradually replaced their commitment to Zionism or to secular Jewish nationalism, which had often substituted for Jewish religious identity and practice. Participation in Zionist political activity and, later, service to the nation—in the diaspora or in Israel—replaced synagogue attendance, the traditional center of Jewish communal identity. In the Yishuv, many religious practices were secularized and became the focus of a new identity. For most Jews in the Yishuv, the holidays of Hanukkah and Passover became celebrations of heroism and freedom.

Table 3.1 shows the distribution of votes and number of seats in the 1949 Constituent Assembly (First Knesset) by competing parties. Table 3.1 shows twenty-one party lists competing for the 120 Knesset seats, with only twelve receiving at least one seat. The labor parties, Mapai and Mapam, gained 65 seats, enough to form a coalition. Mapai also gained two additional seats from its Arab satellite party, the Democratic List. Mapai, with 46 seats, de-

TABLE 3.1 Number of Votes and Seats Obtained in the Constituent Assembly Election, 1949

Party	Number of Votes	Number of Seats
Mapai	155,247	46
Mapam	64,018	19
Religious Front	52,982	16
Herut	49,782	14
General Zionists	22,661	7
Progressives	17,786	5
Sephardim	15,287	4
Communists	15,148	4
Democratic/Arab	7,387	2
Fighters (Lehi)	5,363	1
Women's International Zionist Organization	5,173	1
Yemenites	4,399	1
Workers' Bloc/Arab	3,214	—
Zohar (Revisionists)	2,892	—
Orthodox	2,835	—
Popular Bloc/Arab	2,812	—
Religious Workers/Women	2,796	—
Greenbaum	2,514	—
Religious Workers	1,280	—
For Jerusalem	849	—
Traditional Jews	239	—

Source: Gideon Doron and Moshe Maor, *Barriers to Entry into Israeli Politics* (Tel Aviv: Papyrus, 1989), p. 96.

cided instead to form a coalition with the Religious Front, the Progressives, and the Sepharadim. There were three right-wing parties: Herut, Zohar, and the Fighters. The center was represented by six parties, including the ethnic lists: General Zionists, the Progressives, Sepharadim, the Women's International Zionist Organization (WIZO), the Yemenites, and Greenbaum. There were five lists in the religious camp: the Religious Front, Religious Workers, Religious Workers/Women, Orthodox, and Traditional Jews. The Arabs competed with three lists in addition to the Communists: the Democrats, Workers' Bloc, and Popular Bloc.

In the context of the Israeli political culture, collusion among the non-labor parties seemed impossible. In addition to ideological differences, there were clashing personalities and egos. Many politicians preferred to head their own list rather than be placed in a less prominent position in a larger party; consequently, one- or two-person factions of a larger party would at times run for office independently. There are some notable examples.

Ben-Gurion, the founder of Mapai, formed two such factions, Rafi in 1965 and the State List in 1969. Moshe Dayan of Mapai joined Ben-Gurion in Rafi and in 1981 formed the two-person Telem party. Ezer Weizman, who later became president of Israel, left Likud to form Yahad in 1984. In 1977 another Likud member, Ariel Sharon—until then a leading member of the Liberals—became the head of the two-person party Shlom-Zion. Shulamit Aloni of Mapai formed Ratz in 1973, and Aaron Abuhatzeira of Mafdal founded Tami in 1981.

Ideology tends to harden at the peripheries of each major bloc. Mapam, on the left of the labor movement, adamantly opposes the Orthodox, but the Labor bloc as a whole includes more religious Jews than any of the religious parties. The Religious Workers party's social and economic platform is often closer to Labor than to Likud. Some right-wing Labor leaders are closer to Likud than to Mapam on foreign policy and social issues. Within Likud, some Knesset members' social policy orientation is compatible with the Mapam mainstream.

As parties merge into larger blocs, they tend to deemphasize ideology because of the need to find common ground with other groups. The larger the bloc and the greater the number of factions within it, the greater the pressure for internal ideological compromise. The smaller parties with the least need to reach political compromise remain the most ideologically "pure."

The Dominant Party Era: 1949–1977

Mapai dominated Israel's political scene from 1949 until 1977 in terms of both ideology and government control. Its domination effectively began in 1935 and continued until 1965, when its political influence gradually dissipated, finally disappearing following the 1981 election. From then on, the Israeli party system changed from one-party control to a polity in which two major blocs competed for domination; each could replace the other as the governing power.

Mapai, with its Arab satellites, was perceived as the dominant party in 1949 when it obtained only 38.7 percent of the votes. In 1969, under Golda Meir's leadership, the Mapai-led alignment, together with its Arab satellite party, attracted the support of half of the Israeli voters. In 1974, three months after the Yom Kippur War—an event that was widely perceived in Israel as a military success but a serious political defeat—45 percent of the public continued to support the alignment's veteran leadership. What made Mapai a dominant party during this period?

Three explanations are offered: historical, strategic, and situational. Historically, Mapai and its leaders, in particular Ben-Gurion, were identified as the most responsible for the establishment of the state. Ben-Gurion was perceived as the founder of Israel as well as its party leader, prime minister, and minister of defense. Many new immigrants who were rewarded by the party or the government perceived opposing Mapai to be an act of disloyalty to the state. Moreover, the tremendous economic growth during the early 1950s was attributed by many to effective management by the Mapai-led government.

Because of intergenerational tensions during the late 1950s, when Ben-Gurion decided to raise the political status of his "Young Turks"— especially Moshe Dayan and Shimon Peres—at the expense of Mapai's "old guard," he and his loyalists left the party in 1963 to form Rafi. But Mapai continued its tactical maneuvering and maintained domination. First, it united with Achdut Ha-Avoda, which had split from Mapai in 1944, and later joined Hashomer Hatzair in Mapam. Mapai's union with Achdut Ha-Avoda strengthened it vis-à-vis Rafi's threat. In 1968 the Mapai–Achdut Ha-Avoda alignment absorbed Rafi (without Ben-Gurion) and formed the Labor party.

Labor continued its winning strategy of promoting nonradical "centrist" positions—maintaining the status quo in relations between state and religion, promoting a mixed economy, remaining neutral or pro-West in foreign policy, and choosing coalition partners that could ease pressure on the government. For example, the "permanent" partnership, or the so-called historical alliance, with the Orthodox Mafdal minimized tensions with religious voters. Collaboration with the General Zionists during the period of economic hardship in the early 1950s caused that party, the second-largest at that time, to share the responsibility and the blame for the adverse effects of government policies on the population. Keeping separate Arab lists helped to solve potential contradictions between policies for the Jewish sector and those designed for Arabs.

Mapai domination underscored the inability of other parties to form an alternative government. No party threatened Mapai until Likud gained thirty-nine Knesset seats in 1974. Mapam refused to join a government with the ultra-Orthodox or religious parties; Herut, the General Zionists, the Progressives, and the Free Center could not tolerate the Arab and Communist lists. Only Mapai, because of its size and centrist location, could mediate and bridge these diverse ideological differences. Following the 1974 election, that began to change.

First Transition of Power: 1977

During the era of Mapai political domination, Labor was perceived by many, even its rivals, to be an indispensable permanent fixture. When Likud became the largest party following the May 1977 election, shock waves radiated throughout the entire political system. Some people talked of leaving the country, expecting acts of retaliation against defeated Labor loyalists.

Others anticipated bold policies that would destroy the institutions founded by Mapai governments. Likud was as surprised as others to find itself the leader. It had not prepared new professional cadres and therefore had to continue until 1981 with many of the same officials who had served Mapai. Table 3.2 presents the electoral outcome of the 1977 election.

Several factors led to Labor's downfall in 1977. First and foremost was the establishment of the Democratic Movement for Change (DMC). The fifteen seats obtained by the DMC came mostly from former Labor votes. Even if Labor had obtained a few more seats, it would still have found it difficult to govern. By 1977 the alliance between Mafdal and Labor had ceased to exist because the young religious party leaders were mostly political hawks and Likud supporters. The Council of Sages of Agudat Israel, although basically made up of doves, favored Begin because of his traditional lifestyle. Labor could not rely on the Communists or on Flatto-Sharon because they were not considered legitimate political players and could not attract Ariel Sharon's party, Shlom-Zion. Immediately after the election, Sharon joined forces with Begin and merged with Likud. Thus, Labor spent the next four years on the opposition benches.

The first step in Begin's long route to power had begun in 1965 when Herut and the Liberals (formerly General Zionists) formed the Gahal bloc. The merger achieved two goals. First, Herut found legitimacy as a right-of-center party; second, Gahal, as the largest opposition group, attracted many voters disappointed with Mapai. Begin's final legitimization came on the eve of the 1967 war. During the tense period prior to the war he had publicly

TABLE 3.2   Results of the 1977 Knesset Election

Party	Percentage of Votes	Number of Seats	Membership in Likud Coalition
Likud	33.2	43	Yes
Shlom-Zion	1.9	2	Yes
Democratic Movement for Change	11.6	15	Yes
Mafdal	9.2	12	Yes
Agudat Israel	3.4	4	Yes
Pagi (Agudat Israel Workers)	1.4	1	No
Independent Liberals	1.2	1	No
Labor + Arab List	26.0	32	No
Ratz (Citizens' Rights)	1.2	1	No
Shelli	1.6	2	No
Hadash (Communists)	4.6	5	No
Flatto-Sharon	2.0	1	No

Source: Compiled by authors.

suggested that Ben-Gurion, his longtime archenemy, be brought back to lead Israel through the difficult days ahead. Under public pressure and with Ben-Gurion's approval, Begin joined the government as minister without portfolio in June 1967 and stayed until 1970. His decision to leave in 1970 and rejoin the opposition paid off three years later. Gahal attracted two constituencies: Sephardi Jews, mostly of North African origin, and many middle-class Ashkenazim who voted for the Liberal agenda. Consequently, Begin's bloc obtained thirty-nine seats in 1974.

The Likud gained only four additional seats in 1977. Together with Sharon's party it had a total of forty-five seats, enough to rule effectively, especially since Labor could not adjust to its new opposition role while it rebuilt the party under the leadership of Shimon Peres. Between 1977 and 1981, Likud had two major accomplishments. The first was the peace treaty Begin signed with President Anwar Sadat of Egypt; the second was Project Renewal, a payoff to supporters in poor neighborhoods and development towns. By the 1981 election, Begin had acquired a proven record of leadership. He was rewarded when Likud gained forty-eight seats and soon formed a coalition government with its Orthodox partners and Dayan's new party, Telem. Although Labor won forty-seven seats, it could not attract partners to form a government coalition.

Since 1981, the Israeli polity has been divided into left and right camps. In the 1984 and 1988 elections, the two were about equal in size, forming a national unity government made up of both Likud and Labor with smaller partners. By 1992 the political deadlock between the two camps had been broken, and Labor regained power.

Second Transition of Power: 1992

Between 1977 and 1992, Shimon Peres led Labor but failed four times to restore the party to a position of dominance. In the 1984 election, Labor and Likud were tied; therefore, the post of prime minister was rotated. Peres served the first two years, and then Yitzhak Shamir (who had replaced Begin as Likud leader in 1983) became prime minister. Labor's Yitzhak Rabin had the second-most-important post, minister of defense, under both Peres and Shamir. Following the 1988 election, the two parties decided that even though the Likud had a small edge, they would again form a coalition. One significant difference was that the rotation mechanism was abandoned, making Shamir prime minister, Rabin minister of defense, and Peres minister of finance.

By 1990 Peres felt it was time to break down the existing grand coalition. After three months of extensive bargaining, however, Shamir prevailed as the prime minister. Labor MKs then decided to replace Peres with Rabin as leader of the party. Table 3.3 provides comparative information on the

TABLE 3.3 Changes in Distribution of Knesset Seats Between 1988 and 1992

Party	1988	1992	Difference
Left Camp			
Labor	39	44	5
Ratz[a]	5	12 (Meretz)	2
Mapam[a]	3		
Shinui[a]	2		
Hadash	4	3	−1
Democratic/Arab	1	2	1
Progressive List for Peace/Arab	1	0	−1
Subtotal	55	61	6
Right-Religious Camp			
Likud	40	32	−8
Tehiya	3	0	−3
Tzomet	2	8	6
Moledet	2	3	1
Mafdal	5	6	1
Agudat Israel[b]	5	4	−3
Degel Ha-Torah[b]	2	(United Torah Judaism)	
Shas	6	6	0
Subtotal	65	59	−6
Total	120	120	

[a] Ratz, Mapam, and Shinui combined to run as Meretz in 1992.
[b] Agudat Israel and Degel Ha-Torah ran as United Torah Judaism in 1992.
Source: Gideon Doron, *Strategy of Election* (Tel Aviv: Maariv, 1995).

electoral results in 1988 and 1992 and shows the margin of victory in 1992. The left camp gained six seats compared to 1988, enabling it for the first time since 1974 to organize a blocking coalition to prevent its opponents from forming a ruling coalition. The expectation that Rabin could provide a winning edge prevailed.

Several factors contributed to Labor's 1992 victory. Campaign strategy placed Rabin to the right of voters' preferences. Equally important was the fact that the right lost thousands of votes because several of its leaders did not join forces and could not attract enough support by themselves to pass the vote threshold, the designated minimum percentage required for a Knesset seat. Prior to the 1992 election, the threshold had been raised from 1.0 to 1.5 percent. This marginal increase, although supported by Tehiya, was sufficient to keep the party out of the 1992 Knesset. The result was that the left camp won the election, although more votes were cast for parties to the right.

The introduction of the new electoral system in 1996 in which voters cast two ballots, one for prime minister and one for a party list, led to a setback for Labor. Although the Labor Alignment obtained the largest number of votes (26.8 percent) and the most Knesset seats (thirty-four), its candidate for prime minister, Shimon Peres, was defeated by Likud's Benjamin Netanyahu by less than one percent, or fewer than 30,000, of the nearly 3 million votes cast. Although Labor remained the largest party in the Knesset, under the new electoral procedure Netanyahu became prime minister and formed a coalition government from several right-of-center and religious parties. The events that led to these changes are discussed in Chapter 8.

The Left Bloc

By 1992 the left bloc consisted of four parties: Labor (changed to "Labor Headed by Rabin" in 1992 for campaign purposes), Meretz, and the two Arab parties, Hadash and the Arab Democratic Party. The last two parties were not members of the Rabin government's coalition, although they gave Labor and Meretz the parliamentary support necessary to maintain a majority. With the exception of Shinui, one of the three parties that constitutes Meretz, the other left bloc members have their roots in the labor movement.

The Socialist-Labor Bloc

Jewish socialism and Jewish nationalism fused in early twentieth-century Europe to produce the Zionist labor movement. Socialist Zionists perceived the Jewish community as an "inverted pyramid," with few Jews in primary occupations, such as agriculture or industry, but many as middlemen. An early twentieth-century analysis of Jewish occupational distribution showed nearly one-half of the population was employed in the sale of food and liquor, the clothing trade, the manufacture of jewelry, and the operation of small print shops. Fifteen to 20 percent were employed in building and textiles. Less than one percent were in agriculture, and less than 10 percent worked in basic industry. Jews did not supply society's basic requirements but were concentrated at the end of the production cycle. Many became paupers who worked in highly competitive sweatshops. Zionist theoreticians like Ber Borochov believed diaspora Jews were excluded from the mainstream socialist struggle because they were rootless and needed their own country.

The first socialist Zionist group, Poalei Zion (Workers of Zion), was established in 1907 and later fused its ideas with those of A. D. Gordon, an early Zionist who settled in Palestine at age forty-nine. Gordon's followers considered him to be a saint and a mystic who venerated physical labor for its own sake. Through physical labor on the land, the Jewish nation would regenerate its lost spiritual values. Gordon's thesis, which was much less Marxian than Borochov's, held that the crux of the Jewish problem was not a struggle of capital against labor but was one of production versus parasitism. Attracted by the mystique of Jewish labor on Jewish land, Gordon's immediate followers established Hapoel Hatzair (the Young Worker), a group whose task was to drain swamps, irrigate deserts, and establish new agricultural outposts. The Marxian-oriented Poalei Zion changed its name to Achdut Ha-Avoda (Unity of Labor) after merging with several smaller socialist Zionist groups in Palestine.

The two parties, Hapoel Hatzair and Achdut Ha-Avoda, established Mapai (Workers' Party of Eretz Israel) in 1930, combining theoretical and practical socialist trends. During the mandate Mapai's slogans were "Jewish Conquest of the Land" and "Jewish Conquest of Labor." Most kibbutzim established during the mandate were affiliated with the Mapai-controlled kibbutz federation. The party also helped to establish agricultural cooperatives, or *moshavim*. Jewish labor, Jewish production of essential commodities, a Jewish cooperative movement, and attraction of Jewish youth to the land of Palestine were the Labor movement's chief goals.

In 1920, before Mapai was established, the two Zionist labor parties formed the Histadrut (General Federation of Workers in Eretz Israel), which developed a massive structure parallel to that of the political parties and other Yishuv institutions. Most leaders, activities, and policies of the Histadrut were part of or were determined by the labor parties. All of the large trade unions belonged to the Histadrut.

By the 1930s, about 45 percent of the Yishuv was identified in some way with the labor movement organizations, which carried more weight than all other political groups. Mapai's leaders—like Ben-Gurion, Sharett, and Meir—became central figures in institutions of the Yishuv such as the National Council and the Haganah; they were also leaders of the world Zionist movement. The leaders in the 1930s and 1940s, mostly from kibbutzim, strongly emphasized developing agriculture and expanding the Yishuv.

Until the establishment of Israel in 1948, many leaders and members of labor organizations came from the kibbutzim. From 1930 to 1965, Mapai membership grew from 6,000 to over 200,000. Sixty percent of the original members were farmers, but by 1964 that percentage was only 4.2. By the mid-1970s, over 70 percent of the labor movement members were urban, mostly from large cities. In the mid-1990s the number of labor party members differed little from that of the previous thirty years.

As the economic foundations of the country broadened after 1949, industry, trade, commerce, and services competed with agriculture for the labor movement's attention. Large urban professional groups of physicians, writers, journalists, and engineers joined the Histadrut. In 1964 membership included about one-half of the country's adult population, with two-thirds from industry and nearly one-third clerical and professional employees; the number from agricultural had become negligible. This distribution remained about the same for the next thirty years.

Mapai (Palestine [Eretz Israel] Workers' Party). Mapai, the core party of the Labor bloc until 1965, mirrored the changing social structure of Israel. As the Yishuv became more complex and interest groups multiplied, Mapai had to cater to a larger constituency. Changing attitudes toward class stratification and the country's growing ethnic diversity were reflected in structural changes within Mapai. The Arab communities, now part of Israel, were organized into separate Arab lists affiliated with Mapai.

The growing acceptance of bourgeois values after 1948 was demonstrated in changing lifestyles, values, and political attitudes. Mapai directed more attention not only to urban workers but also to artisans and professionals. Physicians, lawyers, and accountants, formerly perceived as less important to the party than farmers or industrial workers, were organized into Mapai-affiliated professional groups. Recognition of these middle-class members departed from traditional socialist glorification of the proletariat and the tendency to downgrade so-called bourgeois occupations. With the expansion of the public sector in government and national institutions, the value of these professionals and their contributions to the national welfare received greater recognition.

This new situation raised serious ideological problems for Mapai. Physicians, lawyers, and university professors demanded higher wages than laborers, and their lifestyles created class differences within the movement. Tensions generated by these diverse lifestyles appeared when Mapai attempted to reconcile differences between its organizations of professional workers and the affiliated trade unions. Disputes over wage policies divided the Histadrut from the Mapai leadership when union members organized strikes that were not authorized by federation headquarters. In times of economic crises or austerity, when the governing Mapai imposed measures such as higher taxes or reduced food subsidies in opposition to the trade union membership, the rift between the party and unions widened.

Israel's changing demographic patterns are revealed in Mapai membership statistics. In 1954 only 27 percent of the party members were Sephardi Jews; that figure had risen to 45 percent by 1965. Socialization or integration of new immigrants became a party function through departments for North Africans, Yemenites, and Iraqis. Mapai established more than thirty such organizations, at which immigrants learned Hebrew and Israeli culture and values. The party helped new immigrants to find jobs, housing, and bank credit and to resolve family problems.

By the late 1960s, Sephardi Jews represented less than one-third of the party's central committee, no more than 10 percent of the secretariat, and less than 20 percent of the Knesset delegation. Ironically, following Labor's defeat in the 1977 election, Sephardi Jewish representation at the cabinet level increased when the new Likud government appointed several Sephardim to top posts. Mapai has competed successfully with the religious parties for Orthodox Jewish votes and had many Orthodox Jews as members even before the influx of Sephardi Jews. After the large Sephardi immigration, a Mapai religious circle was established to contact local religious councils in Sephardim communities with high percentages of Orthodox Jews.

The local power of municipal party machines affiliated with the labor movement increased greatly after 1948. Through control of vital economic sectors such as the Haifa dock workers and municipal employees in Tel Aviv, local labor leaders acquired control over party branches in large cities, which gave them blocks of votes in the party convention and the central committee. Abba Khoushi, the Mapai leader in Haifa, and the Gush (bloc) in Tel Aviv became strong components of the national party and played important roles in selecting its leaders and in its decisionmaking. Other informal groupings represented distinct interest groups such as university professors and former army officers.

The expansion of Mapai's constituency to include diverse interest groups, factions, and circles tended to undermine the original socialist ideology. The trend was increasingly toward national rather than class interests. The growth of party institutions, both official and unofficial, not only enlarged the bureaucracy but also ended the informality and intimacy of the prestate era. The party bureaucracy was no longer easily accessible to the average member. As some party leaders acquired influence and prestige, they also obtained material advantages that created a social distance between many of them and the rank and file.

Achdut Ha-Avoda (Unity of Labor). Achdut Ha-Avoda represents the nationalist, or "activist," group within labor Zionism. Its political leadership came mostly from the kibbutz movement, and many served as commanders and soldiers in the Palmach. Several of Israel's most security-oriented political leaders, who have taken a hard line toward the Arabs, have their roots in this party; they include Rehavam Ze'evi (Gandhi), the leader of Moledet; Rafael Eitan (Raful), the founder of Tzomet; and Yitzhak Rabin. In 1944 Achdut Ha-Avoda activists who disagreed with the Mapai leadership left Mapai, and in 1948, together with Poalei Zion Smol (Left Zion Workers) and the Hashomer Hatzair, formed the Mapam (United Workers) party.

In the 1949 election, Mapam became the second-largest party, winning nineteen Knesset seats. Mapai and Mapam, the two major parties in the labor movement, failed to form a coalition that would have given labor a comfortable majority of sixty-five members. Even though they were not far apart in their social and economic policies, the two parties were divided over the dissolution of the Palmach and over Mapam's affiliation with the

Communist International and the Soviet Union, which precipitated a major upheaval between 1952 and 1954. Moscow, Israel's strongest supporter during the 1947 UN partition debate and a main supplier of weapons during the War of Independence, began to back nationalist and leftist movements in the Arab states. Forced by Soviet policy to choose between Jewish nationalism and socialist solidarity, Mapam was split: The Zionist nationalists separated from Mapam, resuming their identity as Achdut Ha-Avoda. Most of those who remained in Mapam were affiliated with Hashomer Hatzair.

In the 1955, 1959, and 1961 elections, Achdut Ha-Avoda ran independently and obtained ten, seven, and eight seats, respectively, thereby becoming Mapai's favorite coalition partner. During the 1965 election, Achdut Ha-Avoda accepted Mapai's proposal to combine forces under the leadership of Levi Eshkol against Ben-Gurion, the leader of Rafi. When the 1965 electoral results came in, it became apparent that the Rafi threat had been overstated. The Mapai–Achdut Ha-Avoda alignment lost only five seats (in 1961 the two parties had won fifty seats). Rafi obtained only ten seats, causing its young leadership to rethink ways to pursue their political careers—especially when Eshkol decided to keep them out of government.

In 1968, Mapai's old guard, Achdut Ha-Avoda activists, and Rafi's statists decided to reunite as the Labor party. By then, leaders of Achdut Ha-Avoda such as Yigal Allon, a former Palmach commander, were among Israel's most prominent political figures. By 1974, however, Achdut Ha-Avoda had practically disappeared from the political scene.

Mapam (United Workers Party). Mapam was established in 1948 to represent the left wing of the Labor movement, but over the years it has gone through extensive ideological, tactical, and political changes. In 1949 it was the second-largest party in the Knesset, with nineteen members. In 1988 it received only three seats, a political achievement perceived by many observers at the time as a surprising victory.

Mapam's gradual decline was caused by its failure to adapt to social and political change in Israel. Its Marxist ideology, although somewhat modified after 1948, was still too doctrinaire for the growing middle class. Its moderate position on foreign policy and especially its promotion of a binational solution to the Jewish-Arab problem prior to 1948 kept away nationalist-oriented Sephardi voters, even though many were members of the working class, Mapam's natural constituency. Mapam's long association with the Soviets and international communism caused the split with Achdut Ha-Avoda, mentioned earlier.

Hashomer Hatzair, the core group of Mapam, began as an Eastern European Zionist youth movement with a Marxist orientation and strong devotion to the kibbutz, or collective, ideal. Members considered themselves an integral part of the world proletariat, striving to replace the capitalist system, with its profits and exploitation of the many for the good of the few, with a new economic and social order that had no class distinctions. After its founders had settled in Palestine and established Hashomer Hatzair as a political party, leadership was derived largely from the left wing of the kibbutz movement. Its federation of collectives, Kibbutz Artzi, constituted nearly half of the membership of the kibbutz movement; the party had relatively few urban supporters.

Mapam's many agricultural settlements contributed greatly to the development of frontier areas and to the continued idealization of traditional pioneer, or *halutz,* values. Its strong ideological commitment to rural development led Mapam to overlook both the importance of organizing urban workers and the significance for Israel of large-scale industry. (Many Mapam kibbutzim later developed small industries.) Few of its members played leading roles in industry, and Mapam was thus unable to compete with Mapai in placing members as directors of nonagricultural enterprises.

Before the establishment of Israel in 1948, Hashomer Hatzair ideology strongly emphasized compromise with Palestinian Arab nationalism through the formation of a binational state rather than one that was predominantly Jewish or Arab. When most Zionists supported the 1942 Biltmore Program, which called for the establishment of a Jewish commonwealth in Palestine, Hashomer Hatzair continued to support a Jewish-Arab state. It was thought that binationalism would erase economic and social conflicts between Jewish and Palestinian Arab nationalism, which were exploited by British imperialism. Hashomer Hatzair's binational program isolated it from the rest of the Yishuv on the most vital political issue of the day. Until independence in 1948, the movement continued to oppose the partition of Palestine or the establishment of a separate Jewish state. Eventually, the movement totally reversed its position and stated that Zionism could be realized only in partitioned Palestine.

Between 1955 and 1977, with the exception of the period 1959 to 1961, Mapam was a member of Mapai-led coalitions. In the 1969 election its leaders joined with the newly constructed Labor party in the alignment but retained their separate identity and organizational structure. Mapam's strength, as measured by the outcome of the 1965 election, was preserved within the new alignment by its eight Knesset seats. Its representatives in the Knesset and the government were considered doves, holding the position— especially after 1967—that territorial compromise should be reached with the Palestinians and that they should be permitted to establish their own independent state.

In 1984, when Labor joined the grand coalition with Likud, Mapam felt the distance between its ideological position and that of the government was far too wide. Consequently, Mapam left the alignment and ran independently in 1988. By that time Mapam's new leadership had made several important adjustments to its political image. The leaders abandoned support of the Soviet model of society and adopted a form of Scandinavian socialism. They also emphasized the interests of lower-class industrial workers who were competing with the Likud for support. These efforts resulted in Mapam winning three Knesset seats and a place in the opposition. Prior to the 1992 election, perhaps because of fears that the party would not receive enough votes for even one seat, Mapam joined Ratz and Shinui to form Meretz. Meretz gained twelve seats in the Knesset and became Labor's junior partner in a government coalition; Mapam's share of the Knesset seats was four, and two were held by kibbutz members.

The Rafi Party (Israel Workers' List). To counteract the growing development of special-interest groups, bureaucratization, and leadership inbreeding, Ben-Gurion and a group of young Mapai leaders (*zairim*) began to demand party reform during the late 1950s. An initial step was the election of several *zairim* to the Knesset on the 1959 Mapai List. Impatient with the lack of opportunity for advancement in the party councils, Abba Eban, Shimon Peres, and Moshe Dayan entered the Knesset directly with Ben-Gurion's assistance; later, Ben-Gurion became the group's unofficial spokesman. With such a national figure as their leader, the *zairim* attempted to shift the focus of party activity from internal partisan matters to issues that concerned Israeli society as a whole. The group's theme was loyalty to nation above loyalty to party. Its approach was expressed in the term *mamlachtiyut* (statism), coined by Ben-Gurion. Initially, the group focused attention on the trade union movement and the powerful Histadrut. Challenging a cardinal principle of that movement, the group insisted that business and industrial management had the right to dismiss inefficient labor to lower production costs and increase productivity. Without increased productivity, the group argued, the social benefits received by union members would weaken the country's entire economic structure.

Ben-Gurion and the *zairim* believed it was essential to extend the concept of pioneering (*halutziut*) beyond agriculture and the land to include other sectors of society and the economy. Industry based on science and technology was equally essential for national development. Expertise and efficiency replaced Mapai's traditional glorification of physical labor.

The ideology of statism polarized growing tensions between the government and the Histadrut. Pinhas Lavon, secretary-general of the Histadrut, became a defender of the old land-rooted values. Temporarily discredited by a 1954 "security mishap" (an Israeli intelligence operation in Egypt that misfired), Lavon rose again and became head of the Histadrut in 1956. Some of the Mapai old guard even considered him as a candidate for prime minister to replace Ben-Gurion.

By 1958 the intensity of ideological division in the party had polarized the leadership into factions. The *zairim* assumed the mantle of reformers in opposition to the party's old guard, the Histadrut, and other powerful interests such as the Tel Aviv Gush (bloc) political machine.

Ideological and organizational differences were intensified in the 1950s by sharp personality clashes, especially between Lavon and Ben-Gurion. These disputes came to a head in 1960, when Lavon demanded that Ben-Gurion clear him of any responsibility for the 1954 security mishap. Lavon had been cleared by a cabinet committee, but its authority was challenged by Ben-Gurion, who insisted that only an impartial judicial inquiry could lead to a valid judgment. He threatened to resign unless the cabinet and the party acted on his position. Levi Eshkol, one of the middle-ground Mapai leaders, proposed a compromise that involved dropping Lavon as head of the Histadrut and shelving any further discussion or inquiry into the affair.

When Eshkol succeeded Ben-Gurion in 1963, he downgraded the *zairim* and their "statist" approach and returned to the previous pattern of party politics, with the old guard and the Histadrut at the center of power. Moshe Dayan, a new member of the cabinet as minister of agriculture, threatened to resign if he was not taken into the inner cabinet councils.

With the rapidly rising popularity of Ben-Gurion's reforms, Mapai's control of the Histadrut declined from 80 percent of member votes during the 1930s to 55.4 percent in the 1960 Histadrut election. With a new election scheduled for 1965, the Mapai leadership sought to strengthen its position through an electoral alliance with another strong labor group, Achdut Ha-Avoda.

Many Achdut Ha-Avoda leaders were traditional socialists who were skeptical of, if not outright opposed to, the statist doctrines of the *zairim*. Several had worked closely with the Mapai old guard as cabinet ministers in earlier governments.

Against this background of shifting alliances and new factions among labor organizations, Lavon again asked Eshkol to clear him. His actions angered Ben-Gurion, who had made the Lavon affair an issue of personal trust. Ben-Gurion insisted once more that only an impartial judicial inquiry and not a ministerial committee of Lavon's associates could clear Lavon.

At the tenth Mapai conference in 1964, ideology, tactics, and personality differences converged to create a crisis in the party. The crucial questions were: Who should succeed Ben-Gurion following his resignation; should Mapai realign itself with Achdut Ha-Avoda; how should the party deal with the Lavon affair; and how should the party resolve the fundamental ideological dispute between the traditionalists and the new statists? When the majority of the conference voted in favor of the old guard, Ben-Gurion announced that he and several of the *zairim* would leave Mapai and form a new Labor List, Rafi (Israel Workers' List).

In the 1965 elections the new Rafi List received far less support than anticipated, considering that its leader was Ben-Gurion and that it included attractive young politicians such as Peres and Dayan. Rafi had no well-defined and comprehensive program; rather, it played the role of opposition critic. Above all, it was anti-Eshkol, anti-Mapai, and anti-Histadrut. Rafi challenged many basic and widely accepted values and existing institutions without substituting new ones to compete with Mapai.

Many supporters and opponents of Rafi perceived it as Ben-Gurion's creation, and thus the issue became one of loyalty to "the old man" versus fidelity to the party. Ben-Gurion's charismatic hold on many voters was evident in the transfer of allegiance by many—notably Sephardi—voters from Mapai to Rafi. Rafi appeared as a separate list only once, in 1965; even with the leadership of Ben-Gurion and an array of rising stars, it won only 7.9 percent of the votes and ten seats. Later, Rafi rejoined Mapai and Achdut Ha-Avoda to form the Labor party; a few of its members maintained their separate identity as the State (*mamlachti*) List, which later joined the right-wing Likud.

The 1965 election demonstrated Mapai's institutional strength through a variety of Labor-affiliated organizations. In the contest between traditional party institutions and an array of colorful personalities, the party won. None of the main branches of Mapai defected, although several leaders left to join Rafi. Rafi's major weakness as a separate party was its lack of control over local patronage, government jobs, and the Histadrut. It could enlist only about 25,000 members, less than one-tenth the number in Mapai. Sixty percent of Rafi members were under age thirty-five, demonstrating the extent to which the new party represented opposition to the old guard. The fractious tone of its pronouncements, the bitter personal attacks on Mapai leader Levi Eshkol, and its great hostility toward the Histadrut worried many Labor sympathizers, who otherwise might have agreed with the criticism of the party's entrenched leadership.

The Labor Party. Between 1965 and 1967, both domestic and foreign affairs conspired to weaken Mapai's old guard. On the home front, the country entered a serious economic recession, with nearly 10 percent unemployment. Labor unrest, increased emigration of professionals, and disappointment with Eshkol undermined confidence in the government. In addition to these difficult circumstances, there was an outbreak of much more hostile rhetoric from the neighboring capitals. Israelis feared an imminent Arab attack.

At that critical moment, many Israelis thought the country was adrift without leadership. Eshkol's consensus approach to critical problems, his lack of dynamism in comparison with Ben-Gurion, and his low-key style of crisis management made him appear indecisive and fumbling. Some newspapers and opposition leaders called for Eshkol's resignation; others demanded that he turn the Ministry of Defense over to Dayan or Ben-Gurion. A few days before the eruption of the June 1967 war, a compromise was devised in which Dayan would become defense minister and a coalition of national unity would be formed that excluded only the Communists and several other minor parties. Herut (reconstituted as Gahal) entered the government for the first time, breaking a long-established Labor principle of not participating in a coalition with Begin.

This demonstration of national unity healed many deep rifts both among factions in the labor movement and between Mapai and other parties. With all labor groups from Mapam to Rafi once again serving in the same government, hopes of establishing a united Labor party were revived. Prior to elections for the Seventh Knesset in 1968, Mapai, Achdut Ha-Avoda, and Rafi merged into a new Labor party. Mapam, guarding its independence and distinctive ideology, did not join the new party but became affiliated with it in a single Knesset list called the Labor Alignment, or Ma'arach.

It took several more years for the three Labor components to abandon their separate identities and merge their party machines. After Prime Minister Eshkol's death and the succession of Golda Meir in 1969, the trend was toward domination by the Mapai old guard except in the realms of defense and the occupied areas, which were controlled by Defense Minister Dayan. The old guard was reinforced by Meir's frequent consultations with and reliance on her old party colleagues and Achdut Ha-Avoda in her informal "kitchen cabinet."

The 1973 war created another major shift in the Labor party's internal organization. Following an investigation by the Agranat Commission into the conduct of the war, Meir and several other old-guard ministers resigned. A new government was formed under Yitzhak Rabin, Israel's first native-born prime minister and the first who was not intimately identified with the traditional Mapai leadership. Rabin's government was actually run by a triumvirate: Prime Minister Rabin, who was not closely or formally identified with any party faction; Shimon Peres, the defense minister representing Rafi; and Foreign Minister and Deputy Prime Minister Yigal Allon, the leader of Achdut Ha-Avoda. Ben-Gurion never returned to the mainstream; after the merger he refused to join the new Labor party.

In 1977 Rabin's government was forced to call for early elections for three principal reasons: mounting pressure for reforms in the aftermath of the Yom Kippur War, actual and alleged acts of official corruption that created widespread mistrust, and disagreement over the status quo with the Orthodox religious partner, Mafdal. Peres replaced Rabin as the Labor leader in the 1977 election; after losing to Begin, he began to rebuild the party for the 1981 election. By then, Labor was almost as large as Likud, obtaining forty-seven seats to the latter's forty-eight seats. Much of this increase, fifteen seats, could be attributed to support from voters who decided to return to Labor in 1981. In 1984 Labor, again led by Peres and with forty-four seats to Likud's forty, became the largest party in the Knesset. However, because the number of seats in the left bloc equaled those in the Likud-led right-wing bloc, Peres could not form a government coalition; therefore, Labor formed a Unity Government with Likud. In 1988 Peres attempted for the fourth time to lead his party to victory and failed again. This time Likud, headed by Yitzhak Shamir, edged Labor out by one seat (forty to thirty-nine), and another Unity Government was formed with Shamir as prime minister, Peres as finance minister, and Rabin as defense minister.

Between 1988 and 1990, when Peres attempted to dissolve the government he was opposed by Rabin, who was second to Peres in the party and to Shamir in the government. A change would not have improved Rabin's political situation; his personal position would only have been endangered if Labor had again failed. Instead, in 1990 Rabin decided to challenge Peres's leadership.

Rabin regained his position as Labor leader in February 1992 through a primary vote. Soon thereafter, he undertook steps to remove the obstacles he believed had caused Labor's defeat in earlier elections. During the June 1992 election campaign, all party symbols, including Labor's "socialistic" red flags, were replaced. Traditional Labor institutions like the Histadrut and the kibbutzim were deemphasized, along with old "leftist" leaders like Peres. The party changed its official name to Labor Headed by Rabin. The idea was to present the voters with a new center-to-right image. The strategy worked, and the victorious Labor party was able to form a left-of-center coalition.

However, Rabin's position as prime minister and head of Labor did not give him control of the party. On several occasions his loyalists lost in intraparty competitions, including the election of the secretary-general and the party's choice for president of Israel. Likewise, the party lost several important mayorships, including that of Jerusalem, to Likud during the 1993 municipal elections. In 1994 the Labor party lost its domination over the Histadrut to a new bloc, Ram, headed by a young Labor dissident, Haim Ramon.

Labor in the mid-1990s is different in structure, orientation, and impact on society from the party of the 1970s. It is gradually assuming a U.S. style, recruiting politicians and mobilizing resources to finance political campaigns. It is a catch-all party with no unified ideology or single orientation toward major items on the national agenda. Perhaps the most important issue that unifies its supporters today is the desire to deny rule to Likud.

Ratz (Citizens' Rights Movement). Ratz, a splinter party of Labor, is the product of the personal and ideological ambitions of its founder, Shulamit

Aloni. Dovish in foreign affairs, between 1973 and 1984 Ratz emphasized issues such as the status of women in society and the separation of state and religion. Since 1984, Ratz has expanded its ideological bases by emphasizing moderate and compromising positions on the Israeli-Palestinian conflict.

Ratz scored surprisingly well in the 1973 elections, winning three Knesset seats with 2.2 percent of the vote. Aloni acquired a following in 1973 by appealing to women, secularists, and those discontented with government bureaucracy. She became a cabinet minister without portfolio in Rabin's coalition; however, she was sacrificed when Rabin decided to broaden his base by including the National Religious party, which adamantly opposed Aloni's secularist orientation. Ratz's three Knesset members combined briefly with another independent-minded maverick, Arie Eliav, who left the Labor party in 1974, to form a Knesset faction called Yozma (Initiative). Eliav, a former Labor party secretary-general, was critical of many government policies, especially in foreign affairs. Once elected to the Knesset he could not be deprived of his seat, but he lost standing within the Labor party and was not included on its 1977 election list. Instead, he ran on a new list called Shelli (Peace and Equality for Israel).

Within a few months, disagreements between Eliav and Aloni had split the small band of Knesset members. Eliav and one of Aloni's former followers formed a separate two-person Knesset faction called the Israeli Socialist party. Aloni and her only remaining partner reconstituted their two-seat Citizens' Rights Movement. In 1977 Eliav joined forces with Moked, another peace group, to form Shelli, which won two Knesset seats; Aloni's party obtained only one seat. The list of separate factions formed in this manner is long and is one of the more colorful aspects of Israeli political life.

In the 1981 election, Aloni obtained only one Knesset seat. To improve her chances of entering the next election, she joined with the doves of Shelli, formally adding the words "for Peace" to the name of her party. With these combined forces Ratz obtained three Knesset seats, which increased to five when a member of Labor, Yossi Sarid, who disagreed with the decision to form the Unity Government, left his party and joined Ratz. Later, a member of Shinui, Mordechai Virshovsky, did the same.

Additional forces from the Peace Now movement joined prior to the 1988 election, but Ratz could not increase its five seats. Consequently, it united with Mapam and Shinui to form the Meretz bloc in 1992, which gained two additional seats after combining forces. Meretz became Rabin's junior partner in his 1992 coalition; it was responsible for ministerial portfolios including education and culture, communication, science and the arts, immigration and absorption, and environmental quality. Other Meretz MKs became deputy ministers and heads of Knesset committees. In the 1993 municipal elections, Meretz increased its strength at the local level by joining with either Labor or Likud. In 1994 it joined its most unlikely political rival, Shas, and formed a technical bloc headed by former Labor Minister of Health Haim Ramon to seize control of the Histadrut.

The Communists. Many dilemmas, trials, and tribulations of the Israeli left were epitomized by the career of Moshe Sneh. Born in Poland in 1909, Sneh headed the general Zionist movement there during the 1930s. After immigrating to Palestine in 1940, he became a leader of the Haganah, a member of the Jewish Agency for Palestine Executive, and a director of the Political Department at the agency's European office. When Mapam was formed in 1947, Sneh became a member of its Executive Committee and editor of its daily newspaper, Al-Hamishmar (On Guard). Although his orientation was pro-Soviet, he maintained that he was still a Jewish nationalist, that Israel's future was with the Third World, and that the Soviet Union would play a dominant role in the Middle East. These views were consistent with the strong anti-British feeling in the Yishuv during the period 1947–1948. Sneh was shaken by the massive U.S. efforts to rebuild West Germany so soon after World War II. Furthermore, the Soviet Union supported the UN plan to partition Palestine, and the UN delegates from the USSR were the most outspoken in favor of a Jewish state.

After the split within Mapam, Sneh kept faith with the Communist International. He blamed Israel's difficulties with the Eastern bloc on its overzealous attachment to the United States. In protest against Mapam compromises, Sneh left the party in 1953 and formed Siat Smol (Left Faction), and in 1954 he joined Maki, the Israeli Communist party.

Maki was a blend of several radical non-Zionist perspectives; it grew out of the Palestinian Communist party, formed in 1924. Communist encouragement of the use of Yiddish rather than Hebrew symbolized its opposition to Zionism. According to the Soviet line, Zionism was a bourgeois movement closely identified with Western imperialism. Only a few of its leaders, such as Sneh, considered themselves Jewish nationalists. Despite the fact that most members of the pre-1948 Palestinian Communist party were Jewish, the party could never obtain more than 3 percent of the Yishuv's votes. In 1943 the party split into three factions: the Arab League of National Liberation, which supported Palestinian Arab national aspirations; a Jewish non-Zionist group; and a few individuals who called themselves the Communist Education Association, some of whom later joined the Lehi underground movement. The Jewish and Arab factions were reunited as Maki in 1948, pledging loyalty to the new state but opposition to Zionism.

Maki was in an untenable position in the Jewish community because it followed the Soviet line unfailingly. With the shift from Soviet support for Israel to its unswerving backing of Arab nationalism, Maki attracted a large Arab vote. The strain of reconciling anti-Zionism with support of Jewish nationalism, and loyalty to the State of Israel with Soviet guidance on foreign policy, was too great for the party. In 1965 it again split into two groups: the parent Maki organization and Rakah (the New Communist List), most, but not all, of whose followers were Israeli Arabs.

After 1948 many Arabs identified the Communist party in Israel as a nationalist or liberation movement rather than a Marxist organization. The party was quick to defend the interests of Israel's Arab citizens and to criticize government violations of civil rights, the sequestering of Arab land, and the imposition of military government. The Arab community, which was the most directly affected by these measures, perceived the Communist party as a legitimate expression of nationalist sentiment and dissatisfaction with government.

After the bifurcation of Maki in 1965, Moshe Sneh continued to lead the parent organization, which was left with fewer members than the breakaway Rakah party. Sneh attempted to maintain a neutral position in the Arab-Israeli dispute, as Arab nationalism became more militant and the Soviet Union intensified its hostility toward Israel. Moscow maintained an association with both Maki and Rakah for two years, until the 1967 war. Sneh blamed both Jewish and Arab "reactionary chauvinist" leaders for the conflict, rejecting the Soviet stand on the war. Following an independent line, he attacked Arab terrorism and opposed Israel's evacuation of the Occupied Territories prior to a peace settlement. Sneh said Soviet support of Arab aggression was a "tactical blunder." Even though he continued to regard Moscow as the leader in the struggle against imperialism, Sneh asserted that it should have remained neutral in the Arab-Israeli conflict.

As Sneh became increasingly critical of the Arab states, he shifted back toward Mapam. He recognized the Jewish nation as a cohesive international community with its own distinct aspirations. Before his death in 1972, Sneh reaffirmed a commitment to Zionism and requested a traditional Jewish burial. The funeral was an occasion for his reinstatement as a leader of the Yishuv; it was attended by David Ben-Gurion, Golda Meir, Pinhas Sapir, Moshe Dayan, and representatives of the Labor community from Rafi through Mapam and Maki. Sneh's death raised him once again to the status of an Israeli patriot and an international Jewish figure. Sneh's son, Efraim, was a physician who became an IDF general, military governor of the West Bank, and a trusted member of Rabin's cabinet.

The few Jewish Communists who remained in Maki after Sneh's death were so splintered that the party finally dissolved altogether. One faction was absorbed into the peace group Moked (Focus), formed on the eve of the 1973 election, which also embraced other defectors from Mapam who were dissatisfied with their party's membership in the Labor alignment. Moked's greatest asset was its popular leader, Meir Pa'il, a retired army colonel known for his innovative military strategy and outspoken original political views. In the 1977 election Pa'il joined Arie Eliav and a few other independent radicals to form Shelli, which obtained two Knesset seats.

Rakah continued to gather strength among Israeli Arabs. It obtained over 23 percent of the Arab vote in 1956, 37 percent in 1973, and nearly 50 percent in 1977. Its greatest coup was winning the mayoralty of Nazareth, Israel's largest Arab community, in 1973. Although Jewish Rakah members still served in the party's highest offices and in its Knesset delegation, Rakah continued to represent Arab nationalism and was a respectable voice of dissent for leftists.

To broaden its electoral appeal among Jewish voters, before the 1977 election Rakah decided to offer a safe place on its Knesset List to the leader of the Israeli Black Panthers, an ethnic list formed in 1968 by youths of North African origin from poor neighborhoods and development towns. The Panthers attempted, but failed, to gain a seat in the 1973 election. For strategic reasons, Rakah joined with other Israeli Arab groups and altered its name to Hadash (new), Hebrew acronym for Democratic Front for Peace and Equality). However, Hadash was perceived as either too Communist or too Arab nationalist by its potential Sephardi Jewish voters. Based on its Arab votes, all Hadash could hope for was to maintain the four seats it had received in the three rounds of elections during the 1980s. In 1992 it ran without the Black Panthers. Hadash obtained only three seats but served as an essential part of Labor's blocking coalition against Likud.

By the mid-1990s Hadash had essentially become an Arab nationalist party. Most of its leaders were Arabs, and only a handful were traditional Jewish Communists. The party supported a compromise peace settlement with the Arab states and the establishment of an independent Palestinian state in the West Bank and the Gaza Strip. Labor government policies seemed to be consistent with these goals; thus Rabin benefited from Hadash political support, which was granted even when government policies toward the Arab minority in Israel were inconsistent with those of Hadash or when prevailing official attitudes continued to deny Communists the legitimacy of serving in government offices.

The Arab Lists

A significant difference exists between the Arab lists that were products of the Mapai patronage system, which last gained representation to the Knesset in 1977, and those that emerged after 1984. The former were not genuine parties but were mere electoral lists formed for Mapai's convenience. Prior to each election, Mapai leaders would approach a few Arab notables, such as local leaders, to assess the notables' electoral appeal and offer them a Knesset List of their clients. These notables were able to command a bloc of votes by using their unofficial authority to order clients to vote as they demanded. Several Arab lists would be constructed because it was more convenient for Mapai to finance two or three separate lists than to reconcile personal or religious differences among the Arab factions. At times an unlikely coalition of southern Bedouin and northern Arab farmers would be formed as a Knesset List under titles such as "peace," "equality," "work," "progress," and the like, and ballots would be printed in Arabic. The largest number of seats these lists obtained was five, in 1959. Once elected, the list gave Mapai automatic support with very little payoff in return. Mapai could thus present to its Jewish voters a consistent program that included restrictive measures against the Arabs, such as continuation of the military government, and still receive more Arab votes than the Communists.

The percentage of Arab voters in Israel is usually as high as that of Jews. The Arabs constitute an attractive pool of voters for several parties including Likud and the Orthodox party. Attempts to establish an indigenous Arab party were legally blocked during the 1960s. But with the relaxation of security threats during the 1980s, a group of radical Arab and Jewish leaders formed the Progressive List for Peace (PLP), which promoted reconciliation between Jews and Arabs, equality for all citizens, and an independent Palestinian state coexisting with Israel—issues similar to those promoted by the Communists. The PLP gained two seats in 1984. One was awarded to its Arab leader, Muhammad Meari, and the second to Jewish professor Matti Peled, a former IDF major general. Attempts to legally block the party's entrance to the Knesset were made prior to the 1988 election under allegations that its platform was anti-Zionist, but these attempts failed and Meari was elected. Most Jews gradually abandoned the party. Rather than unite with other Arab lists, Meari ran by himself in 1992 and failed to obtain a single seat.

A new force emerged among the Arabs, headed by Abdul Wahab Daroushe, a former Labor MK. Because of his opposition to Defense Minister Rabin's use of brutal methods to suppress the Arab uprising, or intifada, in the Occupied Territories in 1988, Daroushe resigned from the Labor party and independently gained one seat. Utilizing the old Mapai method of building a coalition of northern and southern Arabs, he ran again as the head of a new Arab Democratic party (ADP) and gained two seats in 1992. Rabin's government had to rely on the ADP to block Likud in Knesset voting. By the mid-1990s Daroushe had become instrumental in facilitating the reconciliation between Israel and the Palestinians by attempting to attract additional Arab nationalist votes. Many of these new voters demanded cultural and even political autonomy and supported traditional Islam and an independent Palestinian state.

The Radical Left

By the 1990s nearly all radical left Jewish groups had disappeared from Israel's political map. These groups had formed during the mid-1960s, and they lasted, with varying intensity, until the mid-1980s when many members joined the PLP. At their peak they consisted of Maoists, Guevarists, and other neo-Marxist factions—some splitting from Communist movements and others incorporating fashionable Western leftist ideas of the time. One small group, the Israeli Socialist Movement, or Matzpen (Compass), attracted more public attention than others. Because of its antigovernment demonstrations and early dialogue with radicals in the Palestinian nationalist movement, Matzpen was perceived as an "antisystem" group whose activities should be legally restricted.

One such group is worth noting because of its leader's untiring efforts to promote peace. Uri Avnery was the editor of the weekly magazine *Ha-Olam Ha-Zeh* (This World), which specialized in sensational political revelations, scandals, expert photography, gossip, and sex appeal. Because of its bold attacks, Mapai's leaders planned to close the magazine in 1965. Avnery then formed his New Force Knesset List, hoping that once he became an MK he would benefit from parliamentary immunity and thus be able to freely promote his program. He won one Knesset seat in 1965 and two in 1969. His platform, which included peace initiatives with the Arab states and welfare services for the needy, was rejected by voters in 1973. In 1977 he was third on the Shelli list but failed to enter the Knesset. In 1984 he helped to found the PLP but again was not high enough on the party list to enter the Knesset. By the mid-1990s he was leading a tiny group of his old guard called the Peace bloc (Gush Shalom). As with groups that belong to the radical right, the left's inability to bridge personal and minor ideological differences and its failure to unite under a single banner cost it the opportunity to affect the political system.

Following the 1967 and 1973 wars, many other small peace groups were formed, most with antigovernment platforms. They failed to pool resources, and their potential impact on politics was negligible.

The Center

Over the years, four Zionist parties could be considered center-right: the General Zionists (later the Liberals), the Progressive party (later the Independent Liberals), the Democratic Movement for Change, and Shinui.

The General Zionists

When the Orthodox religious and Labor Zionists had split into separate groups, members of the mainstream, who perceived themselves to be the core of the movement, created the General Zionist party following the direction of Theodore Herzl and Zionism's founders. During Herzl's time there were no distinctive Zionist political parties. Chaim Weizmann, Herzl's post–World War I heir as the movement's world leader, saw General Zionism as the bridge between right and left.

General Zionism became a counterforce to the Labor and religious groups, rallying those who opposed particular ideologies. During the 1920s and 1930s, when Jewish workers in Europe and the United States were becoming more class-conscious, middle-class Zionists rallied to General Zionism, which increasingly represented middle-class and private entrepreneurial interests in Palestine as a counterforce to Labor. Owners of small shops in Tel Aviv and Haifa, citrus growers, and operators of the country's new industries and businesses tended to identify with the General Zionists. In Palestine these workers were a minority and were unable to compete with Labor's strong institutional base in the Histadrut. Abroad, where Jewish life in Western Europe and the United States was dominated by upper-middle-class leadership, General Zionism was stronger.

The strain of ideological diversity produced right and left wings within the General Zionist movement. By the 1930s the movement was divided between those who insisted General Zionism should be nonideological and those who believed the movement needed a social program to attract the Jewish working class. At a 1935 world conference of General Zionists in Kraków, Poland, a major division occurred between liberals, who formed General Zionist group A, or the World Confederation of General Zionists, and conservatives, group B, who formed the World Union. The liberals in group A were more aware of organized labor's problems and urged the General Zionist Workers' organization to join the Histadrut. In contrast, the conservative group opposed trade unions. Moshe Sneh's unsuccessful efforts in 1948 to merge the two groups may have pushed him toward forming Mapam.

Chaim Weizmann, the longtime president of the World Zionist Organization between World War I and II and the movement's most prominent international personality, identified with the liberals. Most of the support for General Zionism at the time came from American Jewish leaders such as U.S. Supreme Court Justices Louis D. Brandeis, Benjamin Cardozo, and Felix Frankfurter and Rabbis Stephen Wise and Abba Hillel Silver. Ideological disputes within the Yishuv between right and left or capital and labor were of less interest to the Americans than was the larger Jewish national interest. Furthermore, most U.S. Jews were Social Democrats, non-Marxists who distrusted Labor Zionism's class consciousness. In the United States, General Zionism was identified with the Zionist Organization of America and Hadassah, the Women's Zionist movement, which directed its efforts toward assisting the development of "good works" in the Yishuv.

In the first Knesset election there were seven factions of General Zionism: Progressives, General Zionists, the Women's International Zionist Organization, Yemenites, Sephardim, pro-Jerusalem, and the Yitzhak Gruenbaum

List (an independent General Zionist faction). The first five collectively won eighteen seats, the General Zionists leading with seven. During the 1951 election the smaller groups disappeared or merged with the General Zionists; it became the second-largest party, with twenty-three seats. The Progressives kept their separate identity and fell from five seats to four in the Second Knesset.

The General Zionists were gradually replaced as Israel's major opposition party by the more nationalist Herut, an offshoot of the Revisionist Zionist movement led by Menachem Begin. As the Labor party broadened its appeal and constituency, absorbing many professionals, artisans, and other middle-class voters, the General Zionists lost support. Unlike Mapai's Ben-Gurion or Herut's Begin, the General Zionists had no outstanding political figures. Like the Liberal party in England, the group seemed too middle of the road, too moderate, and too "general."

Recognition that their respective constituencies were rapidly declining led the Progressives and General Zionists to remerge into the Liberal party in 1961. The party's leaders hoped the combined strength and a new label would create sufficient appeal to let them compete with Herut, which was now the largest opposition party. The new Liberal party won about the same number of votes as Herut in 1961, which encouraged leaders of the two groups to consider amalgamation. Among the serious questions to be resolved were who would lead the combined Knesset list and how to reconcile differences between liberals at one end of the spectrum and militant nationalists and conservatives at the other end.

The dilemma was lessened when leaders of the Liberals who had formerly been members of the Progressive party decided to leave and retain their separate identity. During 1965, the larger component of the Liberals joined with Herut to form the Gahal bloc. Gahal was overshadowed by Begin's leadership, although Herut and the Liberals had almost equal strength.

Following the Herut-Liberal agreement, Gahal's policies were divided, with Herut responsible for national security issues and the Liberals for the economy. Gradually, Herut became the larger component. Although they kept their ranks open to new members, the Liberals decided to conduct their affairs as a closed shop. Virtually no one was admitted to the party's decisionmaking bodies, and political spoils were divided among a small group. Thus, whereas Gahal and, later, Likud grew from election to election, the Liberals remained a very small faction. This situation was worthwhile for Begin; he and Herut were legitimized in the eyes of moderate voters, which allowed him to move to the political center.

Liberal ministers served in the 1967 and 1969 grand coalitions but left the government in 1970. During the 1974 election Gahal added two new components, the State List and the Free Center. This new bloc, called Likud (Unity), gained thirty-nine seats in the 1973 election and for the first time became a real threat to Labor's domination. Ultimate success came when Likud won the 1977 election.

The Liberals became the second-most-important group in the government, controlling finance and less important ministries. It gradually became apparent that the Liberals were a party that had no followers. Herut members thus demanded revision of the 1965 Gahal agreement. Following Begin's resignation in 1983, the proportion of Liberals within the Likud decreased relative to that of Herut. Personal conflicts among Liberal leaders further weakened the party's bargaining position within Likud.

In the early 1990s intraparty conflict reached new highs. Consequently, a group of Liberals headed by Itzhak Modai, a successful finance minister in the 1984 Unity Government and the person most responsible for halting Israel's runaway inflation, threatened to leave Likud and join the Labor coalition. To attract Modai's group back to the fold, Prime Minister Shamir nominated Modai to his old position as finance minister. Modai believed there were many potential Liberal voters in the Israeli electorate and ran with the "new Liberals" in 1992 but received insufficient votes to secure even one Knesset seat.

The Progressive Party

German Jewish professionals and other middle-class immigrants who came to Palestine after 1933 formed still another middle-of-the-road liberal party, Aliya Hadasha (New Immigration). The party was moderate in domestic and foreign affairs, advocating policies similar to Weizmann's. Its philosophy was similar to that of the World Confederation of General Zionists: It was non-Marxist, prolabor, and in favor of compromise with Great Britain and the Arabs in attaining Zionist goals. When the disputes occurred between militant nationalists and moderates, Aliya Hadasha became the Progressive party and represented the liberal wing of General Zionism in the new State of Israel after 1948.

The Progressives kept their separate identity from 1949 until 1981, except during the 1961 election when they merged with the General Zionists to form the Liberal party. By 1977, however, much of their appeal had shifted to the DMC, and they were able to obtain only one Knesset seat. The decision to break out of the alignment with the General Zionists in 1965 resulted from refusal to compromise with Herut over issues such as women's rights, separation of state and religion, and a compromise peace settlement with the Arab states. The group became the Independent Liberal party and was the minority in the 1969 and 1974 government coalitions, advocating middle-of-the-road positions in both domestic and foreign policy. The party's foreign policy followed the line of the Labor doves. In domestic affairs, the group advocated nonstatist social welfare programs and policies to improve working-class conditions. In 1981 the party disappeared from the political scene.

Democratic Movement for Change

A few months before the 1977 Knesset election a new political party, the Democratic Movement for Change (DMC), was established by former General Yigal Yadin. The DMC evaded traditional Israeli political classifications. It was neither left nor right, Labor or anti-Labor, nationalist or anti-nationalist. Its leaders and membership came from a wide spectrum of nonreligious Zionist parties ranging from Labor to Herut. One issue distinguished DMC from other parties—its insistence on electoral reform as the key to revitalizing Israel's political system. The common theme that united this coalition of hawks and doves, conservatives and liberals, and zealous and moderate nationalists was their demand for change in the political environment. The members focused their campaign on the Labor party's mismanagement of the country, protesting against corruption, nepotism, and cronyism under the previous Labor-led coalitions.

Yigal Yadin, the second IDF chief of staff, had refrained from political activity for nearly a quarter of a century, during which time he acquired international fame as an archaeologist and a professor. He also became known as a member of the Agranat Commission that investigated Israel's setback in the 1973 war. Yadin was joined by law professor Amnon Rubinstein, a liberal with dovish views who was leader of the Shinui movement, established after the 1973 war to protest government ineptitude and a series of military mishaps. Other leaders included a former general who had previously headed one of the large industrial complexes of the Histadrut, a former adviser to Labor prime ministers on Arab affairs, a former general who had directed the Israeli Land Authority, and Shmuel Tamir of the Free Center movement that broke away from Menachem Begin's Herut party in 1967. This coalition of people with diverse and often contradictory political and social perspectives was disenchanted with the old guard in Israeli politics.

The DMC's primary emphasis on electoral reform resulted in fewer votes than anticipated. This issue was not rated a top national priority in public opinion polls prior to the election. However, DMC leaders believed the power of the governing establishment could be broken if the existing system of at-large candidates was replaced by dividing the country into separate electoral districts. The proposed reforms, they believed, would facilitate the formation of a stable two- or three-party system in which it would no longer be necessary to assemble coalitions of diverse, even conflicting programs, which led to compromises that thwarted effective government.

There were few major differences between DMC and the large, nonreligious Zionist parties on other issues. DMC's stance on a peace settlement and on the Occupied Territories resembled that of the Labor party—it advocated the return of some territory in exchange for a conclusive peace settlement. Because of the diverse background of its leaders, DMC had no clear-cut domestic platform, although it was sharply critical of the Histadrut and other Labor-run agencies.

In the 1977 election, DMC won less than 12 percent of the votes and only fifteen Knesset seats, too few to bring about the changes it advocated. Its major impact was to diminish the strength of the Labor alignment in the Knesset and to force Labor into the opposition. Most DMC support came from middle-class professionals, who shifted their allegiance from Labor; DMC received little support from the working class, Sephardi Jews, or Arabs.

After the election, DMC was invited to join Menachem Begin's coalition government. The leaders debated for several months; many believed cooptation into the government would vitiate their principles. In the end, DMC joined Begin's coalition with permission to vote independently on certain issues such as religion and Israel's continued presence in the Occupied Territories. Yigal Yadin became deputy prime minister, and three other DMC leaders accepted cabinet posts under Begin.

The Likud government made no commitment to DMC's principal goal of electoral reform. The major dilemma facing DMC after the election was whether it would fragment into diverse factions once the mood of protest had passed. DMC had thrown the traditional party system askew because of public disenchantment with Labor, but its own future was also very much in doubt. Perhaps by making possible Likud's accession to power with only one-third of the vote, DMC had accomplished something significant. The party system was now in a state of transition, because no single party had received more than a third of the votes.

In the shadow of Begin, Yadin turned out to be a weak and uninspiring leader. The party divided into several small factions; some remained in the coalition, and others joined the opposition. Prior to the 1981 election, Yadin dissolved his party. Only one component, Shinui, remained active and participated in the election.

Shinui (Change)

Shinui was the first new political group to form with the organization necessary to mobilize resources and formulate a platform advocating major reform after the 1973 election. It was also the first faction to leave the DMC after 1977 and join the opposition. Headed by Amnon Rubinstein, Shinui was the only Liberal-centrist party of consequence from 1981 to 1988. It won two Knesset seats in 1981 and three in 1984, and Rubinstein became minister of communications in the Unity Government.

Although it supported free enterprise, privatization, and electoral reforms, Shinui announced that it considered itself part of the Labor-left camp. Shinui's identification with a dovish position regarding the Arab-Israeli conflict led many to mistake it for a left-wing party. To add to this confusion, prior to the 1992 election Shinui's party leadership decided to form the Meretz bloc with Ratz and Mapam, two left-wing parties identified most strongly with peace issues. Shinui is the junior partner in this bloc, although its leader became the minister of education and culture. As a result of Shinui's position, the formal ideological center on the Israeli political map had virtually disappeared by the mid-1990s.

The Nationalist Camp

In the mid-1990s the nationalist right-wing camp consisted of three parties—Likud, Tzomet, and Moledet—essentially Zionist secular parties allied with the religious bloc in direct opposition to the Labor-left bloc. The largest nationalist party is Likud, whose roots are in Herut and the Revisionist Zionist movement. The two other parties are derived from activist factions in the Labor movement.

Herut (Freedom)

Herut was established in 1948, although its doctrinal roots were in the Zionist Revisionist movement founded by Vladimir Zeev Jabotinsky during the 1920s. Jabotinsky, like his follower Menachem Begin, was a militant nationalist and a firm believer in Jewish activism. Weizmann's policies during the mandate seemed to Jabotinsky to constitute appeasement of Great Britain. He believed the Zionist mainstream had not reacted strongly enough to the "anti-Jewish" attitudes and policies of the colonial office. Zionism, Jabotinsky's followers asserted, was a political movement rather than a society through which to colonize Palestine. "Buy acres, build houses, but never forget policy!" they admonished.

In 1922, when Great Britain unilaterally decided that the Jewish national home concept in Palestine was applicable only west of the Jordan River, Jabotinsky and his followers vehemently protested. A fundamental Revisionist tenet had always held that the 1922 separation of Transjordan from Palestine was illegal and that both banks of the Jordan River were integral parts of the Jewish national home.

The Revisionist movement opposed all partition schemes and insisted on the immediate establishment of all of Palestine as a Jewish state, in contrast to other Zionist parties that were willing to accept compromise solutions. The movement objected to mandatory regulations based on economic grounds, which limited Jewish immigration to Palestine because the British government thought the country lacked the resources to support a large immigration. Revisionists consistently opposed the social policies of the Labor bloc, advocating larger middle-class colonization and more private investment to encourage national development. Their ideological hostility toward Marxism had once been expressed in proposals to outlaw class struggle and to insist on compulsory arbitration of labor disputes. During the mandate, the Revisionists formed their own separate labor federation, but they lacked an extensive network of social and welfare services and economic enterprises and were unable to compete in any real sense with the much larger Histadrut.

Jabotinsky formed the World Union of Zionist Revisionists in 1925. Its organizations—intended to compete with the labor movement—included movements for students, Jewish war veterans, Orthodox Jews, athletes, laborers, and women. An independent political action called the World Petition movement was started in 1934; it appealed to all governments to allow free Jewish immigration to Palestine. The Revisionists were suspended from the World Zionist Organization and responded by forming the New Zionist Organization, with Jabotinsky as president. In defiance of mainstream Zionist compliance with British restrictions, Revisionists organized illegal immigration to Palestine and brought 30,000 Jews to the country between 1935 and 1942. (After the 1939 White Paper, the official Zionist organization also organized illegal immigration.)

The best-known component of the Revisionist network was the Etzel, or Irgun Zvai Leumi (IZL) (National Military Organization), formed in 1937 to challenge the official Zionist policy of *havlaga* (restraint) in reaction to Arab guerrilla activity expressed by Haganah's policy of limited retaliatory attacks. The IZL organized "preventive strikes" against Arab attacks on the Yishuv. By "taking the action to the Arabs," the IZL believed it could intimidate and prevent them from supporting guerrilla fighters.

During World War II, the IZL announced that it would suspend military activity in Palestine and concentrate on fighting the Germans. Jabotinsky and a small delegation of IZL he sent to the United States, known as the Bergsonites (after their young leader Peter Bergson [Hillel Kook]), began to organize a Hebrew army that would give the Jewish people belligerent rights alongside other "exiled" Allied groups. After Jabotinsky's death in 1940, the United States became the main center of the Revisionist movement. The Bergsonites continued their efforts to rally public opinion and U.S. congressional support, hoping to pressure the U.S. administration into action that would save European Jewry. Following World War II, many U.S. Zionist leaders demanded immediate recognition of the Jewish people as a member of the United Nations and replacement of the mandate with a Jewish state. The conflict between Jews and Arabs in Palestine, many argued, could be resolved with population transfers: "Palestine for the Jews, Iraq for the Arabs!"

World events and the traumatic experience of European Jewry brought the Revisionists back to the official Zionist movement at the Twenty-Second World Zionist Congress in 1946. Mainstream and Revisionist Zionists joined forces to support illegal immigration, a Jewish army, the anti-Nazi war effort, and the Biltmore Program, which called for a Jewish commonwealth.

After the war, Revisionists again opposed mainstream Zionism. In Palestine the IZL renewed its fight against both Great Britain and Arab guerrilla forces. When the Jewish Agency for Palestine and Haganah devised a program of peaceful resistance to British immigration restrictions, the IZL resumed its military activities. Retaliating against arrests, trials, and death sentences imposed by British authorities on Jewish guerrillas, the IZL blew up British military installations and executed British soldiers captured in retaliatory raids. When civil war broke out between the Palestinians and the Yishuv during 1947, the IZL conducted actions against the Arab community.

The IZL was transformed into the Herut political party by Menachem Begin when Ben-Gurion, in forming the IDF, outlawed all other military groups. A small Revisionist party received so few votes in the first Israeli election in 1948 that it disbanded and gave its support to the newly formed Herut party. At the international level, the Revisionists remained intact, with affiliates represented in various national associations and in the World Zionist movement. It was understood that Herut would represent the movement in Israel.

After 1948, Herut deemphasized, but did not abandon, claims to Jordan. When the West Bank and Gaza were captured in 1967, the party urged their incorporation into Israel, with civil rights for the indigenous Arab population. Arabs who so desired would be given Israeli citizenship; others would be permitted to remain as nonvoting residents. Herut leaders maintained a "flexible" position on the future of the Syrian Golan Heights and the Egyptian Sinai, offering "meaningful" concessions in these territories to obtain a full peace settlement with the Arab states.

In domestic affairs, Herut and other nonsocialist groups advocated a national health service and insurance system to replace the Histadrut-controlled *Kupat Holim* (Sick Fund). Herut adamantly insisted that the complex of Histadrut organizations and economic enterprises be separated from trade union control. The fusion of unions with management and their ownership of a substantial part of the economy, Herut leaders believed, fostered corruption, inefficiency, and an expanding bureaucracy. Herut favored compulsory arbitration of labor disputes, especially in essential industries and services, to avoid the annual strikes that had become customary in Israel. In contrast to their counterparts in many Western countries, Israeli conservatives have urged nationalization of major industries and public services as the only way of wresting them from the Histadrut.

Special circumstances have forced the Labor opponents into positions not usually associated with conservatism. In many respects, the ideology of the non-Labor bloc has resembled classical European liberalism. For example, Herut supported legislation to terminate the military government in Arab-populated areas of Israel in 1966 and has advocated laws to protect civil liberties.

The formation of the Gahal bloc in 1965 greatly helped to legitimize Herut. This fusion of General Zionism, the Liberals, and Herut moderated some of the vehement Herut rhetoric and made the new bloc more acceptable in a Labor-dominated cabinet. When the coalition cabinet of national unity was formed during 1967, Begin became minister without portfolio and temporarily abandoned his characterization of the political struggle as one between socialists and patriots.

Headed by Begin, the Herut List for the 1949 election consisted of IZL headquarters members and the four U.S. Bergsonites, among others. Herut obtained fourteen seats and a safe place in the opposition until 1967. In the next four elections, Herut was unable to expand its Knesset representation much beyond its original size; in 1951 it obtained eight seats, in 1955 it won fifteen, and in the next two Knessets it stabilized with seventeen seats. The formation of Gahal helped to make Herut the principal opposition party, but with only twenty-six seats in 1965 and again in 1969, its route to power seemed long, if not inaccessible. Begin's charismatic leadership, however, attracted many voters, especially among North African immigrants who were frustrated by Mapai's policies. By opening its ranks and organization to less affluent residents of poor neighborhoods and development towns, Herut made serious inroads into local politics. By the late 1960s, Herut had begun to benefit from its political investments at the local and national levels and was soon receiving most of the ethnic protest vote.

As in Mapai, intraparty conflicts based on intergenerational tension did not escape Herut. Challenges to Begin's leadership were raised as early as the First Knesset. During the 1960s a group of young party members headed by Shmuel Tamir, an independent-minded lawyer, was expelled from Herut for questioning Begin's absolute leadership. Tamir formed a new party, the Free Center, with a more radical position toward the Arab-Israeli conflict than that of Gahal. In 1969 the Free Center gained two Knesset seats. Tamir was able to sustain his political following through 1977, when he joined the DMC and became minister of justice under his traditional political rival, Begin.

The State List (Mamlachti List)

The State List was an important political party, less because of its leadership or size than because of its significance as the first group from the labor movement that transferred its alliance to the nationalist camp. Formed in 1969 under Ben-Gurion's leadership, the State List became an integral component of Likud in 1974 and thus helped to legitimize Herut as a possible ruling party.

When Rafi was integrated into the Labor party, Ben-Gurion, by his own choice, remained outside. He then agreed to head a new party, the State List. Its program was fairly simple: It included loyalty to the old man and continuation of the Rafi platform. The party, which was more nationalist than socialist, obtained four Knesset seats, but Ben-Gurion soon resigned from the Knesset and retreated to his kibbutz, Sde Boker, in the Negev. Unable to develop any broad electoral appeal, the leaders of the party decided to join Likud; as members they obtained a rightful place on the Likud Knesset List. Their leader, Yigal Horovich (Moshe Dayan's cousin), served as finance minister for a short time in 1980; Rafi's spiritual hero, Dayan, had become Begin's foreign minister. In the 1981 election, the remnants of Rafi pooled forces as the Telem party under Dayan's leadership and obtained two Knesset seats. Following Dayan's death in 1981, Telem again became part of Likud.

The Likud (Unity)

The person most responsible for Likud's formation was former general Ariel Sharon, a Yom Kippur War hero. A product of the labor movement, Sharon was briefly a leading member of the Liberals, where he began to consolidate various nationalist forces. As a result of his efforts, Likud was formed from the union of Gahal—the dominant bloc—and the Free Center, the State List, and the Land of Israel movement, with Begin as leader of the new bloc.

The bond that held Likud together was its opposition to the return of territory seized in the 1967 war. The movement was headed by a group of ideologically diverse personalities, including former members of Mapam, Mapai, Achdut Ha-Avoda, and the non-Labor parties. Differences over other issues and growing disagreement on foreign policy weakened unity, and by 1977 Likud was still a very loose alliance.

These disagreements caused Sharon to run independently as leader of his Shlom-Zion party. The two seats he gained were transferred to Likud immediately after the election, making it the largest party with forty-five Knesset seats.

The person who masterminded Likud's 1977 victory was Ezer Weizman, the nephew of Israel's first president, a former commander of the air force, and for a short time a Gahal minister of transportation in the 1969 wall-to-wall coalition. After the 1977 victory Weizman became Begin's minister of defense and, together with his brother-in-law, Moshe Dayan, was instrumental in convincing Begin to sign the Camp David Peace Accord with

Egypt's President Anwar Sadat. Like Dayan, Weizman resigned his post prior to the 1981 election. He competed again in 1984 with a new party, Yahad (Together), and obtained three seats. Weizman "gave" Yahad's three seats to Labor, helping it to form a blocking coalition that forced Likud to create a unity government. In return, Weizman's Yahad MKs received a "safe place" on the 1988 Labor Knesset List. In 1992 Benjamin Ben Eliezer, second on the Yahad List, headed the important Ministry of Housing, and in 1993 Weizman was elected president of Israel.

Begin, the former "terrorist" who ruled Likud and the government in an autocratic manner (his followers called him "the commander"), equaled his arch rival Ben-Gurion in popularity. He signed Israel's first peace treaty with Egypt, Israel's most powerful enemy. He also ordered the 1981 bombing of Osirak, site of Iraq's nuclear reactor where preparations were believed to be underway to develop an atomic weapon. His following increased as a result of development programs in poorer neighborhoods undertaken through Project Renewal. The overall performance of the economy under Likud, however, was below par. The programs initiated by the Liberals resulted in runaway inflation that reached over 400 percent. Nonetheless, Likud, led by Begin, retained power in 1981, and Sharon became minister of defense. He convinced Begin to initiate a war in Lebanon in 1982, the outcome of which was one of the factors that caused Begin to resign, transferring power to Yitzhak Shamir in 1983.

Under Shamir, Likud Knesset representation decreased from forty-eight seats in 1981 to forty-one in 1984, but the party was still powerful enough to form a government with Labor. In 1988, with forty seats, it edged out Labor by one seat. After the coalition crisis in 1990, when Labor quit the government, Shamir prevailed as leader of a right-religious coalition that permitted Likud to follow an aggressive settlement policy in the West Bank in direct defiance of U.S. interests. Nonetheless, by the end of 1991 the Likud government had received U.S. approval for its restraint during the Gulf War in the face of Israel's bombardment by Iraqi missiles. Thousands of new immigrants poured in from the former Soviet Union and were assisted by the government, a comprehensive peace process with surrounding Arab states had begun by the end of 1991, and the economy performed well under the Liberal Modai's leadership.

On the eve of the 1992 election, a bitter intrafactional conflict erupted that destroyed the delicate equilibrium among the several Likud factions. The Shamir- and Sharon-led factions joined forces to obtain a majority among the party leaders and defeated members of a third faction led by David Levy, Israel's foreign minister. Levy's followers, mostly Sephardi Jews of North African origin, constituted about one-third of the party center, but their share of power was considerably less. Their defeat, which involved explicit accusations of discrimination against the Sephardim, caused many

Likud activists—including Levy—to remain passive during the campaign. This situation permitted the Rabin campaigners to enter areas from which they had been virtually excluded since 1977. Consequently, Likud lost eight seats in the 1992 election.

Immediately after the election, one of the Likud's junior leaders, Benjamin (Bibi) Netanyahu, challenged the old guard and called for open voting for the post of party leader. The method adopted was similar to that used earlier by Labor; that is, it consisted of primaries in which all party members participated. Netanyahu was elected decisively against the challenge by Levy and became Likud's candidate for prime minister in the 1996 election (see Chapter 9). Under his leadership, Likud rebuilt the party and in 1993 gained important victories in municipal elections, including the mayoralty of Tel Aviv and Jerusalem.

Tehiya (Revival)

Tehiya is a splinter party of Herut, formed in opposition to the Camp David peace agreement with Egypt and Begin's decision to remove Jewish settlements from the Sinai Peninsula. Several Likud members, including Yitzhak Shamir, opposed Begin, and two MKs left the party and joined the opposition prior to the 1981 election. They organized Tehiya with internationally renowned scientist Yuval Ne'eman at the head. Tehiya won three seats in the 1981 election and in 1982 was invited to take part in Begin's coalition government. In the 1984 election Rafael Eitan, IDF chief of staff during the 1982 war in Lebanon, joined Tehiya. The party obtained five Knesset seats but no place in the National Unity government.

Tehiya consisted of several groups including a militant faction of Herut, many secular and religious West Bank settlers, and a few activists of the Labor movement who were led by Eitan. During the 1988 election, Eitan and his followers left Tehiya to form Tzomet. In that election Tehiya obtained three Knesset seats and Tzomet won two. Shamir kept Tehiya and Tzomet outside the 1988 coalition, but when Labor left the government in 1990 he invited them in. In the 1992 election the militant nationalist vote was divided several ways, and Tehiya obtained too few votes for a Knesset seat. After the election its leaders decided to disband the party.

Tzomet (Crossroad)

Tzomet, founded by Rafael Eitan, first ran independently in 1988, gaining two Knesset seats. Eitan, a farmer and a product of the Labor movement, developed a political strategy that stressed security and "clean government." While serving as minister of agriculture (1990–1992), he emphasized electoral reform and the urgent need for water as a security imperative. His ideology was conveyed to the public in short, bold sentences that attracted many younger voters and soldiers.

In 1992 Eitan constructed an election list of several unknown candidates and astonished most observers by winning eight Knesset seats. His dictatorial leadership caused a split in 1994, when three Tzomet MKs left the party and formed Yi'ud. In 1996 Eitan's Tzomet party joined the Likud list.

Moledet (Motherland)

By the mid-1990s Moledet, with its three MKs, was the most strongly nationalist party in the Knesset. It was formed shortly before the 1988 election when the Supreme Court denied Rabbi Meir Kahana's Kach List the right to compete in the election because of its racist program. Led by Rehavim Ze'evi, a retired IDF general and a product of the Labor movement, Moledet (much like Kahana) called for the "transfer" of Arabs from the West Bank and the Gaza Strip to other Arab countries. Ze'evi was careful to talk in terms of voluntary transfer and to legitimize his message with references to the founding fathers of the Labor movement, including Ben-Gurion. His ideology was therefore considered to fall within the legal parameters of the Israeli polity. Shamir's 1990 call to Ze'evi to help form a government coalition legitimized Ze'evi's platform, and in 1992, with expanded appeal, Moledet gained an additional Knesset seat.

The Radical Right

During the 1950s several small extremist groups—many descendants of the IZL and Lehi—were outlawed for antisystem activities. Among the most militant of the outlawed groups was Kach, founded by Meir Kahana. Kahana was an American rabbi who founded the Jewish Defense League (JDL) in the United States in 1968; he began to run for the Knesset in the early 1980s and won a seat in 1984. His platform was simple and attracted many young Israelis: Eretz Israel belongs to the Jews, and all Arabs must leave. Kahana also argued that a contradiction exists between the concept of a Jewish nation and democracy and that the former takes precedence over the latter. His teachings were translated into action when he and his followers entered Arab villages and demonstrated, beat residents, and disturbed the public order.

By the end of his first and only term, polls showed that Kahana's political appeal had expanded greatly—especially among first-time voters, the unemployed, and residents of poor neighborhoods. Parties in the nationalist camp, Likud and Tehiya, felt threatened by Kahana's projected ten Knesset seats. An appeal to the Supreme Court resulted in a verdict that Kach had promoted an illegal racist ideology and therefore could not compete in the 1988 election, whereupon many followers shifted their support to Moledet.

Meir Kahana was assassinated in New York in the early 1990s, but hatred of Arabs, Israelis, or Palestinians has continued to propel several small groups, including the Kahana Chai (Kahana Lives) led by Kahana's son. Jewish supremacy, dedication to the land, a racially "pure" country cleansed of non-Jews, and the right to settle in every corner of Eretz Israel remain central ingredients in the ideological framework of the radical right.

The Religious Parties

The religious parties nearly always compete among themselves. Generally, they do not try to appeal to secular voters, even though secular parties—most notably Mapai and Likud—attempt to attract moderate and nationalist religious voters. Until the early 1980s, the most important religious party was the National Religious party (NRP), or Mafdal. The smaller Agudat Israel was second in importance and served as a coalition partner less often than Mafdal. Mafdal began to lose its political influence during the 1980s, whereas the ultra-Orthodox Agudat Israel gradually expanded. During the 1990s these two parties and a third, Shas, formed in 1984, were basically equal in size.

The National Religious Party (Mafdal)

Religious Zionism began as a separate faction in 1902 when a group of rabbis opposed plans to found a secular school system for Jews. They remained in the Zionist movement as a faction called Mizrachi, the Hebrew acronym for "spiritual center" (Mercaz Ruchani); Mizrachi also means Oriental.

In 1922 younger members of Mizrachi who were close to the working class formed Hapoel Hamizrachi (the Mizrachi Workers), which was intended to win the support of Orthodox laborers in Palestine and to foster the development of religious kibbutzim. Mizrachi and the Mizrachi Workers joined in most Israeli elections to form the National Religious party (NRP); in the first 1949 election Mafdal joined with Agudat Israel and Poalei Agudat Israel to form the United Religious Front, which won sixteen Knesset seats.

On issues other than religion, Mafdal's program has been general enough to allow it to collaborate with Labor in most cabinet coalitions since 1948 and with Likud between 1977 and 1992 and in 1996. In 1992 Mafdal was an opposition party member of the nationalist camp.

Mafdal strongly emphasizes the fostering of Jewish education, forbids any violation of the Sabbath, demands strict enforcement of Orthodox dietary laws in public life, and insists on the preservation of legislation that gives the Orthodox rabbinate control over Jewish marriage, divorce, inheritance, adoption, and other family matters. The Orthodox bloc adamantly opposes secular marriage in Israel and insists that in all matters that pertain to Jewish law, the country's Rabbinical Council should have the final say. Both Mizrachi and Hapoel Hamizrachi have important affiliates abroad in the world Zionist movement to assist them in fund-raising and in developing a network of religious schools (*yeshivot*) and other institutions.

The religious nationalists believe separation of state and religion distorts the essence of Judaism. Proponents believe that only through the Torah has Israel become a national entity and that only the Torah can preserve Jewish identity and traditional culture. Like Ben-Gurion, Mafdal maintains that the Jewish people have an ethical mission that cannot be fulfilled except in Israel. Therefore, the Orthodox parties have strongly emphasized education, insisting on maintaining their own school system. One of the first cabinet crises was caused by disagreement between the religious parties and the rest of the government over the education of new immigrants. Mapai leaders wanted to establish a secular system; the religious parties demanded control over the education of immigrants from religious families. The religious parties maintain their influence over society through the Rabbinical Council and the Chief Rabbinate despite constituting a minority in the Knesset.

Religious Zionists abroad perceive the religious parties as a bulwark against secular trends in Israel, as a link with traditional Judaism that preserves the Jewish character of the state. After 1967, when disputes arose in the cabinet over the establishment of Jewish settlements on the occupied West Bank, Mafdal leaned toward affiliation with Likud. Ultimately, fear of liberal secular trends in Likud brought about the decision to maintain a separate identity. Although they have generally been in accord with the Labor party on socioeconomic and foreign policies, the religious parties have found Labor's ambivalence about the future of the West Bank difficult to accept, which has caused serious strains in the coalition. Mafdal, with strong support from the Chief Rabbinate, opposed surrender of the West Bank, which it regards as an integral part of historical Eretz Israel.

Until 1981, Mafdal held ten to twelve Knesset seats, which made it an attractive coalition candidate for two reasons. First, Mafdal concentrated on issues that were not directly related to security or economics and thus permitted the ruling party to act freely in these areas; second, the mere addition of a party its size could help to secure a minimum winning coalition. Hence, Mafdal was courted as a coalition partner by both Likud and Labor. In the 1981 election, however, its strength was cut in half with the creation of Tami (Movement for Israel's Tradition)—an Orthodox Sephardi ethnic list—and the loss of Orthodox votes to Likud and Tehiya.

Tami was founded just before the 1981 election by Aaron Abuhatzeira, one of Mafdal's young leaders. Abuhatzeira, a member of a highly respected Moroccan Jewish family, argued that as a leader of thousands of North Africans, his people deserved a larger share of power and should be included among the first ten names on the Mafdal Knesset List. When the Ashkenazi leadership refused his demands, Abuhatzeira quit Mafdal and formed Tami. He won three Knesset seats and became a cabinet minister in 1981. In the 1984 election Tami lost two of its three seats and later joined Likud. Much of Tami's support went to the newly established Shas party.

Prime Minister Begin strongly backed religious issues and interests; hence, a typical Mafdal voter could support Likud against Labor without fear of damaging his or her interests. The most radical religious nationalists—the members of Gush Emunim—decided to vote for Tehiya, however, because of its strong support for Jewish settlement in the Occupied Territories.

Members of Gush Emunim (Bloc of the Faithful), the West Bank settler movement, were mainly graduates of the Mafdal youth movement (Bnei Akiva) and of the Mercaz Ha-Rav (the Rabbinical Center founded by Rabbi Kook in Jerusalem), the political spearhead of the movement. The group was motivated less by security than by the "holiness" of the Promised Land. According to Gush Emunim, Eretz Israel was promised to the Jews by God; therefore, it is their exclusive patrimony.

In 1984 Mafdal continued to shrink, losing two seats to Tehiya and one to a militant religious faction, Morasha. Since that time several Mafdal factions have returned, and the size of the party has stabilized at between five and six seats. The party's influence over the Ministry of Education and the Chief Rabbinate has considerably diminished. Another Orthodox party, Shas, has become the influential factor in determining relations between state and religion.

Agudat Israel Parties

The Agudat Israel movement was formed in Frankfurt, Germany, in 1912 as an organization of Orthodox Jews with a constitution based on the Torah. The organization's purpose was to further the common ideals and social tasks of the Jewish community. Every member had to unconditionally accept the supreme authority of the Torah and affirm that Jewish law rather than the Jewish nation was the heart of the Jewish people.

The movement was formed when nationalism appeared to be a threat to most Orthodox Jews. Throughout the mandatory period, members of Agudat Israel refused to formally identify with the Yishuv and were considered anti-Zionist. Israel's role, they believed, was to act as "the territorial tool of providence for the realization of Divine planning for Israel and for the whole of mankind." Their strong belief that all Jewish problems could be solved by the Torah made them indifferent, if not hostile, to other Jewish movements, including Zionism.

After the establishment of Israel in 1948, Agudat Israel recognized the country as the Jewish homeland and joined the first coalition cabinet. Like other political groups, the Agudaists have youth groups, women's groups, and overseas affiliates. The Labor wing of the movement, Poalei Agudat Israel, was formed during the mandate as a vehicle for obtaining land for settlement from the Jewish National Fund. Agudat Israel and Poalei Agudat Israel have combined forces during several elections to form the Torah Religious Front. Although the Agudaists have their own separate rabbinical organization, the Council of Sages, they maintain contact with the mainstream of the Yishuv through Mafdal, with which they frequently vote on matters of Jewish law.

The Council of Sages consists of very senior rabbis, some in their nineties, who represent several Jewish Orthodox trends including Hasidim and Mitnagdim (opponents). The MKs that represent the Aguda party are chosen by the sages according to their strength within the Orthodox public in Jerusalem—Bnei Brak—and other Orthodox communities. Towering among the sages is Rabbi Eliezer Shach, the leader of the Mitnagdim and of Lithuanian origin. Shach labored for years to develop an extensive educational system for children and young adults. In 1984 Shach left the Council of Sages to help form Shas, ordering his followers to support the new party and to oppose Agudat Israel. Shas obtained four Knesset seats, and Aguda fell to two. Two Shas seats came from Ashkenazi votes and two from Sephardi Jews, many of them former Tami supporters.

The official leader of Shas is Rabbi Yosef Ovadia, former Sepharadi chief rabbi of Israel. Ovadia established his own "Council of Wise in Torah," which Shach controlled. In 1988 Shach dominated two parties: Shas for Sephardi Jews and Degel Ha-Torah (the Torah Flag) for the Ashkenazi. Shas obtained six seats, and Degel Ha-Torah won two.

Agudat Israel also fared well in 1988, winning five seats. Agudat's gain reflected the hostility between Shach and his greatest enemy, Rabbi Menachem Shneerson of New York—better known as the "Lubavicher Rebbe," the spiritual leader of the Habad movement, who was believed by his followers to be the Messiah. Shneerson was envious of Shach's success and ordered his well-organized Habad followers in Israel to vote for Agudat Israel. Their votes resulted in three seats. After the 1992 election, Shas broke away from Shach and joined Rabin's government coalition.

Realignment of the Party System

The party map described in this chapter is by no mean complete. Several small parties were mentioned only briefly, others not at all. This description demonstrates the dynamism of the Israel polity, which shapes and reshapes itself and yet exhibits stability. Many political organizations that competed against each other during the Yishuv period were still at odds several decades later, often under different names and leadership and with modified ideologies but nonetheless the same parties with different labels.

By the end of the 1990s, certainly at the beginning of the twenty-first century, the Israeli polity will likely undergo significant realignments. An extensive analysis of these factors is provided in Chapter 9, but five factors are relevant to party politics.

1. With prospects for peace, the security dimension may no longer dominate. Social and economic problems will replace issues of personal and group safety and territory-related nationalist issues. The old political structures and ideological platforms may lose importance.

2. Public interest groups that represent civil society may become effective political forces. These groups represent women, new Russian immigrants, Arabs, and others—all of whom have been grossly underrepresented. Labor's loss of its Histadrut stronghold in 1994 is indicative of a trend in which organized labor and other groups will pursue their interests in a more decentralized manner, through direct political lobbying and otherwise.

3. The consequences of the new electoral reforms adopted in the 1990s and discussed in Chapter 4 are still unclear. The primary system adopted by Labor and Likud has already brought new forces to the Knesset, local governments, and the Histadrut. A direct election of the prime minster, scheduled for 1996, will facilitate voting in Knesset elections according to sincere preferences (see Chapter 8). The system may continue to fragment into many small parties or, alternately, may form even larger political blocs. Four such potential blocs are the religious, Arab, liberal, and conservative blocs.

4. In the 1990s Israel experienced an electronic media explosion. Several Hebrew and Arabic radio and television channels began to operate at the national, regional, and local levels; there was only one state-controlled television channel in the 1980s. Politically minded individuals can now gain access to wider exposure. This situation will call for more articulate, dynamic, and "media attractive" politicians. More professional help and financial resources will also be required to convey public messages.

5. Beginning in the mid-1970s and with increased intensity during the 1980s, the Israeli polity underwent a rapid process of both deliberate and unintended liberalization. Evidence can be found in Supreme Court rulings, in the decision to privatize the public sector at the national and local levels, in the electoral reforms that emphasize direct accountability to citizens, and in the retreat from the comprehensive "welfare state" Israel had attempted to become. With emphasis now on the individual, issues of party loyalty—considerably weakened since the mid-1980s—will become secondary. Consequently, parties will no longer be able to rely on past performance and will have to cater to the changing needs of their supporters.

4

The Electoral System

The average Israeli participates in the formal process of government through elections. Although citizens may have little or no voice in actual decisionmaking, they have a wider range of choices in selecting representatives than is the case in most Western democracies. The large number of parties and the system of at-large elections by a countrywide constituency are features inherited from the Zionist movement. Through proportional representation (PR), the Israeli voter has access to a wide and diverse spectrum of political views from which to choose.

Since the first election to the Constituent Assembly, or First Knesset, in 1949, Israeli politicians have become dissatisfied with the existing electoral system. Electoral reform has been high on the agenda of some renowned politicians, including Ben-Gurion. Concern with reform was widespread during the mid-1980s because of the negotiating excesses in forming and maintaining the government coalition during the Twelfth Knesset. Consequently, Labor and, later, Likud adopted a U.S.-style primary system to select their candidates for prime minister and for the Knesset. Beginning in 1996, the prime minister was to be elected in a direct popular election.

Israeli Proportional Representation Schemes

The Israeli political system is an extreme example of representative democracy with its frequent problems of governability, such as the formation of coalitions from parties with opposing programs. Citizens elect a new Knesset at least once every four years. As a single voting district with 120 representatives, Israel is one of the largest such districts among Western democracies. Citizens do not vote for individual candidates but for party lists, which represent each party's list of nominated candidates. Except for the names at the very top of each list, most candidates are unknown to the average voter.

Originally, every party that obtained at least one percent of the ballots (since 1992 at least one and a half percent) was awarded a Knesset seat. The seats were assigned according to the proportion of votes each party obtained.

There have been up to fifteen parties in the Knesset (in 1951 and 1981) and no fewer than ten (in 1973 and 1992). No party has ever obtained a majority of popular votes; therefore, governments rely on coalitions.

Israel's political system is a descendant of the prestate system used by the World Zionist Organization. Politicians favored by the old system, which was based on proportional representation and made possible representation by diverse minority groups, continued to employ that system after the state became independent. From its inception at the end of the nineteenth century until the end of World War II, the members of the Zionist group constituted a minority among the various Jewish groups in the diaspora. To obtain political credibility, Zionist leaders needed to create the impression that they represented all Jewish people. The generous PR scheme they adopted was almost all-inclusive because it permitted the representation of many groups and individuals from places of all sizes where Jews resided. Although the Zionist movement created the image that it represented and spoke for the majority of world Jewry, actual Zionist interests were managed by a small number of the organization's executives. The broad representation made possible through the electoral system was not indicative of each group's political leverage.

When the sovereign State of Israel was established, this inclusive system continued by default. In fact, the main goal of the 1949 election was to form a Constituent Assembly that would ratify a constitution and design the electoral system of the new state. Once elected, however, the representatives transformed the assembly into a parliament (the Knesset). It became very difficult for the parties in power to acquire the Knesset majority needed to change the electoral system because politicians had been selected by a method they had a vested interest in preserving; a change would entail a risk to their existing or prospective political gains. Consequently, proposals for serious reform of the electoral system, even when initiated by Ben-Gurion, were rejected.

Ben-Gurion, who stood behind the decision to transform the Constituent Assembly into the Knesset, soon became a proponent of an electoral change that would have enabled him to rule without a coalition based on other parties' support. The model he had in mind was the British two-party system. However, Ben-Gurion did not get enough political support, even within his own party, to institute this plan. The closest he came was in 1952, when, with the General Zionists, he planned to set a 10 percent threshold that would have excluded almost all of the other parties from the Knesset.

Threats by the small Progressive party to deny Labor future political support and the inability to predict electoral results after such a proposed change were presumably the reasons Ben-Gurion abandoned his plan.

The demand to reform the laws that guided electoral competition continued, and many small changes in the election process were introduced over the years. Some, such as the Party Law, were mentioned in Chapter 3. Others, such as party financing laws and laws that regulate political campaigns, are discussed later.

In 1969 all Zionist factions of the Labor movement (Mapai, Achdut Ha-Avoda, Rafi, and Mapam), led by Golda Meir, competed in the election as the unified Labor Alignment (which consisted of the Labor party and Mapam). The alignment obtained fifty-six seats, but even combined with its four Arab-affiliated MKs it was short of an absolute majority by a single seat, tempting it to change the electoral method so a future majority could be secured. Gahal, then the second-largest party and, until 1970, a coalition partner, was more than willing to help. The formula adopted in 1973 was called the Ofer-Bader Law after its two architects: one from Labor and the other from Gahal. The Ofer-Bader method of dividing surplus votes is customarily used in Western democracies. In this system, extra Knesset seats (i.e., seats resulting from surplus votes or votes a party obtains that are insufficient for an additional Knesset seat) are distributed to the party lists with the highest average votes. Any two party lists can agree before the election to combine their surplus votes, whereby the numbers of seats the two parties receive are calculated together. Only then are the seats allocated to each party to the agreement determined.

If the Ofer-Bader Law had been utilized in 1969, three small parties—the Free Center, Ha-Olam Hazeh, and the State List—would have been direct victims. The first two would have lost half of their power, and the third would have lost a quarter of its power. The two large parties, Gahal and Labor, would have gained one and two seats, respectively, at the expense of these three small parties. No other party would have been damaged by the new scheme. It is little wonder, then, that the three small parties led the opposition to the Ofer-Bader Law in 1973. Had the law been employed in 1969, Gahal would have gained one seat more than the actual number it obtained. These projected extra votes constituted a strong incentive to reform the electoral system.

The Labor Alignment would have gained two extra seats, which together with the automatic support of its Arab-affiliated lists would have given Labor the absolute majority of sixty-one Knesset seats. The alignment could thus have ruled alone without political partners. Although Meir continued in a wide coalition with Gahal and other smaller partners, with an even larger party base political considerations regarding the size of the coalition and the composition of partners may have been different.

The Ofer-Badar Law was in use in 1977 when three extra Knesset seats were awarded to Likud and two to Labor. The DMC also obtained two more seats. With a Likud base of forty-five seats (including the two of Shlom-Zion), Prime Minister Begin constructed a coalition of sixty-one MKs that included Mafdal and Agudat Israel. Moshe Dayan later joined, increasing Begin's coalition base to sixty-two members. Under these conditions the DMC was left with no bargaining power.

If the 1977 electoral outcome had been determined by the old largest re-mainder formula, the political picture might have been rather different: Labor would have had thirty seats, Likud forty, Shlom-Zion two, Agudat Israel four, Pagi two, Mafdal twelve, Hadash six, Independent Liberals two, Ratz two, DMC fourteen, Peace and Development (Arabs) three, and Flatto-Sharon and another Arab list one seat each. According to this count, both Labor and Likud would have lost two seats each in comparison to the extra seats they gained with the Ofer-Badar procedure, and the DMC would have lost only one seat. Consequently, the ruling coalition would have had to be constructed differently.

The Party List Nomination Process

Israelis do not vote for individuals or even for a party; they select a letter or combination of letters that represents a party. Aleph, Mem, and Taph (AMT) are the letters that signify Labor (they also mean "truth" in Hebrew); Beth, Gimmel, and Dalet (BGD) usually belong to the religious parties; Vav belongs to the Communists, and so on. A veteran party has the legal right to use its "own" letters in subsequent elections. A new party must choose from a pool of vacant letters with one exception: the fifth letter of the Hebrew alphabet, although not legally disqualified, is not used because it stands for God's name. Representatives of the religious parties on the board of the Central Election Committee, which supervises all issues related to elections, would not permit such blasphemy.

Some trivial competition occurs over the selection of letters, but the politics that surround the placement of a candidate on a party list are not at all trivial. As described in Chapter 3, Ratz was created in 1973 because Golda Meir placed Shulamit Aloni in a position on Labor's List that did not guarantee a Knesset seat. The creation of Tami in 1981 was also the result of competition for "safe" positions on the Mafdal List.

Once approved by the Central Election Committee, changes and replacements of candidates on a list are not permitted unless a listed candidate cannot fulfill his or her obligation to the Knesset. An MK who dies or resigns or who cannot serve because of a pre-election commitment makes room for the next person on the list. Two notable replacements occurred in 1992 when Moshe Arens, the Likud minister of defense (1990–1992), resigned from the Knesset to take an executive position in business, leaving his top position to a younger MK who had been thirty-third on the list. Similarly, the Council of Sages of the Ya'hadut Hatorah (United Torah Judaism) party ordered Rabbi Itzhak Peretz, who had served as the interior minister from Shas, to vacate his seat in favor of an Ashkenazi member of Degel Ha-Torah. A party list may consist of up to 120 names (the law does not require that many) and can be divided into four parts.

The first part of the list is the safe zone. For example, if a party obtained ten seats in the previous Knesset and is expected, based on surveys and analysis, to regain a similar number of seats in the next election, the first ten positions on its list are considered safe. The higher a candidate is on the list, the safer his or her prospects for election.

The second part is the uncertain zone. It may begin, using the first example, with position eight and end at position thirteen. Three additional seats may be obtained by chance or by the effect of the voting scheme.

The third zone includes candidates who have no chance to enter the Knesset. A person in position fifty on the list of a party whose size has fluctuated between eight and twelve seats could not anticipate being elected, although some surprises do occur. In 1992 Tzomet increased the number of its MKs from two to eight.

The fourth zone is symbolic; it honors former presidents of Israel, elderly party leaders, or statesmen and women associated with a party who do not seek to become MKs. Number 120 is sometimes the most respected position on a list, but it carries no political power.

Shortly before an election, each party constructs its list, hoping it will appeal to a targeted population. Small parties usually follow their ideological tendencies. It is unlikely, for example, that a party composed of ultrareligious voters would nominate a secular candidate or that a Jewish nationalist party would be headed by an Arab. The situation is more complicated for the large parties, since they must appeal to a wider constituency that has a variety of often contradictory interests. Likud attempts to attract the very poor, the very rich, ultranationalists, various ethnic groups, the young, and the old. Labor targets these same groups in addition to its more traditional base of support in the agricultural and Arab sectors. The two big parties thus play the numbers game, and ideological consistency is secondary.

Each of the large parties attempts to build a winning proto-coalition prior to the election, simultaneously presenting positions acceptable to its various support groups even though their interests may conflict. To cover these differences, party positions may be presented in an ambivalent manner and in very general and abstract terms. For example, in 1992 Rabin promised that he was going to change "the national order of priorities" without specifying what order he was talking about and the order to which he would like to change. Such broad objectives necessitate the inclusion of candidates who represent national issues alongside those who represent narrow and local interests. The distinction is not always clear; local or special interests may be manipulated into salient national issues, and local or sectorial leaders may maneuver themselves into positions of national prominence.

Likud and Labor thus engage in creative efforts to project images of both liberal and populist representation. The populist message is: "Our group of candidates is exactly like you and will take care of your specific needs." The liberal message is: "Our people are better than any available alternative for securing Israel's national interest." The Likud has been more effective in transmitting the former message. In the late 1960s, for example, Herut opened its leadership ranks to social groups including young people, native Israelis, those of Asian or North African ethnicity, and those with lower levels of education and income. When Likud took over the government in 1977 and initiated Project Renewal as a form of payoff to its low-income supporters, it made David Levy (a Moroccan Jew) minister of housing and Moshe Katzav (who was born in Iran) minister of welfare in an attempt to convincingly convey the populist message.

During the 1970s and 1980s, none of Labor's senior Sephardi leaders (Yitzhak Navon, who was the president of Israel and the minister of education; Shlomo Hillel, minister of police and chair of the Knesset; Shoshanah Almozlino, minister of health; Israel Keisar, general-secretary of the Histadrut and, after 1992, minister of transportation; and Benjamin Ben Eliezer, minister of housing after 1992) came from Israel's largest ethnic group, the North Africans. Until 1992, Labor's Sephardi leaders remained a product of the quasi-representation practiced by Mapai during the 1950s. The primary system adopted by Labor in 1992 (discussed later) helped to change this image.

The following sections describe the technical aspects, including the primary system, of the procedures used by various Israeli parties to nominate candidates for their lists.

Herut

Until 1977, Menachem Begin and a small group of loyalists formed Herut's list according to a single criterion: who could expand the party's electoral appeal. People who challenged Begin's leadership were not included. In 1977 Herut adopted the method of "sevens" by which members of the party convention selected candidates in groups of sevens. This method was used in 1992 when the Likud bloc became the Likud party, thus expanding the 2,100-member party convention to over 3,000 members. Before 1992 the Likud bloc was formed by several separate organizations, each selecting its candidates using its own nomination method. Names were then placed on the bloc's list of Knesset candidates according to a predetermined key.

For example, a Liberal candidate would be placed second on the Knesset list because of the 1965 Gahal agreement, which established the terms of co-operation between the Herut and the Liberal parties that formed Gahal (the Gush Herut Liberals).

The 1992 decision to integrate all political segments of the bloc into one party necessitated the expansion of the party convention. Leaders of the Liberals, Tami, and Ometz (the last remnant of the State List) and Efraim Gur (a Labor MK who crossed party lines in 1990) were asked to submit to Herut a list of names weighted according to their relative political strength within the bloc. Thus, convention members of the new party were required to compete for positions on the list as Herut members had done until 1992.

In the first stage of the method of sevens, members elect the party leader to head Likud's list of candidates. Menachem Begin and, after 1984, Yitzhak Shamir have won the top slot unopposed, although different "objective" conditions affected the victories of the two leaders. Begin, the founder of Herut, ran unopposed because no one dared to challenge him. Shamir was unopposed because, together with Moshe Arens, he controlled the largest faction—more than half of the members—within Herut's party convention. The Ariel Sharon and David Levy factions shared the remainder of the support. In 1992 Sharon joined the Shamir-Arens faction and drove out many of the Levy loyalists, most of whom were of North African origin. Consequently, Levy's followers felt they had been discriminated against by the Ashkenazi members and remained passive during the electoral campaign. The Labor campaign headed by Rabin benefited greatly from their inaction.

After the list leader has been chosen, each member of the party convention votes for twenty-one contestants. The thirty-five candidates who receive the most votes then proceed to the final stage, which is divided into three rounds and takes place a few days later. In each round every convention member chooses and ranks seven names. Based on his or her relative strength in the screening stage and on the deals made with other candidates and factions, each contestant announces the place on the list and the group of sevens in which he or she intends to compete. A candidate may overestimate or underestimate his or her relative strength at the party convention and thus may lose a better position on the list or be dropped completely.

The method of sevens was perceived as one of the most innovative democratic steps undertaken by the Herut leadership, especially compared to Labor's continued selection of its candidates by the party arrangement committee, a small group of leaders who decided who would be included on the list and where—the same procedure used by Herut prior to 1977. Herut's final list of candidates has not always been attractive. For example, in 1988, although the final list reflected the relative strength of Likud's three factions, it did not include women, Druze, or representatives of traditional special interest groups. In 1992, however, the list was somewhat more compatible with the party's electoral interests; it included two women and one Druze placed high on the list. Levy's faction, estimated at about 35 percent of the party convention members, was virtually wiped out. Likud adopted a modified version of the Labor primary system for the 1996 election.

Labor

For many years, the Labor party followed the pattern designed by Mapai: A small oligarchic nominating committee selected Knesset candidates. The committee ensured that all groups in the party coalition were represented on the list and that individuals chosen complied with the leaders' preferences. Labor's dramatic defeat in 1977 led to some modification of the process. Safe places on the list were now allotted to representatives of geographic districts, and a 60 percent approval rate at the party convention was required for members who had already served two Knesset terms.

Continuing failures in the 1981 and 1984 elections convinced party leaders—particularly the new secretary-general, Uzi Baram—that substantial reform was needed to change Labor's image as an old, stagnating party. In 1988, under the banner of democratization, Labor adopted a modified version of Herut's nominating procedure, which Labor called the method of "tens." In the first stage, the 1,269 party convention members voted for the party leader, and Shimon Peres was elected unanimously. Peres then chose Rabin, the leader of the largest opposition faction within the party, and Yitzhak Navon, Israel's former president, to join him at the top of the Labor list. The next three places were reserved for Knesset speaker Shlomo Hillel, party Secretary-General Baram, and Histradut chief Keisar. A place was also reserved for Ezer Weizman, leader of the Yahad party, which had gained three Knesset seats in 1984 and later joined Labor. Two of Weizman's followers were given spots, and two places were reserved for Arabs— one Muslim and one Druze. Thus, even before the selection process began, more than a quarter of the forty-two safe seats were committed.

In the second stage, the convention decided on thirty-three candidates. Eleven districts chose one each, and the three largest districts—Tel Aviv, Jerusalem, and Haifa—selected two candidates each. The agricultural sector, including the kibbutz movement, chose six candidates. Ten candidates were chosen by women, youth, residents of poor urban neighborhoods, and Arabs. In comparison to Likud, which kept no place for special interest groups except as required by interparty agreement within the bloc, Labor reflected the "objective" strength of its various sections and their symbolic value.

In the third stage, all convention and district candidates were pooled into a group of fifty to compete for about thirty safe spots. The four rounds of competition were conducted in groups of ten, similar to the process used by Herut. Unlike Herut, however, in 1988 the Labor procedure resulted in a balanced outcome, with new faces, youth, Sephardim, women, and Arabs—all of the necessary elements to help capture the government from Likud. Labor adopted the primary system in the 1992 election.

Other Parties

When the method of sevens had been adopted by Herut and had scored some success between 1977 and 1988, other small parties changed their procedures. In 1988 and 1992, changes in the Labor party's nominating method also influenced other small parties including Mafdal, Mapam, Ratz, Shinui, Tzomet, and Tehiya, which adopted a system that resembled Herut's. A single leader or a small arrangement committee continued to choose candidates in the ultrareligious parties, Moledet, and the Arab parties.

Party Financing

In a democracy, citizens are generally asked to pay for elections, party systems, and representative bodies through direct voluntary contributions, taxation, or, as is the case in Israel, both. The legislation that provides for financing the activities of Israeli parties during and between elections is the Party Financing Law of 1973.

The origins of the Party Financing Law can be traced to Knesset debates that began in 1956. The Knesset was asked to formulate legislation that would protect the interests of workers against employers who withheld wages, and in 1958 the Guaranteed Income Law was passed. This law permitted employers to deduct from workers' salaries "agreed upon" membership fees that were to be paid to the workers' union. This provision was extended in 1965 to cover nonunion workers as well; thus, all organizations that protected workers' interests were covered by the law, including political parties.

Three years later, the original intent of the law was altered to explicitly permit deductions for political parties. Public criticism of the law by workers and academics led to new legislation in the form of the 1973 Party Financing Law, which determined who is eligible for financing, how much can be legally spent during elections, how to keep books for the comptroller to review, and so on. The most important element in the law is paragraph one, which legally defines the receiver of the monies as a "faction," separates election financing from funds needed for routine party operations, and determines the so-called financial unit. Under the law, a faction obtains funds from the state according to the number of its financial units as determined by its Knesset seats. Whenever Israeli parties are under economic stress as a result of electoral campaign overspending or mismanagement of daily activities, they press to change the law so they will receive more money; hence, the Party Financing Law is constantly being amended. In 1994 each MK was entitled to about $30,000 per month during the official election period for political activities.

Table 4.1 provides information about the amount of money spent by Israeli parties during the 1984 campaign within the framework of the 1973 Party Financing Law. The 1984 election was very costly: The funds reported in the table were spent in less than three months and often in less than a month.

Table 4.1 reflects some interesting features of electoral politics in Israel in general and of party financing and the dynamics of the 1984 campaign in particular. First, although some parties did not spend all of the money legally available, others were restricted and thus overspent, in violation of the law.

Second, because the financial unit is computed on the basis of the number of seats a party obtained in the previous Knesset, an aggressive party—hoping to expand its base—will tend to overspend. Tami is a prime example. In

TABLE 4.1 Expenditures of Israeli Parties During the 1984 Electoral Campaign (thousands US$)

Party	Number of Seats	Legal Limit	Reported Expenditures	Amount Overspent	Expenditure on Media
Labor	44	7,217.2	7,388.8	171.6	1,601.0
Likud	41	6,775.2	6,904.8	—	1,734.2
Yahad	3	330.0	4,792.0	4,462.0	55.0
Mafdal	4	883.0	1,848.0	965.0	507.7
Shinui	3	442.0	390.0	—	363.9
Ometz	1	330.0	330.0	—	186.6
Tami	1	442.0	1,529.2	1,087.2	175.9
Agudat Israel	2	589.2	226.0	—	164.8
Tehiya	5	736.4	450.8	—	160.7
Hadash	4	589.2	336.4	—	106.1
Ratz	3	442.0	228.8	—	78.4
Shas	4	442.0	214.8	—	78.2
Morasha	2	330.0	355.2	—	78.2
Progressive List for Peace	2	330.0	163.2	—	53.2
Kach	1	330.0	330.0	—	32.8
Total	120	20,208.2	25,488.0	—	5,376.7

Source: Gideon Doron in Daniel Elazar and Shmuel Sandler, eds., *Israel's Odd Couple* (Detroit: Wayne State University Press, 1990), pp. 146–147.

1981 it had three Knesset members, and its leaders were certain the party would do as well or better in the 1984 election. They could not, however, anticipate the competition from Shas. Yahad is another illustration. Its leaders believed their center-oriented party would repeat the success of the DMC. However, they obtained only three seats and amassed a huge budget deficit; thus, they were forced to join with Labor and eventually to completely integrate with it. Labor, in return, covered Yahad's deficit.

Third, party expenditures on mass media were relatively small compared to overall spending because of legal limitations that allowed each party 10 minutes of free prime air time and an extra 6 minutes for each seat it had in the previous Knesset. For example, Labor, which had fifty members prior to the 1984 election, received 310 free minutes; Shinui, with only two seats, received 22 minutes. The costs included preparation of messages, artists' performance fees, and press advertisements.

Fourth, not all of the figures in Table 4.1 accurately reflect reality. Rabbi Meir Kahana of Kach, for example, refused to submit a report to the state comptroller listing his party expenditures. Short of denying further transfers of funds to a delinquent party, little can be done legally.

Perhaps the "purest" party in terms of its public appeals for clean government was Shinui, headed by law professor Amnon Rubinstein. Shinui could have legally spent $442,000 during the 1984 election. Five items from the Shinui 1984 campaign budget are shown in Table 4.2.

These figures cover only the three months during the campaign. They do not include costs for radio advertisements, workers' salaries, office expenses, payments to advertisers and pollsters, costs of billboards, letters to voters, and the like. Election day expenses are also not included; these involve taxis to bring voters to the polls and workers' food and time. Such expenses can amount to between 25 and 33 percent of campaign expenses.

Often, expenditures of major parties are so vast and uncontrolled that unless the parties do very well in an election they run the risk of bankruptcy.

TABLE 4.2 Shinui Expenditures During the 1984 Campaign (selected items)

Type of Expenditure	Amount Spent (US$)
Television time	66,000
Newspaper advertising	180,000
Office space	13,000
Lecture halls	10,000
Booklet	25,000
Total	294,000

Source: Compiled by Doron from discussions with Shinui.

In the 1992 election Likud, which had based its budget on forty MKs, over-spent by several million dollars. Since the party obtained only thirty-two Knesset seats, it lost state funding for eight MKs and was unable to pay contractors it had employed during the campaign. Among the principal reasons Benjamin Netanyahu was elected party leader was the hope that he would raise funds from abroad. His primary mission during 1993 was to restore Likud's financial base.

Electoral Advantages of Large Parties

One reason for the remarkable political stability of the Israeli polity is a direct function of the extensive and elaborate system of "barriers" established by Zionist parties, especially the large parties, to undermine both veteran and new small parties. Without being labeled as such, three effective barriers to entry have been mentioned in this chapter: the threshold (1.5 percent) percentage, the Party Financing Law, and the law that regulates advertising in the electronic media. Many barriers appear as "laws" that require approval by a coalition formed with at least one of the two major parties.

In 1992 the vote threshold was raised from one to one and a half percent. Labor won the election, but the right-religious camp received more votes than the Labor-left camp. Most of the almost 75,000 right-wing votes were wasted because the parties those votes could have represented obtained less than the 1.5 percent threshold. The new threshold was low enough to encourage these small parties to compete, but it was high enough to create an incentive among politicians who were adverse to risk to overcome their personal and ideological differences and constitute technical blocs. Thus, for example, Shinui and Mapam joined Ratz to form Meretz, and the ultra-Orthodox groups tabled their differences to form the Ya'adut Hatorah party. Had the threshold of one percent not been raised to one and a half percent, Tehiya would have obtained a place in the Knesset. With its 31,957 votes, the party passed the old one percent threshold but not the new one and a half percent mark. With Tehiya in the Knesset, Labor could not have formed a coalition to block the right-wing parties.

The Party Financing Law works on a simple principle: The bigger the party, the more money it gets from the state. It costs much less for a large party to obtain an extra seat in the Knesset than it does for small and new parties. The information presented in Table 4.3 shows the differences in campaign expenditures by "average" large (i.e., Labor and Likud) and small and new (i.e., Yahad, Ometz, Shas, Morasha, PLP, and Kach) parties.

Table 4.3 shows that new parties paid 22 percent more than small veteran parties for each seat obtained in the Knesset and about 250 percent more than was paid on average by the two large parties for each of their

TABLE 4.3   Average Expenditure for a Knesset Seat by Type of Group, 1984

Type of Group	Number of Parties	Number of Seats	Average Cost of One Seat (US$)
Large parties	2	85	168,168
Small parties	7	22	349,846
New parties	6	13	428,372

Source: Compiled by Doron from interviews.

seats. Moreover, new parties, even if they were led by prominent personalities, could not enter the Knesset without resources to invest in their electoral campaign.

According to election law, political advertising is restricted to the last month before an election. New parties receive ten minutes of free television time and twenty-five minutes of free radio time, whereas veteran parties receive the same amount of time plus six minutes for each of their MKs. This obviously favors the large and the veteran parties on several counts.

First, the prohibition on advertising political messages prior to thirty days before the elections does not permit new parties to introduce themselves effectively to the public. The veteran parties, especially those whose members are cabinet ministers, have no such exposure problem; the policies they enact constitute an effective advertisement for their causes.

Second, the greater amount of time allocated to the large parties permits them to repeat their messages again and again; hence, their "product" is easily identified. The large parties can transmit complicated messages on several issues; the small and the new parties, which have little time, must either repeat one theme or present their program in a comprehensive manner. If their single message reaches a target population effectively, then one of the large parties is likely to adopt it for its own campaign. If the message is too comprehensive, it may not be transmitted effectively.

Third, although transmission is paid for by the state, the costs associated with the production of messages are especially high during campaign time, when most advertising companies are involved in the campaigns. Large parties finance these costs with funds obtained from the state; new parties must borrow money or use personal resources.

Fourth, because access to electronic media is limited, new parties must use alternative routes to transmit their messages and introduce their leaders. The printed media is one such route; in 1977, for example, the DMC spent about a quarter of the total expenditures of all of the other parties combined on private printed media because its access to television was limited. Finally, limited air time does not permit the small parties to alter messages after they evaluate their effectiveness.

These and other barriers give the large parties a legal and structural advantage at the expense of the small and new parties. On three occasions citizens have appealed to the Supreme Court, arguing that these laws violate the principle of equality grounded in paragraph 59 of the Basic Law: Knesset, which states: "The Knesset will be elected by general, national, direct, equal, secret and proportional elections." The Supreme Court has denied these appeals, stating that the legitimacy of laws is based not on the principle of equality among competing parties but on the absolute majority in the Knesset.

Electoral Reforms in Israel

In their book *A Strategy of Decision,* David Braybrook and Charles Lindblom distinguish between small and large political changes. A small change occurs within a political structure, whereas a large one changes the structure itself. A change in interest rates is small; a transformation from a barter to a money economy is large. From this perspective the electoral reforms reviewed thus far concerning vote counting and the threshold establishing a minimum percentage of votes required to obtain a Knesset seat are small. The nominating procedures and primary systems adopted by both Labor and Likud and proposals to change the electoral method for the Knesset can also be considered small changes. However, the proposed reform to elect the prime minister by popular vote is a major structural change, similar to the transition in France from the Fourth Republic to the Fifth. Such a reform is often referred to in Israel as a "regime change" or as a "prime minister regime."

Although proposals for electoral reforms have been made since the early days of the state, they became salient during the mid-1980s and intensified in 1988 and 1990. Among the explanations for this sudden desire for electoral reform, most stress the ineffectiveness of the government decision-making process, the long period of bargaining required to form coalitions, the unresponsiveness of politicians to public demands, the substandard behavior of politicians, and so on. The impetus of these desires for change is related largely to the coalition situation in Israel during the second half of the 1980s.

In 1984 the Likud and the Labor-led camps were about equal in size; instead of calling for a new election to break the tie, the leaders of the two parties decided to form a grand coalition. They repeated this decision in 1988, but the second grand coalition dissipated in 1990. It was almost inevitable that these coalitions would encounter severe problems in governing. Such a wide-based coalition requires a greater degree of compromise from its members on basic ideological positions and material payoffs than is the case in a smaller coalition. The distance between the ideal positions of the coalition partners was too great, and because of its size members were bound to receive fewer rewards for participation. Moreover, the public was uncomfortable with the coalition because the leaders of Labor and Likud continually undermined each other's policy initiatives. As a result, the government was locked in a stalemate, and the public began to demand more effective administration.

The two "villains" responsible for the government's failure were the electoral system, which permitted the selection of small parties—especially religious parties—as coalition partners, and the legal requirement that the government had to obtain Knesset support for its policy initiatives. The lack of political accountability and responsiveness to citizens' desires, the high degree of politicization of public administration, government involvement in various aspects of social and economic life, intolerable interference in people's personal lives by government-supported institutions, and the inability to bring peace to the country or to ensure security for the citizens were all identified as by-products of a deficient political system. Consequently, grassroots action was taken to reform the system, and three types of reform were proposed.

Proposals to Reform the Electoral Method for the Knesset

Among the many individuals who called publicly for reform, two were dominant: Gad Ya'acobi and Uriel Reichman. Ya'acobi, a prominent Labor MK until 1992 and at times a government minister, began lobbying for electoral change in 1975. Reichman, former dean of the law school at Tel Aviv University and the head of the "Constitution for Israel" group, began working on his own reform design in 1985. Ya'acobi proposed the establishment of local district lists in addition to the prevailing national party lists. The Reichman initiative was more ambitious; it offered a modified version of the German two-layer electoral scheme, a method once used in Denmark.

Assisted by Israeli volunteers and with funds raised in the United States, Reichman joined forces with Ya'acobi; together they recruited enough support to pass both proposals through the first Knesset reading of the law (three readings are necessary to transform a bill into a law) at the end of the 1988 term. During the bargaining that preceded the formation of the 1988 grand coalition, Labor and Likud agreed to form a committee, headed by Ya'acobi, to examine the two proposals; in 1990 the committee offered a design that combined elements of both proposals into a single system.

The proposed system divided the country into twenty voting districts, each of which would select three Knesset members for a total of sixty MKs, or half the Knesset membership. The other sixty members would be elected on a nationwide basis according to the existing PR system. Only parties able to win at least 3.3 percent of the total votes (or four Knesset seats) would qualify for representation in the Knesset. Thus, for example, if a party won three district seats and 5 percent of the total national vote, it would obtain six Knesset seats. The district representatives would replace members from the national list. This design favored the districts, but the proportion of representation in the Knesset would be determined by the success of parties at the national level. Because of the March 1990 coalition crisis, the Ya'acobi committee was dissolved, and its proposals were not approved by the Knesset as a whole.

Proposals to Constitute a Prime Minister Regime

The proposal for direct election of the prime minister became salient during the three months (March–June 1990) when both Labor and Likud were trying to form their own minimum winning coalitions. At that time, four MKs proposed identical schemes. Yoash Zidon, a member of the two-MK Tzomet delegation, offered one model. Tzomet had conditioned its participation in the Likud coalition upon the adaptation of a law for the direct popular election of the prime minister. When Prime Minister Shamir refused to honor the agreement, Tzomet left the coalition briefly, first in 1991 and again in 1992, which led to an early election.

Zidon's reform, the model that was accepted, called for separating the prime minister's office from a Knesset vote. Instead, voters would directly chose the prime minister, who would form his or her own government. The prime minister would thus be less dependent on coalition politics, and small parties could not undermine the government or demand additional spoils. The government could select professionals to implement its policies, although the prime minister would need a majority of Knesset votes to pass legislation.

The four proposals differed on several technical points, especially on the number of Knesset members necessary for a no-confidence vote. These votes set political limits on the prime minister's powers and can bring down the government when wide disagreement exists between parliament and the government.

Proposals for direct election of the prime minister were adopted in March 1992. They borrowed important elements from both the U.S. and the French systems, including two-stage majority rule and limitations on tenure. The number of ministries permitted was legally restricted to eighteen.

Fearing they would lose a direct contest with Rabin for prime minister, Shamir and his followers opposed the proposal. However, the reform issue had become a political weapon of Labor against Likud, and polls taken during the campaign showed wide support for the reform; therefore, Shamir was forced to accept the proposed bill. Implementation was delayed until the 1996 election; Shamir announced plans to retire after the 1992 election.

The Primary Scheme

The idea of conducting U.S.-style primaries to select Labor front-runners and candidates to the Knesset was introduced after the 1988 election when the party examined reasons for its recurring failure to secure electoral victory. The method of tens had not met expectations, so Rabin agreed to spearhead an opposition to Peres, who was blamed for Labor's inability to form a winning coalition. Led by Micha Harish—Labor's secretary-general—and some Rabin loyalists, a plan to conduct primary elections was proposed to the party convention. The scheme was intended to bypass Peres's domination of the convention by appealing to the larger body of party members; Harish and his group believed Rabin was more popular than Peres with most members and with the general electorate.

The primary scheme was structured in two stages. The first stage called for a runoff election to select the party front-runner, or list head. The first candidate to obtain 40 percent of the votes would be declared the winner. If more than one candidate passed this threshold, the one with a plurality would win. If no one obtained 40 percent of the votes, a second round of voting between the two candidates who had obtained the most votes in the first round would decide the winner. The second stage, to be held several days after completion of the first round, utilized a simple plurality scheme. The final ranking of the candidates on the Knesset List was predetermined. Thus, candidates could choose to compete on the national list or on a district list. Winning first- or second-place positions at the district level would place candidates in a predetermined place on the Knesset List, which was calculated according to the size of the district, the district's weight in the party power structure, and other political considerations.

The Labor primaries were held in February 1992. Four candidates competed in the first stage: Peres, Rabin, and two "spoilers"—Israel Keisar and Ora Namir, who later became minister of labor. Rabin barely edged out Peres and passed the 40 percent threshold; therefore, a second round was not required. In the second stage Peres came in first, capturing about 83 percent of the nearly 100,000 votes of party members who participated. Only two of his followers secured positions among the first ten on the Knesset List, and none except Peres later served as a minister in Rabin's government.

The primaries focused public and media attention on Labor's democratization process, which was in tune with the general demand for reform. Likud's failure to follow suit and the tension that erupted in March 1992 when the party convened to choose its Knesset List reinforced the positive image of Labor, especially of Rabin. This may explain why Shamir decided to end his opposition to the bill for direct election of the prime minister. However, Likud's support of the bill came too late. By March 1992, Rabin's political strategists were already laying the foundations for a campaign that presented their leader as though he were running directly against Shamir for prime minister. When election results were tabulated on June 23, it became evident that the strategy had been effective.

Netanyahu was the only major Likud politician who explicitly supported the direct election bill. He argued that since Likud was a pluralist, democratic party, he should not be punished for his minority views. He reminded everyone that Shamir had opposed Begin on the Camp David agreement with Egypt and not only was he not penalized but he became the party's leader when Begin resigned in 1983. Soon after the 1992 election, Netanyahu began to campaign for instituting primaries in Likud to select the party chair. In the Likud primaries in early 1993, Netanyahu faced three challengers led by David Levy. The almost 200,000 voters chose Netanyahu, and thus he became the head of Likud and leader of the opposition in the Knesset.

Later in 1993, primaries were used in municipal elections. Several competing candidates had to be elected by their party members and then to compete against candidates from other parties. Several local Labor leaders did not accept the primary outcome, and a so-called intervention committee, headed by Rabin and party Secretary-General Nissam Zevili, replaced the elected candidates with those of its choice. In Haifa the incumbent mayor, Arie Gurel, controlled the local Labor party branch and was sure to win his party primary but was likely to lose to his rival from Likud. Consequently, the intervention committee ordered an "open primary" between Gurel and Rabin's candidate, former general Amiram Mitzna. Mitzna, supported by Likud and Ratz voters, won the primary and later became mayor. In other places Labor supported Likud candidates who lost in their own party primary or opposed Labor party members who ran on an independent ticket.

If the prevailing process did not yield the desired outcome, politicians changed it. Voters did not seem to mind these massive violations of the rules. Perhaps the most notable example of such a violation occurred during the Histadrut election in May 1994. Prior to this election, the Labor party had conducted a primary race between acting Histadrut Secretary-General Haim Haberfeld and Amir Peretz, an MK strongly associated with Labor's minister of health, Haim Ramon. Haberfeld won by a two-to-one margin and prepared to compete for Histadrut secretary-general against the Likud challenger. But Ramon resigned his government post and competed against Haberfeld by forming a new party, Ram, made up of followers of Peretz, Meretz, and Shas. Ramon won the election and became the first non–Labor party Histadrut chief while continuing to serve in the Knesset as a Labor MK.

Voting and Elections

Before each election the Ministry of Interior informs all Israeli citizens of the date and location at which voting will take place. Parties often provide free transportation for voters who are elderly or who live far from their designated polling sites. Because politics are so important and the multiparty system offers so many options, few citizens abstain; the Israeli voting turnout rate is among the highest in the Western democracies.

Table 4.4 shows several features concerning elections and voter turnout in Israel. Although the law explicitly fixes a November date for Knesset elections, only three of thirteen elections have been held then. In reality, the time span between elections has been variable. The law requires that Knesset elections be held every four years, but that rarely occurs. The election to the Second Knesset occurred after thirty months and that to the Fifth Knesset after twenty-one months. Elections in 1977, 1984, and 1992 were held less than four years after the previous election because of coalition crises or other causes. MK's terms were more than four years in the Third, Fifth, Seventh, and Eleventh Knessets because of adjustments made between a shorter Knesset term and the date of election required by law. In the 1973 election the legal date could not be met because of the October War, and the election was postponed to the last day of that year.

The numbers in Table 4.4 are somewhat misleading. Few people who are present in the country on election day do not vote. The difference between

TABLE 4.4   Voter Turnout in Israeli Elections, 1949–1992

	Election Date	Number of Voters	% Voters of Those Eligible	% Valid Votes
First	January 21, 1949	440,095	86.5	85.3
Second	July 30, 1951	695,007	75.1	74.0
Third	July 26, 1955	876,085	82.8	80.2
Fourth	November 3, 1959	994,306	81.6	78.9
Fifth	August 15, 1961	1,037,030	86.6	78.7
Sixth	November 2, 1965	1,244,706	83.0	79.9
Seventh	October 28, 1969	1,427,981	81.7	77.5
Eighth	December 31, 1973	1,601,098	78.6	76.5
Ninth	May 17, 1977	1,771,726	79.2	77.9
Tenth	June 30, 1981	1,954,609	78.5	77.6
Eleventh	July 23, 1984	2,091,402	79.8	78.9
Twelfth	November 1, 1988	2,305,567	79.7	78.7
Thirteenth	June 23, 1992	2,637,943	77.4	76.6

Source: Statistical Abstract of Israel (Jerusalem: Government of Israel, Central Bureau of Statistics, 1992), p. 566.

the numbers of eligible and actual voters is accounted for by people who die between the time the Ministry of Interior determines eligibility and election day, those who have not obtained a formal notice from the ministry, and people who are outside the country on election day.

Since 1988 voting booths have been placed in prisons to allow inmates to vote in their place of "residence." In 1988 a prisoners' list ran for the Knesset but did not pass the one percent threshold.

There is no procedure for absentee voting in Israel except for members of the diplomatic corps and sailors serving on Israeli ships. Soldiers on active duty use their civilian address for registration, but they vote at their camps or in the field in mobile booths. Their ballots are usually counted a day or two after the civilian votes; most parties have to wait for the final count to know how much support they obtained from the military and how that support affects the distribution of Knesset seats.

The difference between votes cast and those that are valid also affects the outcome. Until 1977 about 2.5 percent of the votes cast were usually invalid; the largest invalid percentage (4.2 percent) was recorded in 1969. Since 1977 the average percentage of disqualified votes has decreased to less than one percent. Votes can be invalidated because of markings on the ballot paper, empty envelopes, or envelopes with more than one ballot. The law permits any citizen to protest election outcomes by calling attention to improprieties. Such protests can be made only after the election outcome is official and has been made public; by that time a new Knesset and a new government are already at work. Agudat Israel, for example, protested the outcome after the Fifth Knesset election because it claimed the voting booth in one religious neighborhood was closed much earlier than indicated by law, thus preventing its party supporters from casting their ballots. In another case, Aguda protested the disqualification of 148 votes submitted in unsealed and unsigned envelopes. Protests are presented to a Knesset committee, which assesses the charges and decides on remedial actions, and political considerations often affect the committee's decisions. These protests are usually ignored because they would not change the overall results.

If elections are planned earlier than designated by law, the season of the year becomes politically significant. The summer months are best for Likud, and winter months are better for Labor. Labor voters tend to be more affluent than those of Likud; thus, many of the former are away on vacations during the summer and are absent for the elections.

Table 4.4 does not indicate significant differences between the rates of various Jewish-sector votes or between Jewish and Arab rates of participation. The ultrareligious sector tends to vote in unified blocs. The turnout rate in the Jerusalem and Bnei Berak neighborhoods is usually higher than that of secular Jews. The turnout rate in the 1988 election, when the intensity of competition for religious votes was at its peak, was notable. Religious

Jews holding Israeli citizenship were flown from New York to vote, which affected turnout rates and the election outcome. Arabs too, especially many affiliated with Mapai, voted in unified blocs, although Arab voting became more independent and had lower turnout rates after 1977. The greatest gap between the Arab and Jewish rates was 10 percent in 1981.

Overall, voter participation in Israeli elections has been very high. Comparative voting studies show that in addition to attitudes voters hold toward candidates and parties, preferences are affected by a multiplicity of factors including status, class, religious affiliation, and ethnicity, among others. Likud and Labor are catch-all parties, whereas the small parties provide special services to their constituencies. It is easy to predict that the national cleavage between Jews and Arabs will cause many Arab voters to favor so-called left-oriented positions. Obviously, the religious-secular cleavage affects the preferences of the ultrareligious voters. It is more problematic to explain why Sephardi Jews, women, senior citizens, the rich, and similar groups prefer one party or one political position over another. Explanations by students of Israeli politics are often based on intelligent rationalization of statistical findings rather than on causal relationships between the observed variables.

The following analyses utilize political rather than sociological factors that influence voters' choices. They include the issues (either in a policy or an ideological sense) over which an election evolves, candidates' personalities as perceived by voters, and voters' loyalty to party.

Issues

Unlike other Western democracies, where economic and social issues dominate the political scene, in Israel the most salient election issue has been national security. In Chapter 3 we used the left-to-right spectrum to categorize the Israeli polity and to discuss the ideological position of the parties. Attitudes about security correlate highly with positions on economics. Voters who tend to be dovish on security issues also tend to support government involvement in the economy, whereas security hawks generally prefer a free economy. According to the prevailing perception in Israel, left attitudes usually equate to moderation on security matters, after which other dimensions become relevant. It is therefore very difficult for a party (perhaps with the exception of the ultra-Orthodox) to succeed in politics without an explicit position on the security issue.

Table 4.5 illustrates the influence of various issues on voter behavior. The information in the table was compiled after the 1988 election.

One security-related issue in Table 4.5 involves the intifada, the Palestinian civil uprising that erupted in December 1987 and continued, with various levels of intensity, until 1993. Only 12 percent of Israelis, mostly Arab

TABLE 4.5 Influence of Issues on Israeli Voter Behavior, 1988

	Degree of Influence (%)	
Issues	*None*	*Strong or Very Strong*
Future of territories	9	69
National security	6	57
Force against intifada	7	55
Economic policy	10	50
Other domestic policies	33	43
Foreign policy	40	30

Source: Gad Barzilai in Asher Arian and Michal Shamir, eds., *The Elections in Israel—1988* (Boulder, Colo.: Westview Press, 1990), p. 68.

citizens and leftists, opposed the use of military force to suppress the uprising; the other 88 percent supported IDF actions but were divided over how much force should be used. Left-oriented voters usually supported moderate use of force; those on the right generally demanded greater force. At the extreme right, 10 percent of Jewish voters considered the "transfer" of Palestinians from the territories to be the only solution to the intifada. Was the transfer solution a natural reaction of frustrated Jews to Arab violence?

Table 4.6 is based on data gathered in 1987 from 2,400 survey respondents' answers to the question: "Which of the following is closest to your position?" Positions one through five in Table 4.6 are considered right wing and combined were favored by a majority (67 percent) of the population in 1987. These preference profiles changed little in the 1992 election. The first position that favored transfer of the Arabs—the official ideology of Moledet—was favored by 20 percent of respondents. However, Moledet gained only two Knesset seats in the 1988 election and three in 1992. Position two was

TABLE 4.6 Israeli Popular Opinion on National Security, 1987 (%)

Position	*Percentage of Those Polled*
1. Territorial annexation with transfer	20
2. Territorial annexation without transfer	20
3. Territorial annexation with rights for Arabs	8
4. Continuation of the status quo	11
5. Autonomy for the people but not for the land	8
6. Territorial compromise with Jordan	25
7. A Jordanian-Palestinian federation	5
8. An independent Palestinian state	3

Source: Gideon Doron, *Rational Politics in Israel* (Tel Aviv: Ramot, 1988), p. 112.

usually held by religious voters who believed in the Jewish historical and biblical right to control all of Eretz Israel. Their attitudes differed from those of the radical right, who supported the first position. The third group constituted traditional Herut loyalists who had been socialized by Revisionist Zionism and believed Arabs and Jews could respectfully coexist within a Jewish state. The fourth category was the official position of the Shamir government. It appealed to those who preferred the status quo because of uncertainties about future relations with the Palestinians. The fifth position was Begin's following the Camp David agreement, which called for Palestinian autonomy within five years—that is, autonomy for the people but not for the land. This is also often called "functional autonomy."

Position number six is often called the "Jordanian option." It reflects Peres's idea for the solution that should be reached between the Israelis and Palestinians to allow Jordan to assume responsibility for the West Bank, with provisions for Israeli security and the future of West Bank Jewish settlements. In 1987 Peres, then the foreign minister, signed the London agreement with Jordan's King Hussein, who at the time was willing to accept responsibility for the territories. However, Prime Minister Shamir invalidated the agreement, and in 1988 Hussein declared that the territories were the sole responsibility of the Palestinians. During the 1988 election the Jordanian option was Labor's official position.

Until the early 1990s the seventh position was supported by several leftist members of the Labor movement and those who voted for Mapam or Ratz. The last position was supported by Israel's Arab citizens, but after the 1993 agreement between Israel and the PLO it became more of a center-left position and was backed by many in Labor and Meretz.

To win an election a leader needs to hold a position closest to that of most citizens—the moderate middle. Shamir came closest to the median in 1988 and was able to edge out Peres. Shamir failed to repeat his success in 1992 after the intifada had reduced Jewish support for the status quo; most voters felt new policy initiatives were required. Shamir was perceived as moving closer to the right (position three), which allowed Rabin to project a median position.

Many Likud status quo supporters favored Rabin over Shamir. Rabin adopted Begin's solution (number five) but called for the removal of political settlements from the territories, leaving only those required for security. The funds channeled by Likud to political settlements would be directed to a new "national order of priorities," by which Rabin meant economic and social concerns that were usually secondary to security.

Candidates

In a garrison state like Israel, a distinguished military record is always a political plus. Generals are prominent among Israeli politicians: Yitzhak

Rabin, Ariel Sharon, Rafael Eitan, Rehavim Ze'evi, Mordechai Gur, Benjamin Ben Eliezer, Efraim Sneh, and Uri Or are a few of the high-ranking reserve officers elected to the Knesset in 1992. Moshe Dayan, Yigal Allon, Ezer Weizman, Haim Bar-Lev, Yigal Yadin, Matti Peled, Aaron Yariv, Haim Herzog, and others were elected in earlier Knessets. However, a military record is not sufficient or necessary for the highest political post of prime minister. David Ben-Gurion, Moshe Sharett, Levi Eshkol, Golda Meir, and Shimon Peres all had no military record; Menachem Begin and Yitzhak Shamir headed terrorist organizations in the prestate era. Even the post of minister of defense does not require military credentials. Although Dayan, Rabin, and Sharon held this office, several have not been career military personnel including Ben-Gurion, Pinhas Lavon, Eshkol, Begin, Peres, and Moshe Arens. A military record may provide a higher entry point on a party's list of candidates, but it does not guarantee political success.

Family ties to prominent politicians at times provide a competitive edge in Israeli politics. The importance of family has been stronger in Likud than in other parties. For example, Benjamin Begin, Dan Meridor, Uzi Landau, and Ehud Olmert, who were elected in 1992, are sons of members of Herut's "fighting family." In Labor, Moshe Dayan's daughter, Yael, and other prominent MKs, including Ezer Weizman and Yigal Horovich, are related to the Dayan family. Uzi Baram, minister of tourism after 1992, is the son of Moshe Baram, who served as minister of labor under Rabin in 1974. Abba Eban, Israel's former foreign minister, is the brother-in-law of former president Haim Herzog. Some young MKs have joined parties other than those of their parents. For example, the sons of Geula Cohen of Tehiya and Joseph Burg of Mafdal served as Likud and Labor MKs, respectively. The list of family ties is substantial enough to indicate that second- and third-generation relatives of Israeli politicians have easier access to politics than those without family connections.

As noted earlier, since 1992 a secure position on the lists of the two major parties has required success in the primaries. Therefore, most politicians who are members of these parties make every effort to attract public attention through the mass media. Until 1992 the general public usually knew only the party leaders and had little, if any, knowledge about other members of the Knesset. In 1992 the surprising victory of Tzomet brought seven new MKs to the Knesset; of this group only the party leader was well-known, even to the press.

Table 4.7 is based on a survey conducted in August 1990—two years after the Twelfth Knesset—of a random sample of 465 Jewish respondents. The information shown is based on answers to the question: "This is a list of MKs; please note to which party each belongs." The list was selected at random from among Twelfth Knesset MKs who were not in the cabinet. Clearly, the vast majority of respondents could not identify the MK.

TABLE 4.7   Public Recognition of Knesset Members, 1990 (%)[a]

Name of MK	Party	Don't Know	Incorrectly Identified MK	Correctly Identified MK
Gedalia Gal	Labor	88.2	4.1	7.7
Tamar Gruzinski	Hadash	82.0	9.1	8.9
Yosi Goldberg	Likud	79.8	6.2	14.0
Yair Levi	Shas	79.6	5.2	15.2
Avraham Poraz	Shinui	69.4	20.5	9.9
Rafael Pinhasi	Shas	64.9	10.0	25.1
Haim Oron	Mapam	60.8	27.8	11.4
Uriel Lin	Likud	56.8	12.4	30.8
Shimon Shitrit	Labor	42.2	24.8	12.7

[a] Totals may not equal 100 percent because of other responses.
Source: Compiled by Doron from August 1990 survey.

Table 4.8 shows that of five cabinet posts, most Israelis polled in the 1990 survey could correctly identify only one minister, David Levy, the deputy prime minister who was also the foreign minister. The public did not know there was a second deputy prime minister, the Liberal party's Moshe Nissim, who was also minister of industry and commerce.

Some politicians represent a small sector or interest group. Although they may be well-known to their interest constituency, they are unknown to the general public. They may represent a kibbutz movement, a rabbi's community of believers, a local municipal establishment, or an ethnic group such as Druze, Georgian, or Russian Jews.

Party leaders' personal attributes, as perceived by the voting public, often become campaign issues. Personal attributes—real or perceived—such as decisiveness, wisdom, determination, credibility, courage, and so on may help or damage a given party's chances. Ben-Gurion's personal public image was presumably strong enough to help him create three successful parties—Mapai, Rafi, and the State List. Moshe Dayan's charismatic appeal helped

TABLE 4.8   Public Recognition of Ministers and Their Posts, 1990 (%)

Ministerial Post	Don't Know	Incorrectly Identified MK	Correctly Identified MK
Economic planning	80.5	14.5	5.0
Industry and commerce	56.0	22.1	21.9
Tourism	55.4	9.9	34.7
Religious affairs	48.7	30.5	20.8
Deputy prime minister	16.7	6.8	76.5

Source: Compiled by Doron from August 1990 survey.

him to become a leader of Rafi, Labor, and Telem. Rafael Eitan's personality was considered the main factor in Tzomet's success in 1992. Rabin's personal credibility and his image as "Mr. Security" helped him gain an edge over Likud in 1992.

Personal attributes can also constitute an obstacle to success if they become campaign issues. In 1984 Tami did not repeat its 1981 success because party leader Aaron Abuhatzeira was perceived by the public as dishonest. Shimon Peres failed four times against Likud candidates because, among other things, he was seen as having credibility problems. And Yitzhak Shamir lost to Rabin in 1992 because some of his loyal supporters believed he had distanced himself from his followers.

Party Loyalty

It is generally believed that Israeli voters are loyal to their parties and tend to support them regardless of the issues presented and the personalities heading the lists. The perceived relative stability of electoral outcomes has led some scholars to assume that Israeli behavior is guided largely by habitual factors. Indeed, socialization studies and actual observations of the behavior of Likud, Labor, and other loyalists seem to confirm this proposition. The idea that Labor voters would cross party lines was inconceivable until 1974, when—after his death—Ben-Gurion's State List joined Likud, or until 1977 when Labor loyalists supported the DMC.

The belief that Israeli voters tend to be loyal to their party is somewhat overstated. An examination by Gideon Doron of loyalty in the four elections between 1969 and 1984 showed that the highest identification with party (32 percent) occurred in 1984 and the lowest (17 percent) was seen in 1969, when Labor obtained the largest percentage of votes in Israeli political history. A "hard core" of voters support a political party regardless of ideology, policies, or leadership, but this group is relatively small compared to voters who are influenced by the other factors. It is expected that the older a person is and the longer he or she has supported a given party the more likely it is that he or she will continue that support. Thus, the percentage of old voters in a party's hard core is higher than that of younger voters.

Young voters who cast ballots for the first time have not yet developed a voting habit. A study Doron conducted of political choices by young Israelis showed that they were as likely to vote for their parents' party as they were to vote for other parties. Usually, young "independents" tended to vote for radical parties within their parents' political camps. This may explain why Ratz, Moledet, Kach, and Tehiya—all new Israeli parties—have followed the example of the old Zionist parties and established youth movements to train future political cadres.

Party leaders can no longer rely on continued loyalty from their supporters. Today, issues—both those that are real and those that have been manipulated for campaign purposes—seem to have the greatest impact on
most Israeli voters. In many instances, both new and old voters seem to be
moving toward the extreme parties within their respective camps.

From Ideological Competition to
Electoral Strategy

Many Israelis considered the results of the May 1994 Histadrut election to
be as significant as the fall of the Berlin Wall. The veteran Labor leadership,
which had controlled the Histadrut for over seventy years, lost to a young
challenger, Haim Ramon, who organized a new party, Ram. Ramon's success was a function of his personality, his perceived managerial abilities, and
a program that seemed to better meet the needs of Histadrut members than
did that of Labor. As Table 4.9 shows, even Labor voters who continued to
support the old establishment had high regard for Ramon in comparison to
his rival, Haim Haberfeld, the Labor party incumbent. Table 4.9 is based
on data in a 1994 Labor party study compiled from answers to the question: "Which candidate do you trust more to address your personal needs?"

Haberfeld was a veteran union leader with a long record of success in obtaining benefits for organized workers and securing their interests. Ramon
was a maverick politician in his forties with no record in the labor area. His
supporters came from Meretz and Shas, and he attracted about one-third of
traditional Labor voters; Haberfeld's supporters were exclusively Labor
party members. Labor's campaign strategy—which relied on loyalty, ideological commitment, traditional voting habits, and professional interests—
proved largely ineffective. The Labor old guard split their votes between
Haberfeld and Ramon, who seemed to sense the desire for change.

The dramatic results of the 1994 Histadrut campaign were a good indicator of a trend that had been developing in Israel since the mid-1970s:

TABLE 4.9   Distribution of Preferences for Histadrut Candidates, 1994 (%)

	Voted for Haberfeld		Voted for Ramon	
Issue	*Preferred Haberfeld*	*Preferred Ramon*	*Preferred Haberfeld*	*Preferred Ramon*
Day care	35	25	3	77
Guaranteed wage	42	22	78	9
Unemployment	41	19	80	4
Pension	40	23	81	5

Source: Labor Party Study, May 1994.

Voters who are less dependent on political parties for their livelihood tend to make voting decisions on the basis of party policy positions, credibility of candidates, and candidates' chances of winning. Rather than follow party guidance blindly, they ask who can do a better job and who is most capable of delivering on his or her electoral promises.

In the 1992 Knesset election the candidates' personal appeal and campaign strategy contributed to Tzomet's surprising success and to Labor's victory over Likud. Tzomet's gain of six Knesset seats, in addition to the two it won in 1988, can be attributed to the personality of its leader, Rafael Eitan, a former IDF chief of staff who in 1982—together with defense minister Ariel Sharon—had planned the invasion of Lebanon. Since that time Eitan had been perceived as a superhawk who was opposed to the return of the West Bank and the Golan Heights. His political ideology is based on total mistrust of Arabs. Eitan's simplistic view of the Israeli-Palestinian conflict attracts many young voters who hold a position more hawkish than that of Likud. He has benefited from his position to the right of Likud on security issues, but Eitan has positioned himself to the left of Labor on other issues including the separation of state and religion; he argues that the religious establishment should be abolished.

Rabin's nonideological approach was bolder than that of Eitan. Little remained of socialism in his 1992 campaign. In fact, the Labor party and its traditional leaders, Peres and Keisar, were hidden from view so the public would not be remained of the old regime. The symbols of the party were changed: "Nationalist" blue replaced red as the party's color. The rhetoric was also altered; from the usual collective "we," Rabin turned to the charismatic "I" ("I'll lead," "I'll guide," "I'll determine," "My government of professionals," and so on). Votes would not be cast for the Labor party but for "Labor Headed by Rabin," the party's official new name. Statistics and other scientific tools revealed the positions Rabin had to support to gain advantage over Likud; when these positions seemed to contradict earlier stands, ambivalence became the "official position," as in a typical U.S. presidential campaign. Rabin thus became the issue, and Labor's ideology surfaced only after victory had been secured and steps to form a ruling coalition were underway.

5

Interest Groups

Interest groups in Israel are both part of the ruling state apparatus and independent actors; they are often identical to competing political parties or their factions. The Histadrut (Federation of Labor Unions), for example, is considered by most students of Israeli politics to be the ultimate interest group because its goal is to protect its members through legislation and in other ways. The Histadrut, which is an important part of the ruling system, influences public policies in favor of its members both outside and within the political system; its secretary-general and senior officials are often MKs or leaders of Mapam, Likud, or the Labor party. Likewise, associations of farmers, industrialists, new immigrants, veterans, educators, invalids, and women are also represented in more than one party and thus affect policies from both within and without the formal boundaries of the political system.

Many small political parties represent particular interest groups and often play important roles in governing coalitions. In Israel, therefore, distinctions between interest groups and social movements often seem irrelevant. Because politics dominate social affairs and access to politics is often perceived as easy and rewarding, in Israel interest groups—which tend to stay out of the political system in other countries—are tempted to become involved.

The Political Economy of Israel

Jewish settlers of the first *aliya* came to Palestine during the 1880s with no professional knowledge of agriculture, the sector upon which they planned to base their national revival, and without working capital. Goodwill and high motivation were insufficient to "conquer the land." It was only with the assistance of Baron Edmund de Rothschild that Jewish settlement survived at the end of the nineteenth century. Between 1884 and 1900, the famous Jewish philanthropist invested about 10 million English pounds in Palestine. He bought land, built industries, and sustained the Jewish community by guaranteeing workers a minimal income. At the beginning of World War I, almost 60 percent of the Jewish land in Palestine was owned by Rothschild. The new community was dependent on and controlled by him and his French managers.

With the establishment of the World Zionist Organization in 1920, the Jewish settlers chose another form of dependency. Land was purchased by the movement as public property, and Jews organized politically to use Hebrew labor. Consequently, cheap Arab labor was gradually pushed out of the market. The leaders of the second *aliya* established parties and became professional politicians. They provided for immigrant needs with public funds collected from world Jewry and through dues for membership in Zionist organizations, which led to the politicization of the economic, social, educational, and health systems. The idealized pioneers (*halutzim*) conquered the land, guarded Jews against Arabs, and built a new nation, but they relied on others for their livelihood.

Members of both labor and civic groups began to organize to protect their interests. The teachers' union was established in 1903, the workers' union in 1920, the united kibbutz movement in 1927, and the *moshav* organization in 1930. The medical association was formed in 1912, the industrialists' association in 1920, and the farmers' and engineers' associations a year later. All of these groups, and others including those in the religious sector, attempted to advance the specific interests of their members but nonetheless considered fulfillment of the Zionist or communal goals to be of primary importance.

During the 1930s, when Mapai began to dominate the Yishuv and international Zionist politics, its socialist ideology prevailed. Proposals to build the Yishuv based on rational economics and private capital offered by U.S. Zionists were rejected by the socialists. The plans seemed too slow, and their results did not necessarily benefit the power brokers in the Labor movement; immediate needs required collective rather than private action. The need for a coordinated communal effort was supplied by Mapai.

After independence and even in the 1990s, few Jews in Israel argued against the right or the responsibility of government to provide an effective security system, support new immigrants, maintain a welfare system, and provide employment and public education. Israel's political system determined what resources were directed to these and other priorities, and political preferences determined who got what.

The first few years after independence were the hardest. Israel had to build the IDF, which consumed about a third of the national budget, and provide for thousands of new immigrants as well. Survivors of Nazi concentration camps and Jews from Arab countries often had no other place to go. New immigrants were frequently in poor physical and mental condition, and they lacked special skills. Upon arrival, they constituted a serious welfare problem.

Financial support from world Jewry and foreign governments helped to remedy the situation. With the increased population, demand for goods and services grew. By the mid-1950s the rate of growth had increased 50 percent over the rate in 1948. The per capita gross domestic product (GDP) increased by 15.9 percent in 1954 and 10.2 percent in 1955.[40] At the time, these were world records for economic expansion.

All groups did not benefit equally from this economic growth. When Jews arrived from the Middle East and North Africa, they were placed in transition camps (Ma'abarot), deserted pre-1948 Palestinian Arab housing, or newly established development towns located in border and remote areas. Public housing programs were coordinated by the Housing Ministry and administered by the government and Histadrut construction companies. Construction often proceeded too slowly for the rapid influx of North African immigrants, and housing allocation was often arbitrary and even discriminatory. At times, apartments that were planned and constructed for Sephardi immigrants were given instead to Polish and Romanian immigrants who arrived unexpectedly between 1956 and 1958.

These and similar political decisions created a sense of deprivation and frustration that on July 9, 1959, erupted in violent riots in a Haifa slum area, Wadi Salib, and quickly spread to other areas. In response to the riots, a law was passed on July 21 that guaranteed income maintenance to large families.

The national budget relative to gross national product (GNP) has always been high in Israel compared to other democracies. The Israeli-Arab wars resulted in an expansion of security expenditures in the national budget. Thus, for example, the 1967 war brought the portion of the national budget in Israel's GNP to over 55 percent, compared to less than 40 percent during the 1950s and the earlier 1960s; the security component reached 44 percent of the national budget, compared to about 25 percent during the preceding period. In 1973 the budget reached a record 77.5 percent of GNP; security expenditures made up almost half.[41]

Following the political embarrassment caused by the 1973 war, the massive need for new military equipment, the high price of oil in world markets, the necessity to keep a higher percentage of the labor force on active military reserve, and the intensification of social demands made on the system by the poor led to annual inflation of about 40 percent, which resulted in a major economic crisis. The situation was exploited politically by the opposition, which led to a change in government.

When the inexperienced Likud assumed power for the first time in 1977, it tried to do too much too quickly; it attempted to correct all of Labor's mistakes during its years of domination and to fulfill its election campaign promises. Likud was soon trapped in a major contradiction: On the one hand, it offered ambitious new programs that were to be financed by the national budget; on the other hand, it attempted to "liberalize" the economy by transferring public functions to the private sector. The liberalization targets failed, and the rate of privatization was about the same as Labor's. National budgets, which represent an approximate estimate of government involvement in the economy, were not reduced; in fact, they increased to 85 percent of GNP in 1977 and remained high, although at somewhat lower levels, during the following few years.

Several grandiose programs were placed on Likud's agenda. They included Project Renewal to clear slums in cities and development towns, major increases in the number of settlements in the Occupied Territories, and construction of an ultramodern jet fighter—the *Lavi*. Many other projects had to be canceled because of the cost of these three, including an old plan to connect the Mediterranean with the Dead Sea to generate electrical power. Initially, the government had been prepared to devote resources that amounted to 10 percent of GNP for a period of ten years to the *Lavi* project, but it too was canceled in 1987 because of its cost.

The Israeli national budget can be divided roughly into three components. The first covers security, the second is devoted to social welfare, and the third includes repayments of loans and interest on past government loans. Because of Israel's special military requirements, social expenditures are often cut to balance the budget. However, Likud's promises to poorer voters obligated it to maintain a high level of social expenditures. Consequently, deficit planning led to excess printing of currency that was not solidly backed, and in 1980 the annual inflation rate escalated to a record high of 139.9 percent. Plans to liberalize the economy were officially buried.

Yigal Horovich, an industrialist and a founder of the State List, became Begin's minister of finance and was able to temporarily reduce inflation by creating a mass psychology of scarcity. He refused to allocate funds demanded by cabinet ministers and used the media to convince the public to alter its spending behavior. In spite of his effectiveness, Herut ministers were not impressed; six months before the election planned for July 1981 Horovich was replaced by Yoram Aridor, a homebred Herut economist. Under the banner of supply-side economics, Aridor began to allocate resources to one and all. This "corrective economy," as it was labeled by proponents of the policy, or "election economics" as it was called by its opponents, quickly increased the national debt by 11 percent—which had no precedent in Israel. Aridor's 1981 policy was almost standard operating procedure during an election year, but its intensity and scope were far too bold even for many Israelis. Nonetheless, the policy was effective and helped Likud regain power, even though the rate of inflation was four times as high in 1981 as it had been in 1977.

After the 1981 election, Likud seemed to lose control of the economy. The 1982 war launched against the Palestinians in Lebanon added more pressure to the already staggering economy. In 1984 annual inflation reached 445 percent; in some months of that year the projected annual rate reached a world record of about 1,000 percent. The national budget now exceeded GNP by several percentage points. The erratic nature of this hyperinflation made it impossible to plan; business managers could not project the future value of investments and therefore could not determine the current value of their goods and services.

In 1984 a recovery plan was masterminded by Prime Minister Peres and Finance Minister Itzhak Modai within the framework of the Likud-Labor coalition. The plan had several components. First, credit and loans were obtained from the United States to create a safety net in case the plan backfired. Next, all consumer prices, salaries, and income were frozen by law at a fixed level and could not be changed except by special, rarely granted permission. The value of the shekel was linked to the dollar. Further, all political leaders pledged their commitment to the plan and accepted substantial reductions in their ministerial appropriations. A legally binding "package deal" was signed by the three major employers in the country—government, Histadrut, and the heads of industry—prohibiting them from breaking the agreement and thereby causing an unequal distribution of the plan's costs. These costs involved an increase in unemployment from 5.9 percent in 1984 to 7.1 percent in 1986 and a real reduction in profit levels and salaries. The plan also relied heavily on media support, strict enforcement, and, above all, a publicized time schedule for the projected stages of achievement.

By the end of 1986 the inflation rate had been reduced and had stabilized below 20 percent; it remained between 16 and 20 percent for the next five years. When Likud transferred power to Labor in 1992, inflation was 9.4 percent. During the first two years of renewed Labor control, inflation again reached double digits, ranging from 11.2 to 14.5 percent.

The remarkable achievement of curbing inflation in such a short time without major civil unrest was a function of the particular structure of Israel's economy, which is highly centralized and regulated and is therefore easy to control. The government and Histadrut employ about half of all workers; agricultural production is managed by cartels; the three major banks (Leumi, Ha-Poalim, and Discount), in which 90 percent of the country's financial activities are conducted, are essentially nationalized; some companies (tobacco and coffee) have a monopoly position in the market, and a few others export most of the country's industrial products; health services are nationalized; and transportation is heavily subsidized. In short, there is little room for individual entrepreneurs outside the public sphere.

The Histadrut Workers' Union

By far the largest and the most influential Israeli interest group is the Histadrut (General Federation of Workers) in Eretz Israel. Until the defeat of Labor in the 1977 election, the Histadrut had a quasi-official status because of its intimate relationship with the governing party. Frequent interchanges of personnel occurred among the Histadrut leadership, the Labor party, and the government. Several secretaries-general of the Histadrut had also headed the Labor party or had been prime ministers or cabinet members. Labor's broad social programs and welfare legislation were inspired by Histadrut. These laws assured workers of the right to strike and included the National Insurance Law of 1954, the Hours of Work and Rest Law, the Annual Holidays Law, the Youth Employment Law, the Employment of Women Law, the Pay Severance Law, and the Labor Exchange Law.

With the defeat of Labor and the accession of Likud to power in 1977, the Histadrut lost its quasi-official status and became part of the opposition as a nongovernmental interest group, with much the same status as labor unions in Western countries in which labor is not part of the government. The Histadrut exerted great pressure on those in power, becoming more relevant as a separate interest group than it had been before. In October 1977, when the Likud government announced that it would lift many economic and fiscal controls and terminate the subsidies the Labor government had adopted during the previous three decades, the Histadrut threatened the new government with strikes sanctioned by its leaders. The leaders argued that the abolition of tight currency controls, devaluation of Israeli currency, and reductions of subsidies on bread, oil, margarine, eggs, milk, poultry, and public transportation would raise the cost of living between 10 and 25 percent without substantially reducing the inflation rate, which reached 38 percent in 1976. The consequences of this turnabout in social policy seemed to the union leadership to call for concerted and decisive action by interest groups outside government, a difficult accomplishment considering how low the Labor party had fallen in public esteem by 1977.

The Histadrut is important not only as a labor federation; it is also Israel's largest social organization, its largest single economic entrepreneur and employer, and a major influence on cultural and educational life. In 1977 more than a half of all Israeli workers were members of Histadrut or one of its affiliates. Ninety percent of the country's organized workers belonged to one of the Histadrut trade unions. More than two-thirds of the population was insured by the federation's health fund (*Kupat Holim*). Nearly a quarter of the total labor force was employed by one of the Histadrut enterprises.

By 1992 over 1.5 million people were affiliated with the Histadrut. This number combined with the vast range of its activities made the Histadrut Israel's most influential organization, more important than any single political party. Histadrut affiliates include professional unions, workers' councils, a social insurance program, consumer groups, and Na'amat—a semi-independent women's organization. Various departments deal with labor legislation, working women, professional training, Israeli Arabs and Druze, neighborhood and community activities, regional integration, social welfare, and international relations. Four agricultural movements—the Moshavim (agricultural cooperatives), the Alliance of the Kibbutz Movement, the United Kibbutz Movement, and the Kibbutz Ha-Artzi—are Histadrut affiliates. Its educational network contains a system of comprehensive high schools, colleges for technicians and engineers, industrial schools, and professional training programs for adults. The Histadrut also runs a school for its own officials and a teachers' college with several campuses and thousands of students; further, it conducts research at academic institutes. It maintains hospitals and pension funds and finances sport associations and youth movements. Its most important divisions are those that deal with professional unions, its massive economic holding company—Hevrat Ovdim—and Na'amat.

A partial list of the Histadrut's professional unions includes groups composed of nurses, construction workers, press workers, pilots, garment workers, diamond workers, state workers, musicians, teachers, tourist guides, food workers, child-care providers, metal and electricity workers, sanitation workers, social workers, security employees, mass-media workers, journalists, IDF civilian employees, medical doctors, actors and directors, gas station employees, and paramedical technicians. Some of these unions, especially those for electricity workers and teachers, are so powerful that they do not really need Histadrut protection. However, Histadrut's control of thirteen large unions provides a credible threat to government and private-sector employers.

Through Hevrat Ovdim, at some point the Histadrut has owned—completely or partially, directly or indirectly—the two major transportation companies, the largest supermarket chain, the largest savings and credit banks, the largest insurance company, the largest construction company, the largest industrial conglomerate, and the largest agricultural food marketing cooperative. The Histadrut also owns an undisclosed amount of land and number of buildings in some of the most expensive areas of Israel.

Na'amat, the women's section within the Histadrut, is actually quasi-independent. Its head is elected by its members during the same time period as the general Histadrut election. Na'amat runs kindergartens, day-care centers, and professional and agricultural schools; cares for families and provides activities in the Jewish and Arab communities; and protects the status of working women and educates and trains them. The organization offers the same protection, services, and rights as those received by male Histadrut members.

Although the Histadrut was established by the two largest Labor parties in 1920 and was dominated by Mapai until the 1960s, the strength of other parties has been rising, as demonstrated in recent elections to the governing body, the National Convention. All Histadrut members can vote for delegates to the convention. The various parties form lists for the Histadrut Convention, as they do for the Knesset, with the goal of attaining as much influence as possible within the organization. Between the seventh Histadrut National Convention election in 1949, when Labor parties won more than 90 percent of the vote, and the thirteenth election in 1977, Labor representation fell by 35 percent to just over 55 percent of the vote. Ironically Likud, the major critic of Labor hegemony in Israel, won 28.2 percent of the votes in 1977. Many voters who participated in both Knesset and Histadrut elections split their votes to demonstrate their dissatisfaction with the government, supporting Likud in the Knesset and Labor in the Histadrut.

Israeli trade unionists and leaders of local labor councils have become increasingly independent and resentful of the central leadership, which remained unchanged for nearly two generations. Several national unions that belonged to the central federation frequently ignored directives of the Histadrut Executive and secretary-general. Physicians, teachers, airline pilots, and port workers have struck—without authorization from Histadrut leaders—when they opposed wage guidelines established by the Labor government in collaboration with the Histadrut.

The Histadrut was greatly weakened during the 1980s by its inability to sustain its industrial empire, its failure to reform itself and project a modern image, the crisis in the health and the pension fund systems, and the Likud government's opposition. Clearly, the economic hardship of the 1980s was the prime factor that adversely affected the Histadrut's ability to protect member interests. Almost all of its industrial network was on the verge of collapse; several companies had to be dissolved or sold, undergo bankruptcy, or ask for government assistance. Although many Likud government leaders were veteran ideological rivals of the Histadrut, they provided monetary help for its enterprises to prevent a major catastrophe and to reduce the country's high unemployment. Koor, the Histadrut industrial conglomerate, for example, was saved from bankruptcy and dismantling by financial assistance from a Likud government.

Many surviving Histadrut components were forced to make reductions and to adopt new industrial, managerial, and marketing methods; others were perceived by the public as out of touch. The Histadrut headquarters in Tel Aviv was popularly labeled the "Kremlin," and its organization was notorious for inefficiency, redundancy, waste, and, at times, corruption. The Labor leadership that had controlled the Histadrut since 1920 seemed to have no intention or incentive to change. The only potential threat to its domination was the Likud, but Likud representation in the Histadrut Executive was smaller than the 33 percent required to veto or block any decisions of the general council. It made little difference that Labor obtained less than 66 percent of the seats in the 1985 election or less than 60 percent in 1989 because it could join with the Communists or Ratz, Likud's ideological rivals, to defeat any proposals for change.

To finance its operations, from the 1930s to 1994 the Histadrut relied on a portion (about 28 percent) of membership fees paid to *Kupat Holim*. As long as the health system worked well, few members complained. The only serious opposition to this method of financing both the health system and other Histadrut activities came from the Likud and from those who supported the statist ideology. Some prominent Likud members and statists demanded nationalization of the health system—similar to the British model—and others, including Likud Minister of Health Ehud Olmert, called for privatization. The Histadrut was able to deflect much of this opposition, but with new technologies, medicines, methods of treatment, and the gradual increase in Israeli life expectancy the cost of health care became very high. *Kupat Holim* branches and hospitals found it increasingly difficult to finance their operations.

By 1992 the Histadrut had become an electoral liability rather than an asset for the Labor party; during the campaign it was rarely mentioned. Histadrut Secretary-General Israel Keisar was appointed the minister of transportation in Rabin's government, and his former post was taken by Haim Haberfeld, a veteran union chief. Haberfeld, an old-style Labor leader, opposed any reform, and in the February 1994 party primaries he easily defeated his young challenger, Amir Peretz. Haberfeld refused to accept plans to change Histadrut's health program that were suggested by Minister of Health Haim Ramon, who subsequently resigned from the government. Ramon and Peretz joined members of Ratz and Shas and formed the Ram (New Life for the Histadrut) party.

During the campaign that preceded the May 1994 election, Prime Minister Rabin projected a double message: On the one hand, he was a devoted Labor party member; on the other he claimed he liked Ramon's programs and personality. This ambivalent message caused about a third of traditional Labor voters to shift their support to Ramon, who won over 46 percent of the votes; Labor's strength was reduced to 32 percent.

From his new position as secretary-general of the Histadrut, Ramon was able to force his health plan on the government and the Knesset. A health insurance bill, which went into effect in 1995, was passed by the Knesset that required all citizens to pay 4.8 percent of their salary directly to the government rather than to *Kupat Holim,* thereby ensuring that all money paid for health would be used for health and for no other purpose. The government now became responsible for citizens' health, although *Kupat Holim* continued to supply the service. With the adoption of this bill, the Histadrut lost much of the income needed to support its operations.

Israel has other unions, some established since the early 1990s to capitalize on the weakness of the Histadrut and its *Kupat Holim.* These unions include the National Labor Federation (NLF), which has fewer than 200,000 members. The NLF is not officially affiliated with any party but is an outgrowth of the Revisionist movement. The group was formed in 1934 in opposition to the socialist policies of the Histadrut; it advocates compulsory national arbitration in all labor disputes, the establishment of non-party labor exchanges, and a shift in labor ideology to one of unity in the national struggle rather than one based on class conflict. Instead of the red flag used by the Histadrut, the NLF uses the blue and white Zionist colors; its anthem is the Zionist "Hatikva" ("the Hope") rather than the "Internationale"; and its annual workers' holiday is the anniversary of Theodore Herzl's death rather than the first day of May.

Like Likud, the NLF strongly objects to Labor ownership of industrial and commercial enterprises and insists that employer functions cannot be combined with those of trade unions. The NLF also objects to intervention by political parties in labor disputes and demands that such disputes be settled by a national institution for compulsory arbitration. The NLF has its own insurance and funds for unemployment, disability, labor disputes, mutual loans, pensions, and members' credit. Its housing company has constructed thousands of apartments and shopping centers, synagogues, and public buildings for veterans and new immigrants. In the future, the NLF could pose a serious challenge to Histadrut domination of Israeli workers.

The Army and Politics

In 1992, when Rabin became prime minister for the second time and minister of defense for the third time, he placed many military personnel in policymaking positions. Negotiations with the Palestinians and the Arab states were conducted by high-ranking officers under the PM's direction. Their involvement raised the question of whether it was possible for army generals to take over the government. Several factors in the history of the relationship between the IDF and the state make a potential military takeover highly unlikely.

There is no entrenched bureaucracy or officer elite in the Israeli army because of the nature of officer recruitment. Rapid promotion for gifted officers and a relatively short tenure in senior ranks before retirement at an early age ensure that rotation prevents the formation of a permanent officer cadre. There is no elite service academy such as West Point or Annapolis. The only chief of staff who graduated from a military-oriented high school, Amnon Shahak-Lepkin, was nominated to his post in January 1995. Recruitment at the top grades occurs mostly among a cross section of young Ashkenazi and Sabra men. Until the 1970s, no general staff officers had come from the Afro-Asian Jewish community. Since that time, several Sephardi Jews have served as generals and one, Moshe Levy, as chief of staff. An exceptionally large percentage of high-ranking officers and pilots—about 25 percent—have come from kibbutzim and *moshavim,* although the population of these settlements constitutes less than 8 percent of the total population. The policy of rapid turnover has produced a relatively large number of young, retired, high-ranking officers who are available for civilian posts.

Until 1973, especially after 1967, high-ranking retired military officers were held in high esteem, and they had relatively easy access to politics and managerial positions in industry: The higher the military rank, the more likely the person was to secure his or her desired "second career" position. A survey of seventy-five senior officers (colonel and above) who retired between 1950 and 1973 showed that about 33 percent became senior officials in industrial and economic institutions, 25 percent worked for the Ministry of Defense and defense-related institutions, over 10 percent became senior officials in government or in public institutions, 10 percent worked for political parties, and the rest were involved in university teaching, research, administration, diplomacy, and foreign service.

After 1973, many retired officers began to find it difficult to locate suitable jobs. The rapid expansion of the army and the need to increase the top ranks created an abundance of high-ranking officers. Therefore, the army placed more emphasis on preparing its personnel for civilian life and on investing in their professional education; a placement agency was established to help younger officers, mostly in their forties, to find jobs.

Some turned to politics and entered almost every Zionist party. When entry at the national level of politics became more difficult, officers moved into local levels. In 1949 there were twenty-four active military officers on the Knesset Lists of the Zionist parties. The Mapam List included eleven officers, Mapai had six, Herut had five, and two were members of the Progressive party and the Religious Front. Of these, only four members of Mapai and two of Herut were elected. After the 1949 election, the nomination of active officers as Knesset candidates was prohibited, and officers who wanted to run had to resign from the IDF at least one hundred days before an election. As a rule, Labor movement parties had a higher proportion of reserve officers in the Knesset and the cabinet than did other parties.

Until 1967, retired officers were appointed to ministries of only secondary importance such as labor, tourism, transport, and agriculture. But when Moshe Dayan became minister of defense on the eve of the Six Day War, his military peers occupied more important posts including, in 1974, the position of prime minister. In 1974 and again in 1977, there were five retired generals in the government. But in 1981 Dayan, Ezer Weizman, and two DMC former generals did not return to government, and only Ariel Sharon remained as the Likud's top-ranking military officer. Even though it controlled the government, the Likud was less rooted in the IDF than was Labor. Except for Sharon, all generals who served in the Labor-Likud coalitions between 1984 and 1990 were from Labor. In the 1992 Labor coalition, only Rabin and his deputy minister of defense, Mordechai Gur, were former major generals and former chiefs of staff; two others—Benjamin Ben Eliezer, the minister of housing, and Efraim Sneh, the minister of health—were retired brigadier generals.

High-ranking reserve officers in the Knesset have had diverse political perspectives; some were ultrahawks, others have been ultradoves, and several were centrists. Among the most hawkish have been Rehavim Ze'evi of Moledet, Rafael Eitan of Tzomet, and Sharon of Likud. Among the most dovish have been Matti Peled of PLP and retired colonel Meir Pa'il of Shelli. Most others were centrist members of Labor movement parties. Ze'evi, Eitan, and Sharon headed their own party lists and were members of Shamir's 1990–1992 government. Other generals who headed Knesset party lists included Rabin (1992, Labor), Weizman (1984, Yahad), Dayan (1981, Telem), and Yadin (1977, DMC).

Until 1969, no retired high-ranking officer had headed a party list in local elections. Labor then nominated a former officer, former Colonel Joseph Nevo, as its candidate for city mayor of Herzlia, and he won the election. In 1973 former General Shlomo Lahat was elected mayor of Tel Aviv on the Liberal ticket. Since then, many officers of various ranks have run at the local level representing most parties. The most notable success in 1993 was the election of former General Amiram Mitzna as mayor of Haifa.

Surveys of Israeli army officers have indicated that they do not constitute a distinct or separate ideological bloc. More than half voted for the Labor alignment in 1965. Nearly two-thirds had either liberal or moderate attitudes toward nationalism, economics, state and religion, and democracy. In a 1972 survey, retired senior officers expressed a greater willingness to make territorial concessions to achieve peace than did the civilian population. Around 57 percent were ready to grant concessions on the West Bank, and 52 percent were willing to grant self-determination to the Palestinians. These relatively liberal attitudes were also expressed on issues of religion and state, civil marriage, and economics. More diversity of views was reflected in the hawk-dove spectrum of views on foreign and security policies.

Surveys taken in later years have showed essentially similar results. On average, however, senior officers have been more moderate than lower-ranking officers and noncommissioned ranks. Younger soldiers have tended to vote in larger proportions than the rest of the population, usually for Zionist parties of the extreme left or right and for single-leader parties.

Except for the ultra-Orthodox and Arab parties, all parties in Israel are represented in the army. No cluster of distinctive political opinion exists that differs greatly from that of the civilian leadership.

The Security Establishment as a Major Bureaucracy

Various estimates place the IDF's total human resources, including those on active service and in the reserves, at more than 400,000. This number is much greater than armies in many countries whose populations are much larger than Israel's—including the United Kingdom, Italy, Japan, Pakistan, and Indonesia. In terms of the quality of its military personnel, weapon effectiveness, infrastructure and logistics, and organizational quality, the IDF is among the best security forces in the world. It is equipped with state-of-the-art technological weapons including jet fighter planes, helicopters, missiles, tanks, gunboats, and submarines. Many are Israeli-made, with parts imported from Western countries, especially the United States. Israel is said to belong to the exclusive list of countries that have nuclear weapons. It has spent a higher percentage of its GDP than any other country to obtain and maintain the status of a leading military power. Since 1949 military-related spending has consumed an average of about a third of government expenditures.

Until 1967, most Israeli weapons and military assistance came from European countries, notably France. However, following the Six Day War, French President Charles de Gaulle imposed an embargo on weapons to the region, thereby cutting Israel's principal source of supply. After the Eisenhower era Israel's principal military assistance was coming from the United States. In 1959 the United States granted a modest military loan of about $400,000; during the next six years U.S. loans averaged about $6.6 million. Prime Minister Levi Eshkol convinced President Lyndon Johnson to increase the level of aid to $90 million in 1966. Until 1971, U.S. military aid averaged about $40 million per year, but in 1971, when Israel cooperated with the United States in protecting Jordan against an invasion by Syria, U.S. military aid reached $545 million. During the Nixon administration Israel was seen as a regional player on the U.S. side in the Cold War, and it received $300 million in military aid in the early 1970s.

Following the Yom Kippur War, the Israel-U.S. alliance became much closer. In addition to the $800 million Israel had received as loans, in 1973–1974 Washington provided a grant of $1.6 million to replace Israel's destroyed war machines. Since that time, the military aid package to Israel has been a mixture of loans and grants. When Israel signed the peace agreement with Egypt in 1979, it received $2.6 billion, including $600 million in grants from the United States—assistance that has been repeated yearly. Much aid to Israel is invested in U.S. industries that produce weapons according to Israeli specifications, which helps to subsidize the U.S. economy. Also, Israel and Israeli wars have provided a testing ground for new U.S. weapons.

The major burden for security is carried by Israel's citizens through taxation and direct involvement in the military. With some exceptions for Arabs (excluding Druze and Bedouins), ultrareligious Jews, and the disabled, every Israeli must serve in the army. Young men serve for three years and women for about two, but a high percentage of youths are exempted for a variety of reasons, and about a third of the young men do not serve the full three years required according to the law. Most men continue to serve in the reserves until their mid-forties or early fifties. Reliance on reserve forces is a heavy burden on the economy and directly affects military doctrine. Israel cannot afford to station large numbers of troops on its borders because of personnel shortages; thus, it must rely on sophisticated intelligence and early warning systems, develop a first-strike capability, and find adequate technological substitutes for the territorial depth or strategic land area provided by the Occupied Territories. In addition, Israel has developed a fighting doctrine in which combat is moved quickly to enemy territory.

The exact size of the military appropriations is not known because, among other things, not all monies for security appear in either the Defense Department or army budgets. Several items appear in other budgets, although they are primarily related to security. Over the years, the IDF in particular and the security establishment in general have been able to evolve as independent budgetary units within the Israeli government. Whereas all other ministries must bargain with the Treasury Department over every line and item in their budgets, military experts determine their own budgets and their internal composition. The Treasury Department may offer overall budgetary cuts, but the Defense Ministry decides where, if at all, these cuts will be made. Often, when proposals for cuts seem too large, the Minister of Defense, assisted by supporters in the media, pressures the Minister of Finance to retreat. The usual argument is that these cuts would place the security of Israel at risk.

The Security Establishment as an Economic Force

The security establishment is also a major economic force that employs thousands of people in the arms industry; it sells its products to the IDF and exports products to other countries. The arms industry began in the prestate era when the Yishuv secretly produced light weapons, some of which were used during the War of Independence; later, the military industry continued to evolve by adding new types of weapons and ammunition. The basic idea behind weapons development was that Israel should become self-reliant. During the 1950s the industry was constructed around three companies: Israeli Military Industry, Israel Aircraft Industries, and the National Weapons Development Authority (Rafael). By 1960 the industry had expanded significantly and had begun to work on aviation and electronic projects, nuclear research, and the development of weapons such as the Uzzi submachine gun and the Gabriel sea-to-sea missile.

The embargo imposed by France in 1967 and the delay in the U.S. supply of needed weapons in 1973 convinced the Israelis that they must rely on their own production to maintain a viable security posture. Consequently, among other projects, the Kfir jet plane, which is a version of the French *Mirage,* went on the assembly line during the mid-1970s. The highly effective *Merkava* tank was produced several years later. Work on the *Lavi* jet fighter began and was then suspended because of its prohibitively high cost. Israel also joined as a junior partner in the Strategic Defense Initiative project, which was responsible for the development of the *Arrow* ground-to-air missile.

In the process, Israel became one of the world's leading arms exporters. Reports of the American Arms Control and Disarmament Agency, based mostly on Israeli official records, greatly underevaluate the true income from Israel's sales. Nonetheless, Israel was able to gain a competitive edge over other countries in certain products because of their low costs, effectiveness, and proven performance on the battlefield. For some countries, knowledge that the IDF used a weapon was sufficient proof of its high quality. Thailand, Taiwan, Singapore, Malaysia, Indonesia, Ethiopia, Ghana, Kenya, Liberia, Tanzania, Uganda, Zaire, Zimbabwe, Morocco, most South and Central American countries, and South Africa have purchased various types of Israeli-produced weapons at one time or another.

In some years weapons industry exports surpass sales from three traditional sectors: tourism, agriculture, and diamonds. Until the 1990s, weapons industry expansion was supported by a strong Defense Department lobby made up of retired officers who had become weapons dealers, civilian industrialists who supplied parts to the industry, and security-minded politicians. In the early 1990s, however, the effectiveness of the arms lobby dissipated because the end of the Cold War depressed international weapons sales. Competition became more aggressive, and producers were more hesitant to transfer arms sales on credit to potentially unstable regimes. As a result, the Israeli arms industry suffered greatly.

The Media

The typical Israeli consumes news hour by hour as a radio listener—where news is transmitted every half hour—a television viewer, and a newspaper reader. Israelis have one of the highest rates of newspaper and book readership in the world. Exposure to the media increased further during the 1990s when commercial and cable television and local radio stations became available. For ambitious politicians, media exposure became imperative; for policymakers the media constituted an effective feedback mechanism by which to formulate and reformulate decisions.

The daily press presents a broad array of views—from radical to conservative; from sports and fashion periodicals to highly technical, scientific, and philosophical journals. Table 5.1 shows the readership rates of the main daily newspapers in Israel during 1994.

Party-oriented newspapers (*Davar, Ha-Tzofeh, Al Hamishmar,* and others) have very small readerships. In 1995 Mapam's *Al Hamishmar* closed, and the Histadrut-subsidized *Davar* was shut down in 1996 because of financial difficulties. *Davar,* first published in 1925, had traditionally reflected Labor's viewpoint; until Labor's defeat in 1977, it also expressed the government view on most issues. *Davar* once had a large circulation because Histadrut members received the paper. When that distribution was canceled for financial reasons, the newspaper had difficulty competing for readers. *Al Hamishmar* always had a small circulation. Its frequent

TABLE 5.1   Public Readership Rates of Daily Newspapers in Israel, 1994 (%)

Newspaper	Weekdays[a]	Weekends[a]
Globus (financial)	3.7	1.5
Jerusalem Post (general, in English)	1.8	2.4
Davar (Histadrut)	1.5	1.2
Ha-Aretz (general, morning)	6.1	6.3
Ha-Tzofeh (National Religious party)	0.6	0.5
Hadashot (general)	3.6	6.3
Yediot Achronot (general)	52.2	68.7
Maariv (general)	21.1	27.4
Al Hamishmar (Meretz-Mapam)	0.2	0.2
Another Hebrew paper	1.7	1.9
Another non-Hebrew paper	4.9	4.3
Did not read yesterday/weekend	8.6	3.5
Did not read last week/month	4.0	1.1
Did not read last two days/month	11.7	6.4

[a] Totals exceed 100 percent because many Israelis read more than one newspaper.
Source: Geocartographia Media Survey (1994). Tel Aviv: Geocartographia.

criticism of the government and rather doctrinaire approach made it the paper of the Kibbutz federation Kibbutz Artzi. During the 1980s it relaxed its essentially socialist orientation and in 1992 became the main vehicle for expressing the Meretz position. *Ha-Tzofeh,* the newspaper of the NRP, has been the most durable Orthodox Jewish press organ. Other dailies in the Orthodox community belong to Shas, Agudat Israel, and Degel Ha-Torah; they serve as the voice for leading Orthodox rabbis to launch attacks against other parties.

The *Jerusalem Post* is the principal English-language newspaper and is read widely by the diplomatic and foreign communities, as well as by many English-speaking immigrants. The paper has a substantial clientele abroad, especially in Great Britain and the United States. The *Post,* once subsidized by the Histadrut, was sold to a private entrepreneur and for the past few years has represented a militantly nationalist, anti-Labor perspective.

About 5 percent of the population reads non-Hebrew newspapers in various European languages: Spanish, French, Bulgarian, German, Hungarian, Polish, Romanian, and Russian. With the recent influx of Russian Jews, there are now more than half a dozen new Russian dailies and several weeklies. The Arabic press is read mostly by Israeli Arabs.

Ha-aretz and *Yediot Achronot* are owned by the Schocken and Mozes families, respectively, who also dominate several local newspapers through their parent companies. In 1994 the Schocken network and the Mozes empire controlled over 50 percent of the local press and 33 percent of independent local publications. The Schocken and Mozes networks each circulate well over a million "locals" throughout fifteen distribution districts; the two families also have important shares in the weekly and monthly press. A third family, the Nimrodis, who publish the daily *Maariv,* also owns substantial shares of the press. Since late 1993 the Mozes and Nimrodis families have become major stockholders of second-channel commercial television.

The general press is not only independent, it is also relatively free of political bias. Although the three families described in the previous paragraph are known to be liberal or right wing, their newspapers attract all types of readers (and advertising companies) because they permit publication of all political opinions including columns by both left- and right-wing journalists, opposition opinion next to that of the government, and politically diverse letters to the editors.

Until 1968 there was no Israeli television, although many Israelis owned sets and watched programs aired from the neighboring Arab countries. To combat the effect of these stations, the Israeli government formed an Arabic-speaking broadcasting department. News and many other types of "utility programs" were aired in the evening just before the Hebrew programs. From 1968 until 1993, all television programs were under the direct control of the Israeli Broadcasting Authority. Although the television staff has been highly professional, its board of directors has included political appointees according to party strength in the Knesset—that is, the stronger the party, the more board members it has. At times, the board has intervened in specific programs, but in general only professional editorial choices have prevailed. Although not always neutral, Israeli television has usually been perceived as a source of reliable and unbiased information because it has maintained a generally balanced political position.

Beginning in 1995, commercial radio stations were also allowed to operate; until then, there had been only seven public stations. Four were run by the Israeli Broadcasting Authority, two were controlled by the IDF, and one was "independent," belonging to national-religious interests. Until 1993, another "pirate" station, "the Voice of Peace," broadcast from a ship in the Mediterranean.

In 1994 about 94 percent of the Israeli public listened to the radio. About 65 percent listened to one of the four Broadcast Authority's stations, 30 percent listened to the IDF stations, and the rest listened to the "independent" station. On average, about 30 percent of the population listened to the radio in both morning and afternoon; during evening hours most listeners switched to television. Most adult radio listeners focused on news or news-related programs. An additional 10 percent enjoyed other types of programs. There were also news programs for youth, but young people tended to listen to general programs.

Israel's Arab-speaking population is also exposed to the powerful transmitting stations in the neighboring Arab countries, which, in addition to their regular programs, broadcast Hebrew hours. Israel, in turn, broadcasts political propaganda to the Middle East and to distant places like Iran and the former Soviet Union. With its *Voice of Zion to the Diaspora,* Israel reaches Jewish communities throughout the world.

Israel's political leaders follow diverse press currents closely because the papers are widely read and are considered a fairly accurate gauge of public opinion. Press exposure of bureaucratic inefficiency, mismanagement, and corruption puts government officials and politicians on guard. The press is a vital defender of the public interest and of individual rights. Over the years, the electronic and print media, as a matter of practice, have issued public opinion surveys of the relative popularity of political leaders. This feedback affects the behavior of politicians and the formation of public policy.

Diaspora Jewry

In an address to the Twenty-Fifth World Zionist Congress in 1960, Prime Minister Ben-Gurion stated: "The State of Israel was not established for its citizens alone. It is the foremost bulwark for the survival of the Jewish people in our generation." The interests of world Jewry in Israel received international recognition through the League of Nations' Mandate for Palestine and the UN Partition Resolution. This interest was officially sanctioned by the government of Israel through its Declaration of Independence and subsequent legislation, especially the 1952 law that gave special status to the Jewish Agency and the World Zionist Organization.

The U.S. Jewish community is the largest and most influential in the diaspora and constitutes the most visible foreign interest group. The most important diaspora institutions are the World Zionist Organization and the Jewish Agency, which have executive committee members in both Israel and the United States. Representatives to the periodic congresses of the World Zionist Organization are elected by members of Zionist groups in many countries; most are members of groups affiliated with political parties in Israel. Between congresses, the Zionist Executive manages business with the government of Israel through departments headed by its members; they include Torah Education and Culture in the Diaspora, Information, Youth Aliya (Immigration), Aliya and Absorption, and External Relations. Through these contacts the Israeli government makes its needs known to world Jewry, raises funds, propagates educational and informational themes, and rallies political support. Although theoretically Zionists in the diaspora can influence Israel's political system, in practice the Israeli government usually determines the nature of the contact. Israel's dominant role in this relationship is facilitated by the large number of Israelis on the Executive and in the administrative apparatus of the World Zionist Organization. In countries with large Jewish populations, Israeli embassies and consulates actively rally support for Israel, assist or guide local Zionists and other Jewish organizations, and maintain ties between Jewish communities and the Jewish state.

Because of its size and its extensive organizational apparatus, U.S. Jewry has a unique relationship with Israel. Dozens of Jewish religious, cultural, and fund-raising organizations in the United States have special ties with Israel; many are informal, but others have been institutionalized in written agreements. Groups such as the American Jewish Committee and the American Jewish Congress help to disseminate favorable information about Israel and to explain its policies to the U.S. public. Leaders of these groups are in frequent contact with Israel's representatives in the United States and have direct access to the country's political leaders.

Because of the prestige and wealth of its members, the American Jewish Committee (AJC) has been especially cultivated by Israel's leaders. The committee is the only private organization with which the Israeli government has reached a quasi-official agreement that defines a "proper" relationship with diaspora Jewry. In the agreement, signed in 1950 between Prime Minister Ben-Gurion and AJC President Jacob Blaustein, the Israelis accepted the fact that U.S. Jews have only one political attachment and that is to the United States of America. They owe no political allegiance to Israel, the agreement asserted. The State of Israel represents and speaks only on behalf of its own citizens and in no way presumes to represent or speak in the name of Jews who are citizens of any other country.

To reconcile AJC support for the Law of Return with its opposition to automatic Israeli citizenship for Jews, the agreement stipulated that the immigration of U.S. Jews to Israel would occur at the free discretion of each individual Jew. Blaustein called on Israel to recognize that the matter of goodwill between its citizens and those of other countries is a two-way street, that Israel also has a responsibility to not adversely affect the sensibilities of Jews who are citizens of other states by what it says or does. He rejected Ben-Gurion's concept of the role for diaspora Jews by emphasizing that U.S. Jews vigorously repudiated any suggestion or implication that they were in exile. U.S. Jews—young and old, Zionists and non-Zionists— were profoundly attached to the United States and considered it home, Blaustein insisted.

U.S. Zionist interests are consolidated through the American Zionist Federation, which coordinates the efforts of fourteen Zionist organizations and ten Zionist youth movements, most of which are affiliated with political parties in Israel. These groups include Likud-affiliated Zionist Revisionists of America; Americans for Progressive Israel, affiliated with Mapam; the Zionist Organization of America, associated with the former Liberal party wing of Likud; the Religious Zionists of America, affiliated with the National Religious party; the Labor Zionist movement, related to the Israeli Labor party, and others.

The American Israel Public Affairs Committee (AIPAC), known as the "Israeli lobby," is financed and supported by diverse U.S. Jewish groups. AIPAC is one of the most powerful and effective lobbies in Washington, D.C., where it has access to and frequently influences members of the U.S. Senate and House of Representatives on matters related to Israel. AIPAC originated in the American Zionist Council and acquired its present name in 1954, when it became autonomous. Through its close contacts with U.S. Zionist and other Jewish organizations and with diplomatic representatives of Israel, AIPAC informs U.S. legislators and officials of the views and desires of the Israeli government regarding important U.S. legislation that affects the Jewish state.

The highest-level U.S. Jewish organization that reflects Israel's interests in the United States is the Conference of Presidents of Major American Jewish Organizations, which represents thirty-two U.S. Jewish groups. The conference, or Presidents' Club, was organized in 1955 by the president of the World Zionist Organization and the World Jewish Congress, Nahum Goldmann, and other Jewish leaders. The conference represents the collective will of U.S. Jewry on matters related to their relations with Israel.

Many differences within the U.S. Jewish community in its relations with Israel, such as the distinction between Zionists and non-Zionists, have been obscured since 1967. The trauma of the 1967 and 1973 wars led to a consolidation of efforts by most U.S. Jewish organizations, the emergence of near unanimity in policy, and a common perspective toward their relationships with Israel. For most Jews in the diaspora, as well as for many of their non-Jewish friends, the wars evoked memories of the Holocaust. To many, not only the existence of Israel seemed imperiled but the future of diaspora Jewry as well. As the international Jewish community became galvanized in massive efforts to support Israel, both materially and politically, there was a tendency to evoke the slogan of one former non-Zionist, the editor of AJC's monthly magazine, *Commentary*, who wrote, "We are all Zionist now." When Israel was endangered, differences with the Jewish state, such as those over the monopoly of the Orthodox rabbinate over personal-status matters or the exclusion of Reform and Conservative rabbis from official recognition, were relegated to second place.

After 1967, many Jews in the Soviet Union and elsewhere in the diaspora expressed a new interest in Israel, its language, and tradition; many began to study Hebrew and practice Jewish religious customs and observances. Thousands of Soviet Jews requested permission to emigrate to Israel. At first, the position of the Israeli government was ambiguous, but increasingly it urged support for Soviet Jewish dissidents, especially those who wanted to emigrate to Israel. Although a fundamental credo of Zionism holds that the Jewish state was established to provide a home for Jews such as those in Russia, the government of Israel was cautious about meddling in the internal affairs of the USSR. Rather than intervene directly on behalf of Soviet Jews, Israel helped to organize efforts in Western countries to assist them. In the United States, the National Conference on Soviet Jewry became an effective lobbying group that persuaded U.S. legislators to pressure the Soviet government to authorize Jewish emigration. Many of these efforts were taken in consultation with Israeli government officials, whose role was given little visibility.

In the early 1970s a small immigration wave arrived, mainly from Russia and Soviet Georgia. The group included several "refuseniks" who had been imprisoned by the KGB but who, with the help of U.S. intervention, had been freed to leave for Israel. With the collapse of the Soviet Union in 1990, a massive immigration brought hundreds of thousands of Russian Jews, making them the largest Jewish ethnic group in Israel.

Following the 1988 election, leaders of the religious parties pressured Prime Minister Yitzhak Shamir to sign an agreement promising to tighten religious legislation and to enact a change in the Law of Return that was favorable to Orthodox Jews in exchange for their participation in his coalition government. Delegations of U.S. Jewry immediately arrived in Israel to convince the newly elected prime minister to reject these demands because of their adverse impact on relations between Jewish communities in Israel and those in the diaspora. To prevent a major confrontation with the diaspora communities, Shamir had to back down on his promises to the religious parties and form a grand coalition with Labor. Thus, the status quo between the religious and secular parties continued as a result of external Jewish pressures, which demonstrated external influence on Israel's internal affairs.

Among diaspora leaders who had a substantial impact on Israeli politics, the most influential was the late Lubavicher Rabbi Menachem Schneerson, who ordered his Israeli followers—members of the Habad movement—to vote for the party of his choice. In 1988 Habad support gained at least three additional Knesset seats for Agudat Israel. The political impact of some individuals is dependent upon the kinds and amount of resources they can mobilize for their favorite Israeli politicians or parties. Some U.S. Jews have been important financiers of Zionist causes, from support for the late Meir Kahana's ultraright-wing Kach party to aid for more moderate Israeli politicians on both the left and the right. After being chosen the Likud leader in 1993, Benjamin Netanyahu mobilized enough funds from U.S. supporters to completely erase his party's multimillion-dollar debts caused by overspending during the 1992 electoral campaign. Likewise, rich Jews from France, Canada, and Morocco have given financial help to Israeli politicians of North African origin for their political activities.

Ethnic Groups

Until the end of the 1970s, ethnic interest groups in Israel were largely ineffective; attempts to organize themselves into separate parties had failed. Instead, major parties had co-opted influential ethnic leaders, and their supporters had followed them into the various political parties. An interesting example is the Black Panthers.

After 1970, when poverty among Israeli Jews of Afro-Asian origin (Sephardic Jews) became a salient national issue, a group of young men from Morocco and Iraq organized the Israeli Black Panthers as a protest movement that was seeking greater opportunity and fair treatment for Sephardim. During its first years, the group attracted attention to the plight of the Sephardi Jewish community, especially to the youth. Black Panther leaders who were invited to testify before parliamentary committees were written up in the press and received audiences with cabinet ministers, including Prime Minister Golda Meir.

As the Panthers evolved from a protest movement into an organized political group, they began to splinter into factions, divided more by personality differences and jealousies than by ideology. By 1977 the movement was no longer cohesive. During the 1977 election its former leadership scattered among three or four competing groups. Panther or former Panther leaders appeared on lists that included Hofesh (Freedom) and a new group called the Zionist Panthers. Rakah—the former New Communist List, now called the Democratic Front for Peace and Equality—gave its number-three "safe" position to a former Panther leader. Shelli gave its fourth-highest position to an ex-Panther.

A small group of Yemenites continued its unsuccessful attempt to create an ethnic pressure group. In every election until 1977, the group attempted to foster ethnic separatism with its own Knesset List. But the Yemenite List was able to win a single seat only in the First Knesset. Since then, it has failed to obtain even the one percent of votes required to win a seat in parliament.

The Sephardim, identified with the Ladino-speaking elite of the old Yishuv and with some Jews from the Balkans and Asia Minor, have maintained their own interest group since mandatory times. In the first Knesset election in 1949, they ran a separate Sephardic List, but it was absorbed into the General Zionist party, predecessor of the Liberals. The Sephardic Community Council in Jerusalem was active until 1977, thanks to the energy of a handful of individuals. Through its close association with the Sephardi chief rabbi, the council has maintained visibility and is still treated respectfully by political leaders, although it has lost most of its following to the major parties. During Israel's first thirty years, the council supported efforts to encourage Jewish immigration from Muslim countries; it also demanded compensation for Jewish property left in Arab countries and favored diplomatic relations with Spain. In the 1970s, when the social and economic conditions of Afro-Asian Jews became a major public issue, some Sephardi leaders supported the youthful Black Panthers. "We are all Panthers now," a senior council leader once exclaimed in a burst of enthusiasm.

There are other parties that are essentially ethnically based but are not labeled as such. Prime among them are the ultra-Orthodox parties. Degel Ha-Torah (Torah Flag) mobilizes many supporters from the Latvian community. Agudat Israel is a coalition of several Ashkenazi rabbis, each of whom heads an Orthodox group that has origins in different parts of Europe. Some secular parties' support is ethnic-based. The former Progressives (Independent Liberals) were a party of German and Romanian Jews. Mapam was originally largely Polish-based and later added a Bulgarian constituency. The two major parties, Labor and Likud, attempt to mobilize supporters from various ethnic sectors. New immigrants who arrive from a given country in large numbers immediately attract their interest. The Russian immigrants in the 1990s became a prime target because they had enough electoral weight to affect the political makeup of the established parties and to influence those parties' chances to obtain control over the government for many years.

Extra-Parliamentary Movements

The term *political movement* is often synonymous with a political party. Ratz began as a movement to protect citizens' rights, but its leaders decided to attain their objectives from within the parliamentary system. Likewise, Tami, Moledet, and others officially labeled political movements were actually political parties. Many other citizens' movements try to influence the parliamentary and governmental systems from outside the official political establishment.

It is customary to define the territorially oriented extra-parliamentary movements as hawks and those that advocate "land for peace" as doves. Hawks in general do not believe peaceful compromise with the Arab states, especially the Palestinians, can occur if the cost is territorial concessions. Doves hold the opposite position. They generally believe peace with the Arabs is a necessary condition for Israeli security, whereas hawks hold that a tough position on security—one based on territories—is a necessary condition for peace.

After 1967, the future of territories Israel seized from Egypt, Syria, and Jordan during the Six Day War became a focus of national debate and the basis for establishing several new groups—some affiliated with established political parties, others independent citizens' organizations. The spectrum of views ranged from those that called for the return of all lands acquired in 1967 to advocates of incorporation of all of the occupied areas into Israel. In the middle were those who supported the gradual return of occupied territory in exchange for peace on a step-by-step basis.

The Land of Israel, or Greater Israel, movement was formed shortly after the 1967 war and included prominent members of all Zionist parties, from Mapam to Herut. The movement opposed the return of any territory, stating that no Israeli government was "entitled to surrender any part of this territorial integrity, which represents the inherent and inalienable right of our people from the beginning of its history." According to the movement's spokespeople, the new boundaries would guarantee peace and security and "open up unprecedented vistas of national, material and spiritual consolidation."

The Greater Israel movement became an influential pressure group because it had a wide variety of prominent members, including many from the governing Labor establishment, the nationalist opposition, and the religious bloc. The movement's activities in arousing public opinion against the return of the Occupied Territories helped to prevent the Labor government from taking a clear-cut and unambiguous position on the issue. The movement lost political neutrality when its members joined the Likud bloc before the eighth Knesset election in 1973. By the 1977 Knesset election, the Greater Israel movement had been totally absorbed into Likud. Its original objectives were modified considerably after Likud came to power, especially following Egyptian President Anwar Sadat's visit to Jerusalem and the beginning of direct peace talks with Egypt.

In 1968 graduates and students of Mercaz Ha-Rav, a theological school (*yeshiva*) once headed by Rabbi Zvi Yehuda Kook, established Gush Emunim (Bloc of Faithful). Most members belonged to the National Religious party. Gush Emunim's objectives resembled those of the Greater Israel movement; however, its rationale was based not only on the strategic value of the occupied lands but also on "God's Divine promise" to the people of Israel. Its leaders represented a young, militantly nationalist group within the religious bloc who were opposed to the cautious outlook and policies of the older Orthodox leaders. Gush Emunim began as a religious revival movement seeking messianic redemption of the Jewish people through their ties with the Land of Israel. The leaders focused on Judea and Samaria (the West Bank) and gave little attention to Gaza, Sinai, or the Golan Heights. The territories taken from Egypt and Syria in 1967, although significant for strategic reasons, lacked the deep emotional and spiritual connotations associated with Judea and Samaria.

A major thrust of Gush Emunim was to establish Jewish settlements on the West Bank, frequently without government sanction. These settlements helped to revive a pioneering ethos among young people, and the movement quickly expanded beyond the National Religious party. Many of the new settlements included both Orthodox and secular settlers, working together and living side by side.

The movement created a serious dilemma for the Israeli government. Its unauthorized settlements, often in heavily populated Arab regions beyond areas approved by the Labor party, aroused fears and apprehension among the indigenous Arab population. Many officials believed these settlements would undermine peace negotiations. Indeed, one of Gush Emunim's objectives was to preempt Judea and Samaria and thus to prevent or make more difficult the return of the region to Arab control. The consensus of the Gush Emunim settlers was that areas in which they established their new homes would not be surrendered and would remain part of Eretz Israel. Gush Emunim was an effective pressure group that made it difficult for the government to formulate definitive policies about the future of the occupied West Bank.

After Menachem Begin became prime minister in 1977, his sympathy and support for Gush Emunim cooled considerably. When its leaders threatened to continue to build new settlements without the approval of the Likud government, a rift appeared imminent. Once in power, Herut and National Religious party leaders began to regard unauthorized actions by Gush Emunim as a threat to democracy and orderly government.

Several other hawkish organizations associated with the settlers also operated in the West Bank. Some tiny groups were close to the Kahana movement. Following government attempts to negotiate a peace treaty with Syria that began in Madrid at the end of 1991, a new hawkish group of Labor party activists—the Third Way—was formed. Its single objective was to prevent Israel from giving up the Golan Heights. The Third Way has often coordinated activities with Judea and Samaria settlers in opposition to government policies. Utilizing a well-designed media campaign in 1994, the Third Way was able to convince over 70 percent of the public that retreat from the Golan Heights would place Israel's security in jeopardy.

The influence of dovish interest groups has been less apparent. Their following has been much smaller and their allies in government have been less outspoken than those of the hawkish groups. Groups like the Movement for Peace and Security, established in 1968 to oppose Israel's annexation of the territories, and the Israel Council for Israeli-Palestinian Peace, which advocated recognition of and negotiations with the PLO, have included members from across the political spectrum—among them several former high-ranking army officers.

Many Israeli peace factions have been divided by personality differences and disagreements over tactics and strategy. These groups have supported one of the small peace parties, such as Moked or Shelli, in Knesset elections. But disputes over the acceptability of Communist support, recognition of the PLO, and the uniting of forces during elections have prevented any of the peace parties except Meretz from winning more than one or two Knesset seats.

The doves' effectiveness gradually improved with the establishment of the Peace Now movement in the 1970s. A notable achievement was the organization of 400,000 demonstrators in Tel Aviv in 1982 to protest the massacre of Palestinians in two refugee camps, Sabra and Shatilla, by the Lebanese Phalange militia, which had been allied with Israel during its 1982 invasion of Lebanon. After the demonstration, Peace Now continued to apply pressure on the political establishment, which led to the formation of an inquiry committee that later found Generals Sharon and Eitan accountable for the murders of innocent Palestinians because they failed to prevent the Lebanese militias, which were allied with Israel, from entering refugee camps in Beirut.

Peace Now continued its activities with relative success during the 1980s and early and mid-1990s, when some of its young leaders decided to become politically active. Labor and Ratz were the two beneficiaries. Two of the most notable leaders of the movement who became professional politicians were Avraham Burg, elected to the Knesset in 1992, who became chair of the Education Committee and, in 1995, chair of the Jewish Agency, and Dedi Zucker of Meretz, later chair of the Knesset Constitutional and Law Committee.

Because of their impact on the political system, the shaping of public policy toward the Arabs, and their importance as reflectors of the changing values within the Israeli polity, Gush Emunim and Peace Now are also discussed in Chapter 8.

Civic Organizations

There are many organizations in Israel whose interests are not related to a specific political orientation, camp, or party but that are very active politically. They include groups with an agenda directed toward the betterment of society as a whole and those that focus on specific issues. By the 1990s lobbying had become a permanent feature of the political landscape in the Knesset and the various ministries as attempts were made to convince MKs and policymakers to actively support the cause of concerned groups. Examples of generalist lobbying groups include those that seek to promote electoral reforms, clean government, a written constitution, protection of the environment and of nature, consumers' interests, preservation of history and tradition, health and the struggle against specific diseases (e.g., cancer), art and culture, and the like. Groups with more specialized interests include those that seek to abolish rent control; prevent privatization of a specific industry; develop a certain part of the country (e.g., the Negev); mobilize resources for a rabbinical or an educational institution; improve the welfare of invalids, veterans, or prisoners; generate resources for townships or departments in hospitals; and obtain funds for academic research or sports activities.

It is difficult to tell how many such groups operate in Israel because there are no official estimates. Such groups can easily be formed by taking the status of *Amuta* (Association). All that is needed are seven signatures on an official form approved by the registrar of nonprofit voluntary organizations. The law is supposed to regulate the scope, content, and mode of behavior of groups that are approved. Practically, there is no limit to the number of such groups a person may form or serve on as a board member.

6

How the Government Works

Israel's government institutions and constitutional system have developed within a structure established formally through parliamentary legislation and government regulations and informally through practices and procedures that have become constitutional law. The Declaration of Independence called for a constitution to be adopted by an elected Constituent Assembly, but fundamental ideological differences over the purposes and content of the constitution blocked its adoption. The Constituent Assembly became the First Knesset and deferred the task of drafting a formal document. Instead, at its first session in 1949, the Knesset passed the Transition Law—also called the "small constitution"—which provided the foundations for government and defined the powers of and relations among the president, parliament, and the cabinet. Periodically, the Transition Law was amended to adjust to the requirements of the system.

The task of drafting a formal constitution was given to the Knesset Constitution, Legislation, and Judicial Committee. The committee constructed a series of articles, each of which became a fundamental Basic Law. By the 1970s the Knesset had adopted four Basic Laws that pertained to the Knesset, Israeli lands, the president, and the government. By 1995 a few other Basic Laws had also been adopted.

The Transition Law and the Law of Return

The Law and Administration Ordinance, enacted by the Provisional Council of State on May 19, 1948, defined the composition and function of the council and the provisional government. The ordinance declared that local government would continue and that all laws in force in Palestine on May 14, 1948—the final day of the mandate—would also continue unless they conflicted with legislation enacted by the new provisional government. Courts were to operate under existing mandatory legislation.

During the few months of provisional government rule, mandatory legislation that conflicted with the Zionist goals and objectives of the new state, such as laws that limited Jewish immigration and land sales, was amended or abolished. Emergency legislation passed by the mandatory government to deal with civil unrest was maintained, however, and became the basis of the military government in Arab sections of the country.

Elections for the Constituent Assembly were held during January 1949, and the assembly convened in February. The first legislation passed was the Transition Law, which established the principal organs and offices of government and defined their powers, prerogatives, and duties. As in most constitutional systems, practice did not always conform with the provisions of the basic documents, and constitutional custom frequently deviated from the original document.

The Transition Law required that all acts of the legislature had to be signed by the prime minister, the minister(s) responsible for their implementation, and the president of the state. Acts were to be published in the *Official Gazette* within ten days after approval by the Knesset.

The Transition Law accepted the validity of some legal instruments used by the mandatory authorities, especially administrative regulation. According to the Israeli legal system, once a state of emergency was officially declared, the government, the prime minister, or any other minister could enact "emergency regulations" as they saw fit for the "welfare of state security, the safety of the public and the maintenance and supply of essential services." An emergency regulation could alter the conditions of or temporarily suspend any state law for at least three months and could also be used to raise taxes or other payments. From 1949 to the mid-1990s, the official state of emergency was not lifted; hence, this legal instrument was employed frequently by the government for various activities.

One legislative piece stands out: The Law of Return, adopted on July 5, 1950, granted every Jew the right to immigrate to Israel. There were only two formal restrictions: Jews who acted against the Jewish people, such as concentration camp capos, and those who might endanger public health or national security. When the Law of Return was adopted, the legislature did not consider the full implication of the term *every Jew,* and attention was not given to possible embarrassment that could result if Israel became a safe haven for Jewish criminals. Consequently, on August 23, 1954, the law was amended to include a paragraph that allowed denial of citizenship to Jews with "a criminal record who may endanger public peace." Meyer Lansky, the notorious Mafia associate, and several other U.S. and French Jews have been extradited to their former countries because of this provision in the Law of Return.

Questions have arisen about Jews who converted to another religion but nonetheless wanted to become Israeli citizens, children of Gentile mothers and Jewish fathers, and spouses who married Jews and wanted to join them in Israel. Disputes have also occurred over accepting people who were converted to Judaism by Reform rabbis or Jews from Ethiopia and India whose religious practices differed from those in Israel. These and many similar issues did not occur to the original designers of the law. According to Orthodox religious doctrine, only the offspring of Jewish mothers or people converted by an Orthodox rabbi are Jews; others are not.

Israel is not a theocracy, even though the act of granting citizenship is administered by religious bureaucrats employed in the Interior Ministry. A way had to be devised to bridge the differences between the Orthodox and secular definitions of a Jew. Israeli lawmakers usually move slowly on such sensitive matters, especially since they must rely on the religious parties to sustain their political power. Several Supreme Court decisions, however, forced Israeli policymakers to redefine the Law of Return on March 10, 1970. Accordingly, rights of citizenship could now be awarded to "a child or a grandchild of a Jew, to his or her spouse and to the spouse of a child and grandchild of a Jew, except for a person who was Jewish and willingly converted to another religion." The "Jew," according to this redefined law, need not be alive and was not required to have had any connection to Israel. Moreover, if he or she was born to a Jewish mother or had been converted to Judaism by any rabbi and was not a member of another religion, then he or she was legally Jewish. To obtain citizenship, non-Jews who did not qualify according to Jewish religious law (*halacha*) could be naturalized.

Knesset Supremacy

Although the prime minister and the cabinet dominate the political system in Israel, their authority is more circumscribed than that of a British cabinet or a U.S. presidential administration. Unlike the British system, which was a model for Israel, the prime minister, the president, or any other authority cannot dissolve the parliament. Only the Knesset can dissolve itself—even if the government falls—and only the Knesset can set a date for new elections. Until the Basic Law of 1958 was passed, there was no fixed term or tenure for the Knesset; each session determined its own longevity. Since 1958 a Knesset term has been fixed by the Basic Law at four years, unless the Knesset itself decides to advance elections to an earlier date.

Unlike the U.S. system, no one can veto legislation passed by the Knesset; all of its laws are supreme. The Knesset, a single-chamber parliament, is the supreme authority in Israel. Its legislation cannot be altered by the executive or the judiciary, and its laws cannot be declared unconstitutional by any authority. Like the British Parliament, it can pass any law it desires. In reality, however, the Knesset—like the British Parliament—is controlled by whatever government is in power. That government, in turn, is dominated by a prime minister, as long as he or she can command a majority of votes in the Knesset.

The name Knesset (assembly) was taken from the ancient 70-member Jewish Knesset ha-Gedola (Great Assembly) of the early Second Temple era. The modern Knesset was increased to 120 members to provide for broader representation. The First Knesset opened in Jerusalem in 1949, but because of the divided city's insecure location bordering Jordanian Jerusalem, the Knesset met in a Tel Aviv cinema building. When the government moved to Jerusalem in 1949, the Knesset was accommodated in a converted bank until 1966 when a new parliament building was constructed in Jerusalem, which had become Israel's official capital.

Knesset candidates must be Israeli citizens who are at least twenty-one years old. Active civil servants above a certain grade, anyone who has been a permanent officer in the defense forces within a hundred days of the election, the president of the state, the Ashkenazi and Sephardi chief rabbis, judges in the civil and religious courts, the state comptroller, and rabbis and priests who receive government remuneration for their services are disqualified as Knesset candidates.

Knesset members are not chosen individually but are selected from lists compiled by leaders of the diverse political parties and in primary elections. They do not represent specific geographic constituencies or districts; representation exists on a national basis. All Israelis who participate in national elections vote for one of several lists of candidates.

After being sworn in, the members of a newly elected Knesset choose a speaker and his or her deputies, who represent the main parties and constitute the Knesset presidium. The speaker is usually a respected and uncontroversial member of the party that leads the coalition. In 1972, in an effort to broaden ethnic representation, Israel Yeshayahu of the Labor party became the first Sephardi Jew to be selected speaker. An Arab from one of the Labor-affiliated minority parties was chosen deputy speaker with the same intent.

Sometimes the smaller the party, the greater the individual Knesset member's influence. If a party has only one or two representatives in the Knesset, they may carry more weight as individuals than do members of parties with many Knesset representatives. In larger parties, a Knesset member's influence depends on his or her position in the party. By virtue of their freedom of speech, individual members of small parties are often better known nationally than lower-ranking Knesset members in the large parties.

The Knesset's major function is to pass legislation that becomes Israeli law. Most legislation is originated by the government and is presented by the cabinet to parliament for discussion and approval. Members of the government, who are usually also Knesset members, lead legislation through the parliamentary process, explaining and defending it. Occasionally, individual Knesset members introduce private bills, although these bills rarely pass the required gauntlet of committees and other formal procedures.

Few MKs who belong to the government parties attack legislation introduced by the cabinet. Until 1992, government and party leaders could take reprisals against dissidents by removing them from the party list before the next election. Even when selection of the list was moved from the small arrangement committee of party leaders to the party convention, the leaders could still influence the members' decision in favor of a loyal MK and against a dissident. In 1988, for example, Abba Eban, a renowned former foreign minister, was abandoned by his senior Labor colleagues when the party's convention elected the Knesset List. Eban was penalized because as chair of the Knesset Foreign Affairs and Security Committee (1984–1988), he had produced a report concerning the Pollard affair that was embarrassing to the party leader, Shimon Peres. (The Pollard case dealt with the activities of Israeli agents who had recruited a U.S. Defense Department employee to spy for Israel.) After the introduction of primary elections in 1992, MKs no longer needed to fear senior leaders; hence, party discipline was considerably weakened, and some individuals did not hesitate to dissent when their own government proposed new legislation.

Until the 1970s, the Knesset passed an average of seventy to a hundred laws a year. A large part of its work had been to update and modify, in effect to "Israelize," legislation from the mandatory and Ottoman eras that was in force when the state was established. During the nearly three decades of the mandate, much Ottoman legislation remained on the books. Until the 1970s, much Israeli law, such as that pertaining to landholding and ownership, came from Ottoman legislation that was derived from a variety of sources: traditional Islamic law based on the Koran and Sharia, French law adapted by the Ottoman Empire during the nineteenth century, and personal-status law drawn from various non-Muslim countries. Mandatory law was based on acts of Parliament and on English common law.

During the first two years of the Thirteenth Knesset, elected in 1992, the number of proposals for private bills increased manyfold compared to the first two years of the Twelfth Knesset. One member proposed a tax reduction for suntan lotion, another asked for a legal ban on the use of cellular telephones in public restaurants, a third proposed that one-third of the spaces in public parking lots be reserved for women, two others demanded that women should obtain twice as many seats as men in new public toilets, and others proposed to ban anti-Semitic books and tree climbing. The introduction of thousands of proposals to legislate many minor aspects of life is a result of the primary election method adopted by Labor in 1992 and by the Likud in 1993. MKs who want to be reelected must show that they have been productive or at least get necessary media exposure. Whereas some of these proposals address real needs, others are simply gimmicks that help MKs gain public exposure through the printed and electronic media. Knesset members can modify, amend, improve, and discuss government legislation and bring it to the public's attention.

The legislative process is long and complicated, as is the case in most parliamentary democracies. Formal disposition of a bill introduced by the government follows this path: (1) The bill is introduced by the responsible cabinet minister who puts it on the table, where it stays for at least forty-eight hours before being debated; (2) at the first reading, the responsible minister introduces the bill with an explanatory speech, after which debate is opened by an opposition member (the length of debate is fixed by the Knesset committee); (3) the bill is voted on and either "returned to the government"—that is, defeated—or "sent to committee," meaning it has passed the first reading; (4) in committee, the bill is discussed in detail, and amendments are proposed for adoption or rejection; (5) the bill is returned to a plenary session for a second reading by the responsible committee chair or his or her deputy, with amendments adopted in committee, and members whose amendments were defeated in committee may reintroduce them with a short speech; (6) the bill, with all approved amendments, is voted on by the Knesset in a third reading. If approved and signed by the prime minister, the responsible minister, and the president, the bill becomes law and is published in the *Official Gazette*.

Most Knesset legislative work occurs in the organization's nine permanent committees. Each committee is like a small parliament of nineteen MKs appointed in approximately the same ratio as that of parties in the Knesset. The committees are constructed around legislative issues; they include (1) the Knesset, or Procedure; (2) Constitution, Law, and Justice; (3) Finance; (4) Economic Affairs; (5) Foreign Affairs and Security; (6) Education and Culture; (7) Labor; (8) Internal Affairs; and (9) Public Services.

In the minute examination of bills, Knesset committees can conduct inquiries and summon for questioning senior civil servants, ambassadors, army officers, and ministers (with government permission). In addition to their legislative duties, the committees monitor the operations of the government and conduct administrative inquiries. Membership in some committees is more prestigious than in others, and preference is given to certain parties. For example, Arab and Communist MKs are traditionally excluded from the Foreign Affairs and Security Committee.

Plenary sessions of the Knesset are held three days a week, leaving three days for committee meetings, which occupy the largest amount of time. Plenary sessions are not held on Fridays, Saturdays, or Sundays because these are the Sabbath days of Muslim, Jewish, and Christian members, respectively.

During their work, MKs gain public visibility by asking questions and making speeches, and they take initiatives through several parliamentary devices. Any member may submit a question to a minister, who is obliged to reply in the Knesset within twenty-one days. The MK who asked the question may ask one supplementary question after the minister's reply to the original inquiry. In a ten-minute speech, a member can propose a motion requesting debate on any subject the government has not placed on the agenda. The concerned minister replies, following which a motion can be offered to refer the matter to committee for consideration and a report, or a motion can be made for further debate.

Members can submit motions requesting permission to introduce a bill on any subject. After introduction a minister replies, and the Knesset then votes on whether to reject the bill or send it to committee for further consideration. Before introducing a bill, a Knesset member usually obtains approval of his or her party. One session a week is reserved for introductions of private members' motions and bills. These sessions give smaller parties the opportunity to raise controversial issues or ask embarrassing questions; they also deal with matters the government is likely to avoid in its day-to-day business, such as treatment of the Arab minority, civil rights, or misuse of authority by an official.

Rights of MKs who represent minority, opposition, or dissident views are protected by a law passed in the First Knesset in 1951. This law protects all MKs from prosecution for any vote cast, opinion expressed, or act in or out of the Knesset in fulfillment of their duties as members of parliament. This immunity continues even after a member has left the Knesset. Members are immune from search of their property and persons; their mail cannot be opened or confiscated; and MKs cannot be arrested unless they are caught in the act of committing a crime that involves the use of force, treason, or disturbance of the peace. In these cases, arresting authorities must notify the speaker of the Knesset about the arrest within ten days. No Knesset member can be brought to trial for any offense committed while a member or before he or she became a member unless the Knesset itself withdraws this immunity. Members are not required to obtain permits to travel abroad, except during wartime, and they receive special service passports.

These immunities and privileges can be withdrawn only by a majority Knesset vote after the member has been given the opportunity to state his or her case. During the early days of the state, these privileges were especially helpful to Communist members because they exempted those members from the restrictions and interference by security authorities to which other Communists were subjected.

Other fringe benefits Knesset members receive include free public transportation, a home telephone installed free of charge, free calls and priority in long-distance calls, franking mail privileges from the Knesset building, and free receipt of all government publications. Knesset privileges and immunities add to the prestige of being an MK and guarantee an open forum for debate in which members will not be penalized for exercising their right to criticize the government. Until 1991, when MKs broke with their party to form a new faction or parliamentary group, they could not be removed until the next election, although they were likely to be removed from their party's electoral list. Several new parties or factions were formed by MKs who broke with party discipline. A few such independents became influential enough to run their own separate list, thereby becoming a new political party with a new and distinctive identity.

Since 1991 an individual MK has been forbidden to leave his or her party, join another party, and then be included in that party's list for the next election. Two such "switchers" were elected to the Knesset in 1992 because they had joined another party before this legal provision was adopted. One, Yossi Sarid, left Labor in 1984 to join Ratz. In 1993 he became minister of environment. Another MK, Efraim Gur, was elected on the Labor list in 1988. In 1990 he joined Likud and became deputy minister of housing. Public disapproval of Gur's move led the Knesset to pass the "switching" ban.

The Legal System

The Knesset passes regular laws and basic laws. Only a simple majority of participating MKs is required to pass or defeat a regular law. Even if only three MKs participate in a session, a majority of two is sufficient to pass a law. Such a majority could pass a law prohibiting people with one leg from taking part in an election. That law would be legal, and no other state institution could nullify it.

Basic laws can be passed or amended only by an absolute majority of at least sixty-one MKs; thus, the laws acquire constitutional status. It is assumed that once a set of basic laws has been passed, it will serve as a "chapter" in a future constitution. When all of these chapters have been adopted by the Knesset, they will be assembled in one volume and will become Israel's constitution. In addition to the Basic Law: Knesset, Basic Law: Government, Basic Law: The President of Israel, and Basic Law: Judgements, which are referred to throughout this chapter, several others provided a partial constitutional framework for the Israeli polity by 1995. They are described in the remainder of this section.

Basic Law: Lands of Israel

This law, adopted in July 1960, provides that ownership of state lands may not be sold or transferred to nonstate owners. Since only about 5 percent of the land in Israel is private property, the scope of this law is comprehensive. Furthermore, the law defines lands as including "houses, buildings, and everything that is permanently connected to the land."

Basic Law: State Economy

This law, adopted in July 1970, is similar to other systems of laws that concern public finances in Western democracies and provides the legal framework for taxation and public expenditures through the national budget. Taxation cannot be arbitrary, and the budget must be approved as law by the parliament. Of special interest is the statement that the Ministry of Defense budget should not, as required for all other parts of the national budget, be shown to the Knesset but only to "a joint committee [made up of members] of the Finance and the Foreign Affairs and Security Knesset Committees." Thus Arabs, Communists, and others who are not members of these two committees are considered security risks and are prevented from viewing the security budget.

Within any approved budgetary year, the government can present proposals requesting additional spending or taxation; it can also request an intermediate budget to provide for security or other unexpected crises. The government is not legally restricted by an original annual spending plan. In January and April 1992, the Basic Law: State Economy was amended twice. First, in addition to a detailed annual plan, the government was required to propose a multiyear budget. Implementation of this requirement was scheduled for 1996. In case of Knesset disapproval of subsequent budget proposals, the second amendment enabled the government to operate without Knesset permission on the basis of the previous year's budget, although it cannot spend more than one-twelfth of the previous budget per month. This provision assured that the government could pay its national and international debts and sustain vital services. The Knesset would supervise these activities through the state comptroller.

Basic Law: The Army

This law was adopted in 1976 and specifies the relationship between the army and the state. The IDF is the only armed force permitted by the state, and it is subordinate to the government. The IDF's direct supervisor is the minister of defense who, with government approval, nominates the IDF's head, the chief of staff.

Basic Law: Jerusalem

This law was adopted in 1980. The law has a high degree of symbolic value and international significance (few countries recognize Jerusalem as the capital of Israel; nearly all countries place their embassies in Tel Aviv with consular services in Jerusalem). This law states: "The united and complete [including West and East, formerly Jordanian] Jerusalem is the Capital of Israel." Accordingly, the president, prime minister, Knesset, and most government ministries are located in Jerusalem.

Basic Law: State Comptroller

This law, adopted in 1988, provides the legal framework for the activities of the state comptroller, who supervises the activities of the government and reports directly to the Knesset. In Israel, unlike other countries, the state comptroller also serves as an ombudsman in charge of handling complaints against the government and other public institutions. The state comptroller cannot be removed from his or her post unless two-thirds of the MKs approve, which provides protection against political retaliation.

Basic Law: Individual Freedom and Dignity

This law was adopted in March 1992 to "protect personal freedom and dignity." The legislation seeks to "anchor in a basic law the values of the State of Israel as a Jewish and democratic state." The fundamental normative contradiction that exists between the Jewish state and democratic doctrine is not resolved by this law; rather, the law deals with the preservation and protection of life, body, personal dignity, private property, individual freedom, and the right to privacy. Israeli minorities (Arab citizens, other non-Jewish citizens, women, and similar groups) can seek redress from racial, sexual, and other discrimination under the auspices of this law.

However, the law explicitly imposes several limitations on individual freedoms. The law does not apply to employees of the state security forces (i.e., the IDF, the police, prison services, and other security organizations). Presumably, when a person becomes a part of the security system, he or she surrenders individual freedoms and must follow orders.

From a liberal perspective the most disturbing feature of this law is the statement "nothing in this basic law should violate the validity of *din* [religious law] that existed prior to the beginning of this basic law." In some respects, this law creates more restrictions than existed before it was adopted. Prior to 1992, the relationship between secular laws and *dins* was often vague enough to permit the Supreme Court to provide liberal interpretations in certain cases. With the institution of this Basic Law, such freedom of interpretation became more restricted.

There are additional qualifications. The law explicitly states that emergency regulations cannot alter this law in any way or form "unless" a state of emergency is declared. In such a case, emergency regulations may be applied "negating or limiting" any individual right. Therefore, any of the rights of this Basic Law can be violated at any time.

Basic Law: Freedom of Occupation

This law, also adopted in March 1992, permits Israelis to work in any occupation they wish as long as no legal restriction is imposed on their choice. These restrictions can involve issues of security, public safety, public order and health, the environment, and the protection of public morals. Emergency regulations cannot affect the law's validity.

In 1994 religious parties in the Knesset, which were part of the government coalition, demanded a change in this law to prohibit occupations involved in the importation of nonkosher food. To appease the Orthodox contingent, the Knesset approved an amendment that effectively banned the importation of all nonkosher meat to Israel.

The validity and stability of the Israeli system of Basic Laws differ from the U.S. constitution, which is very difficult to amend. In Israel, no special majority protects these Basic Laws; their continuity is assured only by absolute majorities of at least sixty-one MKs. Thus, the government can decide whether a Basic Law should be changed.

The Supreme Court

The Israeli court system is similar to the British. Israel has four levels of courts. The highest is the Supreme Court, which serves as a court of appeal and as the High Court of Justice (HCJ). The second level includes district courts, and the third is made up of the justice of the peace courts for minor offenses. The fourth level includes religious, labor, family, and other special court systems. The law that guides the judicial system is Basic Law: Judgements, adopted in 1984, which is immune from emergency regulations. This law specifies that the president of Israel will appoint judges upon the recommendation of a Committee for the Selection of Judges that consists of nine members including the president of the Supreme Court and two other Supreme Court judges, two MKs, two lawyers chosen by the National Bar Association, a cabinet minister, and the minister of justice, who serves as chairperson.

The HCJ, which is located in Jerusalem, deals with all issues that are not addressed in any other legal jurisdiction. The HCJ may intervene in all kinds of state decisions at all levels; it can order officials to take an action or to stop acting, free people who were unlawfully arrested, order lower-level courts to change their decisions, and order religious courts to cancel decisions they were not authorized to make. Furthermore, when a contradiction occurs between existing laws, the Supreme Court can ask the lawmakers to find the proper legal bridge. In establishing legal precedents, the HCJ functions as a lawmaker parallel to the Knesset.

According to a study conducted by the International Social Science Program in 1991 that investigated the level of citizen trust in fifteen countries regarding the rule of law and their court systems, Israel ranked number one, ahead of the U.S., British, and Italian systems. Almost 70 percent of Israelis expressed high levels of trust in their legal system. Although the Supreme Court is the flagship of the Israeli judicial system, it was not the most popular institution in the country. The court ranked third among the leading Israeli institutions, with the IDF in first place and the State Comptroller in second. (See Table 6.1.)

The prestige of the State Comptroller was a function of the personality of its head, former Supreme Court Judge Miriam Ben Porath, and the highly visible media campaign she conducted against bureaucratic inefficiency and corruption since her appointment in 1989. Few people, however, could identify the names of Supreme Court judges. The study on which Table 6.1 is based asked people to identify the names of three Supreme Court Judges from a list of seven people. Meir Shamgar, president of the court, was recognized by only 28 percent of respondents; his highly respected deputy, Aaron Barak, was identified by only about 25 percent. The high trust and respect judges receive from the public is not a function of their personalities but is rather a blind trust in the impartiality of the institution and its goal of justice for all. The method by which judges are selected is almost a complete mystery to the public.

Access to the HCJ is rather easy to obtain. In his 1983 book, *Paths of Government,* Zeev Segal calls the HCJ "the Fortress of the Citizen" and the "daily and living voice of the Israeli democracy." The HCJ intervenes on be-

TABLE 6.1   Degree of National Legitimacy of Leading Israeli Institutions

Institution	Ranking	Positive Contribution (%)	Positive and Negative (%)	Negative Contribution (%)
Israeli Defense Force	1	94.9	4.0	1.1
State Comptroller	2	91.1	7.0	1.9
Supreme Court	3	83.6	10.2	2.1
Police	4	75.2	19.9	4.8
Knesset	5	57.7	32.8	9.6
Government	6	51.6	35.8	12.6
Media	7	37.3	40.7	22.0
Parties	8	25.1	25.9	29.0

Source: Gad Barzilai, Ephraim Yuchtman-Yaar, and Zeev Segal, *The Israeli Supreme Court and the Israeli Public* (Tel Aviv: Papyrus, 1994), p. 69.

half of Jewish and Arab citizens, as well as Palestinians in the Occupied Territories, against government decisions. In cases for which there are no laws or a wide and liberal interpretation of existing law is permitted, the Supreme Court does not hesitate to assume the role of lawmaker. Since the early 1980s, the court has been an active and major reformer. A sample of decisions taken during the late 1980s and early 1990 illustrates the HCJ's scope and character.

- It is a soldier's absolute obligation to serve in the Occupied Territories even if he or she conscientiously objects to doing so.
- The Kahana "Kach" list should be banned from the 1988 election because it is racist.
- The Progressive List for Peace should qualify for the 1988 election because it did not violate any state law.
- The security authorities' decision to release Palestinian terrorists should be upheld.
- Government orders that violate basic principles of democracy should be invalidated.
- It is unlawful to deny women the right to serve on the boards of rabbinical councils.
- Reform conversions to Judaism made abroad should be accepted as valid.
- The Ministry of Defense decision to release Yeshiva students from army service should be approved.
- The government decision to expel terrorists from Israel without a court hearing should be upheld.
- The government decision to destroy or seal with cement the homes of terrorists' families is legal.
- Gas masks should be provided for Palestinians in the Occupied Territories during the Gulf War.
- The prime minister must discharge a minister and a deputy minister—members of Shas—who were accused of conducting unlawful acts.

These and many other decisions were not always welcomed by the Israeli public. Yet because of the wide respect for the court, even those opposed to particular decisions upheld its status as the principal protector of the citizens against the arbitrariness of government.

The Presidency

The president of Israel is elected by the Knesset for a five-year term and may be reelected for one additional successive term. He or she signs all laws except those that concern presidential powers. In forming new governments before 1996, the president consulted with leaders of the various parties, then called on a member of the Knesset to head a new regime. He or she accepts the accreditation of foreign ambassadors and ministers; appoints Israel's ambassadors, ministers, judges, and state comptroller; and has the right to pardon or commute prison sentences.

The Basic Law: The President of the State, adopted in 1964, provides the legal framework for this post. The president is legally Israel's highest-ranking official. Drafters of the Transition Law tried to find a compromise between efforts to place an internationally recognized Zionist at the head of the new state and the realities of political power. In practice, the role was soon seen as symbolic, with the presidency becoming an honorary position rather than one vested with political power. Since 1949 the post has been given to individuals of stature who have served the nation in an unusual capacity and have remained above political controversy. The most important political function of the president—designating the head of government, or prime minister, when a new cabinet was formed—was so circumscribed by constitutional convention that it became a symbolic act, resembling the appointment of a prime minister by the British monarch.

Personality differences between David Ben-Gurion, the state's first prime minister, and Chaim Weizmann, the first president, helped to shape these developments. When the state was formed, the presidential role could have developed in one of four ways. Under initial legislation the president could have shared broad executive powers with the cabinet; he might have been elected, like the U.S. president; he might have assumed supreme power, like the president of France, with a prime minister who served him; or, as actually happened, he could have been a symbol of national sovereignty with ceremonial functions only.

Ben-Gurion, already the head of the strongest political party in the Yishuv, automatically became head of the provisional government. As leader of the Mapai party, he headed the most influential group in the National Council and was also a leading figure in the world Zionist movement; consequently, he was the logical choice to head the new government. His job began even before the state had been established.

The office of president was not set up until the provisional government was formed, and Weizmann was chosen to fill the post. Weizmann was abroad, and Ben-Gurion quickly assumed actual power. When Weizmann arrived to take up his duties, relations between the president and prime minister had already been established. Weizmann, who was ill and aging, was unable to assume a vigorous role in day-to-day affairs. In contrast to Ben-Gurion, who dominated the political apparatus of Mapai and the Histadrut, Weizmann had no strong political base in Israel. His strength was in the World Zionist Organization, which he had headed for many years, and its non-Israeli leaders had little influence in the new state.

As a figurehead removed from the politics of the day who spent much of his time in various ceremonial activities, Weizmann complained that the only real place he could stick his nose was his handkerchief. Indeed, Israeli presidents have largely been apolitical, attempting to represent all walks of society as much as possible. Often, when a president has taken an explicit political stand in favor of an issue, the political system has quickly reminded him of his legal boundaries. Albert Einstein rejected Ben-Gurion's offer to become Israel's president; hence, Weizmann's successors have also been chosen for their past contributions to the development of the Zionist movement or contributions to the state. Six presidents have followed Weizmann, all associated in some way with Mapai and the Labor establishment.

Weizmann's immediate successor in 1953, Izhak Ben-Zvi—a Zionist leader of lesser stature—was restricted by illness, as Weizmann had been. Ben-Zvi attempted to make the presidency a center for scholarly discussion of subjects that interested him, including religion and Israel's minority communities. The third president, Zalman Shazar (1963–1973), also a scholar, formalized these discussions, founding the Bible Study Circle and the Circle for the Study of the Diaspora. Ephraim Katzir, the fourth president, who assumed office in 1973, headed scientific research projects at the Weizmann Institute of Science and in the Israeli Defense Force. Younger than his predecessors, more vigorous in health, and more assertive in his political views, Katzir created speculation that the presidency might become a more active post. Events in Israel overshadowed any such aspirations, however, and by the end of his term in 1978 Katzir was ready to return to his academic pursuits. He was succeeded in 1978, after one term, by Yitzhak Navon, Israel's first native-born (*sabra*) president and the first Sephardi Jew to attain the position.

Navon's election by the Knesset to the country's highest post, even though largely honorific, was regarded as a prestigious achievement by the Sephardic community. The honor was even greater since Navon, a former Labor party MK and aide to Ben-Gurion, ran unopposed and was chosen during the reign of a Likud government when Navon's own Labor party was in the opposition. When Navon retired in 1984, Labor party officials believed he still had great potential. They calculated that if Navon headed the Labor party list, he could attract many of the Likud Sephardim and thus win the election. But Peres outmaneuvered Navon, and he was placed third on the party list. Navon later obtained the post of minister of education in the Unity government.

Navon's successor, Haim Herzog, was Irish-born, a former general, a former ambassador to the United Nations, and a former Labor MK. He was also the son of a former chief rabbi. Herzog, like Navon, was, chosen by the Knesset even though it was dominated by Likud and its coalition supporters.

One of the best-known and most controversial presidents is the seventh, Ezer Weizman, Chaim's nephew, elected by the Knesset in 1993. A former general who built up the Israel air force, Weizman was the person most responsible for Labor's defeat in 1977, when he managed Likud's election campaign. Prime Minister Begin appointed Weizman minister of defense in 1977 (he had served as minister of transportation between 1969 and 1971), and together with his brother-in-law, Foreign Minister Moshe Dayan, he convinced Begin to risk signing a peace treaty with Egypt. In 1980 Weizman and Dayan resigned from Begin's cabinet because of disagreement over Likud's foreign policies. Weizman, a former hawk turned dove, left Likud to form the Ya'ad party. Following the 1984 election, Weizman and Ya'ad joined Labor. Of the seven presidents who have served in this post, Weizman seems to be the most "political"; he often remarks on government's policies and decisions.

The Prime Minister and the Cabinet

The powers of the prime minister are not defined by law, and his or her relationships with other cabinet ministers are only loosely described in the Basic Law, which establishes the prime minister as "head of the government." Actual power depends on the prime minister's conduct in office and the strength of his or her personality.

Until 1996, when a prime minister resigned because of dissatisfaction with the government or because the government failed to receive a vote of confidence in parliament, the president called on another Knesset member to form a new government. The president could go through the formality of consulting several Knesset members from various parties, but the person finally selected was usually the leader of the party with the largest number of Knesset seats. A prime minister was chosen after every parliamentary election and between elections when a prime minister resigned. After 1996, the prime minister was to be replaced by a new election.

Until 1966, when a prime minister resigned because his or her government failed to receive a majority vote in parliament, the president asked the prime minister to form an interim government until the results of the next election determined who would form the new government. This interim, or caretaker, government could serve for several months. The precedent for this was established in 1951, when Ben-Gurion's government received a no-confidence vote on an education issue. The religious bloc members of the coalition refused to support government legislation that allowed immigrant parents free choice in the selection of schools. These members insisted that all children of religious immigrants had to be sent to religious schools. Failing to receive Knesset support for his government-proposed legislation, Ben-Gurion resigned, but he continued as prime minister for eight months until the next election. During this interval the religious bloc left the cabinet, and Mapai governed without a parliamentary majority.

The cabinet has both policymaking and administrative functions. Cabinet members supposedly serve with, rather than under, the prime minister in making crucial decisions. As heads of their respective ministries, they are responsible for implementing government policy. Neither the composition nor the powers of cabinet ministers are strictly defined in the Transition Law or in the 1968 Basic Law that lays out the structure of the government. Until 1996 there was no fixed number of cabinet posts; the number depended on coalition requirements. In 1949 there were twelve posts; this number increased to twenty-four in 1969 and decreased again later. A 1991 amendment allowed the prime minister to discharge cabinet members. Before 1991 they left only of their own accord or if the prime minister resigned, in which case the entire cabinet had to resign and the government fell. Under the 1992 amendment to the Basic Law: Government, the cabinet must have at least eight and no more than eighteen ministers, including the prime minister.

Ministries are divided among parties of the government coalition in proportion to their influence. Frequently, ministers without portfolio are named if more cabinet appointments are required than there are ministries. In smaller coalitions, cabinet members can hold more than one ministry. Although traditionally cabinet members have belonged to the Knesset, the prime minister, at least half of the ministers, and deputy ministers are required to be members. Between 1965 and 1970, six of eighteen cabinet members were not Knesset members. In 1992 only one minister was not a Knesset member.

Cabinet posts are usually political appointments given to leaders of Knesset factions that are represented in the government. Certain ministries— such as foreign affairs, finance, and defense—are always assigned to knowledgeable and experienced individuals. Because of their dominant position in all government coalitions until 1977, the Labor party and, before it was formed, Mapai always held the prime ministry, defense, foreign affairs, and finance portfolios. Certain other ministries are customarily assigned to specific parties if and when they join the coalition. Thus, the Ministry of Justice has often been assigned to the Independent Liberals, and the Ministry of Social Welfare has gone to the religious bloc.

Between the first cabinet in 1949 and the 1977 elections, there were eighteen governments. Until 1973, many of the same faces appeared in every cabinet because all governments were led by the Labor party or Mapai; the National Religious party also served in most of these cabinets.

Government coalitions have been based on elaborate and detailed agreements that set out the principal lines of government policy, major items for legislative and administrative action, and the division of cabinet posts. Parties in the coalition designate which of their leaders will participate in the government, and the leaders receive posts on the basis of the agreement among coalition members. Cabinet members must be confirmed by the Knesset.

The cabinet usually meets once a week to discuss major policy issues, new legislation, and other government affairs. Decisions, supposedly secret, are taken by majority vote and are covered by collective responsibility; all members of the cabinet must support them in parliament. The day-to-day business of government is managed by the ministries or by committees of relevant cabinet members. There are many cabinet committees that deal with a variety of issues, from security and foreign policy to agriculture and social welfare. The government secretariat, which is within the prime ministry, provides clerical services to cabinet committees; it also prepares agenda, takes minutes, circulates decisions, and informs the press of cabinet actions. Despite the secrecy rule, discussions in cabinet meetings and in committees have frequently been leaked to the press. At one time the government considered introducing legislation that would have made leaking information a criminal offense.

Collective responsibility requires that all members of the cabinet and the parties they represent support the government in parliament or resign from the government. The fall of the Labor government in 1976 was precipitated when two of the three National Religious party members refused to support the government against a motion of censure introduced by the Agudat Israel party. The motion charged that the Sabbath had been desecrated when an official ceremony was held on a Friday afternoon to celebrate the arrival of fighter planes from the United States. Prime Minister Rabin demanded resignations from the ministers who abstained on the censure vote. The resignations of the National Religious party members left the government with a minority in the Knesset, although Labor continued to govern until its defeat in the May 1977 elections.

The 1968 Basic Law has been amended several times over the years. Some of these amendments were introduced after the March 1990 coalition crisis, when both Likud and Labor attempted to form a minimum winning coalition by convincing MKs from rival parties to join forces with them in exchange for government positions. Switching sides in this manner was prohibited for individual MKs, and so was the practice of demanding a money guarantee to assure that a political deal made between parties was consumated. Furthermore, no written deal stating a promise of payoff—in-kind or otherwise—made by one party with another in the context of coalition formation or a non-confidence vote was permitted after 1991.

Another amendment specifies how the government operates in the area of permanent, temporary, and ad hoc committees. One permanent committee for national security consists of the prime minister, the minister of defense, the treasury minister, the deputy prime minister (if there is one), and—upon request of the prime minister—other ministers. The amendment also includes an instruction to form a national security team, similar to the U.S. National Security Council, to advise the prime minister. Yitzhak Rabin felt he did not need such advice, and in 1994 he moved to dissolve the security team.

The most comprehensive amendment to the 1968 Basic Law: The Government was its replacement with a revised law adopted in 1992. Under this new law the prime minister is elected directly by the voters rather than by the Knesset. Regardless of the selection method and the source of legitimization for the prime minister, Knesset approval is still required to pass laws, so the prime minister will still need a majority of MKs to support his or her cabinet policies. Because no single party has ever obtained a Knesset majority, it is likely that future Israeli prime ministers will still be required to govern on the basis of coalitions formed by several parties.

Coalition Governments in Israel

Since the formation of the first government in 1949, the prime minister has had to rely on a coalition of parties that together constituted a majority of sixty-one MKs or that at least was able to block the formation of a potential majority of MKs from the opposition.

In May 1967, when Egyptian President Nasser blocked the Straits of Aqaba, expelled the UN peacekeeping forces from Sinai, and replaced those forces with his own army, Israel's security seemed to many to be seriously threatened. Following public and parliamentary pressures, Prime Minister Levi Eshkol was convinced to broaden his coalition and include opposition politicians from Rafi and Gahal. Moshe Dayan of Rafi became the minister of defense, and Menachem Begin of Gahal was appointed minister without portfolio. Both men were instrumental in the government's decision to undertake a preemptive strike against the Arab armies. This was Israel's first grand, or wall-to-wall, coalition that included all of the major parties in the government.

After a reduction in the level of the threat, the size of the coalition could be reduced. However, this happened only gradually: As shown in Table 6.2, the size of the coalition was reduced from 106 members to 104 and then to 102. After the 1969 election the government continued the coalition's extended size—especially during the war of attrition with Egypt—but soon thereafter politics returned to normal, and as shown in Table 6.3, a typical "oversized" coalition (a coalition with many more members than necessary to obtain a majority in the Knesset) was formed.

The grand coalition formed in 1984 was initiated by a combination of real and perceived problems, including the expense caused by IDF involvement in Lebanon, hyperinflation, a deteriorating balance of payments, and

TABLE 6.2 Grand Israeli Coalitions by Size[a] and Year of Formation

Size[a]	Year of Formation	Size[a] of Principal Party	Size[a] of Other Participants
106	1967	Alignment (44)	Gahal (26), NRP (11), Rafi (10), Mapam (8), IL (5), PAI (2)
104	1969	Alignment (44)	Gahal (26), NRP (11), Rafi (10), Mapam (8), IL (5)
102	1969	Labor (60)	Gahal (26), NRP (12), IL (4)
97	1984	Likud (41) Labor (40)	NRP (4), Shas (4), Shinui (3), AI (2), Morasha (2), Ometz (1)
95	1988	Likud (40) Labor (39)	Shas (6), NRP (5), AI (5)

[a] Size equals the number of Knesset members.
Key: NRP = National Religious party, PAI = Poalei Aguda Israel, IL = Independent Liberal, AI = Aguda Israel.
Source: Compiled by Doron.

other issues. Also, as shown in Table 6.2, the two large parties and their respective political blocs were almost equal in size. Rather than call for a new and costly election and risk losing to the rival, the leaders of the two parties—Shamir of Likud and Peres of Labor—decided to form a unity government, thus employing a strategy of "not losing." This type of coalition was effective only in certain crisis situations.

The Labor-Likud Unity government had two important achievements between 1984 and 1988: Inflation was curtailed, and the IDF was withdrawn from Lebanon. In other areas the government was almost paralyzed. Low payoffs to its members, ideological differences, and the unwillingness to permit the "rival-turned-partner" party to gain any political victories that could be transformed into votes on election day were responsible for the government stalemate. Under a rotation agreement between Likud and Labor, Peres, serving as foreign minister, signed an accord in London with King Hussein of Jordan. Prime Minister Shamir, who replaced Peres as prime minister in 1986, rejected the accord.

The 1988 grand coalition was established, like the one four years earlier, for political reasons rather than because of a unifying national crisis; thus, it could not be expected to survive for long. Soon after it was formed, three Likud members—David Levy, Ariel Sharon, and Itzhak Modai—tried to terminate the coalition. The three assumed that in a small coalition their personal political weight would be greater and that they would therefore receive better ministerial posts. Similarly, on the Labor side some Peres loyalists, together with Shas, began to work for a smaller coalition. Consequently, the Unity government collapsed, and a Likud-led small coalition was formed.

Why do major parties that are capable of ruling without the help of a minor party ask the latter to participate in an oversized government? There are three reasons to form coalitions that have excess numbers, such as those shown in Table 6.3.

Dummy Party. A dummy party is one that joins a coalition even though it is not needed to assure winning a decision in the Knesset. When its participation is essential to win, the party is pivotal. The Independent Liberals were a dummy party; they usually obtained very little political payoff for their participation in oversized coalitions (e.g., they were awarded the Ministry of Justice or Ministry of Tourism for joining the government coalition).

Regardless of a coalition's structure, the principal party keeps most of the spoils: the prime minister's office, Ministry of Defense, the Foreign Ministry, Ministry of the Treasury, Ministry of Education and Culture, Ministry of Agriculture, Ministry of Communication, and Ministry of the Police. The NRP, Mapai's historical ally, almost routinely obtained the ministries of religious affairs, interior, and welfare. Moreover, even when an important ministry fell under the control of a minor dummy party, Mapai made sure several of its important functions were transferred to a Mapai ministry.

TABLE 6.3   Oversized Israeli Coalitions by Size[a] and Year of Formation

Size[a]	Year of Formation	Size[a] of Principal Party	Size[a] of Other Participants
73	1949	Mapai (48)	RF (16), Progressives (5), Sephardim (4)
87	1954	Mapai (50)	General Zionists (23), Mizrachi (10), Progressives (4)
80	1955	Mapai (45)	NRP (11), AA (10), Mapam (9), Progressives (5)
86	1959	Mapai (52)	NRP (12), Mapam (9), AA (7), Progressives (6)
75	1966	Alignment (49)	NRP (11), Mapam (8), IL (5), PAI (2)
76	1970	Labor (60)	NRP (12), IL (4)
77	1977	Likud (45)	DMC (15), NRP (12), AI (4), Dayan (1)
69	1979	Likud (25)	Same as 1977 less 8 DMC

[a] Size equals the number of Knesset members.
Key: NRP = National Religious party, RF = Religious Front, AA = Achdut Ha-Avoda, PAI = Poalei Aguda Israel, IL = Independent Liberal, DMC = Democratic Movement for Change, AI = Agudat Israel.
Source: Compiled by Doron.

Mapai was thus able to control between 75 percent and 90 percent of the national budget.

Internal Stability. Because Israeli coalitions consist of parties that are composed of factions (e.g., Labor includes Mapai, Achdut Ha-Avoda, and Rafi; Likud was formed from Herut, the Independent Liberals, and the Free Center), there is always a danger that the leaders of some faction might bargain for more power or threaten to defect. To prevent this from occurring, an additional party is brought into the coalition, thus eliminating pivotal advantages the threatening party may possess. For example, to lower the bargaining power of Dayan and his supporters in the early 1970s, Labor party leaders had to rely heavily on Mapam support, which diminished Dayan's threat to defect from the coalition.

External Stability. Once a winning coalition has been formed, the opposition attempts to bring it down. The principal instrument used for this purpose is the no-confidence vote. The opposition also attempts to approach dummy parties, offering them payoffs according to their potential pivotal position and number of safe seats in the next Knesset. The principal party often finds it difficult to match such offers. Peres was able to lure two Likud members in 1983; in 1990 Shamir convinced Efraim Gur of Labor to become a deputy minister in the Likud government and, after 1992, a Likud MK. In 1991 making promises and assurances to individual MKs (but not to factions whose size is at least a third the size of the faction's party) became illegal, which restored some measure of stability to the system.

The presence of surplus partners helps the government to survive. Some partners may leave because the payoffs in an oversized coalition may not be sufficiently satisfying, but the government can still function with other partners. The DMC and the General Zionists illustrate this dynamic. In 1977 the DMC became a dummy party with fifteen members. Begin could rule with or without the DMC, much as Ben-Gurion could rule with or without the General Zionists. The DMC began a process of self-destruction when it entered Begin's coalition. Some of its leaders joined the opposition; others split into several small factions because they received little payoff and had little impact on national issues. Similarly, the General Zionists, the hope of the middle class in the early 1950s, had little importance in Mapai coalitions and had little say in public policy. Unlike the DMC's meteoric rise and quick decline, the General Zionists were able to sustain their existence by integrating into other parties until they disappeared in 1992.

David Ben-Gurion—Founder of the State

Many institutional precedents were established by Israel's forceful first prime minister, David Ben-Gurion, and the directions in which he led the state during its first precarious years. A major reason Israel had no constitution was that Ben-Gurion simply did not want one. He found he had a freer hand without a formal document and thus discouraged the hasty drafting of a constitution. The British system, he argued, had taken centuries to develop. Thus, in Israel customary procedures evolved from the day-to-day work of the government, as was the case in the British system. Experience eventually showed that government could operate without a formal constitution by working under legislation passed by the Knesset.

Ben-Gurion extended his influence by assuming the post of defense minister as well as prime minister. He also took over management of foreign affairs, immigration, and development. During his tenure the prime minister became the keystone of government—overshadowing the rest of the cabinet, the president, and parliament, although he was still responsible to the Knesset.

In time, the state itself rose above the interests of parochial ideologies and groups and developed into the object of loyalty for most citizens. The centrality of state authority was determined within a few weeks of the government's establishment when Ben-Gurion took control of the several Jewish military factions that had fought the 1948 war. Toward the end of the mandate, at least three military groups coexisted in the Yishuv. Haganah, the Yishuv's official military arm, operated under the Jewish Agency for Palestine and the National Council. Two dissident factions split from the Haganah because of political disagreements and differences over tactics. The Irgun Zvai Leumi (IZL) was associated with the Revisionists and favored more militant tactics against the British and Arabs. Its offshoot, the Lohamei Herut Israel (Fighters for the Freedom of Israel), or Lehi—also called the Stern Gang after one of its founders—refused to halt its actions against the British during World War II. After World War II it resorted to even more militant measures than the IZL. When Israel was established, Haganah became its official army, but initially the other two groups refused to give up independent actions, including conducting terrorist attacks on Arab and British civilians and importing private military supplies.

A showdown between the government and the separate military factions occurred a month after independence. A shipment of arms destined for the IZL arrived from Europe on the ship *Altalena* at an embarrassing moment for the provisional government, which ten days earlier had signed a UN truce halting military activity—including arms imports. When IZL leaders insisted on unloading the arms against the orders of the cabinet majority, Ben-Gurion, as defense minister and prime minister, ordered the army to prevent the cargo from landing. During the struggle that ensued between the army and *Altalena*'s crew, the ship was shelled; it sank, and several of its crew were killed or wounded. Most of the arms were destroyed. Two cabinet members representing the Orthodox Mizrachi party resigned in protest of the incident. Ben-Gurion responded by ordering the army to take command of all military groups. Thereafter, no independent or autonomous armed factions were permitted. The state alone has been responsible for military security.

During the encounter, many Israelis feared a civil war would erupt, and rumors circulated that the IZL intended to set up a separate Jewish state in Jerusalem. Instead, IZL leader Menachem Begin gave orders not to fire on fellow Jews and agreed to dissolve his military organization. Later, he converted the IZL into the country's principal opposition party, Herut. The much smaller Lehi also dissolved its military forces, and its leader, Nathan Friedman Yellin-Mor, established the Lohamim (Fighters) party, which had a one-member delegation in parliament. The party ceased to exist after the First Knesset.

After the *Altalena* incident Ben-Gurion also decided to absorb the Haganah's elite striking force, Palmach, into the army against the wishes of its leaders. Although Palmach was not an independent military organization, it had been created by left-wing members of the kibbutz movement; it maintained a distinctively leftist political orientation and an elite membership. Eight of the Palmach's thirteen commanders were from the leftist Achdut Ha-Avoda and Mapam parties.

Through these acts, Ben-Gurion established supreme authority over all military factions and concentrated armed power and the use of force in government hands. But he also antagonized some of the country's political and military leaders. The *Altalena* incident created such discord between Begin and Ben-Gurion that the two broke all contact, thereby establishing a precedent in which Mapai, later the Labor party, refused to form a coalition with Herut for nearly twenty years.

During Ben-Gurion's tenure, highest priority was given to developing the country's military machine, with the understanding that the military would always be subordinate to the civil administration. To maintain civilian control, Ben-Gurion became defense minister; he personally selected leaders of the armed forces and guided their military strategy and political orientation. A close personal bond was forged between the young commanders and the chief of state, and Ben-Gurion became an intermediary and a spokesperson for their interests in the cabinet.

Ben-Gurion saw to it that the armed forces received not only the lion's share of the national budget but also the cream of the country's youth. Universal conscription of men and women was adopted with little controversy, despite Orthodox opposition to drafting women. The objections of Orthodox Jews were honored; women who requested exemptions for religious reasons and married women with children were not required to serve. Ben-Gurion envisaged the military forces as a socializing agent in which class distinctions would be obliterated and new immigrants integrated. The army's educational activities became one of its significant features.

The army was one of the few institutions in the new state that remained relatively free of party politics. Promotions in the forces and positions in the Defense Ministry were based on merit rather than on party dealings, although most high-ranking officers were from the Labor movement. The military became one of the few state institutions that was respected by all factions.

Ben-Gurion was not a doctrinaire socialist. In keeping with the principle of state above party, he frequently compromised on economic and social policy. Unable to win a majority in any national election, Mapai was forced to rely on coalitions that always included nonsocialist parties, which were opposed to socialist doctrines. Because large amounts of foreign funds were required to fuel its rapid economic growth, Israel established close ties with capitalist countries and Jewish communities in the West. Although social welfare was an accepted credo, other socialist policies, such as central economic planning and income redistribution, were diluted in deference to nonsocialist domestic and foreign alliances formed by the Mapai-led coalitions. Emphasis was on a mixed economy with many sectors under government control. Many institutions, such as the Histadrut and the Jewish National Fund, were quasi-public. The public sector coexisted with private enterprise, resulting in the mixed economy. Overcoming the sharp ideological differences between socialists and nonsocialists would probably have been much more difficult without Ben-Gurion's leadership.

A sharp ideological split between Orthodox Jews and secularists also threatened national unity in the early years. Ben-Gurion was intimately associated with traditional Jewish values and consciousness, but he did not hesitate to deliver heretical views on Old Testament commentary and did not shun contact with other creeds and dogmas. He epitomized the learned secular Jew with traditional roots, whose mind grasped for broader knowledge of the world. Realizing that feelings in Israel were deep enough to precipitate a *Kulturkampf,* or religious war, Ben-Gurion felt compromise was necessary to protect both Orthodox Jews and secularists. As a result, many aspects of Orthodox Jewish observance were maintained, but they were circumvented when required by national emergency. Strict Sabbath observance and kosher cuisine were maintained in public institutions, but enough private leeway was allowed to avoid major discomfort to secularists. Personal-status matters such as marriage and divorce remained under the control of the clerics, but marriages contracted abroad were recognized. Rather than impose either a secular or a religious educational system on the country, both types of schools were supported with government aid. Raising pigs was banned in Jewish sectors, but leftist kibbutzim raised the animals and called them giraffes or rabbits. Many secularists objected to these evasions or deceptions, yet such compromises avoided serious constitutional crises. In effect, Ben-Gurion achieved a constitutional dualism in which the state was simultaneously secular and Jewish.

198 • *How the Government Works*

The relationship between Israeli Arabs and the government was determined largely by Ben-Gurion's early policies. During the mandate he attempted to make personal contact with Palestinian Arab leaders, at one time proposing the establishment of a binational federation in which the two communities would share sovereignty in separate cantons. Before the mandate ended, however, Ben-Gurion had concluded that the Jews could not give what the Arabs were willing to accept and the Arabs would not accept what the Jews were willing to give. He retained the negative view of the Arab personality and character derived from stereotypes that existed not only in the Yishuv but in the West as well. Although he was widely read in the classics of several non-Jewish cultures, Ben-Gurion never regarded Islamic philosophy or literature as having major significance. He learned Greek and Spanish but never mastered Arabic. His attitudes toward Middle Eastern culture were revealed in his evaluation of Sephardi Jewish culture and in his policies toward Israeli Arabs; neither group became part of the mainstream of life in the Jewish state. Throughout Ben-Gurion's tenure, policies toward Israeli Arabs were improvised by a special office in the prime ministry headed by an adviser on Arab affairs.

Ben-Gurion's closest associates in government were not the Labor party old guard but young members of the movement who agreed with him on the supremacy of the state over partisan ideologies. Many younger advisers and followers, such as Moshe Dayan and Shimon Peres, came from the military sector as either officers or high-level technocrats. They broadened many of the prestate Zionist themes and dogmas, introducing concepts that had never occurred to the leadership prior to 1948. The idea of pioneering, or *halutziut,* which focused on Jewish settlement on Jewish land, was extended to nonagricultural sectors including high-tech industry. National security required that Israel's economy be integrated with the nonsocialist Western world. The development of technology would meet defense needs through national industrial expansion. Scientists and technicians were also considered pioneers, or *halutzim,* whose contributions were at times more valuable than those of kibbutz members or farmers.

Ben-Gurion set a personal example in pioneering when he established residence at one of the newer kibbutzim, Sde Boker, in the undeveloped Negev area of southern Israel. The government continued to encourage youths and new immigrants to form settlements in sparsely populated rural areas, although as time went on the relative importance of the collective settlements declined along with the overall contribution of agriculture to national development.

Zionist security and humanitarian factors influenced Ben-Gurion's decision to rapidly expand immigration and to develop national policies to stimulate it. Political and social rather than economic considerations received priority in early decisions to double the country's Jewish population within a decade. In Eastern Europe after World War II, Jewish communal life was so disrupted and the number of displaced Jews was so great that the moment was ripe for "in-gathering" before new Communist regimes in Romania, Poland, Bulgaria, Hungary, and Czechoslovakia adopted restrictive emigration policies. In the Arab world, clashes between Israeli and Arab nationalism exacerbated local prejudices against indigenous Jewish communities, making life insecure if not untenable.

In Israel, social and political conditions were sufficiently fluid to facilitate the rapid improvisation of new policies. The Yishuv was still euphoric over its newly won independence. A spirit of sacrifice and ideals of egalitarianism were strong enough to overcome second thoughts about the economic wisdom of bringing in such large numbers of immigrants in so short a time. The unanticipated flight of Arab refugees left a windfall that could help to provide for the new immigrants; tens of thousands of acres of agricultural land, large blocks of urban property, and entire towns and villages left by the departing Palestinians were available for Jewish settlement. These diverse circumstances stimulated the early decision to bring in as many Jews as possible. In 1950 the Law of Return was passed, which guaranteed every Jew (with minor exceptions) the right to immigrate; in 1952 the Nationality Law came into effect, conferring automatic citizenship on those who entered the country under the Law of Return.

Without Ben-Gurion's urging, those who placed more emphasis on the economic absorptive capacity might have had greater influence. If immigration had been geared to the pace of economic growth, the rapid rate of Jewish movement into the new state would have slowed, and many who immigrated between 1948 and 1953 might have come later or not at all.

Efforts to speed up immigration required sacrifices by the Yishuv, the immigrants, and the world Jewish community. During their early years, many immigrants lived in Ma'abarot (transition camps), which were often little better than the displaced person's camps they had left in Europe. Sephardi Jews usually remained in the Ma'abarot much longer than European immigrants, a situation that became the source of social unrest.

Doubling the population in so short a time was costly to the state. Israel's narrow economic base and lack of preliminary planning for such large-scale immigration caused serious economic repercussions that led the country into its first recession during the early 1950s. This was the first era of major financial contributions from diaspora Jewry. (Later periods, including the 1967 and 1973 wars, required even greater efforts in overseas fund-raising.)

Israel's first prime minister was also influential in establishing the general direction of foreign policy despite fundamental divisions within the cabinet. In the early days of the Cold War, Israel required and received the support of both the United States and the Soviet Union. Without support from both the Eastern and Western blocs, the UN partition resolution could not have passed the General Assembly. U.S. economic assistance to the new state was as essential as military supplies from the Soviet bloc during the 1948 War of Independence.

Initially, Israel attempted to follow a nonaligned, or neutral, foreign policy. Political opinion was divided between advocates of closer ties with the Soviet Union and those who favored a Western orientation. Soviet policy and Ben-Gurion's own analysis of the situation soon compelled a major reorientation from a position of neutrality to one of identification with the West, especially the United States. Once Israel had brought about diminished British influence in the Middle East, Soviet support shifted rapidly to the Arab states. Within a year or two of Israel's foundation, the USSR perceived the new state as another tool of imperialism and an ally of Western forces in the region. In time, changes in Soviet policy undermined the once extensive support the USSR had enjoyed among significant groups in the Israeli Labor movement.

Relations with the United States were also difficult because of broader U.S. interests in the Middle East. The two countries remained cordial, however, and developed increasing intimacy. The United States was the home of the world's largest and most affluent Jewish community, which provided extensive political and economic support to steer the country through its perilous first years. Under Ben-Gurion's guidance, foreign policy moved toward closer identification with the West while avoiding another area of possible internal political warfare.

Not all of Ben-Gurion's policy objectives were realized; despite major efforts, there were two significant failures. Ben-Gurion's failure to integrate Sephardi Jews was a keen disappointment. He personally attempted to raise funds to facilitate their absorption and strongly encouraged affirmative action in the promotion of army officers of Sephardi origin, in their admission to higher education institutions, and in advancement of their government careers. But his efforts could not overcome the broad cultural chasm between Sephardi and Western Jews. This problem remains one of the most serious issues confronting Israel.

Another of Ben-Gurion's unrealized aspirations was to populate the Negev and other regions sparsely settled by Jews. Few individuals followed Ben-Gurion's example by moving to the underpopulated regions, and his vision of Negev reforestation remained a dream. Water shortages contributed to the limited settlement of the undeveloped areas. Internal population movement continued toward urban areas and pursuits. Ben-Gurion's vision of one million Jews in the Negev may have been the reason he showed little enthusiasm for plans to establish large numbers of Jewish settlements in the Occupied Territories in 1967.

Ben-Gurion's strong leadership was decisive in shaping the role of prime minister as Israel's most powerful office. His energy and dynamism, the network of political lines he controlled, and the initiatives he seized were so great that he overshadowed all other officials, including President Weizmann.

Despite Ben-Gurion's dominant role, the coalition basis of his cabinets and the constitutional stipulation of collective responsibility required that he consult frequently with government colleagues, although he often took decisive action without them and merely informed the cabinet of some policy he was about to implement. A threat to resign was usually sufficient to win over dissenting members.

Ben-Gurion's Successors: Labor Party's Prime Ministers

The political styles and powers of Ben-Gurion's successors have varied. Moshe Sharett, who served for the brief period of Ben-Gurion's "retirement" between December 1953 and February 1955, concentrated on foreign affairs and turned other policy decisions over to his cabinet colleagues. During this era the prime minister lost control of the Defense Ministry for the first time in Israel's brief history. Sharett complained that Defense Minister Pinhas Lavon failed to consult him about reprisals taken against neighboring Arab states for raids into Israel. The lack of centralized control became even more of an issue when it was revealed that an espionage and sabotage operation had been conducted in Egypt without the knowledge of the defense minister. This episode later became a cause célèbre that led to quarrels in the cabinet, deep personal animosity between Ben-Gurion and his colleagues, and factional strife within Mapai. When Ben-Gurion returned to power in 1955, he again imposed his strong personality on the government, and the prime minister again became the government's paramount officer.

Levi Eshkol, Ben-Gurion's successor, did not command the latter's prestige or extensive influence. Eshkol made decisions based on cabinet consensus. During the most critical period of his tenure—the eve of the 1967 Six Day War—public opinion and pressure from his colleagues forced him to turn the Defense Ministry over to former General Moshe Dayan, a leading competitor for the post of prime minister. During and after the war, Dayan seized the initiative in matters concerning defense and administration of the Occupied Territories. He operated with little influence or intervention from the prime minister or the cabinet. In matters related to these two areas, his power was equal to, if not greater than, Eshkol's.

Golda Meir, one of the first women in the world to head a democratic government, was chosen by the Labor party as a stopgap measure following Eshkol's death in 1969. She remained in power until the political turmoil following the 1973 war. A long-time party leader who had been among the heads of the Histadrut, as well as the minister of labor and a foreign minister under Ben-Gurion, she demonstrated a strong personality and a forcefulness that placed her in a commanding cabinet position, although her position was not as strong as Ben-Gurion's. She relied heavily on a small group of advisers in the cabinet, often called "Golda's kitchen." Because this closed circle did not include all cabinet members, several—including Dayan—felt excluded from vital decisions. Dayan threatened to resign in protest several times during Meir's tenure.

Israel's first native-born prime minister, Yitzhak Rabin, had never been a part of the Labor party's inner circle. His only high office outside the army, where he was chief of staff during the 1967 war, was ambassador to the United States. In the 1973 election, before he became prime minister, he was not even among the party leaders heading the Labor ballot. His appointment was an unexpected compromise that resulted from the party's desire to select a leader who was not identified with the 1973 war reversals. Throughout his tenure, it often appeared the government was run by a triumvirate made up of Prime Minister Rabin, Defense Minister Shimon Peres, and Foreign Minister and Deputy Prime Minister Yigal Allon—each of whom represented a different Labor party faction. Rabin was the compromise candidate of the old-guard Mapai politicians. He had never been active in party affairs, although as a young Palmach officer he had had close ties to Achdut Ha-Avoda. Rabin's administration suffered from factionalism not only among different parties in the coalition but also within his own party.

The Labor alignment, theoretically headed by Rabin, was divided over policy for the Occupied Territories and the terms of a peace settlement with the Arab states. In addition, there were disputes between supporters of a strong Labor movement and those who wanted to curb the Histadrut's power during the country's increasing economic difficulties. What was perhaps Rabin's most decisive action toppled the government: He demanded that members of the religious party in his coalition resign because they had failed to support him in a Knesset vote. Consequently, elections scheduled for the end of 1977 were advanced to May, which supposedly gave the incumbent Labor party an advantage. Instead, Labor was turned out of government, and the opposition Likud came to power for the first time in Israel's twenty-nine-year history.

Shimon Peres, who replaced Rabin as the head of the Labor party, failed to win the post of prime minister in both 1977 and 1981. Peres, former mayor of Jerusalem Teddy Kollek, and Israel's fifth president, Yitzhak Navon, were among the few Israeli politicians most closely associated with Ben-Gurion. When Peres was director general of the Ministry of Defense, he was instrumental in developing diplomatic and military relationships with France that led the two countries to embark upon the 1956 Sinai campaign; France also helped with the construction of Israel's nuclear reactor in Dimona. Peres left Mapai, together with Ben-Gurion and Dayan, to form Rafi; later, he and Dayan played a major role in forming the Labor party, whereas Ben-Gurion headed the small State List. In his third attempt to become Israel's prime minister in 1984, Peres and his party could only obtain a tie with Shamir and his bloc. In the resultant new Labor-Likud Unity government, Peres served as prime minister between 1984 and 1986 and as foreign minister for the next two years.

Beginning in 1974, when Peres and Rabin competed to chair the Labor party, the two were involved in a seemingly symbiotic relationship; although they did not trust each other, they shared a mutual respect and tended to depend on each other. Peres served as minister of defense under Rabin from 1974 to 1977, and Rabin was Peres's minister of defense between 1984 and 1986. After the 1992 election, Peres was Rabin's foreign minister. Over the years both leaders' political orientations changed. Peres was initially much more hawkish than Rabin, then he moved to Rabin's left; after 1992 both were somewhat left of center in the Israeli political spectrum. They shared the Nobel Peace Prize with Yasser Arafat for the 1993 agreement between Israel and the PLO.

Menachem Begin: The Perfect Gentleman

Menachem Begin, the first non-Labor prime minister, took full charge of the government when he assumed power in 1977. To many observers his style at first seemed like Ben-Gurion's—assertive, innovative, and personal. There was no doubt that the prime minister was in charge. During his first months in office, Begin made few significant changes in the upper levels of the bureaucracy; he retained most directors of ministries, department heads, and diplomats—including ambassadors. Nevertheless, appointees from the Labor era were clear as to where authority lay and who would make significant policy decisions.

Begin's appointment of Moshe Dayan as his foreign minister underscored his emphasis on national rather than party considerations. The appointment was such a deviation from traditional political behavior that it shook the Labor party and sent tremors through Begin's own coalition. It was unheard of to appoint a leader of the opposition to such a post. Even the Labor opposition considered it unacceptable for Dayan to accept the post under Likud.

Begin's personal style illustrated his government's political orientation. He was the most conservatively dressed prime minister in Israeli history; he seldom appeared in public without a suit and tie and was always courtly in manner and firm and unambiguous in his policy statements. Begin removed many of the uncertainties that had surrounded Israel's foreign policy since

1967 by clearly stating his party's opposition to the surrender of any territory in Palestine and its refusal to recognize the Palestinians as a partner in the peace negotiations. But these positions did not preclude possible Israeli concessions in seeking peace with Egypt, Syria, and other Arab states. After Egyptian President Anwar Sadat's visit to Jerusalem in November 1977 and his attempts to open direct peace negotiations with Israel, many of Begin's Israeli critics believed he had not been forthcoming enough in his response to Sadat and that he was too much of a nationalist ideologue to make the concessions required for a settlement.

On the domestic front, Likud made efforts to reverse the socialist measures of the Labor governments that had preceded Begin. By the end of Likud's first year in power, however, few, if any, improvements had been made in the economy. Moreover, between Likud's 1977 victory and its victory in 1981, few of its economic promises were implemented. In 1981 the cumulative inflation rate was over 1,200 percent, unemployment had doubled, and Israel faced the largest foreign debt in its history. The public-sector bureaucracy—one of the largest in the West—had not been reduced, and there had been little success in diminishing the large government enterprises and the industrial and other holdings of the Histadrut. Public opinion polls taken six months before the election showed Likud at a low point, projected to win no more than eighteen Knesset seats to Labor's fifty-six.

In July 1980 the Likud government supported a new law that annexed Jerusalem, although the city had essentially been annexed by Labor in 1967. Begin's support was given in response to the initiative Tehiya took in the Knesset to demonstrate its own patriotism. Although the new annexation sparked a chain of international protests, UN censure, U.S. criticism, a demand by Sadat for suspension of autonomy talks, and removal of thirteen foreign embassies from Jerusalem to Tel Aviv, it was received with enthusiasm by the Israeli public.

In the June 1981 election a turnaround occurred. Instead of the Likud defeat predicted in 1980, the party increased its margin of victory compared to 1977 by nearly 4 percent of the votes and was returned to power. The "miracle" that saved Likud was Begin's charisma—not as prime minister but as a campaigner. Despite four years of inauspicious governance of internal affairs, Begin emerged as the dominant personality in the 1981 campaign. Both friends and critics acknowledged that his fiery, aggressive, and highly rhetorical style made him the best orator in Israel. Begin capitalized on his position as the first Israeli leader to sign a peace treaty with an Arab state, on the internal weakness and divisiveness in Labor's ranks, and on Labor's inability to field a leadership team that had wide public appeal.

Begin's forceful style, his apparent resistance to foreign pressures, and his patriotic speeches were important assets. Concessions made to Egypt in the peace treaty, particularly the agreement to return all of the Sinai Peninsula, were counterbalanced by a hard line on the remaining territories and on other issues in which Begin showed he was not a dove.

Another Begin action that aroused international ire but was popularly supported at home was the air strike on Iraq's nuclear reactor in Osirak, near Baghdad, in June 1981. The surprise attack was necessary, stated Begin, to prevent production before the end of 1981 of atomic bombs similar to those dropped on Hiroshima. Within a short time, he asserted, the reactor would have become "hot"; a later attack "would have caused a huge wave of radioactivity over the city of Baghdad, and its innocent citizens would have been harmed." The attack, which took place a few weeks before the Tenth Knesset election, captured the electorate's imagination because, according to Begin, it prevented another Holocaust. Even some of Begin's severest critics cheered the escapade.

Nearly six months after the 1981 election, Begin further enhanced his image as a patriot and consolidator of the homeland at the expense of international reprimand by annexing the Golan Heights, which had been captured from Syria during the 1967 war. The region was among the areas of growing Jewish settlements, many from the Labor alignment; thus, annexation was welcomed by critics as well as supporters of the prime minister.

Then, in June 1982, Begin ordered the IDF to launch a full-scale invasion of southern Lebanon. Initially, Israel stated that its objective was to push the PLO twenty-five miles north of the border, a goal that received general public acceptance. As the war expanded, fighting also broke out between Israelis and Syrians, and Begin extended his objectives to the removal of Palestinian *and* Syrian forces from Lebanon.

In 1983 Operation Peace for Galilee was still unresolved. The previous October Begin had announced that the war had established, "for the first time," a state of security on all of Israel's borders. But the price was high. By the end of 1982 more than 460 Israelis were dead and over 2,500 had been wounded in the invasion. The deaths of his wife and of the young Israeli soldiers in Lebanon might have led Begin to leave his post in 1983. He withdrew from the public and died several years later.

Begin's Successors

Begin's successor as prime minister was Yitzhak Shamir, one of Lehi's three principal leaders. During the 1950s and 1960s Shamir worked for the Mossad and was little involved in politics, but when he entered the arena he ascended rapidly. With Begin's approval he became Knesset speaker in June 1977 and Israel's foreign minister in March 1980. These posts are very prestigious, but Shamir was a newcomer and had no real power base within the Herut. At the time, there were three competing factions in the party: one composed of Begin's followers, one led by David Levy, and one headed by

Ariel Sharon. With Begin's departure, the younger members associated with his faction feared an intraparty war would erupt.

Shamir seemed to be a compromise choice among the different Likud factions. He was much older than most other politicians, who thought he would last only a year or two in office. However, Shamir served as prime minister from 1983 until 1992 (except between 1984 and 1986, when he was deputy prime minister and foreign minister in the Likud-Labor coalition government), longer than any prime minister other than Ben-Gurion. During this period Shamir built a strong base in the party, which assured him of continued leadership.

Shamir's decisionmaking style was conservative and status-quo oriented. Between 1984 and 1990, many state problems were solved cooperatively between his Likud and the Labor party. When Likud formed a coalition without Labor as a member in June 1990, however, Shamir's relaxed style seemed more an asset than a liability. During the Gulf War, for example, Shamir decided not to attack Iraq even though Moshe Arens, his minister of defense, pressured him to do so.

The economy did well under Likud Finance Minister Itzhak Modai, immigrants were coming by the thousands, and peace talks between Israel and the Arab states were initiated in Madrid. By the end of 1991 Shamir and the Likud seemed as strong politically as had been the case under Begin.

In 1992 Rabin replaced Shamir as prime minister. Rabin dominated his government and operated it in the style of a military commander (he was the former IDF chief of staff), personally making nearly all crucial decisions. During his administration attention was focused on peace negotiations, especially with the Palestinians and with Syria. Although Labor's second-most-prominent leader, Shimon Peres, was foreign minister, Rabin kept tight control of foreign policy.

Perhaps Rabin's greatest achievement was the initiation of negotiations with the PLO. Until 1992, negotiations with the PLO and its leader, Yasser Arafat, had been eschewed by both Labor and Likud. Nevertheless, secret negotiations between Israel and PLO representatives began in January 1992 and led to the Oslo agreement and mutual recognition of Israel and the PLO in a public ceremony in Washington, D.C., in September 1993.

The Washington meeting and the Oslo agreement were followed by direct negotiations between the Rabin government and Arafat, the establishment of a Palestinian authority and elected council, and continued contacts that were designed to lead to a full-scale peace agreement by the late 1990s (no specific date). Although Peres conducted much of the negotiation process, Rabin was a full participant, and all phases of the process had to be approved by him. Initially, Rabin had been skeptical about contacts and negotiations with Arafat; by 1995, however, Rabin appeared convinced that peace with the PLO and a Palestinian entity were achievable.

The negotiations with Syria were less successful. A major obstacle to a settlement was Israel's continued occupation of the Golan Heights, which had been seized from Syria during the 1967 war. Rabin was ambivalent about whether to return the region to Syria, and Syria was adamant that there could be no peace without the return of the Golan.

In November 1995, shortly before the campaign for the 1996 election was to begin, Rabin was assassinated at a peace rally in Tel Aviv by an Orthodox Israeli Jewish student who was opposed to Rabin's policies, especially to Labor's program of "land for peace."

Shimon Peres succeeded Rabin as prime minister. Peres was committed to continuing Rabin's program to attain a comprehensive peace settlement with all of Israel's neighbors and the Palestinians. The 1996 election campaign began as soon as Peres ascended to the prime ministry. The new electoral system called for the direct election of the prime minister and a separate ballot for members of the Knesset. The campaign was largely a contest between the two candidates for prime minister, Labor's Peres and Likud's Netanyahu. Likud focused on security issues, maintaining that Rabin and Peres—especially the latter—were lax in security matters and had placed too much trust in Arafat. Likud opposed Labor's program of land for peace, and Netanyahu promised to continue Jewish settlement in the Occupied Territories.

Public opinion was almost equally divided, as seen in the vote for prime minister: Netanyahu was elected with 50.4 percent of the vote, and Peres obtained 49.5 percent. Despite the close division, Netanyahu became prime minister for a four-year term. Although a major objective of the new electoral system was to free the prime minister from bargaining with coalition partners, thus weakening his or her authority and ability to implement government policies, Netanyahu was faced with a Knesset that was more divided than ever before and was forced to construct a cabinet coalition of seven or eight different factions (for further discussion, see Chapter 8).

7

Government Administration and Public Policy

There is a story, probably apocryphal, that Ben-Gurion decided to examine the economic feasibility of his vision to transform the Negev into a luxuriant garden region. Because the Negev was empty and constituted about half the area of the state, Ben-Gurion believed it had to absorb many of the new immigrants. "Conquest of the desert" thus became a central policy goal in Ben-Gurion's concept of the Zionist enterprise. He and his family moved from Tel Aviv to Sde Boker, a kibbutz in the northern part of the Negev, to provide a personal example. To assess the cost and identify the means by which to realize his vision, Ben-Gurion assembled a committee of experts who studied the issue. The experts recommended against pursuit of this far-reaching goal, but Ben-Gurion refused to accept their advice. He assembled another committee, which arrived at similar conclusions. A third commission was formed—this one made up of international scientists—and again the answer was negative. Ben-Gurion nonetheless continued to pursue the vision and to emphasize the centrality of the desert in the development of the new state.

The Policy of Improvisation

The story illustrates the determination of some Israeli policymakers to overcome obstacles in spite of unfavorable odds and, in this case, against the recommendations of scientists. When all rational methods used to arrive at a decision had failed, imaginative decisions were taken based on vision, intuition, experience, emotions, and faith. For Ben-Gurion and some of his successors, extra-rational decisions that had unexpected outcomes became almost routine. Some of these include the decision to declare independence of the state in 1948 while anticipating attacks by the surrounding Arab states; to almost triple the population within the country's first few years, even though means to sustain the newcomers were scarce; to build development towns with no industrial infrastructure, no experienced workers, and no capital; to defeat the Arab states in a six-day period in 1967 and again in 1973; and to bring in thousands of immigrants in the early 1990s without jobs or places prepared to integrate most of them.

The successful outcomes of these decisions were a function of many factors, including luck, but most important was the human element. As a country with few natural resources, Israel had to rely on its most important asset—highly qualified people, many from abroad. Economically, Israel benefited greatly from the influx of individuals educated in the West or in the Soviet system. (See Table 7.1.)

Israeli government administration personnel came from several sources. There were veterans of the Jewish Agency for Palestine, Histadrut officials, and party members who obtained jobs through personal connections. Personal familiarity led to favoritism, or *Protektzia,* in which a note from a minister would be sufficient for a person to receive a job in national or local government. There were also professional bureaucrats who had been trained in the mandatory administration, many of whom were employed in the postal service and in lower ranks of the police. The records of some suspected as "Anglicans"—those employed by, and considered sympathetic to, the British—were screened to determine how loyal they were to the British.

TABLE 7.1   1991 Immigrants from the USSR by Occupation

Occupation in Country of Origin	Absolute Numbers	Percentage
Scientific and academic	28,318	36.2
Engineers and architects	18,267	23.3
Physicians and dentists	3,429	4.4
Other professional, technical, and related workers	26,021	33.2
Nurses and paramedics	3,603	4.6
Managers, clerical, and related workers	3,375	4.3
Salespersons	1,932	2.5
Service workers	3,018	3.9
Agricultural workers	96	0.1
Skilled workers in industry, construction, and transport	11,641	14.8
Unskilled workers	3,906	5.0
Occupation not known	1,430	—
Total	79,743	100.0

Source: Statistical Abstract of Israel (Jerusalem: Government of Israel, Central Bureau of Statistics, 1992), p. 179.

By 1952 there were about 27,000 state employees, less than 10 percent of whom were police officers. Twenty years later the number of state employers had increased by 20,000. In 1985 almost 78,000 people were employed by the national government. Three years later the number had been reduced to about 70,000, but it rose again to over 76,000 in 1992. In more recent years the police and the prison service have constituted about 30 percent of government personnel. These numbers do not include the 30,000 workers in local government, a similar number employed in welfare and other community services, over 100,000 in public health service, and 200,000 in education. The total number of public employees, excluding the army, has been close to half a million since the early 1990s.

Government Administration

When Israel was established, only four ministries had an organized civil service: the Ministry of Foreign Affairs, which was a continuation of the Jewish Agency for Palestine's Political Department; the Ministry of Defense, which descended from the Haganah; the Ministry of Social Welfare, developed from the Welfare Department of the Yishuv's National Council; and the Ministry of Education and Culture, the National Council's (Vaad Leumi) Education Department. Most ministries were new, but several were carried on from the mandatory government or the Jewish Agency for Palestine. Although many mandatory government files had been destroyed or removed to England, several agencies' records and facilities were intact. The newly established government of Israel took over the railroad stock of the former government, many of its police facilities, the telephone and telegraph services, landholding records, and broadcasting services.

Under Mapai, the Israeli government greatly extended the functions for which the British mandatory authorities had been responsible. Although Mapai governments formally had a socialist orientation, in reality a mixed economy developed that included a very large public sector. The number of government ministries and their subsidiary agencies involved in business, trade, commerce, and financial activity increased.

At first, the prime minister was in charge of the civil service; control was later shifted to the Ministry of Finance, as is the case in Great Britain. In the mid-1950s an independent Civil Service Commission was established, headed by a cabinet-appointed commissioner who was responsible to the finance minister. The commission attempted to depoliticize government service through competitive examinations, civil service training and education, and more efficient organization. However, party politics remained an influential factor in appointments to high-level posts in the ministries and agencies that remained under the jurisdiction of a single party. After Likud's defeat of the Labor party in 1977, Prime Minister Begin, head of Israel's first non-Labor government, made surprisingly few changes at top levels. He retained several directors general, ambassadors, and other high officials who had served in the previous Labor governments.

Prime Minister Begin could have done little to institute changes and place his people in high-ranking government positions even if he had wanted to. Herut, which had been an opposition party for about thirty years, had prepared too few highly trained professional cadres to replace the administration appointed by Labor. By 1981, however, new cadres had been formed of people who switched their alliance from Labor to Likud. By the end of the 1980s, political appointments made by both Likud and Labor had led to the designation of active party members, many of whom were unqualified for their posts. Consequently, a 1993 amendment to the 1959 Civil Service Law prohibited high-ranking government employees from participating in any "voting" body—that is, any political group that elects Knesset candidates or candidates for local government, the World Zionist Organization, or the Jewish Agency. The amendment also forbade employees from taking part in any other political activity.

Day-to-day administration of the government is carried out by the ministries, the number of which has varied since 1949. Nine ministries have always been part of the administration: The Prime Minister's Office, Defense, the Foreign Affairs Office, the Treasury, Justice, Interior, Education and Culture, Religious Affairs, and Transport. In addition to this group, the first government, formed in 1949, had other major ministries: Supply and Rationing, Police, Labor and Social Welfare, Insurance, War Casualties, and Immigrant Absorption. The second government, formed in October 1950, introduced the Ministries of Industry and Trade, Agriculture, and Health. The Post Office and the Ministry of Development were established in 1951. Development was combined with Agriculture and was later attached to other ministries or independently operated. The Construction and Housing Ministry was created during the tenth government, formed in 1961; the eleventh government appointed a deputy prime minister in 1963. During the national Unity governments of the 1980s, the status of cabinet deputies was lowered somewhat to make room for a substitute prime minister. Tourism was established in 1964, Information—a ministry whose sole purpose was to explain government policies—and Communications were organized in 1974. When Likud came to power in 1977, it introduced Ministries of Social Betterment and Energy and Infrastructure. The Ministry for Environment Quality was started in 1988, and a Jerusalem affairs ministerial function began in 1990.

At times there have been over twenty ministries and special agencies, but the number has varied because of amalgamations and shifts of party alignments. For example, after the 1977 election the Ministry of Police was absorbed by the Ministry of Interior, and earlier Industry and Trade absorbed Tourism.

Often, no administrative rationale, need, or social pressure exists to form a new ministry or eliminate an old one. The guiding logic for creating a new ministry is usually political and is related to coalition payoffs. A new ministry may be formed to take over some functions from one or several other established ministries and may assign those functions to a coalition partner the prime minister wants to reward with the title of minister. At times, several ministers have had no ministerial portfolio or function. There are also several deputy ministers, some of whom are assigned responsibility for important functions (e.g., sports, development of towns, the Arab sector); others have only a title and a government limousine.

Although the prime ministry is at the apex of Israel's administrative pyramid (as shown in Figure 7.1 [the president's position is honorary]), on many occasions ministries headed by members of other parties carry out policies that are seemingly uncoordinated with those of the ruling party. Since each ministry and special office has a wide array of functions, coordination has often been difficult unless a strong prime minister is in office. Figure 7.1 represents an official presentation of the government and its branches, but it does not show the true importance of each agency. To better understand the actual relationship among ministries, one must classify them according to criteria such as importance in terms of administrative prestige (as perceived by the authors and others), size of budgets, and number of personnel employed.

Another way to understand the status of a given ministry within the administrative network is to look at its utility as perceived by politicians, who consider government portfolios a payoff for personal achievement. Are certain ministries assigned to senior or only to junior politicians? Are they assigned to a small coalition partner, or do they belong to the dominant party? Table 7.2 classifies ministries according to the general functions they are intended to serve.

The table lists ministries according to their political rather than their substantive importance. Clearly, the four most important ministries are the Prime Minister's office, the Ministry of Defense, the Foreign Ministry, and the Ministry of the Treasury. The principal party in the coalition (i.e., Labor or Likud) usually retains these ministries. Often, the prime minister has also assumed the role of defense minister; Ben-Gurion, Eshkol, Begin (for a short time), and Rabin served in both posts. Moshe Sharett, who replaced Ben-Gurion as prime minister, also served as foreign minister. The Foreign Ministry and the Treasury have seldom been given to ministers who were not members of the ruling party. Moshe Dayan was an exception; he became Eshkol's minister of defense in 1967 even though he was a member of Rafi,

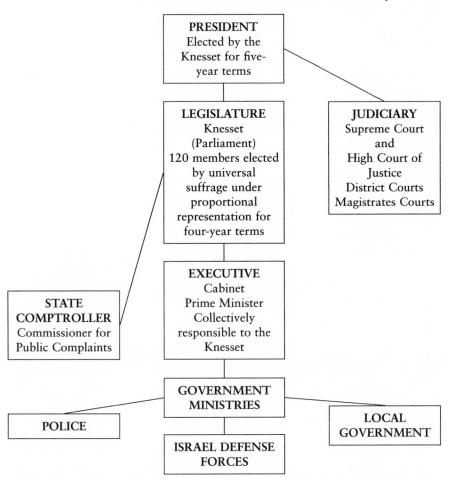

FIGURE 7.1   Relationship Among Various Israeli State Institutions.
Source: Adapted from *Facts About Israel, 1975.*

and he was Begin's foreign minister in 1977 when he was a Labor MK. Note that the prime ministry and the foreign offices do not have the most personnel and do not control the largest budgets.

Table 7.2 organizes ministries into five groups by function. Except for the treasury, the first class includes the three principal ministries—the Prime Minister's office, the Ministry of Defense, and the Foreign Ministry. The four other groups are economic, social, infrastructure, and other, which includes three special ministries. The ranking of the ministries is not necessarily an accurate or objective description of their importance but is rather Doron's impressionistic understanding of their value in 1992 when the

TABLE 7.2   Israeli Ministries Ranked According to Prestige, Function, Number of Personnel, and Size of Ordinary Budget (in million NIS), 1994

Rank	Name	Number of Personnel	Size of Budget	Control[a]
1	Prime Minister	1,015	170	P
2	Defense	2,063	20,392	P
3	Foreign Affairs	910	572	P
Economic Ministries				
4	Treasury	6,990	689	P
9	Industry and Trade	585	73	P
10	Labor and Social Welfare	3,493	13,822	J/P
15	Agriculture	2,072	493	P
16	Tourism	245	254	J
22	Economy and Planning	52	9	P
Social Ministries				
6	Education and Culture	2,784	12,574	J/P
11	Religious Affairs	421	927	J
13	Health	22,659	1,808	P
18	Immigrant Absorption	599	1,411	J/P
Infrastructure Ministries				
7	Construction and Housing	2,569	530	P
8	Transport	939	83	P
17	Communication	135	24	J
19	Energy and Infrastructure	229	469	J
20	Environment Quality	229	59	J
21	Science and Technology	54	57	J
Other Ministries				
5	Interior	774	142	J
12	Justice	2,443	393	J/P
14	Police	41	1,887	P

[a] P stands for principal party; J stands for a junior partner.
Source: Statistical Abstract of Israel (Jerusalem: Government of Israel, Central Bureau of Statistics, 1994).

Labor coalition was formed and ministerial portfolios were assigned. A ministry's status and, consequently, its ranking may change because of changing circumstances or the visibility of the person who heads it.

The Ministry of Police, for example, has not usually been considered important; from 1949 to 1967 it was headed by Bechur Shetrit of Mapai and was considered a political payoff of lesser value given to Sephardi Mapai members. Consequently, a general public impression evolved that police was a Sephardi ministry and hence was not very important. This impression was later strengthened because the two ministers of police who succeeded

Shetrit, Eliyahu Sasson and Shlomo Hillel, were also Sephardim. Perhaps because of this image, the Ministry of Police became part of the Ministry of Interior from 1977 to 1984. As circumstances changed, especially following the outbreak of the intifada in December 1987 when the police force was asked to perform militarylike security tasks, police gradually became an important ministry.

Among the "others" in Table 7.2 the most important ministry is interior because, among other things, it manages citizenship and local government issues. Traditionally, interior has been assigned to a coalition partner such as the religious parties (NRP and Shas), which also control the religious affairs ministry. Ministries such as economy and planning, science and technology, and environment were "invented" to satisfy a particular coalition need or to solve a personal problem.

On occasion, a minister has controlled two or even more portfolios that were not in the same functional class. When the coalition was formed in 1992, Moshe Shahal, the minister of police, was also minister of communications. He later became the minister of energy when communications was awarded to Shulamit Aloni of Meretz. Aloni served as minister of education but was replaced by another member of her party, Amnon Rubinstein. She then became the minister of communication, science and technology, and the arts.

The Prime Minister's Office

The Prime Minister's office is the most important ministry in the government. It has also adopted functions that previously belonged to other ministries, such as the National Council for Research and Development. The range of activities within the prime ministry is extensive. A government secretariat is charged with coordinating interministerial interests, keeping the prime minister in touch with government activity, and maintaining contact between the cabinet and parliament. The secretariat is also responsible for the Government Press Office, one of Israel's most strategic points of contact with the outside world and the principal agency in providing information and services to foreign journalists. The prime minister's adviser on Arab affairs determines policies that relate to Christians, Muslims, and Druze who are Israeli citizens. Prime Minister Rabin terminated the post after 1992.

An important agency within the prime ministry is the Central Bureau of Statistics, which collects, processes, and publishes economic and social data. Its impressive array of publications—including the annual *Statistical Abstract of Israel*—is extensive and scientific and is by far the most reliable statistical collection in the Middle East.

Other responsibilities and units include coordination of the various ministries, management of the state archives, the Atomic Energy Commission, and the War Against Drugs Authority. Since November 1990 the prime minister has also been the minister for Jerusalem affairs in recognition of the special status of Jerusalem.

Two of the most important units in the Prime Minister's office are the Shabach and the Mossad. The Shabach (Shin Bet, or General Security Service) is Israel's secret service; it is responsible for identifying potential hostile activities against the state by extreme local Jewish groups or Israeli and Palestinian Arabs. The Mossad (Institute) is responsible for preventing hostile activities outside Israel. (Shabach functions like the U.S. Federal Bureau of Investigation and Mossad like the Central Intelligence Agency.) When the prime minister is also minister of defense, he or she controls virtually all of the important security-related information accumulated in Israel.

Prior to 1992 the prime minister had no effective supervision over the Treasury. The Basic Law: Government 1992, which calls for the direct election of the prime minister, places him or her in a stronger position vis-à-vis the Treasury. But it is still not clear how effective the prime minister's control over other ministries will be even though a hierarchical order among them has been formalized by law.

The Ministry of Defense

Because of Israel's precarious security situation, the Defense Ministry has become one of the largest government agencies; it is responsible for organizing and maintaining the defense forces and for coordinating a large military industry. Over the years the ministry has absorbed as much as 40 percent of the state budget and 20 percent of gross national product; it thus is one of the most influential agencies in the national economy in developing industry, science, and technology. Military equipment exported by the Ministry of Defense has become one of Israel's major sources of foreign exchange, and military industries under the jurisdiction of the ministry are among the country's largest employers.

The Ministry of Defense has a virtually independent budget whose components are determined essentially by its own professionals rather than by the Treasury, although the budget is approved by a special Knesset committee. The ministry has delegations in other countries (e.g., the United States, South Africa). An important task is to care for IDF war invalids and their families. In 1994, 336 million NIS (over $100 million) was spent for assistance to war invalids, who in general receive better care than civilian invalids.

After 1967 the Ministry of Defense, acting through the Israeli army, governed the areas occupied during the Six Day War—the West Bank, Gaza, and the Golan Heights. Regional military commanders in each area were designated legislators and chief executives, or military governors. They appointed all local officials, including judges, and were responsible for the military justice system established under emergency regulations in the occupied areas. The military governors were assisted by Israeli civilians who represented various ministries such as the Ministries of Agriculture, Education, Social Welfare, and Industry and Trade.

An Israeli Committee for Coordination of Economic Activities in the Occupied Territories was organized in 1967 to plan and direct civilian activities, but in practice the military directed operational decisions in economic and civilian affairs as well as in military and security matters. The chief executive of the Directors-General Committee for Economic Affairs, which was subordinate to the ministerial committee mentioned earlier, was a senior army officer. When Prime Minister Levi Eshkol attempted to increase the policymaking role of the cabinet in the Occupied Territories in 1968, he was unsuccessful. The most important day-to-day decisions in the territories at all levels remained with Defense Minister Moshe Dayan. Links with the six regional military governors were maintained at the Defense Ministry through a major general (*aluf*) designated as coordinator of government operations in the administered areas and head of the general staff's Military Government Department.

Following the 1967 war, Labor and Likud policy was to enforce security in the occupied areas while maintaining normal day-to-day civilian life as much as possible. Legal systems that had existed before occupation were continued subject to amendment by the military authorities. The existing tax and judicial systems remained; taxes were paid to the military government, and military courts were set up to deal with security offenses. During the 1970s the Israeli military authorities introduced several hundred military orders that fundamentally altered the pre-1967 law of the West Bank and Gaza.

Under the orders of the Ministry of Defense, many public services were reactivated, reorganized, and expanded. Postal and telephone services were linked with the Israeli system and placed under the supervision of Israeli officers. Israeli technicians and engineers improved the water supply system and conducted hydrological surveys to expand the service. Health, social welfare, and educational services were continued under Israeli supervision. Israeli regulations were introduced to license radios, regularize weights and measures, certify Arab tour guides, and implement Israeli road safety standards and automobile registration.

A number of Israeli businesses and commercial operations were permitted to operate in the West Bank and Gaza, and local Arabs were employed as their representatives. The groups included certain Israeli banks and transportation services that were extended into the territories.

Local government was maintained in the West Bank and Gaza. At first, the military government appointed mayors or heads of local councils, but by 1976 local elections were permitted in the towns of the West Bank. Under the Jordanian government the larger West Bank towns had twelve-member councils elected by taxpaying males. Regulations for these elections were modified in 1976, extending suffrage to women and broadening the categories of voters. During the 1976 West Bank elections widespread criticism of Israel was permitted, and several candidates were elected on platforms that supported the Palestine Liberation Organization. However, by the late 1980s Israeli officers had taken over most local government executive posts; many West Bank mayors were discharged, and several were deported for nationalist activities.

Defense Minister Dayan implemented a double-edged policy. On the one hand, he forcefully repressed overt manifestations of political opposition and tried to thwart the organization of Arab movements other than strictly local groups. On the other hand, he attempted to normalize and improve day-to-day life in the Occupied Territories. One of the most innovative aspects of his policy was to open the bridges across the Jordan River, thereby linking the occupied West Bank with the Jordanian East Bank and facilitating the movement of hundreds of thousands of Arabs and other visitors between Israeli-held territory and the Arab world. However, the vast majority of those who fled during the 1967 war and earlier were not permitted to return, although some family visits were authorized, and West Bank students in Arab countries were allowed to visit their homes during vacations if they obtained the appropriate permits from the military government. Extensive trade also developed between the West Bank and the rest of the Arab world. In short, this policy greatly facilitated Israeli contact with the Arab world.

Israel rejected the U.S. and UN view that provisions of the Fourth Geneva Convention that concerned the protection of civilian populations under military occupation should apply to its governance in the Occupied Territories, although it claimed voluntary compliance with most of the convention's stipulations. In Israel's view, the West Bank and Gaza were not Occupied Territories that belonged to some recognized foreign nation but were areas whose legal status was uncertain; therefore, it claimed, the territories were not subject to the Geneva Convention.

The establishment of civilian Jewish settlements has caused great controversy. Both Labor and Likud governments have been deeply involved and have supported Jewish settlements whose population had reached over 130,000 by 1995 (not including East Jerusalem). Although most of these settlements are located near the 1949 armistice borders (the green line), some are in the midst of dense Arab populations. Most notable among the latter is Kiryat Arba, which adjoins the city of Hebron. Many Kiryat Arba residents belong to the most militant right-wing factions of Jewish society; nonetheless, the IDF is responsible for their safety. The Ministry of Defense invests large sums from its own funds—separate from the IDF budget—to develop protective networks for the settlements. In 1994 it invested about 10 million NIS in fencing, lighting, electric gates, reconstruction of roads, security cars, and communication systems for settlements in the Occupied Territories. For further discussion of IDF policies in the Occupied Territories, see "The Intifada" in Chapter 8.

Some important security-related activities initiated by the Ministry of Defense also appear in other ministry budgets. Expenditures for road construction are hidden in the Housing Ministry's budget, and telephones are covered by the Communication Ministry. The government also orders and buys products from companies and factories located in priority areas within the territories, thus enabling them to sustain economic viability.

Over the years, especially after the beginning of the intifada in 1987, thousands of Arabs have been imprisoned in detention camps inside Israel and the territories for "security" offenses. An important component of the Israeli-Palestinian Authority bargaining during 1994 was the release of these prisoners, although several thousand had been freed following the 1993 Oslo agreement.

The Ministry of Foreign Affairs

In one of the disputes between Prime Minister Ben-Gurion and Foreign Minister Sharett, Ben-Gurion was reported to have said, "It is not important what the Gentiles say but what the Jews do!" This attitude toward Israel's international affairs has often been reflected in activities of the Foreign Ministry. The Ministry of Foreign Affairs is Israel's third-most-important ministry, less because of its size, budget, or numbers of personnel than because its activities draw constant international media attention. The head of the ministry is usually among the senior members of the ruling party. Moshe Sharett, Golda Meir, Abba Eban, Yigal Allon, Moshe Dayan, Yitzhak Shamir, David Levy, and Shimon Peres all headed the Foreign Ministry; Sharett, Meir, Shamir, and Peres were also prime ministers. Many Ministry of Foreign Affairs employees have been civil servants in the old British style: They were trained as cadets and joined the diplomatic corps at lower ranks. However, several positions are considered political appointments; it is the foreign minister's prerogative to assign ambassador and consul posts in certain countries such as the United States, Russia, Jordan, Egypt, and France.

In the 1960s, when Israel initiated relations with many Third World countries, the Department for International Cooperation was established to send experts to developing countries to help start intensive agricultural projects in cooperation with local populations. Many students came to Israel from Africa, Southeast Asia, and Latin America for training in special development-oriented programs. Many of these ties were broken, however, following the 1973 October War because of Arab and Soviet pressures. Following the Gulf War, the Oslo agreement, and the collapse of the Soviet Union, Israel renewed or established new ties with at least fifteen states including the Vatican, Vietnam, Laos, Cambodia, and several more remote countries such as Burkina Faso and São Tomé and Principe.

The foreign office has attained close ties with the European Economic Community through a special agreement. Many ministry officials and special appointees serve on boards of international bodies such as the World Health Organization, the International Labor Organization, and the World Bank. The Ministry of Foreign Affairs is responsible for conveying a positive image of Israel, especially in the West. Its most important target is the United States where, in addition to its large embassy, Israel has ten fully staffed consulates with substantial budgets for improving the country's image. Between 1984 and 1987, about $730 million was spent for this purpose in the United States alone.

The Economic Ministries

Treasury Ministry. The minister of finance is one of the most powerful cabinet members because his or her department, the Treasury, raises the funds that pay the government's bills. A strong finance minister such as Pinhas Sapir, who was an influential Labor party leader, can play a large role in directing government policy. Although theoretically major policy decisions are collective, with all cabinet members participating, a strong prime minister in collaboration with a powerful minister of finance can use the power of money to determine priorities. All cabinet members must consult with the finance minister in preparing their budgets, even though they do not necessarily have to consult each other in setting policy. Departments that make the most convincing case to the finance minister and the prime minister have an advantage over those that are less skillful in presenting their plans. National security has always been given top priority and has received as much as 40 percent of the budget; other ministries have had to struggle for the remaining available funds.

The ministry is divided into four major departments: government personnel, state accounting, state income through taxation, and the national budget. The commissioner of the state civil service is responsible for hiring and firing (a difficult task because most state workers are protected by tenure), for promotions, and for the conduct of state employees. The commissioner is, in essence, "the chief bureaucrat" who determines the wage scale based on skills, rank, and administrative experience. He or she is also responsible for the code of rights and obligations for state workers.

The General Accounting Department supervises the flow of expenditures of various ministries. Ministers and directors general of various ministries are not legally free to spend monies as they wish even from their own budgetary appropriations. Every government ministry has a representative of the general accountant's office who must approve and cosign each expenditure beyond a certain sum and obtain receipts. Through this system the Treasury Ministry keeps firm and close control over expenditures.

The department in charge of state income is responsible for assessing the financial framework for government expenditures. This assessment is not always accurate; during Israel's first forty-five years there were as many years with budgetary surpluses as years with deficits. State income relies on five principal sources: current receipts, capital receipts, receipts from the Bank of Israel, business enterprises, and budgetary surpluses or deficits. Israel is one of the most heavily taxed countries in the world. Included among the various taxes imposed during the 1990s were the value-added tax on private nonprofit institutions, a health tax, employee and organization taxes, travel taxes, levies on foreign currency, customs taxes, and others. A large part of Israel's income, however, comes from foreign loans and grants.

A fourth division within the Treasury Ministry, the Department of Budgets, places its representatives, or "referents," in each government ministry. These representatives specialize in every aspect of the daily operations and projects of their particular ministry. This knowledge serves the department heads, as well as the minister of finance, in annual bargaining over budget appropriations. Ministers and directors general often complain that these referents have more authority over policy in their ministries than the ministers themselves.

Many government appointments to various public posts require the signature of the minister of finance. Except for the prime minister, who is formally in charge of the government, only the finance minister can view the entire system. Since 1985, when a law that deals with the basics of the budget was adopted, centralization has also had an impact on local government in areas such as education and welfare, which receive funding from the Treasury Ministry.

The Treasury Ministry also affects activities in the private sector, where it faces conflicting goals. On the one hand, a free and efficient economy requires privatization; on the other, the transfer of public goods and services to private interests results in the loss of some of government's powers in the face of opposition from organized labor. Both Labor- and Likud-led governments have tended to move slowly toward privatization. Between 1968 and 1988, almost equal numbers of enterprises were privatized by Labor and Likud governments. In the 1992 election, the major political parties introduced an explicit commitment to privatization in their platforms. Not until 1994, however, did the Ministry of Finance take serious steps in this direction. Between June 1993 and July 1994, for example, over 2 billion NIS was obtained through privatization by the sale of government interest in two major banks and eight state-owned enterprises.

Other Economic Ministries. Five other ministries also lie within the economic category. The Ministry of Economy and Planning, the least important and the smallest of these, was formed by Begin in 1981 to provide a cabinet post for his prestate underground partner, Yaakov Meridor. Meridor, a successful businessman, was asked to coordinate government economic policy—an area in which the Likud had performed badly between 1977 and 1981. Meridor was designated to become a kind of a "superminister" in charge of several specific areas such as the Division for Economic Planning, which had been transferred from other ministries to his new organization. However, much of the economic policymaking apparatus remained in the Treasury, and Meridor was soon effectively reduced to an ineffective "subminister." Nonetheless, the Ministry of Economy and Planning sustained its position in the government structure and since that time has been awarded as a political payoff to young politicians or to those for whom the prime minister cannot find a better assignment. From an administrative point of view, only ministers without portfolio and the deputy ministers are less important.

Another less important economic ministry is Tourism, which was invented in 1966 as a payoff to the Independent Liberals, a party previously labeled "dummy." Between 1966 and 1977 the leader of the Independent Liberals, Moshe Kol, was the minister of tourism. This arrangement allowed some paid jobs to be given to party loyalists. The Likud abolished the ministry in 1977, but it was reestablished in 1979 to provide a ministerial position for Gideon Pat and later for Avraham Sharir, leaders of the Liberal faction within Likud.

Tourism is an "invisible" export industry whose added value is very high. For many years the Israeli tourist industry relied mainly on Jewish visitors and Christian pilgrims. However, during the 1980s and early 1990s, investments in the construction of new infrastructure and the marketing of tourism yielded great returns. In 1993 almost 2 million tourists visited Israel for an extended period, spending about $2.5 billion.

The economic as well as the political status of the Ministry of Agriculture has been continually declining. In the early days of the state, agriculture was not only a major economic sector and the backbone of the Labor movement, it was also a symbol of renewed Jewish nationalism. Most agriculture ministers were members of *moshavim* (cooperatives) or kibbutzim and had many followers in these institutions. Levi Eshkol, Moshe Dayan, Ariel Sharon, and Rafael Eitan were among the most visible agriculture ministers.

The three most important functions of the minister are to sustain agricultural lands, develop water resources, and coordinate the import and export of agricultural products. During the high-inflation era of the 1980s, when many private farmers and kibbutzim suffered economically, the ministry became their main protector against hostile government forces, especially the Ministry of Finance.

The Ministry of Industry and Trade also represents sectorial interests. Until Likud took power in 1977, the ministry was called Commerce and Industry. Perhaps to symbolize a change in values and orientation, the Likud switched the emphasis from commerce to industry. When the economy was restrictive and highly regulated during the early 1950s, the minister in charge, Dov Joseph, was the least popular person in government because he had to implement rationing of consumer goods and suppress the emerging black market. Thirty years later, when Ariel Sharon served in this post, the Unity government boldly attempted to suppress hyperinflation by reinstating rigid price controls.

The ministry helps to attract new investments and directs them to government-designated areas with the aid of subsidies and tax benefits. It also invests in the development of small business and exports. The ministry's chief scientist undertakes industry-related research and development, which helps individual firms to benefit from new scientific findings and technological innovations. To a large degree, this ministry's initiation and resources have helped to make Israel an international leader in the high-tech industry.

The last ministry in the economic category is Labor and Social Welfare. During the provisional government in 1948–1949 there was a post called minister for labor and construction. In 1949 Golda Meir (then Meyerson) became minister of labor and national insurance and served in that capacity until 1955. Yitzhak Rabin was minister of labor for three months in 1974 until he became prime minister. In 1977 Likud, in an attempt to rationalize the administrative structure, combined labor and welfare and created the Ministry for Social Betterment, which in 1981 again became the Ministry of Labor.

The principal tasks of labor and social welfare are to address unemployment, expand the labor force, train adults and youth in needed professions and skills, provide day care for children of working parents and homes and social centers for the aging, provide shelters for abused women and protection and care for the mentally incapacitated and invalids, rehabilitate prisoners, and similar social functions. The ministry's budget is second only to that of defense (see Table 7.2), and it has more personnel than only two other ministries.

The National Insurance Institute. The National Insurance Institute, an independent agency, administers an extensive array of social security programs, which cover a large portion of the population, under the direction of the labor minister. Payments include pensions for the elderly and for widows and their children, monthly allowances for families with more than one child, maternity benefits, payments for medical treatment and hospital care, payments to the disabled and to families of breadwinners who have been killed, and vocational rehabilitation benefits. The institute is operated by a council of public representatives appointed by the minister of labor and is headed by a director who is also appointed by the minister. National and local insurance tribunals settle contested insurance claims. Appeals from the local tribunals are sent to appeal tribunals headed by district court judges in the civil court system, and final appeals can be made to the Supreme Court.

The Social Ministries

Education and Culture. About a third of Israelis are involved in education as either teachers or students. Most educational institutions are government owned and operated under the Ministry of Education and Culture. A special feature of the system is the division of education for Israeli Jews into secular and religious institutions, both operated by the state. The ministry has a special branch for the school systems in Arab and Druze areas, where instruction is in Arabic; it also supervises education in the Occupied Territories through the military government.

When Israel was established, the only university was the Hebrew University in Jerusalem, a private institution assisted by overseas contributions. As the number of higher education institutions increased and costs escalated, the country's universities became increasingly dependent on government financing. Although universities still receive a large amount of private aid and operate autonomously, the Ministry of Education and Culture now plays an active role in their financing and operation.

The importance of the ministry is underscored by the fact that Mapai and, later, Labor always kept control of it because they viewed education as a means of socializing future citizens and voters. Likud, however, did not regard the ministry as crucial and in 1977 awarded it to the NRP. Labor regained control in 1984 and placed former president Yitzhak Navon at its head, but Likud again transferred the position to the NRP in 1990.

During the bargaining process that preceded the formation of Rabin's coalition in 1992, two potential junior partners—Meretz and Tzomet—competed for the ministry. The leaders of both parties clearly understood the political value of controlling education. When Shulamit Aloni of Meretz obtained the post, Rafael Eitan of Tzomet decided to stay out of the government. Aloni's outspoken liberal ideas irritated the leaders of Shas, another coalition partner that represented the Orthodox community; consequently, Shas threatened to leave the coalition unless Aloni was replaced, preferably by a man. Aloni *was* replaced by Amnon Rubinstein; she became minister of communication and minister of science and technology.

The Ministry of Education determines the curriculum for all levels of schooling and introduces special programs for both the Jewish and Arab sectors such as familiarization with democratic values, social cooperation, Holocaust history, Jewish traditions, and other value-laden subjects. The ministry builds classrooms, trains and finances teachers and management staff, and introduces new technologies to students. In addition to providing support for special education and cultural activities, the ministry supervises sports under a deputy minister for sports nominated in 1990.

Other Social Ministries. The social welfare and health network includes extensive assistance in rehabilitation, community organization, youth work, and services to the blind; it also supports some government hospitals. These services are supplemented by voluntary organizations that are supported by international contributions. The American Joint Distribution Committee supports hospitals, senior homes, child development centers, and mental health services; the Organization for Rehabilitation Through Training (ORT) supports more than seventy technical and vocational institutions; the Women Workers' Council, an affiliate of the Histadrut, focuses on child care and education; the Women's International Zionist Organization is involved in child care and education; and Hadassah (Women's Zionist Organization of America) operates the country's largest hospital—which is internationally known for its health services and research—and provides educational services.

The Histadrut's sick fund, *Kupat Holim,* is Israel's largest voluntary organization; nearly 70 percent of Israeli residents are members. The fund provides free medical insurance for immigrants during their first six months in Israel and maintains over 1,000 clinics, more than 4,000 hospital beds, a number of convalescent and rest homes, laboratories, physiotherapeutic institutes, pharmacies, dental clinics, and a medical research institute. Although it is not a government agency, its close affinity with the Labor party through the Histadrut gave *Kupat Holim* quasi-official status during the era of Labor governance.

During the 1980s, because of the gradual increase in health-related costs as a result of longer life expectancies, expensive technology and medicine, greater public demand for treatment, and staff demands for higher wages, the health system in Israel was in constant crisis. When Likud controlled the Ministry of Health, steps were taken to privatize hospitals and other health institutions, but these attempts failed because the Histadrut opposed the policy. The Histadrut, the country's largest health care provider, depended on the dues *Kupat Holim* members paid for its services. But in fact, 28 percent of health dues were used by the Histadrut to finance its other operations—a practice that became the main issue in Haim Ramon's campaign against the Histadrut old guard. Following his May 1994 victory and takeover of the Histadrut, Ramon forced the government to assume most of *Kupat Holim*'s debts. To finance this operation the government passed a comprehensive health tax bill that required all citizens to pay 4.8 percent of their salaries directly to the government beginning January 1, 1995. *Kupat Holim* was separated from the Histadrut, and universal health coverage was installed.

The special place of Jewish immigration in Zionist ideology underscores the importance of the Ministry of Immigrant Absorption, which works closely with the Jewish Agency for Palestine and the World Zionist Organization. In effect, a division of labor exists between the ministry and the Jewish agency; the latter encourages and directs immigration to Israel and assists in the absorption of new immigrants once they reach there.

Most of the ministry's budget is used to house immigrants. Official policy guarantees every new immigrant family a home somewhere in Israel. Fulfillment of this promise is at times complicated by bureaucratic inconsistencies and administrative problems. Sephardi Jews who arrived in Israel at an earlier time believed housing and employment opportunities provided to them were inferior to those offered to new arrivals from the Soviet Union, who were given jobs as scientists or university professors. Young Israeli couples have complained that Soviet newcomers found apartments more easily than longtime Israelis.

The ministry arranges special courses to retrain new immigrants for employment in occupations needed in Israel; it assists them in finding employment and helps to establish small businesses with low-interest loans. The ministry also organizes transient absorption centers and hostels, where newcomers study Hebrew; it works closely with immigrant associations and other ministries including education, health, agriculture, and housing.

The Jewish Agency for Palestine and the World Zionist Organization were given special legal status in a law passed by the Knesset in 1952 and in a covenant signed in 1954 by the Israeli government and the World Zionist Organization Executive. The law reiterates the fundamental Zionist credo that the State of Israel is the creation of all Jewish people and that every Jew can immigrate to the country in accordance with the law. It notes that the World Zionist Organization led the efforts to establish the Jewish state.

The World Zionist Organization/Jewish Agency (which is not part of the government) is the authorized agency for Israeli development and settlement, and it coordinates Israeli institutions and organizations that are active in immigrant absorption. A joint committee created by the law authorizes the Zionist Executive to enter into contracts; to acquire, hold, and dispose of property; and to enter legal or other proceedings. The law also exempts the Executive from Israeli taxation. A prime objective of the law was to facilitate the use of tax-exempt status in fund-raising, as is the case in the United States, by defining Jewish agency activities as purely humanitarian.

When Ben-Gurion was prime minister, he frequently circumvented the agency because he believed it was dominated by the bickering and political maneuvering of Zionist political parties. He encouraged separate fund-raising endeavors such as bonds for Israel, private gifts to educational institutions, and similar efforts.

The Immigrant Absorption Ministry was established in 1948 and was under the control of the NRP until 1952. Between 1952 and 1967 its functions were carried out by other ministries. The ministry was reestablished in 1967; since that time its importance has fluctuated according to the saliency of the immigration issue and the personality and political weight of its minister.

The last ministry in the social category is the Ministry of Religious Affairs. The nature of Israel's political system, in which coalition governments usually include cabinet members from the religious bloc, gives the Orthodox establishment an important role in government administration through its control of this ministry. The ministry has been at the center of several controversial issues regarding religious and secular matters such as marriage and divorce, the status of immigrant Jews under the Law of Return, Sabbath observance, and the supervision of dietary laws. The Knesset and the Ministry of Religious Affairs are often under pressure from the Chief Rabbinate and the Supreme Rabbinical Council. The rabbinate's judgments are based on traditional Jewish law, or *halacha,* and its followers in the religious parties influence cabinet policy and Knesset legislation.

The organizational structure of the religious hierarchy is a relic of the Ottoman era, when Palestine's religious communities were known as *millets* (nations). Various Christian *millets* of the Ottoman Empire were headed by patriarchs who served as high priests or religious functionaries and as ethnarchs, or national leaders. The Jewish *millet* was headed by the *hacham bashi* (chief rabbi) of Jerusalem, also called *Rishon le-Zion* (first in Zion). The tradition of separate Sephardi and Ashkenazi chief rabbis was established during this period, and each community conducted its own rabbinical courts.

Ottoman practice was continued during the British mandate, which recommended that a board of electors consisting of officiating rabbis and laypeople elect a Supreme Rabbinical Council headed by both Sephardi and Ashkenazi chief rabbis. The council's two joint presidents were assisted by three Sephardic and three Ashkenazic rabbis who were members of the council and three laypeople who acted as advisers.

The mandatory government gave the rabbinical courts exclusive jurisdiction in matters of marriage, divorce, alimony, confirmation of wills, and other personal-status matters and religious endowments. The Supreme Rabbinical Council was authorized to decide on interpretations of Jewish law in matters not within the jurisdiction of the rabbinical courts. Since the mandate, the Supreme Rabbinical Council has been enlarged to include twelve rabbis, among them the chief rabbis of Jerusalem and Tel-Aviv as well as the country's Sephardi and Ashkenazi chief rabbis.

There are eight regional rabbinical courts with sixty-five Jewish religious judges (*dayanim*) and a rabbinical court of appeals headed by the two chief rabbis. The Supreme Rabbinical Council is self-appointed (by its own members); thus, only Orthodox rabbis become members, and only Orthodox jurisdiction is officially recognized in Jewish ritual or legal matters. Because of the Orthodox monopoly, attempts by Conservative and Reform Jewish leaders in the United States to obtain recognition in Israel have been unsuccessful.

In addition to operating the Jewish religious courts and administering *halacha,* the Chief Rabbinate supervises *kashrut,* or ritual purity of imported food and food in kosher restaurants. Its staff of rabbis, ritual slaughterers, examiners, and inspectors travel as far as Argentina, Brazil, Uruguay, Yugoslavia, Bulgaria, Romania, Hungary, and Ethiopia to supervise the ritual slaughter of cattle imported into Israel.

The Ministry of Religion is responsible for nearly two hundred religious councils and over three hundred religious committees in smaller communities, which are given assistance in religious matters by the Supreme Rabbinical Council. The country's thousands of synagogues and officially appointed rabbis are also supervised by the council.

Muslim, Druze, and Christian religious courts operating within the Ministry of Religious Affairs have exclusive jurisdiction in personal-status matters that affect their community members. Until the 1990s, directors of offices for Muslim, Druze, and Christian affairs were Jewish. In matters of personal status involving persons of different religious communities, the president of the Israeli Supreme Court decides which religious court will have jurisdiction.

If there is a question about whether a personal-status case falls within the exclusive jurisdiction of a religious court, the matter is referred to a special tribunal composed of two Supreme Court judges and the president of the highest religious court of the community concerned. Judgments of the religious courts are executed through the civil courts, although the civil courts may refuse to implement such judgments if they exceed the religious authorities' jurisdiction or are contrary to "natural justice."

Although less than a fifth of the Jewish population consistently supports the Orthodox parties in national elections and less than a third of residents are considered consistent observers of Orthodox Jewish traditions and practices, decisions of the Chief Rabbinate affect the total population—especially in matters pertaining to personal status, immigration, and citizenship. Secularists have at times sought to challenge or circumvent religious authority in personal-status or citizenship matters, which has resulted in intervention by the civil judiciary or secular authorities.

Failure to resolve the issue of Orthodox religious authority over personal status and citizenship and the ambiguities surrounding that issue has raised problems for the government in its relations with the large, non-Orthodox Jewish communities that support Israel in the United States. Whereas Reform and Conservative Jewish rabbis and their congregations can hold religious services in Israel, the Orthodox rabbinate has a monopoly over the performance of personal-status rites such as marriage. Because of the large financial and political support Israel receives from non-Orthodox U.S. Jews, complaints from Reform and Conservative rabbis about their exclusion have strained relations between the Jewish state and the diaspora. The Orthodox rabbinate in Israel and its coreligionists abroad adamantly refuse to allow non-Orthodox rabbis to break the monopoly they hold over personal-status matters, overseeing *kashrut,* and supervision of Jewish cemeteries in Israel.

Orthodox refusal to recognize conversions to Judaism unless they were carried out by Orthodox rabbis has created opposition among non-Orthodox U.S. Jews, as well as among the many Russian Jewish immigrants whose spouses are not Jewish or who were converted by non-Orthodox rabbis. The issue was politicized in 1974 when the Supreme Rabbinical Council ordered the National Religious party not to join any new government coalition unless it pledged to amend the Law of Return to exclude non-Orthodox conversions to Judaism. In March 1974 the Supreme Court of Israel ordered the Supreme Rabbinical Council to show why the court should not revoke the council's instructions to the NRP; it also issued a temporary injunction barring the rabbinical authorities from enforcing the ban pending a final decision by the Supreme Court.

In the meantime, a compromise was reached when the NRP agreed to join the coalition government if the cabinet accepted the principle that conversions would be done according to Orthodox religious law and if a cabinet committee settled the conversion issue within a year. The agreement also provided that the minister of the interior would officially state that to the best of his or her knowledge, no non-Jew had been registered as a Jew during the previous four years.

With the defeat of the Labor government in the May 1977 elections, the religious issue again came to the fore. When the leader of the new Likud government, Menachem Begin, approached the NRP to join his coalition, it demanded amendment of the Law of Return so that only Orthodox conversions to Judaism "according to *halacha*" would be recognized in registering Israeli residents and granting citizenship. This demand rekindled the dispute between the Israeli government and its non-Orthodox Jewish supporters in the diaspora.

The dispute erupted again after the 1988 election, which put the religious parties in a pivotal position in Shamir's proposed coalition government. Thus, they felt they could ask for substantial alterations to the Law of Return. To deflect their pressure, Shamir opted for a Unity government with Labor. By joining the Labor coalition following the 1992 election, Shas replaced the NRP as the holder of the religious portfolio, but when Shas left the coalition in 1994, Labor became the principal protector of religious interests and the main provider of religious services.

The Infrastructure Ministries

Of the six infrastructure ministries, construction and housing and transport are the most important. The Ministry of Construction and Housing holds title to most state lands and commands large budgets. Established in 1961 as the Ministry of Development and Housing and headed by important personalities in the Labor party, the ministry initially supplied low-cost homes. It was not until 1979, when David Levy made the ministry his power base within Likud, that it acquired central importance. Between 1979 and 1990, Levy was the minister in charge of the construction of apartments and roads, as well as deputy prime minister. His ministry coordinated all of the activities that were related to Project Renewal and that channeled huge resources to development towns and poor neighborhoods. By controlling these resources, Levy created a cadre of loyal followers at the local level of politics. Most of his followers were Sephardi Jews, many of North African origin. His brother Maxim Levy, the mayor of Lydda, was part of this locally based operation—especially after his election as head of the Center for Local Government, which coordinates the activities of municipal authorities in Israel.

Levy moved to the post of foreign minister in 1990, leaving housing operations to Ariel Sharon, who aggressively initiated construction of new settlements in the West Bank. Sharon also invested large sums to provide quick housing solutions, often in the form of mobile homes called "caravans," for the hundreds of thousands of new immigrants from the Soviet Union and Ethiopia. In 1992 Benjamin Ben Eliezer became the minister of housing and construction and used a $10 billion loan guaranteed by the U.S. government to construct housing and a modern road system.

The housing minister is also chair of the board of directors of the Israel Lands Management organization. In this capacity he or she can order the transfer of agricultural lands into construction sites and can legally confiscate lands for public roads or new settlements. The minister also provides rent and mortgage subsidies to help qualified Israeli citizens purchase apartments.

The Ministry of Transport was established in 1948 and at first was controlled by Mapai. In 1952 the General Zionists obtained control for three years, and the ministry was then taken over by Achdut Ha-Avoda and Labor until 1969. In the 1969 large coalition, former air force commander Ezer Weizman became minister of transportation for about eight months. His major achievement was to increase the speed limit on major highways. Likud controlled the ministry from 1981 to 1992. When Labor returned to power in 1992, Israel Keisar, former chief of the Histadrut, became the minister in charge.

The ministry controls the country's transportation networks including airports, seaports, boat basins, railroads, and the El Al airline. It also licenses automobiles and other vehicles and supervises driver safety. Since 1993 the ministry has assisted the Palestinian Authority in establishing its own transportation network.

The Ministry of Communication includes the former postal service. The first minister of communication was Shimon Peres, who was assigned the post in 1970. Since that time the ministry has been controlled by the DMC, Likud, Shinui, Shas, and Meretz. The ministry supervises all mail, telephone service, and television and radio stations. During the early 1990s its principal organ, Bezek, effectively supplied high-quality telephone service and undertook steps toward privatization.

The Ministry of Energy and Infrastructure was established in 1977 for Itzhak Modai, a Liberal leader within the Likud party. Its main responsibilities were to search for and import oil, coal, and natural gas and to maintain reserves for emergencies. The ministry also supervises the electricity supply and energy preservation. The powerful union of electric company workers, which is the direct beneficiary of the ministry, dictates workers' demands to the energy minister.

The Ministry of Science and Technology was a straightforward political payoff invented by Menachem Begin in 1982 to lure into his government Yuval Ne'eman, leader of the right-wing Tehiya. As with the Ministry of Economy and Planning, once established the Ministry of Science and Technology remained a permanent part of the administrative structure. The ministry initiates international cooperation and exchange programs in science, most notably with Germany and the United States; helps new immigrant scientists find jobs in research institutions; supports research in various areas; and provides aid to research institutions. Ne'eman's favorite project was the relatively small-budget space program, which cost about 23 million NIS in 1994.

The last ministry in the infrastructure group is the Ministry of Environment Quality, established in 1988. One of its functions was taken over from the Prime Minister's office, another was moved from the Ministry of Interior, and a third was newly invented. The ministry deals with waste, water and air pollution, reconstruction of beaches and waterways, and dangerous industrial by-products. Awareness of the importance of a clean environment has been minimal in Israel; however, since the formation of this ministry the subject has acquired a higher place on the public agenda.

The Ministry of Interior

Local government in Israel is supervised by the ministry of Interior, whose responsibilities are divided among the country's six administrative districts, each with its own administrative center. The districts include Jerusalem (centered in Jerusalem), northern (Nazareth), Haifa (Haifa), central (Ramla), Tel Aviv (Tel Aviv), and southern (Beersheba). The ministry drafts legislation that regulates local activities and approves local tax rates, budgets, and bylaws. Local governments oversee municipalities, and local regional councils help to support education, health and sanitation, social welfare, water, road maintenance, parks, and fire departments. Funds for such activities at the local level are raised through taxes or levies on the inhabitants, with extra aid for Jewish settlements provided by the Jewish Agency for Palestine. Because of the allocations for Jewish settlements, local Arab authorities have often charged that they are being discriminated against when they receive lesser matching funds for roads, water supplies, or schools.

The ministry controls many diverse civilian services; it issues citizenship documents, passports, and the ID card Israelis must carry at all times, and it maintains an effective network of the population that keeps records on citizens' eligibility to vote. The ministry also approves permits for building plans and permits to carry firearms.

Elections for local and municipal councils are usually held simultaneously with or close to the Knesset election. All voters who are qualified to participate in the national polls, as well as residents who are not Israeli citizens, may cast ballots in local elections. Thus, since 1967, in elections for the Jerusalem municipality many Arab voters from East Jerusalem have been ineligible to participate in the Knesset balloting because they have not acquired Israeli citizenship; they are, however, able to vote in municipal elections.

Until the 1970s, mayors and heads of local councils were chosen by the councils. In more recent elections, voters have tended to support the party with the most popular local following regardless of how they vote in the Knesset elections. In 1973 several municipalities and towns split their votes, electing Knesset candidates from one party and local government officials from another. Sephardi Jews have been able to obtain positions of prominence in local government as a result of their leadership role in various political parties at the local level.

As in the Knesset, parties at the local level usually govern in coalitions because a single list rarely gains a majority. Candidates for local office, who usually represent the same parties as those in the Knesset, must bargain and make concessions with members of other parties in the council. Smaller parties often hold the balance and thus are influential in local politics. National party headquarters sometimes instruct their local candidates or agree among themselves that one party will obtain a mayoralty in exchange for another. Such complicated maneuvers have even affected negotiations for national coalitions.

Regional councils have been formed to represent villages or to help provide services in thinly populated areas. Kibbutzim, cooperatives, small farms, agricultural schools, and similar institutions are represented in regional councils. Smaller village committees must submit their annual budgets to the regional councils for approval. The councils are also authorized to levy approved taxes and to pass bylaws, a privilege that has rarely been used.

In instances of adjoining municipal boundaries, where services cross town or city borders, towns may form municipal unions to provide hospitals, schools, slaughterhouses, sewers, and other services. The first such municipal union was formed in 1955 between Tel Aviv and some of its suburbs.

The minister of the interior supervises activities of the local authorities through commissioners in each of the six districts and district officers in fourteen subdistricts. The minister has the legal power to remove local authorities because of inefficiency or serious dissension among the councillors. In such cases he or she may appoint a local committee of officials to replace the council until the next election. Proposals have been made to establish a local government court with jurisdiction over disputes between citizens and local authorities. Judges would be members of the public with magisterial qualifications and would have the status of other members of the Israeli judiciary.

The Ministry of Interior has developed several countrywide master plans to unify and coordinate a variety of national services. These include plans for a national highway system, power stations and electricity grids, floodwater storage and dispersal systems, national parks and nature reserves, recreational and tourist facilities, mining, and preservation of farmsteads.

The Ministry of Interior has usually been under the domain of one of the religious parties as a political payoff for their participation in the coalition. The religious parties can channel monies to local government, thus helping to establish bases of goodwill for religious causes. Budgets for sewage and water systems, development of beaches, erection of monuments, construction of internal roads, and provision of fire-fighting services can be transferred to a given municipality along with support for construction of synagogues and religious schools.

The Ministry of Justice

Under the 1948 Law and Administration Ordinance, the mandatory court system was continued in the new Jewish state. Thus, many of Israel's laws and courts that administer justice are based on the British tradition. The system includes local and district courts headed by appointed judges who follow the British legal code. Under this system innocence is assumed until guilt is proven, and bail is provided in criminal cases. In addition to the civil courts there are the religious and military courts described earlier. From 1948 until 1966, when military government was abolished, Israel's Arab citizens were affected most by the military legal system. Since 1967, Arabs in the occupied areas of the West Bank and Gaza have lived under the jurisdiction of the emergency regulations used by the British mandatory authorities, which has made them subject to the military courts.

The court system is organized in the following hierarchy. Each of the major cities has municipal courts with jurisdiction over offenses committed within the municipal area. These courts are authorized to impose small fines and short terms of imprisonment. Magistrates courts are established in each district and subdistrict and have limited jurisdiction in both criminal and civil cases. They may try contraventions or misdemeanors, offenses punishable by no more than three years in prison. Appeals from the magistrates courts are tried by one of the five district courts, located in Jerusalem, Tel Aviv, Haifa, Beersheba, and Nazareth. In addition to hearing appeals from lower courts, the district courts also have unlimited jurisdiction as courts of first instance in all civil and criminal cases not within the jurisdiction of magistrates courts. One judge usually presides at district courts. In capital cases—those in which the maximum punishment is ten years' imprisonment or more—and in certain other matters, three judges serve in district courts.

The Supreme Court is the highest judicial body with jurisdiction throughout Israel. It can hear civil and criminal appeals from lower courts and serves as the High Court of Justice to hear charges of arbitrary or illegal acts by public authorities. At times it serves as a special tribunal or maritime court. Cases are normally heard by three, five, seven, or nine justices. At the discretion of the president, cases decided by three judges may be reheard by five or more justices. When constituted as the High Court of Justice, the Supreme Court can consider petitions presented by individuals seeking redress against administrative decisions or cases outside the jurisdiction of any other court or tribunal. Although the court system is administered by the Ministry of Justice under a director of courts, an independent judiciary is maintained through the 1953 Judges Law.

There are also a number of special courts. Traffic magistrates courts try offenses against the Road Transport Ordinance. Special military courts were established in 1954 to try offenses against the Prevention of Infiltration (Offenses and Jurisdiction) Law. A court martial appeal court was established in 1955 to deal with offenses committed by soldiers or army employees. A national labor court and regional labor courts were set up under the Labor Courts Law in 1969 to deal with disputes between employers and workers, disputes between parties to collective agreements, claims against pension funds, disputes between a worker and a worker's organization, and claims under the National Insurance Law.

A major difference between the British and Israeli civil courts is that Israel has no provisions for trial by jury. As in Great Britain, the courts are subsidiary to parliament and may not invalidate any law it passes. Since there is no written constitution or Bill of Rights, the Knesset, rather than the courts, has the final word. The courts have the reputation for being scrupulously fair, frequently going out of their way to protect the rights of citizens under law in the face of attempted intrusion by administrative authorities. Because of their record of fairness and defense of individual rights, civil courts in Israel are among the few areas of government that have remained untainted by scandal, rumors of corruption, or political bias.

During its first decade, the Israeli court system frequently questioned administrative acts of civil and military authorities toward Arabs. In several instances, administrative authorities were charged with abusing the law or arrogating excessive authority. In one case the High Court of Justice noted that administrative regulations authorizing the government to seize Arab property

> gave the authorities broader power than is warranted in these emergency times. The broad right granted by the legislator to any authority places great responsibility in the hands of those who must often decide on the elementary rights of the interested parties. It makes it essential for them to act only after long and fair consideration and understanding of the results of their acts. Even the broadest authority does not justify arbitrary action and reliance on one's own judgment, which may be prompted by heartlessness or obstinacy.

In another case, the High Court of Justice reminded the military authorities that they too "are subordinate to the law as is any citizen of the State." The court emphatically reminded the military that one of Israel's basic principles was the rule of law and that the interests of both the public and the state would be endangered if the limitations placed upon the use of emergency regulations by the legislature were ignored. The court held that the need to preserve civil rights was no less important than national security. In several of its judgments, the court called attention to English common law, which guarantees individual freedom of movement. The principles of English law were applicable in Israel, the court insisted, and were in keeping with the spirit that motivated the establishment of the state and with Israel's proclamation of independence. In the court's opinion, the most important aspect of individual rights was not their declaration but their implementation. The court called attention to English judicial remedies, which on behalf of imprisoned individuals enable the courts to examine the legality of their arrest. If the court believed such arrests were illegal, it was obliged to order the prisoners' discharge.

A major difference in the relationship of British courts to administrative bodies and that same relationship in Israel is that in England such relations have been worked out over a period of three hundred years. Today, it is an accepted part of the unwritten British constitution that no administrative body will deliberately flout a court order. In Israel the relationship of the courts and administrative tribunals to authorities such as the army is still evolving. Although the spirit of English law pervades the courts and their decisions, it has not been accepted by many administrative authorities who come from different traditions. Administrative authority has frequently flouted or ignored legal decisions in the name of national security or some higher national interest. Because there is no automatic constitutional authority other than habeas corpus to implement writs of the High Court of Justice, these writs remain largely declaratory. Since the first decade of Israel's independence, the courts have become more cautious about intervening lest their authority be undermined by frequent evasion of court decisions by the administrative authorities.

Tribunals, boards, and committees established to deal with special cases or inquiries are frequently headed by judges. The 1967 Commission of Enquiry Law authorizes the government to appoint commissions to examine and report on matters of vital public interest. The president of the Supreme Court appoints the chair, who must also be a Supreme Court justice or a district court judge. The chief justice appoints other members of such commissions. Two notable examples were commissions appointed to investigate the burning of the Al-Aksa Mosque in Jerusalem in 1969 and the Agranat Commission, appointed in 1973 to investigate mismanagement of Israeli operations during the 1973 Arab-Israeli war.

The attorney general of Israel, who is under the Ministry of Justice, has extensive power in legal matters related to parliamentary immunity, in the indictment of judges for improper actions, in prosecution of offenses against state security in foreign relations, and in matters related to official secrets. He or she may transfer cases from civilian to military courts or the reverse or can obtain extradition of persons apprehended in Israel after having committed offenses in the occupied areas.

The Ministry of Justice is also responsible for the registration of title to land in Israel and for other transactions related to landed property. The ministry has continued the practice begun during the mandate in which newly settled land ownership is identified and registered according to precise cadastral survey.

The Ministry of Police

The Ministry of Police has a small staff of only about forty people. From its start in 1948 it was considered an "Oriental" ministry because it employs many Sephardi Jews. The total police force constitutes almost a third of the Israeli state administrative service. In 1994 there were over 24,000 police officers (including about 3,500 in the prison service) compared to about 52,000 other state workers. In 1977 the Ministry of Police was incorporated into the Ministry of Interior; added to its responsibilities were the frontier guard and the national prison system.

The police system in Israel is not local but is organized and administered at the national level, with headquarters in Jerusalem. The force employs women and members of Israeli minority groups.

In the 1984 Unity government, the Ministry of Police regained its independent status, with Haim Bar-Lev, a former IDF chief of staff and a war hero, as minister. The Likud's Roni Milo's appointment to the post in 1990 continued the process of transforming the ministry from a political award to Sephardim into an impartial and professional force. The ministry is responsible for internal security, including the prevention of terrorist activities, responsibility for law enforcement, and prevention of traffic violations. The ministry is extremely busy, constantly understaffed, and perenially underbudgeted. Thus, in areas not perceived as first priority on the internal security agenda, such as violations against property (burglaries and car thefts), private police often provide the desired protection.

Independent Agencies

The Bank of Israel and the State Comptroller's Office are independent agencies that have a great impact on making and executing the public policy of the ministries reviewed in this chapter.

The Bank of Israel. The Bank of Israel was established by the Knesset in 1954. Previously the Anglo-Palestine Bank and later called Bank Leumi, it was the government's bank for issuing currency and was its leading commercial bank. Since 1954, the Bank of Israel has become increasingly responsible for monetary and economic policies, with the sole right to issue currency and to administer, regulate, and direct the monetary system. The bank regulates and directs credit and the banking system according to government-established economic policies. Its primary purposes are to promote economic stability and stimulate capital investment. The bank's most difficult task has been to stabilize the currency. Since Israel was cut loose from the sterling bloc in 1948, the value of Israeli currency (the pound, then the shekel, then the new Israeli shekel [NIS]) has declined from parity with the British pound to only a fraction of its original value.

The Bank of Israel serves the country's banking system as the ultimate credit resource. It can impose credit and liquidity restrictions on the system. Through various measures, the bank can control the quantity of money in circulation and direct the flow of credit to sectors of the economy it designates worthy of investment. All new banks and branches of existing banks must be authorized by the central bank. The Bank of Israel also supervises the banking system; it searches out unsound practices and protects the public interest. State loans are administered by the Bank of Israel, which represents the country at international meetings related to finance and in agencies such as the International Monetary Fund and the World Bank.

The governor of the Bank of Israel, who is also the government's chief economic adviser, is appointed by the president and assisted by a seven-member advisory board. The bank's independence is indicated by the flexibility the governor has to determine monetary policy based on his or her assessment of the country's day-to-day economic situation. The only bank decision that must be approved by the Knesset is fixing the country's interest rate. The governor must also report to the Knesset increases in the money supply of 15 percent or more over the previous year.

During most of its history, the Bank of Israel has been free of scandal and charges of nepotism, party influence, and inefficiency. However, it became a center of national attention when Prime Minister Rabin designated a long-time Labor party leader as governor in 1976. The appointment was withdrawn after a police investigation revealed that the appointee had received large sums in concealed payments for fees and commissions in real estate deals and diverted the money to the treasury of his political party.

The commissioner of the bank and the minister of the treasury frequently coordinate their policies and decisions. On some occasions, however, evaluations of market performance made by the bank's highly respected research department contradict assessments made by the Treasury. In such instances (e.g., in 1994) each organization attempts to bring the other to its position through the media, academia, and politicians. The outcome is usually a compromise between the two opposing views.

The State Comptroller. A second important independent regulatory agency is the office of the State Comptroller, established in 1949 to audit ministries, the defense establishment, state enterprises, corporations and companies partially owned by the state, and local authorities. In 1971 the State Comptroller was also designated Ombudsman of Israel, or Commissioner of Public Complaints. The office has exercised a strong influence on the government by calling attention to many policy inconsistencies, overlapping programs, excessive expenditures or misappropriations of funds, and other irregularities that are the bane of a large bureaucracy. The authority and scope of this office exceed those of similar institutions in other countries because of Israel's extensive government network.

The 1958 State Comptroller Law provides that the president, on recommendation of the Knesset, will appoint the comptroller for a five-year term. The office is responsible only to the Knesset, to which the comptroller must report whenever he or she or the Knesset thinks it desirable. The comptroller must remain above politics, may not be a member of the Knesset or of any local government, and may not be involved in any business operation. To assure his or her objectivity, the comptroller must not be involved in any undertaking supported by, or holding a concession from, the government.

The comptroller's annual reports include findings from investigations of ministries, state agencies, and corporations and from reports on local authorities and corporations. The broad objectives of the office are to assure the legality of state financial transactions, to promote accuracy and orderliness in handling government financial documents and records, and to promote efficiency, economy, and ethical behavior in government.

The comptroller has broad powers under the 1958 law, including the authority to require submission of regular and special reports on the finances and administrative activities of any government office. With the approval of the Knesset Finance Committee, he or she has the authority to launch a commission of enquiry, including the right to compel testimony under oath.

As the number of government activities has increased and the responsibilities of the comptroller have grown, the staff, which is headquartered in Jerusalem, has expanded from about one hundred in 1959 to several hundred. Because of the large number of agencies and offices the agency supervises, inspections are planned so that a number of central units are examined yearly and the remaining bodies are audited at other regular intervals. Inspections of local authorities are carried out every three to five years, and the reports are submitted to mayors, local councils, and responsible government ministries. Each year the comptroller's office handles thousands of complaints from the public. When numerous complaints are received about a common problem, they are likely to spark an investigation.

The range of areas the comptroller has investigated have included practices of the Israeli Football Association, welfare services for Arabs, and veterinary services. Special reports have covered such government institutions as the Israel Mining Industries, the Israel Petroleum Company, the Cotton Production and Marketing Board, and the national lottery. The Israeli Defense Force, usually above public criticism, was the subject of a scathing 1977 report by the comptroller that contained accusations of wastage, slack reserve call-up procedures, and poor maintenance of vital equipment. The report concluded that many of the shortcomings that had contributed to Israel's unreadiness for the 1973 war had not been corrected.

Since 1971, when the Knesset designated the comptroller the public complaints commissioner, or ombudsman of Israel, any person—citizen or not—can lodge a complaint that claims injurious acts of commission or omission or alleges excessive bureaucratic rigidity or flagrant injustice. In such cases the commissioner can undertake an inquiry without being bound by the usual rules of legal procedure. If the inquiry reveals that the complaint is justified, the commissioner must report the findings to the complainant and must also ask the complainant to rectify the fault, and that body or person must notify the commissioner of measures taken to remedy the situation.

During the first five years of its existence, the ombudsman's office handled over 30,000 complaints. Table 7.3 presents the scope of complaints made to the ombudsman in 1993 against the various state institutions.

The totals presented in Table 7.3 reflect, approximately, both the average number of complaints entered every year since the establishment of the ombudsman and the average number of justified complaints. During the early years of operation, an estimated 40 to 50 percent of the complaints entered were found to be justified. Rather than use private attorneys to handle their complaints against the various state institutions, as occurs in wealthy or well-established countries, citizens turned to the ombudsman. Over the years, however, increasingly valid complaints have been handled by

TABLE 7.3   Complaints to the Ombudsman, 1993

Cases Presented Against	Number of Cases Presented	Cases Decided[a]		
		Total	Justified	% Justified of the Number Reviewed
Government ministries	3,166	2,260	651	28.8
State authorities	1,037	1,129	245	21.7
Local authorities	1,547	1,242	300	24.2
Others	1,542	1,598	106	6.6
Total	7,292	6,229	1,302	20.9

[a] Some of the decided cases were presented in the previous year; thus the total number of cases decided may exceed the number of cases presented.
Source: Statistical Abstract of Israel (Jerusalem: Government of Israel, Central Bureau of Statistics, 1994), p. 623.

lawyers, and the rate of justified complaints has gradually reached levels similar to those in other Western countries. The existence of the complaints procedure is often a psychological deterrent to officials and institutions that tend to arrogate to themselves excessive or arbitrary authority.

Perhaps the most effective deterrents used by the State Comptroller's Office are the reports made by its head, Miriam Ben Porath. After her nomination to the post of comptroller in 1989 following a distinguished career as a Supreme Court judge, Ben Porath effectively took advantage of both the media and her personal popularity to influence public opinion. One report published in May 1992 on the eve of the election concerned activities of certain individuals in the Housing Ministry. The report provided effective ammunition for Labor to attack Likud's "corruption"; consequently, it affected voting behavior and the final electoral outcomes.

State-Owned Enterprises. Government involvement in the economy and social life occurs to a much greater degree in Israel than in other Western systems. In addition to the ministries, thirteen regulatory councils, all operating as independent legal entities, are responsible for industrial production (especially those under the authority of the Ministry of Industry and Trade) and for marketing agricultural products. There are also several independent state agencies: the National Insurance Institute, Red Magen David (similar to the Red Cross), the Broadcasting Authority, the Gambling Authority, and others. The state-owned enterprises (SOEs) established under the auspices of the Government Companies Law of 1975 can also intervene in the economy.

By 1994 there were over 170 SOEs, either completely owned by the government or mixed companies. Israel Chemicals is the largest SOE; the Diamond Institute and the Israel Museum are mixed. The list of companies owned completely or in part by the government is impressive, ranging from small firms to huge conglomerates. The list includes SOEs in the areas of agricultural marketing, minerals, theater, communications, housing, education, banking, oil, insurance, research, tourism, medals and coins, sports, development, environmental quality, translation, military, roads, hotels, museums, air and sea travel and transportation, financial funds, consumer goods, and more. The government is present in virtually every area through one of its companies, and it holds a monopolistic position in several.

Each SOE requires the establishment of a board of directors to supervise company activities in the name of the public. Consequently, thousands of directorship positions are available for distribution to party loyalists as political payoffs. Since the early 1990s, the appointment of party members (defined as those who participate in internal party decisions) to directorships has not been permitted if the member has no knowledge of or expertise in the subject matter of a designated company. However, there are enough party loyalists in the country who do qualify for any given position to allow politics to still determine most board appointments.

Reforming the Administrative System

When Shimon Peres was prime minister between 1984 and 1986, a committee was formed to study the structure of and propose reforms in the public administration system. This committee, headed by Haim Koversky and Yehezkel Dror, submitted a two-volume report in 1989 based on the personal testimony and knowledge of dozens of practitioners and academic experts. The report observed that the huge Israeli administrative system was highly involved in the economy and was overcentralized and that the economic system and nongovernmental services were highly dependent on the central government; there was excessive intervention in all aspects of life, paternalism bridged with patronage, too much bureaucratization, and extensive politicization. The report also stated that public administration was not responsive to the urgent need to improve public policy and service. In sum, the administration was found to be ineffective and inefficient. It lacked a strategic master plan, or long-term vision, and was often more responsive to coalition needs and the politics of the hour than to citizen needs; there was often no relationship between the performance and productivity of state employees and their salaries.

The report did emphasize the achievements of the administration, such as its capacity to deal with complex problems and to maintain the framework of the law with little if any corruption. The report made four central recommendations for reform.

1. The role of ministries at the central government level should be redefined. The administration should give up functions better served by the private sector; ministries should formulate and guide, rather than implement, policies. The criterion for the transfer of responsibilities from the public to the private sector should be the "public interest," and the government should reduce the number of personnel employed by the state and in the public sector.

2. The number of friction points between service providers and citizens should be minimized, and citizen rights to hold the administration accountable for mischief should be reinforced.

3. Professionalism in the public service sector and the use of modern techniques, administrative practices, and machinery should be improved to increase employee motivation and improve the overall image of the service.

4. High-quality staff should be added to the cabinet and to each ministry so decisions can be made on the basis of research and analysis. The role of directors general of the ministries should be redefined to make them more effective, and a high-level managerial force should be appointed as a sepa-

rate professional stratum. Finally, a national college should be established to train high-level managers.

Very few of these recommendations have been adopted. Shimon Peres—the ultimate reformer—was out of office when the report came out, and as in other countries, resistance to change made the proposed reforms too costly politically and hence not feasible. However, the document became an important academic textbook.

8

Second Transition of Power

The first transition of power occurred in 1977 when Likud took control of the government from Labor; the second took place in 1992 when Labor regained political domination. Several factors contributed to the second transition, including the social realignment of certain groups, economic conditions, a change in society's value systems, and external events—including three wars. The quality of leadership and effective campaign strategies were also conducive to political change.

Stabilizing the First Transition of Power

Likud's victory over the Labor alignment in the 1977 election marked the beginning of a new era. At first, many observers believed Begin's victory was an aberration in the country's politics caused by the intrusion of the DMC, which had been formed a few months before the Ninth Knesset election from a diverse coalition of political figures who were disenchanted with both Labor and Likud. Many former Labor supporters voted for the DMC or joined its leadership. Thus, it was argued that if the DMC were co-opted into Begin's coalition cabinet or if it disintegrated after outliving its usefulness, the alignment would again capture the votes of those who had defected to the DMC in protest over thirty years of entrenched Labor rule.

During the 1977 campaign, Likud blamed Labor for the national economic plight. Its leaders argued that inflation was the number-one enemy of the people and promised to reduce it from 30 percent to 15 percent within a year. Within five years, Likud said, it would raise the GNP at least 40 percent by encouraging investment, reducing the adverse trade balance, ending bureaucratic interference, and abolishing currency controls. Both state and

Histadrut enterprises would be sold off to the private sector. Public lands would be marketed to raise state funds. The government would allow tax deductions for housekeeping expenses to help make more jobs available to women.

Ariel Sharon joined Likud immediately after the election, and his party was absorbed by it, thus increasing the strength of Begin's faction to forty-five seats. Flatto-Sharon's Development and Peace party, which received more votes than Sharon's Shlom-Zion party, received only one Knesset seat because Flatto-Sharon's name alone appeared on the party list; that seat was awarded to the NRP.

Few of Likud's economic promises were met. Instead of achieving economic recovery, Likud policies generated higher rates of inflation, unemployment, and foreign debt. The size of the public sector increased, and so did the bureaucracy. As discussed previously, six months before the 1981 elections Likud was at its lowest point; according to public opinion surveys Likud was capable of winning no more than eighteen seats. Begin's charisma and effective electoral strategy helped to turn things around between 1977 and 1981, which contributed to Likud's success.

Table 8.1 presents the results of the Ninth Knesset election as they were published in May 1977. The table compares the margin of gains and losses in terms of popular votes and Knesset seats between 1973 and 1977.

TABLE 8.1   Results of Elections to the Ninth Knesset, 1977

Party	Votes		Knesset Seats		Net Gain or Loss
	Absolute	%	1977	1973	
Likud	583,075	33.4	43	39	+4
Labor alignment	430,023	24.6	32	51	−19
Democratic Movement for Change	202,265	11.6	15	—	+15
National Religious party	160,787	9.2	12	10	+ 2
Agudat Israel	58,652	3.4	4	5	0
Poalei Agudat Israel	23,956	1.4	1		
Communists	79,733	4.6	5	4	+1
Shelli	27,281	1.6	2	1 (Moked)	+1
Shlom-Zion	33,947	1.9	2	—	+2
Flatto-Sharon	35,049	2.0	1	—	+1
Independent Liberals	21,277	1.2	1	4	−3
Citizens' Rights	20,621	1.2	1	3	−2
United Arab List	24,185	1.4	1	3	−2

Source: Adapted from Don Peretz, *The Government and Politics of Israel, Second Edition* (Boulder, Colo.: Westview Press, 1983), p. 210.

Begin's major success was in the area of foreign policy, which overcame public awareness of failures in domestic policy. Following through on Sadat's 1977 visit to Jerusalem, Begin not only concluded and signed the 1979 Egyptian-Israeli peace treaty but also, with Sadat, won the Nobel Peace Prize for his efforts. Although the terms of the treaty were so controversial that they sparked the longest Knesset debate in the country's history and split the Likud bloc, the treaty won approval from 95 of the 120 members. Of the 18 negative votes, 7 came from the Likud, with a total of 13 coalition members opposed. Also opposed at the other end of the spectrum were the 5 members of the Communist Democratic Front for Peace and Equality.

The Knesset victory cost Begin two of his most militant supporters, who left Likud to form the zealously nationalist Tehiya. Tehiya's two Knesset members were supported by many members of Gush Emunim and the Land of Israel movement.

Prime Minister Begin's second victory in the Tenth Knesset election in June 1981 showed that the country had experienced an ideological reorientation. The election confirmed that Labor's setback was no temporary phenomenon and that different cultural orientations, political perspectives, and value systems were replacing those that had prevailed in Israel when Labor held power. A shift was occurring from reliance on the government social network to greater emphasis on individual initiative and toward more militant nationalism that emphasized retaining the lands occupied during the 1967 war. Revisionist Zionist leaders of the past, who had been scorned by the Labor movement, were now proclaimed national heros. The founder of Revisionism, Vladimir Jabotinsky, was reburied in Jerusalem, and his picture appeared on Israeli postage stamps.

In the 1981 election, Labor and Likud were about equal in strength. Likud captured 37.1 percent of the votes—a larger share than ever before— and Labor received 36.6 percent, a much smaller share than at the peak of its strength. The DMC had disappeared before the election and could not be held accountable for diverting votes from any party. Even the smaller parties collapsed as potential alternates. Between them, Labor and Likud won 95 of the 120 Knesset seats with nearly three-quarters of the votes— more than the two largest parties had received in previous elections. The NRP, traditionally Israel's third party with enough Knesset seats to swing parliament one way or the other, lost half its Knesset delegation because of internal squabbles and the resurgence of ethnic politics. Labor and Likud now dominated the political scene.

By the end of 1982, Begin had complied with all of the provisions of the treaty that called for Israel's withdrawal from Sinai and the return of the peninsula to Egypt. Although relations between the two countries were cool, Israel and Egypt had instituted formal ties, exchanged ambassadors, established embassies, opened the borders to tourism and commerce, and set up telephone and telecommunications links; Israeli ships were now passing through the Suez Canal. Completing other phases of the peace package proved more difficult, especially the provisions that called for autonomy for Arab inhabitants in the Israeli-occupied West Bank and Gaza.

Egypt, supported by the United States—the third party to the peace treaty—perceived autonomy as meaning Israel's withdrawal from the territories and the establishment of Arab self-government. Begin's interpretation was that autonomy involved the inhabitants of the territories but not the land; that is, the land would remain under Israel's jurisdiction even though the Arab inhabitants would be given control of local affairs. A crucial question was whether permanent Jewish settlement of the Occupied Territories would be permitted. Egypt and the United States called for a halt, whereas Begin insisted that continuation of Jewish settlement was a right. The settlements not only caused diplomatic problems for Israel but also aroused widespread opposition among the indigenous Arab population, whose protests led to severe control measures implemented by Israeli security forces.

Begin's policies and those of post-1981 election Defense Minister Ariel Sharon met with criticism in Israel but won approval from the largest sector of the electorate. The controversial policies also led to the resignation of two key cabinet ministers: Foreign Minister Moshe Dayan and Defense Minister Ezer Weizman.

Two wings within the Likud were in opposition over issues concerning peace, foreign affairs, and the Occupied Territories. The more zealous nationalists grouped around Sharon or defected to Tehiya; the compromisers, or doves, were associated with the former Liberals or, like Weizman and Dayan, left the government. But the public at large approved of Begin's policies. Despite results that showed strong support for some compromise on the Occupied Territories in exchange for a secure peace, Begin consistently led by many points in every poll that sampled preferences for prime minister.

Even though he won the Nobel Peace Prize, Begin was no dove. In July 1980 he supported a bill that annexed Jerusalem. The annexation sparked a chain of international protests, UN censure, U.S. criticism, and the removal of thirteen embassies from Jerusalem. Nonetheless, the public admired Begin's stand on the issue. Six months after the 1981 election Begin also ordered the annexation of the Golan Heights to enhance his image as a patriot and consolidator of the homeland. Because most Jewish settlements in the Golan Heights belonged to the Labor movement, the annexation was welcomed equally by both supporters and opponents of the prime minister.

The Sephardi Revolt

Even though its foreign policies further isolated Israel and severely strained relations with the United States, the policies were internal successes that helped to reinforce Begin's appeal, especially among the Sephardi Jewish population. Sephardi disenchantment with Labor had been growing since the 1960s, and support for the Likud had increased steadily. As the Sephardi became active politically, they moved further to the right, and Begin replaced Ben-Gurion as a father figure, prophet, and fiery-tongued opponent of the Ashkenazi establishment. As Sephardis became more politically sophisticated, they resented what they perceived to be Labor's paternalism. Even though Likud won the 1977 election, Labor was still regarded as the establishment by virtue of its political, social, and economic power. Ashkenazis still dominated the powerful institutions that remained under Labor's control, including the Histadrut, the health funds, and many of the most important economic enterprises.

Attraction to traditional Labor values and symbolism had never been strong among Sephardi Jews. Frontier pioneering, settlement in agricultural collectives, and a strong union consciousness had never appealed to them. Their values and social orientation were derived more from cultures of the traditional societies in the Middle East. They tended to be more family oriented than nation-state oriented; their primary loyalties were to relatives and kin rather than to civic institutions. Earlier attempts to modernize or westernize the Sephardis in line with models of the Labor establishment had met with little success. Often, rather than replacing Eastern values with Western values, old traditions and customs were merely denigrated, with no new values to replace the old. The psychological result was that support given by the family and the close-knit community was often undermined.

Attempts to organize Sephardi unrest into ethnic separatist factions had never been politically successful. Instead, the Sephardis' discontent was expressed by the shift of votes from Labor to the right and by their growing approval of Begin. The attrition of Sephardi support for Labor became significant in 1969 and reached a peak in the 1981 election. Among Sephardis born in Asia and Africa, 51 percent voted for Labor in 1969, 39 percent in 1973, 32 percent in 1977, and about 25 percent in 1981. In 1969, 32 percent voted for Likud; this figure was 43 percent in 1973, 46 percent in 1977, and around 60 percent in 1981. The shift was even greater among Israelis whose fathers had been born in Asia or Africa. Their support for Labor was 49 percent in 1969, 40 percent in 1973, 23 percent in 1977, and less than 23 percent in 1981. Likud strength among this group increased from 37 percent in 1969 to 47 percent in 1973, 65 percent in 1977, and about 65 percent in 1981.[42]

Party profiles drawn by pollsters in 1981 showed that Labor's supporters were mainly Ashkenazi, middle-aged or older, white-collar workers with middle and upper incomes, and better educated than their Likud counterparts. Many members of Likud's constituency were Sephardi youths between ages eighteen and thirty, religious, blue-collar workers, and less educated and with lower incomes than Labor supporters.[43]

During the 1981 election all parties paid increasing attention to the ethnic factor and attempted to place at least one or two Sephardis at the top of their electoral lists. In fact, there were more Sephardis in top positions on the Labor list than on Likud's. But the fact that fourteen of its newly elected Knesset members were Sephardi compared to six for Likud made little difference to Labor's image; the Sephardi population generally viewed Labor Sephardis as having been co-opted by the establishment, whereas Likud Sephardis had more public visibility and popularity.

As the 1981 campaign progressed, the ethnic issue became more pronounced; the Israeli press characterized the phenomenon as "the Sephardi revolt." When election day neared, the intensity of the issue became critical. Likud campaigners alluded increasingly to Labor's discrimination against Sephardis. In one campaign speech, former Chief of Staff Mordechai Gur, then a leader of the Labor alignment, angrily threatened a group of Sephardi hecklers, saying "we will beat you as we beat the Arabs." On another occasion alignment leader Peres nicknamed the hecklers "Khomenists," alluding to the reign of political terror in Iran, and advised them to return to their Arab home countries. Several days before the end of the campaign, a moderator at an important alignment rally declared that "the nice people," the real fighters, and the "army officers" are with the Labor alignment, whereas the Likud camp is supported by *"Chakchakim"* (a derogatory term applied to Moroccan Jewish hooligans or to hooligans in general).

The Sephardi revolt shook up the entire political structure and wreaked havoc in the NRP, then the third-largest party following the disappearance of the DMC. When the NRP picked its electoral list for the Tenth Knesset, some of its Sephardi supporters complained that only two of the top ten positions had been given to Sephardi. Aaron Abuhatzeira—a young Sephardi leader of the NRP who had served in Begin's coalition cabinet—demanded that his name be placed second on the religious party's electoral list, made a bid to become the leader of the NRP, and insisted that half of the party's top ten positions be given to Sephardis. When the party leaders turned him down, he left and formed his own separate party, Tami (the Movement for Israel's Tradition).

Tami won three Knesset seats and claimed to represent Sephardis who were Orthodox Jews, many of whom were former supporters of the NRP. Although Tami's constituency supposedly reflected the diversity of

Afro-Asian Israelis, all but two of its top ten positions were held by Jews from Morocco.

Four other ethnic or Sephardi lists failed to win even a single seat, although Sephardi voters constituted more than 45 percent of the nearly 2 million voters. Most Sephardis voted for Likud, Labor, the NRP, Tami, or Tehiya. Despite the resurgence of ethnicity as a key issue, the ethnic parties were unable to capitalize on the rising consciousness of the Afro-Asians; Begin's charisma and his forceful stand on nationalist issues seemed to outweigh the Sephardis' attraction to voting for their own ethnic politicians. Abuhatzeira's defection from the NRP was the major direct result of the Sephardi revolt and caused the NRP to lose nearly half of its voters. Tami received three of the six seats lost by the NRP in 1981, and the other three were shared by Likud and Tehiya.

With the era of shifting Sephardi voting patterns that culminated in the 1981 election came a substantial increase in the Afro-Asian population. Between the 1960s and 1980, Sephardis had become the majority, constituting nearly 60 percent of the Jewish population. Still, in 1981 they represented only 45 percent of the electorate because a large number were under voting age. Although the number of children in Sephardi Jewish families was decreasing because of a lower fertility rate, they still outnumbered the Ashkenazis.

During the Begin era, government efforts to close the gap between Sephardis and Ashkenazis continued with some success. One major effort was Project Renewal, an attempt to rehabilitate slums in urban areas that were inhabited largely by Sephardis. The Begin government also invested heavily in low-income public housing and raised the age for compulsory education. The number of Sephardis in the professions continued to increase, and a newly emerging middle class of Jews whose parents had come from Africa or Asia asserted itself politically. Despite these developments, the number of Jews living in poverty remained large, and most were Sephardi. Israel's Central Bureau of Statistics reported in 1982 that the gross income of Sephardi urban wage earners was 40 percent lower per capita than that of workers of Western origin and that the gap between rich and poor in the cities was persistent and widening.

Among the untoward effects of Sephardis' frustration in their fight for upward mobility was a marked increase in both political and criminal violence. Statistics in the late 1970s showed that Sephardis made up more than 90 percent of Israel's prison population and were involved in criminal behavior much more often than Europeans. The Sephardi revolt during the 1981 election demonstrated the dangers of this increased frustration. Many observers agreed that the campaign was highly raucous and undisciplined. Although no candidate openly accused Sephardis of being the perpetrators, enough implications existed to link them to the frequent campaign disturbances, and apprehension about these developments was revealed in comments made by election commission members. The commission's chair, Justice Moshe Etzioni, said that much of the electorate was "hot-tempered and still unfamiliar with democracy." Another commission source said that the country's parties resisted electoral changes because "tens of thousands of voters are still illiterate" and cast their ballots "not knowing for whom they are voting."[44]

After the 1981 election the Sephardi revolt seemed to be defused, and the level of political violence declined sharply. The ethnic issue reappeared in 1984 when Shas entered the political scene and followed the initiatives of Rabbi Eliezer Shach, an Ashkenazi Jew. Two of the four Knesset seats that were obtained by Shas in that election came at the expense of Tami; the other two seats were built on Ashkenazi votes. In 1988 and again in 1992, however, Ashkenazi assistance was no longer needed because Shas gained all of its six Knesset seats from the Sephardi vote. In spite of Shas gains in these three election rounds, the party was not instrumental in bringing the ethnic issue to the center of voters' attention; its electoral campaign was directed specifically toward its own supporters in an attempt to strengthen their traditional Sephardi identity rather than toward raising ethnic tensions.

The ethnic issue again became politically salient in 1992 in the context of nominating David Levy's supporters to the Likud Knesset List. These supporters complained that they had been "massacred" by the Ashkenazis in the so-called Shamir-Arens camps and were thus kept off the list. Consequently, many of Levy's followers at the local level remained passive during the campaign. Some even switched sides and voted for Rabin, who projected a strongman image similar to Begin's eleven years earlier. Rabin promised to "change national priorities" to benefit Sephardis in poor neighborhoods and development towns. During the election, many "Likud-disappointees" as they were called, supported Rabin. Labor's victory in 1992 should be accredited in part to the 5 to 6 percent support the party obtained from these former Likud voters.

Economic Issues

The failure of Likud to achieve the economic goals promised in the 1977 campaign had little effect on most of its supporters. Although opinion polls conducted before the 1981 election showed that the public had little faith in the bloc's ability to cope with the economy, most of its supporters were insulated from the impact of inflation, unemployment, and the growing gap between imports and exports. Strong labor unions ensured that Israeli workers would maintain a high living standard through indexation, which linked wages to prices and cushioned the effects of the declining value of Israeli currency. Savings were protected through foreign-currency accounts, pension funds, and saving schemes linked to inflation. In spite of a steady erosion of the public economy, the private citizen did not seem to suffer. Indeed, some observers maintained that private wealth occurred at the expense of the public economy: The only unprotected lender has been and continues to be the state, observed one economic analyst.

Although they were critical of the apparent drift in economic policy, average citizens did not consider themselves to be faring poorly, according to a poll taken shortly before the 1981 election. The number of voters who felt well-to-do had declined since 1977, but a larger number of people considered themselves to be in a "middling" status.[45]

Public skepticism about the economic policies of Labor and Likud was reinforced by the relatively small difference between the two groups' programs. Labor's response to Likud's economic and social programs contained little of socialist Zionism. Labor's economic pundits advocated measures such as stabilization of the exchange rate, incentives for the export industry (Israel's primary growth sector), long-term wage agreements to keep real wages stable, and a gradual alteration of the tax structure to achieve a more equitable distribution of the economic burden. Under Labor, the government would use administrative measures to control inflation, including price fixing. A major thrust was to step up exports through direct incentive payments to producers. Differences between the private-sector–oriented Likud and "socialist" Labor were a question more of degree than of radically opposite ideologies.

Likud's difficulties in dealing with the country's economy were manifested by its three finance ministers during Begin's first term. The first, Simha Erlich, leader of the free-enterprise Liberal bloc, resigned in 1979 shortly after the signing of the Egyptian-Israeli peace treaty. The treaty—which represented Israel's hope for greater security—led to increased defense expenditures: the expenditure of several billions of dollars to replace oil lost from Sinai; the transfer of large military installations, including three of its most modern air bases, from Sinai to the Negev; and the purchase of more sophisticated military equipment. These costs, Erlich charged, would add 20 percent to the already escalating inflation rate. To help meet these expenses, the government imposed sharp reductions in subsidies for basic food commodities, which led to a spate of strikes and further disruption of the economy.

Erlich was replaced by Yigal Hurvitz, an advocate of hard-line economic policies and austerity. Hurvitz demanded even sharper cuts in subsidies, a wage freeze for public servants, and reduction of the civil service by 20,000 workers. But prices continued to shoot upward, leading to an inflation rate of over 100 percent. To mitigate the psychological effects of inflation, the government replaced the Israeli pound with a new unit of currency, the shekel, at the rate of one shekel for every ten pounds.

Hurvitz's austerity measures proved to be politically costly, and he was removed from office a few months before the 1981 election. His replacement, Yoram Aridor, introduced a package of measures intended to increase public support for the Likud. His first major act was to reduce taxes on consumer durables, such as television sets and private cars, and to restrain price increases of some basic commodities. Aridor's supply-side measures were intended to stimulate sales of consumer goods so that future tax revenues would exceed revenue based on existing rates. These measures were obviously welcomed by Israelis, who are among the world's most highly taxed citizens. With a 1977 per capita income of about four thousand dollars, taxation came to 46.5 percent of the GNP. Shortly before the Passover holiday in 1981, Aridor again reduced prices on a number of food items, soft drinks, air conditioners, and motorbikes.

But the temporary solution could not help for long. After the election the inflation rate went out of control until a coordinated effort of the Unity government stabilized the economy in 1984. This joint political effort by Labor and Likud continued until 1990. Itzhak Modai, the minister of treasury who had been so successful in 1986, regained his post and once again was able to lead the economy to progress and growth. Modai's economic success, however, was part of the reason for Likud's political failure in 1992.

In 1990 Modai headed a small party (actually an independent faction within the Likud) called the Movement for the Revival of the Zionist Idea (later the New Liberal party). Modai established a "politically clean" economic policy. Consequently, the macroeconomic indicators were at their strongest during 1991, but Likud supporters—mostly Sephardi and poor—did not feel they were enjoying a fair share of the overall economic success. They therefore succumbed to Rabin's 1992 promises, and many, as noted earlier, switched to Labor. Modai later quit Likud and ran alone in the 1992 election but failed to win a Knesset seat.

Changing Values

Economic conditions, the continued strain of war, and the decline of traditional ideology converged during the Begin era and discouraged large-scale immigration into the country. At the end of 1981, government statisticians announced that for the first time in Israel's history the number of emigrants outnumbered immigrants. During 1980–1981 there was a net emigration of about 20,000 Jews. Immigration totaled about 11,000, the lowest number since the 1963 economic recession. Official figures in 1980–1981 pegged the total number of emigrants since 1948 at 300,000, but unofficial estimates indicated there were at least twice that many. Some counts placed the number of Israelis and former Israelis in North America at about 500,000, with large concentrations in New York City and Los Angeles. Begin raised this painful issue in the Knesset in 1976, pointing out that many of the emigrants were native-born Israelis (Sabras), former army officers, and kibbutz members. Since independence, he cautioned, Israel had lost four divisions, or a dozen brigades, which represented a real bloodletting.

The difficulties in attracting large numbers of Jewish immigrants were underscored by the issue of Soviet Jewry. After protracted negotiations that involved the United States as an intermediary, the Soviet Union agreed to permit the exit of Jews who had families in Israel, ostensibly for family reunions. When the immigration scheme began during the 1970s, most Soviet Jews eagerly moved to Israel, but by the late 1970s a large percentage of the refugees had either left Israel or never arrived. Upon arrival in Vienna, the midstation between the USSR and Israel, an increasingly large number left for the West rather than immigrate to Israel. Efforts by the Begin government to assure that departing Soviet Jews would reach Israel became the focus of controversy between Israeli officials and representatives of Western Jewish aid groups, who were reluctant to force the refugees into Israel against their will. The issue also strained relations between Israel and the U.S. government, which refused to support any coercive measures. The Begin government, however, insisted that the program to rescue Soviet Jewry would be jeopardized if large numbers immigrated to the West rather than to Israel because the Soviet authorities had issued exit permits only for the latter.

Despite difficulties in attracting new immigrants, there was no lack of patriotism among Israeli youth. A 1981 poll of seventeen-year-olds showed that 90 percent would volunteer for the armed forces if conscription were abolished, 73.7 percent were ready to enlist in elite combat units, and 59 percent would agree to serve an extra year to become officers.

The changing value system gathered impetus after 1967 following the extension of Israel's authority into the West Bank (Judea and Samaria), Gaza, and the Golan Heights. As possibilities for a Greater Israel became realistic, the ideology of Begin and his nationalist followers gained support, gradually displacing the old Labor credo. For the nationalists, realization of the messianic message meant the reestablishment of Israel's historical frontiers, territorial reunification, and new pioneering along the extended borders. Before Begin, the Labor government had cautiously avoided making historical claims to Judea and Samaria; rather, it emphasized national security to justify maintaining a Jewish presence in the Occupied Territories.

As discussed earlier, Gush Emunim epitomized the ideological approach to territory. As its influence spread and its clientele grew among non-Orthodox Jews in Israel and abroad, the group became a major political force—not in size but in the extent of its influence among prominent members of the Begin establishment. Some observers believed Gush Emunim attracted much of its following because it filled the ideological vacuum left by the decline of Labor Zionism.

Many of Gush Emunim's themes were derived from the nationalist-religious thought of Rabbi Zvi Yehuda Kook, son of a former Israeli chief rabbi. Israel, the Gush leaders asserted, had been overtaken by lack of resolution and self-doubt. As a result, its leaders had succumbed to vague promises of peace at the cost of territorial integrity. Like Begin's Herut party, Gush Emunim leaders believed the Land of Israel should never have been partitioned. They held that the people of Israel were meant to live in all of biblical Israel and that those leaders who had surrendered part of the holy patrimony, or who would be willing to give up land now, had committed a mortal sin. "Every piece of our land is holy—a present from God," they insisted. The essence of the Jewish claim depended less on international recognition or documents such as the Balfour Declaration, the League of Nations Mandate, and the UN partition resolution than on the covenant between God and Abraham. This right was not transferable because the land in its entirety belonged to the Jewish people and their future generations.

The Gush ideology extended beyond irredentism: Its nationalist doctrines were rooted in religion and in a social critique of modern Zionism. The ideological heart of the movement was the Yeshivat Mercaz Harav Kook, an Orthodox seminary and institution of higher Jewish learning and research in Jerusalem. The two rabbi Kooks, father and son, were the spiritual fathers of the movement. The younger Kook declared that the establishment of Israel had represented the beginning of the messianic era. Resettlement of the land and Israel's revival in that land were a manifestation of "the true Redemption . . . of the rule of our own government in it, and of the adherence of our group behavior to its real holiness."

Gush Emunim leaders criticized Israel's leaders not only for the "suicidal" return of territory to the Arabs but also for permitting the moral and social deterioration of society, the growing indifference to "productive labor," alienation from the land, and the development of a useless and burdensome bureaucracy. The country had acquired a reputation, they stated, as an "international *schnorer* [one who gets something from someone through flattery or by begging but without paying]," rather than an independent, self-sufficient republic.

Gush Emunim was as critical of the religious parties from which it originated as it was of Labor. Whereas the Laborites were taken to task for their infatuation with socialism, which diluted their Zionism, the NRP and religious parties were "no longer spiritual. They are like merchants in the marketplace."

Borrowing from the tactics and slogans of early Labor Zionism, Gush leaders prescribed *hitnahalut,* a combination of frontier settlement and messianism that requires that Jews establish themselves in *all* of Eretz Israel as both a cultural imperative and a religious obligation. The term resembled the old Labor Zionist credo of *halutziut,* frontier pioneering that combined the conquest of labor and land along socialist lines. Gush Emunim settlers frequently replaced the *halutz* (pioneer) settler of the Yishuv in the minds of many young Israelis. Like the socialist *halutz* who battled the Arabs and the British, Gush Emunim struggled against Arabs and the feckless Israeli government. Its volunteers, many of them new immigrants from the United States, deployed dozens of Jewish settlements in Judea and Samaria—at times in conflict with Israeli government policy. Like the *halutzim* during mandate times, they frequently resorted to swift or surreptitious tactics, stealthily occupying Arab areas in the middle of the night without official permission or assistance. Their strong emphasis on self-sacrifice, reluctance to accept government aid, and refusal to request official permission for their settlement endeavors surrounded the Gush members with an aura of patriotism identical to that which surrounded the *halutzim* when they drained the swamps, planted the deserts, and extended the frontiers of the Yishuv during the mandate.

Although the group was not affiliated with any political party, much of the Gush Emunim ethos was incorporated into the program of the Tehiya party, whose founders broke with Begin's Herut prior to the 1981 election. Tehiya received less than 3 percent of the vote and only three Knesset seats in 1981, but among the youthful electorate in the army it won 6.3 percent of the vote—more than twice the amount it received from the electorate as a whole.

The polar opposite of Gush Emunim was the Peace Now movement, which also commanded a large following among the youth, many from the kibbutzim and urban socialist groups. Peace Now emerged from protest groups formed after the 1973 war by young former officers who demanded that the government make more strenuous efforts to achieve peace. A major thrust was the group's opposition to Jewish settlement in the Occupied Territories; one of its slogans was "peace is greater than Greater Israel." Israel had taken major risks in war, so why not "take a risk for peace," the leaders argued.

The movement gained prominence after Sadat's visit to Jerusalem in 1977, when it organized some of the largest political rallies in the country's history to demand that Begin be more forthcoming in negotiations with Egypt. Peace Now later protested Gush Emunim settlements in the West Bank and assisted Arab villagers whose property had been destroyed by Jewish zealots. As the movement gained political focus, it increasingly urged mutual recognition and negotiations between the Jewish and Palestinian Arab nationalist movements. During 1982 Peace Now was in the vanguard of protests against the war in Lebanon, discussed in the next section, especially after the massacre of Palestinians in two Beirut refugee camps following Israel's occupation of west Beirut. When a judicial commission completed its investigation of Israel's role in the massacres, Peace Now staged demonstrations demanding the resignation of Defense Minister Sharon. These demonstrations also brought to the surface deep resentments of Sephardi Jewish supporters of Sharon against the Ashkenazi "elitists" in the peace movement.

Much of the activity of both Peace Now and Gush Emunim became less intense during the six years of the Unity government. Other groups, less well organized and much smaller, came onto the national protest scene. On the radical right, Kahana's Kach and its supporters carried the torch of Jewish nationalism and anti-Arabism. The left included individuals who at first protested the continuous presence of Israeli troops in Lebanon and later refused to serve in the Occupied Territories. These protest movements had no more than several dozen members at any given time on either side of the political spectrum; thus, it was relatively easy for the state to deal with them. However, the issues they supported became a focus of public attention and discourse. The eruption of the intifada in December 1987 further fueled the intensity of these debates, which involved the inherent tension between Jewish and civil nationalism, the right of Israel to control the Occupied Territories, and the rights and obligations of individuals to acquiesce to objectionable policies.

By the mid-1980s another important issue was high on the national agenda; it involved a closer examination of the Israeli democratic system in general and its voting methods in particular. A new Constitution for Israel organization and similar groups began to exert pressure on lawmakers that by 1992 had resulted in a Knesset decision to directly elect the prime minister and to enact the Basic Law: Government.

Even the value of ingathering—the most basic Zionist credo—came under attack toward the end of the 1980s and in the early 1990s, when the wave of Russian immigration greatly strained the economy and society and people were asked to sacrifice actual or potential gains for the newcomers. Many were happy to do so, but some objected, especially those of Sephardi origin who felt once again that their chance to improve their share of the national wealth would pass them by. Some publicly argued against the Russian immigration and even went to Moscow to convince Russian leaders to slow the flow of Jews to Israel.

Consequently, the perceived unity that so often characterized Jewish society in Israel during the 1950s and 1960s seemed to erode in many circles at the beginning of the 1990s. Three principal events contributed to the erosion process: the 1982 war in Lebanon, the four years of the intifada (1988–1992), and the 1991–1992 Gulf War.

The 1982 War in Lebanon

The 1982 war in Lebanon was the first major military expedition to stir extensive and overt political opposition during the period of combat. The 1973 war had also aroused controversy over the government's inadequate preparation to resist an Egyptian and Syrian attack, but that dispute erupted following the war. The Lebanon campaign raised questions regarding Israel's security needs, the extent and length of the military phase, Israel's involvement in Lebanon's internal politics, and the conduct of high-ranking generals and the minister of defense.

Relations between Israel and Lebanon had been quiescent since the 1949 armistice, but this changed with the influx of Palestinian guerrillas from Jordan during the early 1970s. Prior to the 1970s the Lebanon-Israel border was the only Israeli border fully accepted by both sides. When several Palestinian guerrilla groups moved their operations to southern Lebanon, Jewish settlements in northern Israel became the targets of frequent attacks. This situation led to an informal alliance between the Israeli military and the mostly Maronite Christian Phalange militia during the Lebanese civil war in the mid-1970s, both of which were eager to remove the Palestinian guerrillas from Lebanon.

A guerrilla attack on Israel in 1978 sparked an invasion that lasted several months and led to Israel's direct involvement within Lebanon. The establishment of a UN force in southern Lebanon failed to deter the guerrillas, and the establishment of a Lebanese military unit under Israel's control failed to end the conflict. Continued incidents led to escalation of Israeli attacks on Palestinian bases, refugee camps, and political offices of the PLO between 1978 and 1982. A U.S.-initiated truce between Israel and the PLO in 1981 lasted about a year but failed to halt either Israeli attacks or Palestinian reprisals.

Despite the truce, Begin's government was determined to remove all PLO forces in Lebanon, especially from the south. This determination to end the PLO's military potential was reinforced by a string of international political victories scored by the organization in the late 1970s and early 1980s and by continued terrorist attacks on Israelis abroad (although many of the attacks were officially disavowed by PLO leaders). The Begin government increased Israel's commitment to the Phalangists and intervened with air support when Syrian "peacekeeping" units in Lebanon attacked the Phalange.

The precarious cease-fire negotiated by the United States in 1981 fell apart in June 1982 when Israel launched a full-scale invasion of Lebanon following an assassination attempt in which the Israeli ambassador in London was critically wounded. It was established later that he had not been shot by PLO operatives but by a dissident Palestinian terrorist faction.

By the end of June, the IDF had captured much of Beirut—the first Arab capital ever to fall to Israel—and most of the southern third of the country. The Israeli invasion, called Peace for Galilee, ended PLO military and political control of West Beirut and of its large enclaves in southern Lebanon. The invasion also changed the balance of political forces within Lebanon in favor of the Israeli-backed Phalange, which enabled its leader, Bashir Jemayal, to be elected president by the Lebanese parliament. But before he could take office, Jemayal and dozens of his followers were killed by an explosion at Phalange headquarters.

The assassination became the excuse for Israel's reoccupation of West Beirut, ostensibly to prevent chaos. Maintaining that PLO fighters were still concealed there, Israel allowed Phalange units to enter the Palestinian Sabra and Shatilla refugee camps to "cleanse" them of remaining guerrillas—an action Defense Minister Ariel Sharon maintained would save the lives of many Israeli soldiers.

During the next two and a half days, the Phalangists killed several hundred Palestinian men, women, and children in the two camps. News of the massacre raised a storm of protest in Israel, bringing to a head criticism of the entire Lebanese operation that had been simmering among many opponents of Likud government policy. Peace for Galilee was the first Israeli military expedition to cause extensive civilian casualties, and much criticism was heaped on the government because thousands of the victims were innocent Lebanese who were not involved in the struggle between Israel and the Palestinians. Although the government insisted that the civilian casualties should be blamed on Palestinian guerrillas who had placed military targets in installations such as hospitals and schools, many Israelis were appalled by the results. Some cabinet members accused Sharon of having exceeded his authority by initiating large-scale military undertakings that should have required government approval. The Sabra and Shatilla massacre brought much of this disquiet to the surface and led to the largest protest demonstration ever held in Israel. An estimated 400,000 people—over 10 percent of the population—joined in demands for a full-fledged investigation.

Initially, Begin and his cabinet labeled accusations of indirect government responsibility for the massacre a "blood libel" and refused to initiate a full and independent judicial investigation. But after several high officials had resigned—including one Likud cabinet member—Begin asked the president of the Supreme Court, Chief Justice Yitzhak Kahan, to organize an independent panel, established under a 1968 Inquiry Law, that would resemble the Agranat Commission appointed to investigate responsibility for the 1973 war. Both bodies were headed by Supreme Court judges and included retired army generals.

Most political activity in Israel was suspended during the nearly five months of the Kahan Commission's work. Many believed the political future of both Sharon and Begin hung in the balance. Three-party talks among Israel, Lebanon, and the United States eventually led to Israel's evacuation of most of the territory seized in Lebanon, but further negotiations with Egypt over full normalization and the future of the West Bank and Gaza were set back by the 1982 war.

Although the substance of the Kahan Commission's report, issued in February 1983, was not unexpected, the severity of its tone surprised many. The commission concluded that direct responsibility for the slaughter rested fully with the Phalange. Although there was no evidence that the Phalangist personnel involved had received explicit orders from their commanders to perpetrate acts of slaughter, it was evident that the hatred and anti-Palestinian feelings of those who entered the camps were so great that violence was inevitable.

No direct responsibility was placed on Israel or on the officers who acted in its behalf. At the same time, those who had authorized the Phalange to enter the camps clearly had not considered the dangers of such an operation. After the Phalange had entered the area, the Israeli military did not properly heed reports about the massacre, failed to draw the correct conclusions, and did not act immediately or energetically to stop the slaughter.

The commission laid responsibility for these faulty decisions on several individuals, including the minister of defense, the IDF chief of staff, the director of military intelligence, and other generals in the field and called for their resignations or suspension from command positions. Although the prime minister, the foreign minister, and the head of the Mossad intelligence agency were criticized, they were not held responsible because the information they received came late or was indirect. The political repercussions of the report were widespread and cast aspersions on several top government officials, including Prime Minister Begin.

Before the final report was issued, observers had speculated that a harsh judgment might result in Begin's resignation or at least in new elections. Instead, the cabinet approved the findings and recommendations by a sixteen to one vote, with only Defense Minister Sharon opposed, thus obviating the necessity for either action. Given the political climate, only Begin would have profited from new elections. All polls showed that he was by far the most popular choice for prime minister and that his Likud might even win a majority if he called for elections. Begin's continued popularity discouraged all of the small parties, as well as Labor, from supporting new elections because they feared an even greater Begin victory than the one in 1981.

The report reinforced a long-held convention of Israeli politics: that the military must always be subordinate to civil authority. The tradition, established during Ben-Gurion's tenure as prime minister and defense minister, was scrupulously observed until Sharon assumed the latter post. To preserve this tradition even Sharon's predecessor in the Begin cabinet, Ezer Weizman—a former general who had commanded the air force—had prevented the army chief of staff from attending cabinet meetings. After Weizman's resignation and Begin's temporary assumption of the defense post, civil control began to slip. Begin, preoccupied with higher diplomatic strategy, tended to depend increasingly on his chief of staff for military advice and policy. When Sharon took over following the 1981 election, he frequently acted independent of the prime minister and the cabinet—especially in the Lebanon operation, which for all practical purposes he ran as field commander as well as defense minister. The commission report and recommendations assumed that the defense establishment would again be subject to the cabinet rather than to the dictates of a single individual.

Although the report did not topple the Begin government as some had hoped, it intensified bitterness between hawks and doves. Critics felt the report placed a moral responsibility on both Begin and Sharon to resign. Protest demonstrations against the two men became the occasion for counterdemonstrations by their supporters. When the latter attacked dovish demonstrators, the clashes were markedly polarized between Sephardi Likud supporters and their largely Ashkenazi opponents. Thus, the Lebanese episode once again demonstrated that the volatile mixture of ethnicity and class could aggravate the political differences that divided Israeli society.

The number of Lebanese, Syrian, and Palestinian casualties was still unknown, but the total of those killed was expected to reach many thousand, and tens of thousands of new refugees were wounded and homeless. Israel's increasing involvement in the morass of Lebanese internal ethnic squabbles had now had internecine results. Negotiations with Lebanon over withdrawal were stymied by Syrian and PLO reluctance to leave their enclaves in northern Lebanon and by Israel's insistence that withdrawal be accompanied by diplomatic normalization and the establishment of semipermanent Israeli bases in the south. To some Israelis the situation was beginning to resemble the dilemma faced by imperial powers in withdrawing from overseas territories. Occupation had created a series of commitments to various Lebanese factions, but public opinion at home was set increasingly against such involvement.

Israel stayed in Lebanon until 1985 when it withdrew from all but a narrow "security zone" on the Lebanese side of the border. The Likud government, aware of its deep involvement, could not openly admit that the military presence in Lebanon had been a mistake without bearing the necessary political consequences. Prime Minister Shamir, who had replaced Begin in 1983, refused to order an IDF retreat; only the Unity government, headed by Peres, could give such an order. The decision to pull out of Lebanon was made by a cabinet vote in which Likud's David Levy supported the Labor ministers, which resulted in a majority in favor of retreat. However, to protect the northern borders Israel maintained a several-kilometer-wide security zone guarded by the IDF and its clients in the South Lebanese Army, a local militia made up of mostly Christian local Arab villagers.

The Intifada

The Palestinian civil revolt, or intifada, was not planned, and its final outcome could have been predicted. The revolt started in December 1987, sparked by an accident in which several Palestinian workers were killed and injured by an Israeli truck. The incident aroused anger among Gaza youth, who directed their sorrow and hostility against the IDF. Israeli authorities, as well as officials at PLO headquarters in Tunis, were caught by surprise. The intensity of the revolt and the courage of its local participants were new phenomena. Anticipating that he could suppress the revolt within a few days, Defense Minister Rabin ordered the IDF to "break the bones" of those creating disturbances. However, this and other harsh orders not only intensified the conflict but also undermined Israel's international image.

The intifada, which was presented by the international media as a fight of the powerless against a strong oppressor, lasted more than four years. Palestinian children throwing stones at Israeli soldiers symbolized the uprising; the IDF was not prepared strategically, technically, or psychologically to suppress the revolt, which became a full-scale media war. The army was unable to cope with many aspects of Palestinian civil disobedience such as refusing to pay taxes to Israeli authorities; rejecting employment in Israel, where a large segment of the workforce in construction and agriculture had become dependent on Palestinian labor; boycotting Israeli products; flying the Palestinian flag; and staging nationalist demonstrations in violation of military government ordinances.

After the first few months, it became clear that a cohesive national spirit had developed among the Palestinians. They were proud of their achievements under a local, authentic, new, and youthful leadership that forced PLO headquarters in Tunis to coordinate its policies and tactics with those of the intifada in the Occupied Territories. In 1988 Jordan ended all claims to the West Bank, which it had controlled from 1948 to 1967. Thus, PLO leader Yasser Arafat was now recognized as the leader of the Palestinian national cause.

The personal and psychological costs sustained by IDF involvement in the uprising affected Israeli public perceptions of the conflict, as illustrated in Table 8.2. The table shows Israelis' changing attitudes toward the territories according to surveys taken in 1987 and 1989 during the first two years of the intifada.

TABLE 8.2   Changes in Attitudes Toward the Territories 1987 and 1989[a] (%)

Public Attitudes Toward Future of the Occupied Territories	Left Bloc		Labor		Right Bloc	
	1987	1989	1987	1989	1987	1989
Return all or most	59.2	75.7	36.2	52.4	10.3	11.7
Return some	30.9	16.0	43.5	34.6	24.2	24.7
Return none	9.9	8.3	20.3	13.0	65.5	63.6

[a] Number surveyed in 1987 = 1,509, in 1989 = 995.
Source: Ephraim Yuchtman-Yaar, "The Intifada as Viewed by the Israeli Public," *International Problems, Society and Politics,* vol. xxix, 55 (3–4) (1990), p. 25.

The left bloc in Table 8.2 includes voters who supported Mapam, Ratz, Shinui, Hadash, and the Progressive List for Peace. The right includes Likud, the religious parties, Tehiya, Tzomet, and Moledet. Some attitudinal shifts occurred within the blocs. Thus, for example, in 1987—before the intifada—about 31 percent of the left bloc supported the return of some territories; by 1989 that group had been halved, whereas the group that supported total return had increased by the same percent (about 16 percent). Maintaining the status quo, Prime Minister Shamir's option of choice in 1992, represented the preferences of only a minority of the electorate.

The Gulf War

The Gulf War that started in January 1991 ended in a massive military defeat of Iraq. The war marked a significant change in Arabs' perceptions both of each other and of Israel. Israel was not a principal participant or the cause of the conflict. On the contrary, its interests were similar to those of several Arab regimes including Egypt, Syria, and Saudi Arabia—all of which actively joined the U.S.-led anti-Iraq coalition. The war precipitated a U.S.-initiated Middle East Peace Conference in Madrid in late October 1991.

The war also alerted Israelis to the need for decisive leadership and to the country's strategic vulnerability. During the war, strong public sentiment held that the country was leaderless. Prime Minister Shamir rarely appeared in the media, and it was not clear how he planned to respond to Iraqi attacks on Israel's population. About fifty Iraqi ground-to-ground Scud missiles fell on Israel; the missiles caused great damage to property, although there were very few casualties. The public feared the missiles might carry chemical warheads. Many left their homes to find shelter in more secure places or left the country altogether, which was rather rational behavior in the face of the unknown risks and the uncertainty. The IDF deterrent system was totally ineffective, which led to a communal psychological crisis.

Rabin, "Mr. Security," quickly capitalized on this leadership void. When the military spokesperson ordered people to stay in their homes, Rabin was shown in the media defying these "instructions" as he entered his Tel Aviv basement shelter. His stand gained him much respect and admiration, which later translated into political capital. Rabin emerged from the war as the most trustworthy security authority in the country.

The war made many Israelis aware that in the missile age, the Occupied Territories did not constitute effective protection—a fact that called into question the strategic value of the Golan Heights and the West Bank. Negotiations with the Arabs on the basis of UN Security Council Resolutions 242 and 338, which called for peace in exchange for the territories, were now considered feasible. Yet it was Rabin and the Labor party rather than Likud that carried the olive branch in 1993.

Second Transition of Power, 1992

Labor ended decades of political domination in the first, unexpected turnabout of power in the May 1977 election that brought Likud to power. Developments in the 1980s and the early 1990s again made Rabin and Labor competitive with Shamir and Likud by the time of the 1992 election. Labor returned to its traditional position as the largest center party and the core of any potential coalition; that shift in power after fifteen years brought Rabin back to the prime minister's post.

A combination of factors led to the 1992 power shift. Early that year it became evident that Likud could not provide satisfactory leadership to deal with mounting social and economic problems and could not adjust to the new international atmosphere. A second factor was the replacement of Shimon Peres, a four-time loser in electoral bids against Menachem Begin and Yitzhak Shamir, by Rabin as Labor's leader. Rabin had already served as prime minster (1974–1977) and defense minister (1984–1990). His personality, political orientation, and the security myth he represented in the Israeli collective memory evidently influenced the outcome of the election.

When the Shamir government was formed in 1990, it seemed that Likud's domination would last a long time. A huge wave of Jewish immigrants— close to 400,000 people—began to pour in from the Soviet Union. This group, combined with a smaller influx of several thousand Ethiopian Jews who were secretly airlifted in, boosted Israeli morale. These immigration waves helped to enlarge the Israeli Jewish population by over 10 percent in a two-year period. The newcomers provided extra human resources that could be directed to settlements in the West Bank and Gaza and help to expand the economy. They also represented a pool of potential voters in future elections who, it was hoped, would reward the Likud government for its provision of housing, jobs, and welfare with their votes.

By 1991 Israel's international position had improved dramatically. The decision to remain passive during the Gulf War while absorbing the psychological and material costs of Iraqi Scud missile attacks was viewed sympathetically in the West, and relations with the United States and the European community had improved. Israel also formed diplomatic ties with the emerging states of the former Soviet Union and reestablished ties with Eastern European and African states. Even Israel's most hostile neighbor, Syria, a member of the U.S.-led international coalition, moderated its stance because it could no longer rely on Soviet support.

These factors led to overconfidence among senior Likud members, who disregarded both Israeli and foreign public opinion. They failed to respond to the demands of their own loyal supporters, which led to the party's defeat in the 1992 election. Several factors led to Likud's downfall.

1. Although the economy was run efficiently, with virtually no inflation (i.e., less than 10 percent) by June 1992, Likud's priorities were highly debated. Billions of dollars were diverted to housing in the West Bank, but not enough was allocated to the development of new jobs within the green line; consequently, unemployment rates soared. In April 1992 the press reported a jobless rate of about 12 percent of the adult population, including half of all new immigrants, military veterans, and residents of development towns (the traditional power bases of Likud) and about a quarter of Israeli Arabs. (That year the rate did stabilize at 11.2 percent.) Education, communication, and other social infrastructure suffered from lack of funding.

2. Shamir, supported by right-wing extremists in his party and in the government, continued to defy U.S. requests for flexibility and compromise on policy concerning the Occupied Territories. This defiance greatly strained the relationship between the two administrations and raised questions about Israel's ability to withstand regional opposition without U.S. economic, diplomatic, and military assistance. However, he did respond to the U.S. request for a temporary halt in massive building of new settlements in the West Bank.

3. For a variety of personal and organizational reasons, Shamir and Likud were unwilling to comply with popular demands to alter the electoral system and introduce some measure of personal political accountability. During the 1970s Likud had been the first party to democratize its nominating procedures, but in the period 1990–1992 it failed to respond to popular demands for change. Moreover, it did not comply with the law that forbade convention members to hold top positions in the public administration and on boards of governors of state-owned companies. In April 1992 the highly respected state comptroller, Miriam Ben Porath, released a report that severely criticized Likud—specifically employees in the housing ministry—for personal and bureaucratic corruption.

4. The Likud government also failed to provide reasonable answers to security problems. On the one hand, its efforts to contain the intifada were relatively successful. Since the Madrid talks, low-intensity conflict was also in the interest of the PLO leadership. On the other hand, several acts of random terror against both children and adults by desperate Palestinians horrified the Jewish public. After a terrorist attack in May 1992 in the town of Bat Yam, many blamed the government for providing insufficient protection, and local residents there and in Likud strongholds turned to Rabin for answers.

However, the cumulative effects of these factors did not guarantee Labor's victory. In the 1981 and 1984 elections, the Likud came from behind, closing large gaps in the polls and ultimately edging out Labor. This did not happen in 1992, and much of the blame was placed on the party leadership.

By 1992 the Likud was divided into three main factions. The largest was controlled by Shamir and Moshe Arens, the smallest by Sharon. Collaboration between these two camps gave them a majority at the party convention, and they were able to keep the third faction, headed by David Levy, from obtaining strategic positions. Levy, alone among North African Jews, secured a place among the top party leaders. Allegations of ethnic discrimination, which had been directed against Labor in earlier elections, were now directed against the Ashkenazi leaders of Likud. Indeed, on election day many North African Israelis shifted their support to Rabin, which was sufficient to secure the Labor victory.

In the zero-sum electoral game between the two large parties and their affiliated bloc of small parties, Rabin's reappearance as the Labor frontrunner made the decisive difference. Although this development had long been predicted by politicians and experts, Rabin's return to power faced some serious obstacles.

The most immediate obstacle was Peres, who had defeated Rabin in the confrontation at the 1990 party convention. Because of Peres's strength within the party establishment and the public demand for electoral democratization, the party's secretary-general, Micha Harish, along with Rabin's supporters, moved to institute a primary system. They assumed that Rabin would be more popular than Peres with party voters. About 100,000 party members voted in February 1992; Rabin prevailed, barely edging out Peres. Peres, who then competed in the second stage of the primaries to select Knesset candidates, came in first—thus securing the second position, after Rabin, on the party list.

The primaries made Rabin the center of mass media and public attention. All polls indicated that in a head-to-head competition Rabin would prevail against any Likud candidate; however, if Labor as a party were to face Likud, Labor would lose. The inference was clear: The electorate, or rather many Likud voters, was willing to support Rabin but not his party. This situation called for a campaign strategy that emphasized Rabin and deemphasized the role of his party—especially the position of Peres. An election victory required a U.S.-style personalized presidential campaign.

To diminish party visibility, symbols of Labor's traditional socialist orientation were removed; the red flags and party logo were replaced with the national blue. Peres was allowed to appear only once in the party's television commercials, whereas Rabin appeared daily, sometimes two or three times. Most significantly, as discussed earlier, the official name of the party was changed to Ha'Avoda Be'reshut Itzhak Rabin (Labor Headed by Ytzhak Rabin). Pictures of Rabin—and only Rabin—appeared everywhere, and he quickly altered his public lingo; instead of "we" he began to use the charismatic "I" ("I promise," "I am responsible," "I shall change," and so on). The principal slogan and jingle were "Israel Mehake Le'Rabin" ("Israel is waiting for Rabin") and "Rabin Ha'Tikvah Ha'Yechidah" ("Rabin is the only hope"). But slogans and tricks would not necessarily ensure victory; some substantive strategic moves were also required.

On the security issue, where Likud had enjoyed a relative advantage in earlier elections, Rabin emphasized the distinction between "political" and "security" settlements, thus offering a modified form of the 1967 Allon Plan for the West Bank devised by the former foreign minister and Rabin's mentor, Yigal Allon. The plan basically called for the establishment of a security belt around the West Bank and the return of heavily populated Arab cities and towns to Jordanian civil administration. Rabin proposed a broader security zone surrounding a Palestinian autonomous area. The Gaza Strip was included in Rabin's plan, but the Golan Heights was to remain under Israeli control. Public perception of Rabin as the country's foremost security authority who had not been reluctant to take harsh measures against the Palestinians during the intifada gave credence to his position.

Rabin's economic and social program offered a change in the order of national priorities. Funds would be redirected from "useless political settlements" to investments for economic and social development. Rabin promised to confront unemployment; immigrant absorption; the deteriorating education, health, and transportation systems; and other outstanding problems. Because Rabin was attuned to Washington's directives, the public believed he could obtain the U.S. $10 billion loan guarantee denied to the Likud government by the Bush administration. Paradoxically, the leader of the old social democratic party was proposing massive privatization of government-owned companies to generate greater national resources.

On some issues (e.g., the future of Gaza) Rabin positioned himself at the center of the political map not far from Likud, which forced Likud to take a more radical position than its leaders wanted. Rabin captured the center by stating that no extreme left or right parties or extremist politicians would participate in his government. Likud voters took such statements as hints that some of their leaders, such as Levy, might be considered to be actual partners in a Rabin coalition.

To gain the support of Begin's admirers, Likud attempted to reproduce his image, using young Benyamin Begin to deliver campaign messages that were largely ineffective. Rabin's personal myth—IDF commander in the June 1967 war, liberator of Jerusalem—was reiterated. By coincidence, the twenty-fifth anniversaries of the 1967 Six Day War victory and the Liberation of Jerusalem fell during the campaign, much to Labor's delight and Likud's dismay.

The election on June 23, 1992, produced the expected outcome. Most traditional Ashkenazi voters supported Labor; almost half of the new immigrants and about 6 percent of former Likud voters also cast their ballots for Labor. Although those in the last group did not change their political attitudes, they changed their preference for prime minister by supporting Rabin. Labor captured forty-four Knesset seats, and Likud received only thirty-two. But more important, Labor could prevent the formation of a right-wing bloc that would stymie Rabin's government. Together with Meretz, which obtained twelve seats, and the five won by two Arab parties, Labor held a majority of sixty-one seats. The Likud could rely on only fifty-nine: thirty-two of its own, eight from Tzomet, three from Moledet, six from the NRP, four from Ya'hadut Hatorah, and six from Shas. Rabin had regained actual power.

The Second Rabin Era

Preparations for a new government began immediately after results had been officially approved so that Rabin could assume office after the twenty-one days proscribed by law. He hoped for a wide-based coalition that would include all parties willing to accept his basic platform, which included Meretz and three religious parties that together had captured sixteen Knesset seats. Rabin also planned to recruit Tzomet, which had scored the biggest surprise by increasing the number of its seats from two to eight. Tzomet had campaigned with a tough stand on security and the need for an efficient and clean government, electoral reform, strong education, and the recruitment of Orthodox Jews in the army—issues similar to those of Labor.

A partnership with Tzomet would have assured protection against attacks from the right-wing opposition; however, such a partnership did not materialize. Tzomet's Rafael Eitan refused to alter his opposition to negotiations with the Palestinians, and his request to become defense minister or, alternatively, minister of education and culture was refused. Instead, the education ministry was awarded to Meretz leader Shulamit Aloni, who stood for civil rights and the separation of state and religion. Leaders of the religious parties could not abide Aloni's appointment and tried to persuade Rabin to abandon her. He held firm, thus alienating many of the Orthodox. The only religious party to join the government was Shas, which had six seats; that decision was not well received by the other religious parties. But Shas now had a relative advantage over the others, including access to public funding that could be channeled to develop further support.

Faced with these difficulties, Rabin decided to form a minimum winning coalition that consisted of Labor, Meretz, and Shas, with support from the five Arab Knesset members. To maintain this alignment, Rabin had to depend on Peres for political assistance; hence, he awarded the position of foreign minister to his old party rival. Rabin kept the post of defense minister in addition to the prime ministry. Most coalition members were given payoffs in the form of ministerial positions, posts as deputy ministers or heads of important Knesset committees, and other top posts, which created personal incentive to sustain the coalition.

After the 1992 election the government was small, and the distance between the partners on central ideological and policy positions was not great except on issues of state and religion. This situation allowed Rabin to provide clear answers to mounting policy problems inherited from Likud. Internal coalition stability was ensured, and external opposition challenges could be easily checked.

Rabin was a unique politician who was known to be a man of his word. By August 1992 the government had already begun to fulfill some of the prime minister's campaign pledges: New political settlements were frozen in the West Bank, loan guarantees promised by President George Bush had been instituted, and peace negotiations had been resumed with the Palestinians, Syrians, Jordanians, and Lebanese. The government exhibited firmness on domestic issues and flexibility on international problems. After some initial difficulties, a Palestinian Administrative Authority was formed in Gaza and Jericho. Negotiations with Syria over the Golan region were renewed. In 1994 Jordan followed Egypt's example and signed a peace treaty with Israel. Yet by the end of 1994 much of the support Rabin and Labor had enjoyed since 1992 seemed to be evaporating. A gap began to develop among Rabin's promises, public expectations, and the hard realities of economic and security issues.

Much Israeli public attention was directed toward economic recovery. Success would be achieved, Rabin promised, by diverting resources from security-related matters and through borrowed external funds to satisfy the public's needs. But after the first year of government, the positive overall macroeconomic performance was undermined by poor distribution; the same areas and people who had suffered during Likud times continued to be deprived under Labor. By 1994 the public seemed to be losing confidence in the stock market and in the state's economic leadership. Rabin's reputation as the country's most credible politician was badly damaged when in spite of promises not to tax the stock market he did approve taxes, then later canceled his approval, thus shooting down the market. Security problems were also mounting: Both Rabin's Palestinian and Jewish opponents threw into question the prospect of peace. By mid-1995 the right wing, led by Likud's Benjamin (Bibi) Netanyahu, had risen in public esteem; a year before the election for the Fourteenth Knesset it was unclear whether the relative success and achievements of the Labor government would guarantee its reelection to power in 1996.

Likud's Return to Power

Although formal campaigning is limited to the few weeks prior to an election, electioneering for the May 1966 election began months before the date scheduled for voting. Prime Minister Rabin dominated the scene until his assassination on November 4, 1995. Foreign Minister Peres was still a secondary figure, and the new leader of the Likud opposition, Benjamin Netanyahu, was an up-and-coming young politician who had yet to be tested.

With Rabin as its candidate for prime minister, Labor held an advantage. Rabin was a war hero whose military credentials were difficult to challenge. He presented an image of straitlaced honesty, loyalty to country above party, and no-nonsense dedication to duty. But despite Rabin's image, the country was deeply divided over Labor's negotiations with the Palestinians and with Syria. When the Oslo II agreement was presented to the Knesset in October 1995, it was approved by the slimmest majority (sixty-one to fifty-nine). Opinion polls fluctuated around the 50 percent mark between those who agreed with Labor's land for peace approach and those who feared withdrawal from the West Bank or the Golan Heights would undermine national security. Consequently, Netanyahu and Likud made a "retreat" from these territories the major theme in their attempt to displace Rabin and his Labor coalition.

Before Rabin's death, the debate was often acrimonious, with his most militant opponents accusing him of being a traitor. In September 1995, several Orthodox rabbis from the nationalist wing of the religious bloc of parties backed a statement signed by one thousand reserve soldiers and officers pledging to disregard army orders to uproot Jewish settlements in the Occupied Territories.

The intensity of political arguments decreased after Rabin's assassination at a peace rally in Tel Aviv. His murder seemed to shake society as no other event had since the establishment of the state. Some Rabin supporters accused Likud and its leader of doing too little to disavow the support of militant extremists. However, both the mainstream religious parties and Likud disclaimed responsibility for the tragedy. For several weeks following the assassination, leading political figures adopted a more measured tone in electoral pronouncements and public appearances.

Rabin's death shifted public opinion away from Netanyahu, Likud, and the religious parties. Rabin's successor as prime minister, Labor leader Shimon Peres, refused to press his advantage by calling for an immediate election; he waited several weeks before moving the election up to May from its scheduled November date.

In early 1996 a series of catastrophic events again led to sharpened rhetoric, with charges that Peres was lax on security and was too trusting of PLO leader, Yasser Arafat. Several suicide bombings by Palestinian terrorists in Jerusalem, Tel Aviv, and Ashkelon that killed scores of Israeli civilians during February and March 1996 changed the political atmosphere. Labor's ability to maintain security now became the dominant issue.

In an attempt to disprove accusations that he was unable to maintain security, Peres initiated several forceful policies against Israel's enemies. He adopted Rabin's concept of "separation"—that is, cutting Israel off from contact with Palestinians in the West Bank and Gaza. The closure measures that kept Palestinian workers from earning their livelihood in Israel were more strictly enforced. Plans were projected to construct a fence along a buffer zone to separate Israel from the Palestinians. To further display his toughness, Peres called off negotiations with Syria following a terrorist attack on a Jewish bus. Peres's most forceful display was Operation Grapes of Wrath in April 1996 against the Islamic fundamentalist guerrilla force Hezbollah that had attacked Israeli forces and their allies in southern Lebanon. The IDF invasion of Lebanon resulted in hundreds of Lebanese civilian deaths and injuries, displaced thousands from their villages, and destroyed hundreds of homes.

Labor's platform in the 1996 campaign emphasized security while maintaining a commitment to the peace process. The platform emphasized Peres's vision of a "new Middle East" based on a common market, with regional cooperation in irrigation, tourism, transport, and communication systems. The platform stated that although Israel would not rule over the Palestinian people, it would insist on a united Jerusalem under Israel's jurisdiction. The Jordan River would be Israel's eastern security border. No new Jewish settlements would be established in the Occupied Territories, although Israel would maintain jurisdiction over most of the Jewish settlers there.

Netanyahu made light of Peres's vision of a new Middle East, charging that Peres's idealism was misplaced, which led him to misjudge the intentions of Israel's enemies. Likud campaigners maintained that Peres placed too much trust in Syria, Arafat, and the PLO. In contrast to Labor, Likud's platform emphasized the right of Jews to settle in the Occupied Territories and promised to rescind Labor's freeze on Jewish settlements there. Although Likud would honor Israel's previous international agreements and continue with the peace process, it would also act to reduce the dangers to the country from these agreements.

Under the new electoral system, voters could cast one ballot for the party of their choice and a second for prime minister. As a result, many who voted for either Netanyahu or Peres did not vote for Likud or Labor. Some parties, such as Meretz, urged supporters to vote for the party and to vote for Peres as prime minister; the NRP, on the other hand, asked its constituency to vote for Netanyahu. The result of the two-ballot system was a nearly even split for prime minister, with 50.4 percent for Netanyahu and 49.5 percent for Peres.

Voting for party lists resulted in several surprises. Among the most significant was the large increase in support for the three Orthodox religious parties—Shas, the National Religious party, and United Torah Judaism. As Table 8.3 shows, these parties combined received twenty-three Knesset seats, seven more than the religious parties had previously obtained. This growth vastly increased the parties' bargaining power and made them an essential part of any government coalition. The large number of votes for two new parties, Israel ba-Aliya and the Third Way, was also unexpected.

In the year that led up to the 1996 election, several new parties were established and old ones were restructured. Of the twenty-one parties that contested the election, thirteen were new, but only eleven passed the 1.5 percent threshold that entitled them to a place in the Knesset (see Table 8.3). Four of these eleven were new parties or were realignments of older factions. The new parties in the Knesset were Israel ba-Aliya and the Third Way.

Israel ba-Aliya, which received seven Knesset seats, was established by Natan Sharansky, a former Soviet dissident who became the principal leader of the Jewish immigrants who arrived in Israel after the collapse of the Soviet Union in 1991. Sharansky's party rallied Jews from the former Soviet Union who were dissatisfied with the government's treatment of the new immigrants.

The Third Way movement became a political party in 1996; it opposed the return of the Golan Heights to Syria. A large number of its supporters, many from Jewish settlements in the Golan area, were former members of Labor.

Party realignments included the fusion of David Levy's Gesher party and Rafael Eitan's Tzomet party with Likud, as well as the union of the Democratic Arab party with the Islamic Movement in the United Arab List. Likud's realignment saved it from a major loss of support. By uniting with Gesher and Tzomet, Likud was able to keep the same number of seats in the new Knesset as it had held in the Thirteenth Knesset (see Table 8.3). By

TABLE 8.3   Results of Elections to the Knesset, 1996

Votes for Prime Minister
Benjamin Netanyahu—1,501,023 (50.4%)
Shimon Peres—1,471,566 (49.5%)

Knesset Votes

Party List	Number of Votes	% of Votes	Seats, 1996	Seats, 1992
Labor	818,570	26.8	34	44
Likud/Gesher/Tzomet	767,178	25.1	32	32 (Likud)
Shas	259,759	8.5	10	6
National Religious party	240,224	7.8	9	6
Meretz	226,257	7.4	9	12
Israel ba-Aliya	174,928	5.7	7	—
DFPE	129,455	4.2	5	3
United Torah Judaism	98,655	3.2	4	4
Third Way	96,457	3.1	4	—
United Arab List	89,513	2.9	4	2 (Arab Democratic party)
Moledet	71,982	2.3	2	3
Ten other parties[a]	78,616	3.0	—	—

[a] Each of these parties received under 1.5 percent of votes cast.
Notes: Minimum votes required to pass 1.5 percent threshold for election to Knesset—45,774; number of votes per Knesset seat—24,775. Voting by place of residence: cities over 100,000 population, 46.5 percent; development towns, 9 percent; rural villages, kibbutzim, and *moshavim,* 7.5 percent; Arab communities, 10.3 percent; Jewish settlements in West Bank and Gaza, 2 percent.
Source: Compiled by Peretz.

combining the two Arab lists in the United Arab List, Arab strength in the Knesset was also increased.

Although the dual election system was intended to strengthen the prime minister, the resultant fragmentation of the party system diminished Netanyahu's overall authority. To obtain a majority in parliament, Netanyahu had to form a cabinet composed of members of Shas, the NRP, Israel ba-Aliya, the Third Way, and the Gesher and Tzomet factions of his own Likud party. Since the new law permits no more than eighteen cabinet members, fewer than half the members can come from the prime minister's own party.

Netanyahu's new partners could make extortionate demands for cabinet posts, knowing he would have to concede to their demands or lose his majority in the Knesset. The religious parties could intensify pressure to impose their imprint on new legislation. The prime minister faces a challenge in balancing religious party demands against opposition from secular-oriented coalition members such as those in Israel ba-Aliya and Tzomet.

It appears that the system designed to reduce the power of smaller parties may have the opposite effect. Israel's political map has become more diffused than ever before. Simply put, the small parties of yesteryear have become larger and more powerful, and the two main parties—Labor and Likud—have lost their dominating position.

9

Challenges of the Israeli Polity

Since independence, Israeli polity has muddled through from one crisis to another at high cost, including human lives, with the help of its powerful Western ally. Although Israel has met many challenges, some serious issues have not yet been addressed satisfactorily; some remain unsolved intentionally and are likely to become critical in the future.

The Challenge of Diaspora Jewry

The relationship between the Jews in Israel and those in the diaspora is highly problematic. Some observers draw a direct, even an inseparable link between the Jews who live inside Israel and those who live outside. Many say the Jews are "one people," with the same identity and interests. The fact that almost all Jews now live in countries from which they are free to leave but that relatively few choose to come to Israel does not seem to affect this unity. Other observers, fewer in number, consider Israeli Jews a distinctive nation. A major challenge for the future will be to determine the nature of Jewish religion and national identities and the kind of relationship that should exist between them—a difficult task.

According to Israeli law, Israel does not belong to its citizens alone but to the entire Jewish people. Many diaspora Jews share a strong spiritual tie with the Jewish community in Israel. They are eager for news of Israel, some support Israel financially, and some send their children to spend time there. Some call themselves Zionists without moving to Israel. Israeli political institutions are structured to perpetuate these ties: The Jewish Agency, the World Zionist Organization, Hadassah, the Jewish National Fund, and other organizations link the Jewish people.

Should Israeli society and its nationality continue to be mainly Jewish, or should they become Israeli? Even if the choice is to support the status quo and not tamper with nationality, the issue cannot be avoided. Population figures show that Israel is already essentially a binational state. The relaxation of the Law of Return, which allowed many loosely defined Jews to enter the country during the 1990s, added much confusion and created some urgency to resolve the problem.

Several major factors must be considered, the most important of which is the fact that the Jews in Israel are different from most diaspora Jews, even in their religious orientation. In Israel, only the Orthodox tradition is officially recognized by the state; in the diaspora, the leading traditions are Reformed and Conservative. Israel would have to become more pluralistic in its religious orientation to maintain its ties with world Jewry.

Integration of Israeli Arabs

Many Israeli Arabs demand a national identity that assures that the state belongs to all its citizens. This is a reasonable demand, one that is consistent with the values of liberal democracy. The future success of Arab political parties may force the issue onto the national agenda and confront the Jewish majority with the need to deal seriously with this issue of national identity.

Until now, Arabs have had no part in the Israeli corporate national identity. The boundaries of that identity are Jewish, but they are open enough to include the Druze and Bedouins, who are allowed to serve in the IDF. Still, the fulfillment of civil obligations does not assure an equal share of rights and does not necessarily result in a true sense of belonging. In fact, these Arabs feel like outsiders. Little in the Israeli collective and symbolic memory is Arab; there are no new street names, postage stamps, monuments, national holidays, or heros, and there is very little common history. The state is Jewish, built by Jews for Jews.

By the end of the 1990s the Arab minority in Israel will approach a quarter of the population. This minority of "outsiders"—which constitutes a significant part of the population—has been forced to develop its own identity. It is no surprise that many Arabs are asking for cultural autonomy, and some are even demanding political autonomy. A solution to this problem must be formalized in the near future.

The Israeli-Palestinian Relationship

The initiation of the peace process between Israel and the PLO in 1993 was the first serious step undertaken by the two groups to terminate the conflict between them. The 1993 Oslo Accord gave the two sides a legal and conceptual framework upon which they could begin the historic process of reconciliation. The accord even gave the Palestinians a territorial base (Gaza and Jericho) where they could start to build their independent political institutions and prepare for self-rule in the West Bank.

Two years after hopes were raised by the Oslo Accord, these expectations seemed to be replaced with frustration and disappointment. Neither side met its obligations and promises. Continuous terrorist activities showed that opposition to peace negotiations was strong and violent and could subvert the process. Terrorist activities and doubts about the peace process were instrumental in the defeat of Shimon Peres in the 1996 election for prime minister. If peace indeed prevailed between Israel and the Palestinians and the latter were to form their own independent state, what would be the nature of the relationship between the new state and Israeli Arabs? How would the Knesset react if a quarter of its members had a close affinity with a neighboring state? What about the future of Jerusalem, where population estimates indicate that by the year 2010 the majority of residents will be anti-Zionist or non-Zionist—either Arabs or ultra-Orthodox Jews?

Israel has been at peace with Egypt since 1979 and at peace with Jordan since 1994. It maintains an office of "economic interests" in Morocco and has semiofficial relationships with some Gulf states. Israel has been engaged in erratic peace talks with Syria since 1991, but in the mid-1990s the ultimate result of these negotiations was still unclear. Syria and Israel have found it difficult to settle their differences less because of disagreement over territory than because of mutual distrust.

The Israeli-Palestinian conflict is more complex than claims over territory; hence, simple territorial division may be insufficient to resolve the dispute. Arabs live in Galilee, the Negev, Jaffa, the Little Triangle, the West Bank, and the Gaza Strip and are interspersed among Jews in many of the same regions; thus, territorial separation of the two peoples, even if desired by Israeli policymakers, may not be possible or practical.

The Economy

Overall the Israeli economy has been a success. It ascended from an underdeveloped stage to the level of Western European postindustrial societies within a decade or two. Although Israel has moved toward a free economy, it still maintains an essentially mixed economic system in which the government is involved in all aspects and sectors of life. The government is willing to gradually sell off its excessive holdings, more for practical than ideological reasons. Thus, the process of privatization has been slow and complex.

The weakening of the Histadrut has helped privatization. Workers' diminishing organizational power, however, may have an adverse effect;

instead of dealing with one central union, the government and private interests may have to deal with an array of independent unions.

The economy has benefited from the influx of new Russian immigrants, the association with the European Economic Community, the peace process, and the possibility of Arab markets. U.S. economic assistance may soon be greatly diminished, however, which will force Israelis to rely on themselves. In the mid-1990s many economists were optimistic that they could do so.

Society

Several important societal problems that were present during the early days of the state await solution. These include problems of relationships between Arabs and Jews (the problem of Israeli nationality), Orthodox and secular Jews (the problem of state and religion), Sepharadi and Ashkenazi (the problem of ethnicity), men and women (the problem of gender equality), veteran settlers and new immigrants, poor and rich, workers and employers, and others. Some of these issues may be solved in time without government intervention; others require careful evaluation and a state policy. Continual avoidance will lead to a national crisis and societal instability.

For example, the integration of secular Sepharadi and Ashkenazi Jews may not need special attention as long as members of both groups reside in the same areas or belong to the same social class. When these preconditions are absent, the relationship between the groups becomes similar to that between rich and poor, the educated and less educated, and residents of the center and those at the periphery. However, belonging to the same social class or living in the same area may not be a mediating factor for Arabs and Jews. On the contrary, sharing the same social attributes may intensify the conflict when Arabs demand equal rights and treatment.

The Environment

Until recently, little systematic attention was given to the quality of the environment in Israel. Toward the end of the 1980s, some policymakers realized that problems could exist in the general public's attitude toward this issue. Since then, the environment has appeared on the public agenda in statements by politicians, although most Israelis have still not internalized the importance of caring for the quality of their surroundings.

In this respect, Israel is not yet an advanced society. Giving attention to the landscape, air quality, the noise level, water resources, wildlife, and the like has become part of the legal codex, but little has been done to implement the law effectively. Because Israel is so small and has a dense population, this issue will require policy attention in the future.

New Political Rules

In time, Israeli political parties may be less central than they were in the past; in fact, by the 1990s they had already lost much of their importance. Ideology will also become less significant; parties and candidates already offer mixed packages of issues that give little attention to ideology. It is still not clear whether the prime minister will be as independent or as effective under the new rules as he or she was in the past. The power of the office will depend on the prime minister's personality and on the composition of the Knesset.

Notes

1. Robert Famighetti, ed., *The World Almanac* (Mahwah, N.J.: St. Martin's Press, 1994).

2. Cited in Dina Goren, "Why Is the World So Interested in Us." *Otot* (August 1987): 12.

3. Yoram Levi, *Davar* [Tel Aviv], August 11, 1992.

4. Yitzhak Reiter and Geoffrey Wigoder, eds., *The Political Life of Arabs in Israel* (Tel Aviv: Beit Berl, Institute for Israeli Arab Studies, 1992).

5. Sergio Dellapergola, *The Jewish People: A Picture of the Demographic Situation* (Jerusalem: Ministry of Education and Culture, 1994).

6. *Statistical Abstract of Israel* (Jerusalem: Government of Israel, Central Bureau of Statistics, 1994), pp. 180–181.

7. Rebecca Kook, "Dilemmas of Ethnic Minorities in Democracies: The Effect of Peace on the Palestinians in Israel." *Politics and Society* 23, no. 3 (1995): 309–336.

8. *Statistical Abstract*, 1994, p. 340.

9. *Statistical Abstract*, 1992, pp. 346–347.

10. *Statistical Abstract*, 1994, pp. 48–49.

11. Cited in Arthur Hertzberg, ed., *The Zionist Idea* (New York: Atheneum, 1970), pp. 248–277.

12. J. De Haas, trans. *The Jewish State* (New York: Scopus Publishers, 1943).

13. Cited in Israel Cohen, *The Zionist Movement* (New York: 1946), p. 78.

14. Simon Dubnow, *Nationalism and History* (Koppel Pinson, ed.) (New York: Atheneum, 1970).

15. Yehuda Ben-Avner, "Zionism and Autonomism in East Europe at the Beginning of the 20th Century." *Kivunim* 16 (August 1982): 100.

16. J. C. Hurewitz, *The Middle East and North Africa in World Politics: A Documentary Record,* Vol. 2 (New Haven: Yale University Press, 1979), p. 106.

17. Walter Laqueur and Barry Rubin, eds., "The British Mandate (1922)." In *The Israel-Arab Reader* (New York: Facts on File Publications, 1984), pp. 34–42.

18. *Statistical Abstract*, 1994, p. 46.

19. David Wyman, *The Abandonment of the Jews* (New York: Pantheon, 1984).

20. Laqueur and Rubin, eds., "Towards a Jewish State: The Biltmore Program (1942)." In *The Israel-Arab Reader*, pp. 77–79.

21. Laqueur and Rubin, eds., "State of Israel Proclamation of Independence (1948)." In *The Israel-Arab Reader*, pp. 125–128.

22. *Jerusalem Report* 6, no. 26 (May 4, 1995): 30; *Statistical Abstract*, 1992, p. 174.

23. American Jewish Committee, *American Jewish Year-Book,* Vol. 92 (1992); Dellapergola, *The Jewish People.*

24. *Statistical Abstract,* 1994, pp. 328–329.

25. Ibid., p. 336.

26. Ibid., p. 552.

27. Ibid., p. 376.

28. *The Multi-Year Plan for the Israel Economy: 1995–2000* (Jerusalem: Government of Israel, Ministry of Economy and Planning, 1994), p. 37.

29. *Statistical Abstract,* 1994, pp. 324, 328.

30. Ibid., p. 638.

31. Ibid., pp. 58–67.

32. Dellapergola, *The Jewish People,* p. 12.

33. Ibid., p. 14.

34. *Statistical Abstract,* 1994, pp. 328–329.

35. *Statistical Abstract,* 1993, p. 361.

36. Ibid., p. 360.

37. Gideon Doron and Daniella Shunker, *Women's Political Representation in Israel* (Tel Aviv: Ha'Kibbutz Ha'meuhad, 1997).

38. Gideon Doron, "Two Civil Societies and One State: Jews and Arabs in the State of Israel." In Augustus R. Norton, ed., *Civil Society in the Middle East,* Vol. 2 (Leiden: E. J. Brill, 1996), pp. 193–220.

39. Yael Yishai, *Interest Groups in Israel* (Tel Aviv: Am Oved, 1986).

40. *Statistical Abstract,* 1993, pp. 192–195.

41. Gideon Doron and Boaz Tamir, "The Electoral Cycle: A Political Economic Perspective." *Crossroads* 10 (1983): 141–164.

42. Don Peretz and Sammy Smooha, "Israel's Tenth Knesset Elections—Ethnic Upsurgence and Decline of Ideology." *Middle East Journal* 35, no. 4 (Autumn 1981): 512.

43. Ibid.

44. *Jerusalem Post,* May 24, 1981.

45. Peretz and Smooha, "Israel's Tenth Knesset Elections."

Bibliography

Agassi, Joseph. 1984. *Religion and Nationality*. Tel Aviv: Papyrus.

Ahroni, Yair. 1991. *The Political Economy of Israel*. Tel Aviv: Am Oved.

Akzin, Benjamin. 1955. "The Role of Parties in Israeli Democracy." *Journal of Politics* 4: 507–545.

Al-Haj, Majid. 1995. *Education, Empowerment, and Control: The Case of the Arabs in Israel*. Albany: State University of New York Press.

_____. 1995. "The Political Behavior of the Arabs in Israel in the 1992 Elections: Integration Versus Segregation." In Arian and Shamir, eds.

Arian, Asher. 1985. *Politics in Israel: The Second Generation*. Chatham, N.J.: Chatham House.

_____, ed. 1972. *The Elections in Israel—1969*. Jerusalem: Jerusalem Academic Press.

_____, ed. 1975. *The Elections in Israel—1973*. Jerusalem: Jerusalem Academic Press.

_____, ed. 1980. *The Elections in Israel—1977*. Jerusalem: Jerusalem Academic Press.

Arian, Asher, and Samuel Barnes. 1974. "The Dominant Party System: A Neglected Model of Democratic Stability." *Journal of Politics* 3: 592–614.

Arian, Asher, and Michal Shamir. 1983. "The Primary Functions of the Left-Right Continuum." *Comparative Politics* (January): 139–158.

_____, eds. 1987. *The Elections in Israel—1984*. Tel Aviv: Ramot Publishing.

_____, eds. 1990. *The Elections in Israel—1988*. Boulder, Colo.: Westview Press.

_____, eds. 1995. *The Elections in Israel—1992*. Albany: State University of New York Press.

Aronoff, Myron. 1988. "The Failure of the Labor Party and the Emergence of Gush Emunim." In K. Lawson and P. H. Merkel, eds., *When Parties Fail: Emerging Alternative Organizations*. Princeton: Princeton University Press.

Avnon, Dan. 1993. *The Party Law in Israel: Between a Legal Framework and Democratic Norms*. Tel Aviv: Israeli Institute for Democracy.

Barkai, Haim. 1983. *The Early Days of the Israeli Economy*. Jerusalem: Falk Institute.

Bartal, Gabriel. 1986. *The General Histadrut: Structure and Activities*. Tel Aviv: Havad Hapoel.

_____, ed. 1985. *Report to the Fifteenth Convention of Histadrut*. Tel Aviv: Havad Hapoel.

Barzilai, Gad. 1992. *A Democracy in Wartime: Conflict and Consensus in Israel*. Tel Aviv: Sifriat Poalim.

Barzilai, Gad, Ephraim Yuchtman-Yaar, and Zeev Segal. 1994. *The Israeli Supreme Court and the Israeli Public.* Tel Aviv: Papyrus.

Beilin, Yossi. 1992. *Israel: A Concise Political History.* New York: St. Martin's Press.

Ben-Eliezer, Uri. 1993. "The Meaning of Political Participation in Nonliberal Democracy: The Israeli Experience." *Comparative Politics* 25: 397–412.

Ben-Rafael, Eliezer, and Stephen Sharot. 1991. *Ethnicity, Religion, and Class in Israeli Society.* Cambridge: Cambridge University Press.

Benvenisti, Meron. 1988. *The Sling and the Club.* Jerusalem: Keter.

Ben-Zadok, Efraim. 1993. *Local Communities and the Israeli Polity: Conflict of Values and Interests.* Albany: State University of New York Press.

Benziman, Uzi, and Mansour Atallah. 1992. *Subtenants.* Jerusalem: Keter.

Ben-Zvi, Abraham. 1993. *The United States and Israel.* New York: Columbia University Press.

Braybrook, David, and Charles Lindblom. 1963. *A Strategy of Decision.* New York: Free Press.

Brichta, Avraham. 1977. *Democracy and Election.* Tel Aviv: Am Oved.

_____. 1979. "The 1977 Elections and the Future of Electoral Reform in Israel." In Penniman, ed.

Buber-Agassi, Judith. 1982. "The Status of Women in Israel." In Yisraeli Dafna et al., eds., *The Double Bind: Women in Israel.* Tel Aviv: Ha'Kibbutz Ha'meuchad.

_____. 1989. "Theories of Gender Equality—Lessons from the Kibbutz." *Gender and Society* 3: 160–186.

Caiden, Gerald. 1970. *Israel's Administrative Culture.* Berkeley: University of California Press.

Caspi, Dan, and Yehiel Limor. 1992. *The Mediators: The Mass Media in Israel, 1948–1990.* Tel Aviv: Am Oved.

Caspi, Dan, Avraham Diskin, and Emanuel Gutmann, eds. 1983. *The Roots of Begin's Success: The 1981 Israeli Elections.* New York: St. Martin's Press.

Cockburn, Andrew, and Leslie Cockburn. 1991. *Dangerous Liaison: The Inside Story of the U.S.-Israeli Covert Relationship.* New York: HarperCollins.

Cohen, Eric. 1972. "The Black Panthers and Israeli Society." *Jewish Journal of Sociology* 14: 93–109.

Cohen, Israel. 1946. *The Zionist Movement.* New York.

Curtis, Michael, ed. 1971. *People and Politics in the Middle East.* New Brunswick, N.J.: Transaction.

Curtis, Michael, and Chertoff Mordecai, eds. 1973. *Israel: Social Structure and Change.* New Brunswick, N.J.: Transaction.

Danet, Brenda. 1989. *Pulling Strings: Biculturalism in Israeli Bureaucracy.* Albany: State University of New York Press.

De Haas, J., trans. 1943. *The Jewish State.* New York: Scopus Publishers.

Dellapergola, Sergio. 1994. *The Jewish People: A Picture of the Demographic Situation.* Jerusalem: Ministry of Education and Culture.

Dery, David. 1993. *Politics and Civil Service Appointments.* Tel Aviv: Israeli Institute for Democracy.

_____. 1994. *Who Governs Local Government?* Tel Aviv: Israeli Institute for Democracy.

Dery, David, and Emmanuel Sharon. 1994. *Bureaucracy and Democracy in Budgetary Reform.* Tel Aviv: Israeli Institute for Democracy.

Diskin, Avraham. 1988. *Elections and Voters in Israel.* Tel Aviv: Am Oved.

Don-Yehiya, Eliezer. 1975. "Religion and Coalition: The National Religious Party and Coalition Formation in Israel." In Arian, ed.

———, ed. 1991. *Israel and Diaspora Jewry: Ideological and Political Perspectives.* Ramat Gan: Bar-Ilan University Press.

Doron, Adam, ed. 1988. *The State of Israel and the Land of Israel.* Beit Berl: Beit Berl College.

Doron, Avraham. 1990. *Privatization of Welfare Services.* Jerusalem: Hebrew University.

Doron, Gideon. 1984. "Policy Flexibility and Coalition Size: The Case of the Israeli Ruling Party." *Israel Social Science Research* 21: 66–74.

———. 1986. *To Decide and to Implement.* Tel Aviv: Kivunim.

———. 1987. "Party Financing in Israel: The 1984 Election." In Arian and Shamir, eds.

———. 1988. *Games in Israeli Politics.* Tel Aviv: Ramot.

———. 1988. *Rational Politics in Israel.* Tel Aviv: Ramot.

———. 1993. "Labor's Return to Power in Israel." *Current History* 570: 27–31.

———. 1996. *Strategy of Election.* Rehovot: Kivunim.

———. 1996. "Two Civil Societies and One State: Jews and Arabs in the State of Israel." In Augustus R. Norton, ed., *Civil Society in the Middle East,* Vol. 2. Leiden: E. J. Brill.

Doron, Gideon, with Sara Levitov. 1989. "Social Welfare Policy: Israel." In Jack DeSario, ed., *International Public Policy Sourcebook.* Westport, Conn.: Greenwood Press.

Doron, Gideon, and Nurit Adiri. 1994. *Privatization of Service Delivery in Israeli Local Governments.* Jerusalem: Institute for Advanced Strategic and Political Studies.

Doron, Gideon, and Giora Goldberg. 1990. "No Big Deal: Democratization of the Nominating Process." In Arian and Shamir, eds.

Doron, Gideon, and Barry Kay. 1995. "Reforming Israel's Voting Schemes." In Arian and Shamir, eds.

Doron, Gideon, and Moshe Maor. 1989. *Barriers to Entry into Israeli Politics.* Tel Aviv: Papyrus.

Doron, Gideon, and Daniella Shunker. 1997. *Women's Political Representation in Israel.* Tel Aviv: Ha'Kibbutz Ha'meuhad.

Doron, Gideon, and Boaz Tamir. 1983. "The Electoral Cycle: A Political Economic Perspective." *Crossroads* 10: 141–164.

Drezon-Tepler, Marcia. 1990. *Interest Groups and Political Change in Israel.* Albany: State University of New York Press.

Dror, Yehezkel. 1985. "The Politics of the Defense Budget: A Comparison Between West Europe and Israel." In Zvi Lanir, ed., *Israeli Security Planning in the 1980s: Its Politics and Economics.* Tel Aviv: Ministry of Defense.

———. 1989. *A Grand Strategy for Israel.* Jerusalem: Academon.

Dubnow, Simon. 1918. *History of the Jews in Russia and Poland.* Philadelphia: Jewish Publication Society.

_____. 1970. *Nationalism and History.* New York: Atheneum.

Duverger, Maurice. 1972. *Political Parties.* London: Methuen.

Edelman, Martin. 1994. *Courts, Politics, and Culture in Israel.* Charlottesville: University of Virginia Press.

Eisenstadt, Shmuel. 1969. *The Israeli Society.* Jerusalem: Magnes.

_____. 1985. *The Transformation of the Israeli Society.* London: Weidenfeld and Nicholson.

Elazar, Daniel, and Haim Kalhaim, eds. 1987. *Local Government in Israel.* Jerusalem: Jerusalem Center for Public Affairs.

Elazar, Daniel, and Shmuel Sandler, eds. 1990. *Israel's Odd Couple.* Detroit: Wayne State University Press.

_____. 1995. "Who is the Boss?" In Daniel Elazar and Shmuel Sandler, eds., *Israel at the Polls, 1992.* Detroit: Rowmon and Littlefield Publishers.

Etzioni-Halevi, Hava. 1975. "Protests in the Israeli Democracy." *Political Science Quarterly* 90: 497–520.

Etzioni-Halevi, Hava, and Rina Shapira. 1977. *Political Culture in Israel.* New York: Praeger.

Evron, Boas. 1988. *A National Reckoning.* Tel Aviv: Dvir.

_____. 1995. *Jewish State or Israeli Nation?* Bloomington: Indiana University Press.

Freedman, Robert O. 1984. *The Middle East Since Camp David.* Boulder, Colo.: Westview Press.

_____, ed. 1991. *The Intifada.* Miami: Florida International University Press.

Galnoor, Itzhak. 1982. *Steering the Polity: Communications and Politics in Israel.* Beverly Hills: Sage.

Goldberg, Giora. 1992. *Political Parties in Israel.* Tel Aviv: Ramot.

_____. 1994. *The Israeli Voter 1992.* Jerusalem: Magnes.

Goldscheider, Calvin, ed. 1992. *Population and Social Change in Israel.* Boulder, Colo.: Westview Press.

Grinberg, Lev. 1991. *Split Corporations in Israel.* Albany: State University of New York Press.

Gutmann, Emmanuel. 1977. "Political Parties and Groups: Stability and Change." In Moshe Lisak and Emmanuel Gutmann, eds., *The Israeli Political System.* Tel Aviv: Am Oved.

Harris, William. 1980. *Taking Roots: Israeli Settlement in the West Bank, the Golan and Gaza-Sinai.* New York: Wiley.

Hasson, Shlomo. 1993. *Urban Social Movements in Jerusalem.* Albany: State University of New York Press.

Hertzberg, Arthur, ed. 1970. *The Zionist Idea.* New York: Atheneum.

Herzog, Hanna. 1987. "Toward Reassessment of the Role of Minor Parties." In Arian and Shamir, eds.

_____. 1995. "Penetrating the System: The Politics of Collective Identities." In Arian and Shamir, eds.

Horovich, Dan. 1977. "Is Israel a Garrison State?" *Jerusalem Quarterly* 4 (Summer): 58–75.

Horovich, Dan, and Moshe Lisak. 1978. *The Origins of the Israeli Polity.* Chicago: University of Chicago Press.

_____. 1989. *Troubles in Utopia*. Tel Aviv: Am Oved.

Jaffe, Eliezer. 1982. *Giving Wisely*. Jerusalem: Koren.

Jerusalem Center for Public Affairs. 1993. *The Israeli Economy at the Threshold of the Year 2000*. Jerusalem: Old City Press.

Johnson, Paul. 1987. *A History of the Jews*. New York: Harper and Row.

Katz, Ytzhak. 1992. *Privatization in Israel*. Ph.D. thesis, Tel Aviv University, Tel Aviv.

Kellerman, Aharon. 1993. *Society and Settlement: Jewish Land of Israel in the Twentieth Century*. Albany: State University of New York Press.

Kimmerling, Baruch. 1983. *Zionism and the Economy*. Cambridge, Mass.: Schenleman.

_____. 1983. *Zionism and Territory*. Berkeley: Institute for International Studies.

_____, ed. 1989. *The Israeli State and Society*. Albany: State University of New York Press.

Klieman, Aharon. 1985. *Israel's Global Reach: Arms Sales as Diplomacy*. New York: Pergamon-Brassey.

_____. 1990. *Israel and the World After 40 Years*. New York: Pergamon.

Klieman, Aharon, and Reuven Pedatzur. 1991. *Rearming Israel*. Boulder, Colo.: Westview Press.

Kook, Rebecca. 1992. *The Politics and Production of Corporate National Identity Within Democracies*. Ph.D. thesis, Columbia University, New York.

_____. 1995. "Dilemmas of Ethnic Minorities in Democracies: The Effect of Peace on the Palestinians in Israel." *Politics and Society* 23, no. 3: 309–336.

Korn, Dan. 1994. *Time in Gray: Unity Governments 1984–1990*. Tel Aviv: Zmora-Bitan.

Kretzmer, David. 1990. *The Legal Status of Arabs in Israel*. Boulder, Colo.: Westview Press.

Kyle, Keith, and Joel Peters, eds. 1993. *Whither Israel? The Domestic Challenges*. New York and London: Royal Institute of International Affairs and I. B. Tauris.

Landau, Jacob M. 1993. *The Arab Minority in Israel, 1967–1991*. Oxford: Clarendon Press.

Lanir, Zvi, ed. 1985. *Security and the Israeli Economy During the 1980s*. Tel Aviv: Defense Ministry Publications.

Laqueur, Walter. 1972. *A History of Zionism*. New York: Holt, Rinehart and Winston.

Laqueur, Walter, and Barry Rubin, eds. 1984. *The Arab Israeli Reader*. New York: Penguin Books.

Lazin, Frederick A. 1994. *Politics and Policy Implementation: Project Renewal in Israel*. Albany: State University of New York Press.

Lehman-Wilzig, Sam N. 1992. *Wildfire: Grassroots Revolts in Israel in the Post-Socialist Era*. Albany: State University of New York Press.

Libman, Charles, ed. 1990. *Religious-Secular Relations in the Israeli Society*. Jerusalem: Keter.

Libman, Charles, and Eliezer Don-Yehiya. 1983. *Civil Religion in Israel*. Berkeley: University of California Press.

Lustick, Ian. 1980. *The Arabs in the Jewish State*. Austin: University of Texas Press.

_____. 1988. *For the Land and the Lord: Jewish Fundamentalism in Israel*. New York: Council on Foreign Relations.

Mautner, Menachem. 1993. *The Decline of Formalism and the Rise of Values in Israel's Law*. Tel Aviv: Maagale Daat.

Menuchin, Ishai, and Dina Menuchin, eds. 1985. *The Limits of Obedience*. Tel Aviv: Siman Kri's Books.

Migdal, Joel. 1992. "Civil Society in Israel." In Goldberg Ellis, Resat Kasaba, and Joel Migdal, eds. *Democracy in the Middle East?* N. P.

Ministry of Justice. 1988. "Associations Next to Government Ministries." Jerusalem: Report of the Committee (memo).

Modai, Itzhak. 1988. *Erasing Zeros*. Tel Aviv: Edanim.

The Multi-Year Plan for the Israel Economy: 1995–2000. 1994. Jerusalem: Government of Israel, Ministry of Economy and Planning.

Nachmias, David. 1974. "Coalition Politics in Israel." *Comparative Political Studies* 7: 316–333.

Novik, Nimrod. 1986. *The United States and Israel*. Boulder, Colo.: Westview Press.

Pedatzur, Reuven. 1992. *The Impact of "Decision Kitchens" in the Making of National Security Policy: Eshkol Government and the Territories, 1967–1969*. Unpublished Ph.D. thesis, Tel Aviv University, Tel Aviv.

Penniman, Howard, ed. 1979. *Israel at the Polls: The Knesset Elections—1977*. Washington, D.C.: American Enterprise Institute.

Peres, Shimon. 1993. *The New Middle East*. Tel Aviv: Stimatzki.

Peretz, Don. 1960. "Reflections on Israel's Fourth Parliamentary Elections." *Middle East Journal* 14, no. 1 (Winter): 15–28.

_____. 1968. "Israel's Administration and Arab Refugees." *Foreign Affairs* 46, no. 1 (January): 336–346.

_____. 1970. "Israel's 1969 Election Issues: The Visible and the Invisible." *Middle East Journal* (Winter): 31–46.

_____. 1974. "The War Election and Israel's Eighth Knesset." *Middle East Journal* 28, no. 2 (Spring): 111–125.

_____. 1977. "The Earthquake—Israel's Ninth Knesset Elections." *Middle East Journal* 31, no. 3 (Summer): 251–266.

_____. 1984. "Israeli Policy." in Freedman, ed.

_____. 1988. "Intifada: The Palestinian Uprising." *Foreign Affairs* 66, no. 6 (Summer): 964–980.

_____. 1990. *Intifada: The Palestinian Uprising*. Boulder, Colo.: Westview Press.

Peretz, Don, and Sammy Smooha. 1981. "Israel's Tenth Knesset Elections—Ethnic Upsurgence and Decline of Ideology." *Middle East Journal* 35, no. 4 (Autumn): 506–526.

_____. 1985. "Israel's Eleventh Knesset Election." *Middle East Journal* 39, no. 1 (Winter): 86–103.

_____. 1989. "Israel's Twelfth Knesset Election: An All-Loser Game." *Middle East Journal* 43, no. 3 (Summer): 389–405.

Peri, Yoram. 1983. *Between Battles and Ballots: Israeli Military in Politics*. Cambridge: Cambridge University Press.

_____, ed. 1989. *Electoral Reform in Israel*. Tel Aviv: Israel Diaspora Institute.

Pleg, Ilan, and Ofira Selikter, eds. 1989. *The Emergence of Binational Israel*. Boulder, Colo.: Westview Press.

Prime Minister's Office. 1994. *Prime Minister's Report on Government Activities*. Jerusalem: Prime Minister's Office.

Rabinovich, Itamar. 1985. *The War for Lebanon: 1970–1985*. Ithaca: Cornell University Press.

Radian, Alex. 1984. "The Policy Formation Electoral Cycle (1955–1981)." In Caspi, Diskin, and Gutmann, eds.

Rae, Douglas. 1967. *The Political Consequences of Electoral Laws*. New Haven: Yale University Press.

Ram, Uri. 1995. *The Changing Agenda of Israeli Sociology, Theory, Ideology, and Identity*. Albany: State University of New York Press.

Reich, Bernard, and Gershon R. Kieval, eds. 1991. *Israeli Politics in the 1990s: Key Domestic and Foreign Policy Factors*. Westport, Conn.: Greenwood.

Reiter, Yitzhak, and Geoffrey Wigoder, eds. 1992. *The Political Life of Arabs in Israel*. Tel Aviv: Beit Berl, Institute for Israeli Arab Studies.

Rekhes, Elie. 1993. *The Arab Minority in Israel: Between Communism and Arab Nationalism 1965–1991*. Tel Aviv: Ha'Kibbutz Ha'meuhad.

Riechman, Uriel. 1987. *A Proposal for a Constitution for the State of Israel*. Tel Aviv: Tel Aviv University.

Riker, William. 1962. *The Theory of Political Coalitions*. New Haven: Yale University Press.

_____. 1986. *The Art of Political Manipulation*. New Haven: Yale University Press.

Rubinstein, Amnon. 1980. *The Constitutional Law of Israel*. Tel Aviv: Schocken.

Russell, Raymond. 1995. *Utopia in Zion: The Israeli Experience with Worker Cooperatives*. Albany: State University of New York Press.

Sachar, Howard. 1976. *A History of Israel from the Rise of Zionism to Our Time*. New York: Knopf.

Safran, Nadav. 1969. *From War to War*. New York: Pegasus.

Schindler, Colin. 1991. *Plowshares into Swords? Israelis and Jews in the Shadow of the Intifada*. London: I. B. Tauris.

Segal, Zeev. 1988. *Israeli Democracy*. Tel Aviv: Defense Department.

Semyonov, Moshe, and Noah Levin-Epstein. 1987. *Hewers of Woods and Drawers of Water*. Ithaca: ILR Press.

Sened, Itai. 1996. "A Model of Coalition Formation: Theory and Evidence." In Doron, Gideon. ed. *The Electoral Revolution: Primaries and Direct Election to the Prime Minister*. Tel Aviv: Ha'Kibbutz Ha'meuhad, pp. 171–196.

Shaari, Yehuda. 1992. *Toward Social Liberalism*. Tel Aviv: Forder.

Shamir, Michal. 1986. "Realignment in the Israeli Party System." In Arian and Shamir, eds.

Shapira, Boaz. 1993. *Epistemological Authority and the Socialization of Children*. Unpublished Ph.D. thesis, Tel Aviv University, Tel Aviv.

Shapiro, Yonatan. 1976. *The Formative Years of the Israeli Labor Party*. Beverly Hills: Sage.

_____. 1980. "The End of the Dominant Party." In Arian, ed.

_____. 1984. *Elite with No Followers*. Ramat Gan: Revivim.

_____. 1989. *Chosen to Command*. Tel Aviv: Am Oved.

Sharfman, Dafna. 1988. *Women in Politics*. Haifa: Tamar.

Sharkansky, Ira. 1979. *Whither the State?* Chatham, N.J.: Chatham House.

———. 1985. *What Makes Israel Tick: How Domestic Policy Makers Cope with Constraints*. Chicago: Nelson Hall.

———. 1987. *The Political Economy of Israel*. New Brunswick, N.J.: Transaction.

———. 1989. "Israeli Civil Service Positions Open to Political Appointments." *International Journal of Public Administration* 5: 731–748.

Shiff, Zeev, and Yaari Ehoud. 1984. *A War of Deception*. Tel Aviv: Schocken.

Shimshoni, Daniel. 1982. *The Israeli Democracy*. New York: Free Press.

Silberstein, Laurence J., ed. 1991. *New Perspectives on Israeli History: The Early Years of the State*. New York: New York University Press.

Smooha, Sammy. 1978. *Israel: Pluralism and Conflict*. London: Routledge and Kegan Paul.

———. 1987. *Social Research on Jewish Ethnicity in Israel*. Haifa: Haifa University Press.

Smooha, Sammy, and Don Peretz. 1993. "Israel's 1992 Knesset Elections: Are They Critical?" *Middle East Journal* 43, no. 3 (Summer): 448–463.

Sobel, Zvi. 1993. *A Small Place in Galilee: Religion and Social Conflict in an Israeli Village*. New York: Holmes and Meier.

Sobel, Zvi, and Benjamin Beit-Hallahmi, eds. 1991. *Tradition, Innovation, Conflict: Jewishness and Judaism in Contemporary Israel*. Albany: State University of New York Press.

Sprinzak, Ehud. 1981. "Gush Emunim: The Tip of the Iceberg." *Jerusalem Quarterly* 21: 28–47.

———. 1986. "Kach and Kahane: The Emergence of Jewish Quasi-Fascism." In Arian and Shamir, eds.

Sprinzak, Ehud, and Larry Diamond, eds. 1993. *Israeli Democracy Under Stress*. Boulder, Colo.: Lynne Rienner Publishers.

Statistical Abstract of Israel. Various years. Jerusalem: Government of Israel, Central Bureau of Statistics.

Stone, Russell A., and Walter P. Zenner, eds. 1995. *Critical Essays on Israeli Social Issues and Scholarship*. Albany: State University of New York Press.

Tessler, Mark. 1994. *A History of the Israeli-Palestinian Conflict*. Bloomington: Indiana University Press.

Torgovnik, Effrim. 1980. "A Movement for Change in a Stable System." In Arian, ed.

Vital, David. 1978. *The Origins of Zionism*. Oxford: Clarendon Press.

———. 1982. *Zionism: The Formative Years*. Oxford: Clarendon Press.

Wagaw, Teshome G. 1993. *For Our Soul: Ethiopian Jews in Israel*. Detroit: Wayne State University Press.

Wald, Emmanuel. 1992. *The Wald Report: The Decline of Israeli National Security Since 1967*. Boulder, Colo.: Westview Press.

Walinsky, Louis. 1981. *The Implications of the Israeli-Arab Peace for World Jewry*. New York: World Jewish Congress.

Weiss, Shevach, and Yael Yishai. 1980. "Women's Representation in Israeli Political Elites." *Jewish Social Studies* 17: 165–176.

Wyman, David. 1984. *The Abandonment of the Jews*. New York: Pantheon Books.

Yaacobi, Gad. 1980. *The Government*. Tel Aviv: Am Oved.

Yaacobi, Gad, and Ehoud Gera. 1975. *The Freedom to Choose*. Tel Aviv: Am Oved.

Yanai, Natan. 1982. *Political Crises in Israel*. Jerusalem: Keter.

Yaniv, Avner, ed. 1993. *National Security and Democracy in Israel*. Boulder, Colo.: Lynne Rienner Publishers.

Yishai, Yael. 1986. *Interest Groups in Israel*. Tel Aviv: Am Oved.

_____. 1991. *Land of Paradoxes: Interest Politics in Israel*. Albany: State University of New York Press.

Yuchtman-Yaar, Ephraim. 1989. "The Israeli Public and Its Institutions." *Israeli Democracy* 3: 7–11.

Zidon, Asher. 1964. *The House of Representatives*. Tel Aviv: Achiasaf.

Zuckerman, Alan. 1990. "The Flow of the Vote in Israel: A Reconsideration of Stability and Change." In Arian and Shamir, eds.

About the Book and Authors

Israeli government and politics have undergone significant changes since the second edition of this book was published in 1983. Israel withdrew from Lebanon, absorbed hundreds of thousands of new immigrants from the collapsed Soviet Union and Ethiopia, and undertook peace negotiations with the Palestinians and other Arab neighbors that led to a historic peace treaty—the Declaration of Principles. These events were possible because of several institutional, legal, and normative changes in the political system and because Labor resumed its historical role as the country's leading party.

This completely revised edition of *The Government and Politics of Israel* offers a comprehensive and up-to-date overview of the dynamics of Israeli politics. This edition focuses on issues that have become central in the study of Israel's political system, such as new electoral procedures, the formation of new parties, a government administrative reorganization, fresh personalities on the national scene, and the peace process. The book is intended to familiarize those interested in Israel's government with its origins; the evolution of its institutions, practices, and traditions; and the workings of the government today.

Don Peretz is professor emeritus of Binghamton University. **Gideon Doron** is professor of political science at Tel Aviv University.

Index

Absentee Property Law, 57
Abuhatzeira, Aaron, 78, 115, 143, 249, 250
Achdut Ha-Avoda, 72, 79, 84, 86, 87, 90–92, 196, 202
  in government coalitions, 120, 193(table), 194, 231
ADB. *See* Arab Democratic party
Advertising, 129, 130
Africa, 17, 48(table), 50
Agranat Commission, 103, 236
Agriculture, 5, 10, 35, 37, 150, 152, 198
  Arabs, 51, 57–59
  Jews in, 83–84, 146–147
  Ministry of, 211, 214(table), 222–223
Agudat Israel, 25, 37, 71, 73, 113, 115–116, 162, 168, 190
  in coalitions, 121, 192(table)
  in elections, 80(table), 82(table), 116, 127(table), 137, 167, 245(table)
Aid, 63, 158–160, 199, 275–276, 278
AIPAC. *See* American Israel Public Affairs Committee
AJC. *See* American Jewish Committee
Al-Aksa Mosque, 236
Algeria, 49
Aliya, 34–36
Aliya Hadasha, 36, 102
Allenby, Edmund, 21, 26, 27
Allon, Yigal, 87, 92, 141, 202, 219, 267
Almozlino, Shoshanah, 123
Aloni, Shulamit, 65, 73, 78, 93–94, 121, 215, 224–225, 268–269
Altalena incident, 195–196
American Israel Public Affairs Committee (AIPAC), 165
American Jewish Committee (AJC), 41, 164–166

American Jewish Congress, 164
American Joint Distribution Committee, 225
Americans for Progressive Israel, 165
American Zionist Federation, 165
Anglo-Palestine Bank, 21, 237
Anti-Semitism, 14–17, 22, 24, 34, 35, 40, 47, 49
Arab Democratic party (ADP), 83, 98
Arabic language, 31, 40, 52
Arab League of National Liberation, 95
Arab List, 80(table)
Arabs, 51, 55–61, 152, 163, 224, 263, 278
  autonomy of, 58, 59, 61, 276
  and the Balfour Declaration, 27–28, 30, 31
  citizenship of, 7, 56, 60
  conflicts with, 3, 8, 9, 34, 39–40, 42, 56, 57, 219, 259–260
  income of, 8, 56, 59
  Jewish relations with, 11, 56, 58–60, 88, 257, 278
  in judicial system, 185, 234, 235
  and Labor party, 122, 125, 126
  and the military, 57, 106, 107, 159, 195
  and national identity, 60, 61, 276
  nationalism of, 29, 47
  in Occupied Territories, 55, 58, 170, 217–218, 232, 247, 264
  in Palestine, 14, 21, 28–34, 36, 38–44, 55, 57, 195
  policies toward, 56, 57, 112, 171, 174, 198, 215
  political participation by, 58, 59, 69, 98, 117, 137–138, 232, 256–257